# THE COMPLETE BOOK OF
# MATH TIMED TESTS

## GRADES 3-5

AMERICAN
EDUCATION
PUBLISHING™

Columbus, Ohio

Copyright © 2009 by School Specialty Publishing. Published by American Education Publishing™, an imprint of School Specialty Publishing, a member of the School Specialty Family.

Send all inquiries to:
School Specialty Publishing
8720 Orion Place
Columbus, OH 43240-2111

ISBN  0-7696-8562-5

2 3 4 5 6 7 8 9  HPS 13 12 11 10 09

# The Complete Book of Math Timed Tests    Grades 3-5

**Table of Contents**

# Table of Contents

4

# What Is Addition?

You add to find how many in all. The answer is called the **sum**.

3 birds plus 2 more birds equals 5 birds in all.

There are two ways to show the addition.

$$3 + 2 = 5 \qquad \begin{array}{r} 3 \\ + 2 \\ \hline 5 \end{array}$$

You can draw a picture to find a sum.

**Example:** Find the sum.  2 + 4 = _6_

**Step 1:** Draw 2 dots. ⟶  • •

**Step 2:** Draw 4 more dots. ⟶  • • • •

**Step 3:** Count all the dots.

**Answer:** 2 + 4 = _6_

■ Draw a picture to find the sum.

3 + 1 = _4_          2 + 2 = _4_          4 + 2 = _6_

1 + 5 = _6_          2 + 3 = _5_          3 + 3 = _6_

Addition

# What Is Addition?

You can use counters to find a sum. You will need some pennies.

**Example:** Find the sum.  3 + 2 = _5_

**Step 1:** Put 3 pennies in the box. ⟶

**Step 2:** Put 2 more pennies in the box. ⟶

**Step 3:** Count all the pennies. ⟶

**Answer:** 3 + 2 = _5_

■ Use counters to find the sum.

$4 + 3 =$ _7_     $2 + 4 =$ _6_     $3 + 4 =$ _7_

$$\begin{array}{r} 4 \\ + 4 \\ \hline 8 \end{array} \qquad \begin{array}{r} 5 \\ + 1 \\ \hline 6 \end{array} \qquad \begin{array}{r} 2 \\ + 5 \\ \hline 7 \end{array} \qquad \begin{array}{r} 2 \\ + 1 \\ \hline 3 \end{array} \qquad \begin{array}{r} 3 \\ + 2 \\ \hline 5 \end{array}$$

You can use a number line to find a sum.

**Example:** Find the sum.  5 + 3 = _8_

**Step 1:** Put your finger on 5.

**Step 2:** Move your finger 3 spaces to the right.

**Step 3:** Read the number your finger is on.

**Answer:** 5 + 3 = _8_

■ Use the number line to find the sum.

$4 + 1 =$ _5_     $5 + 3 =$ _8_     $3 + 5 =$ _8_

$$\begin{array}{r} 5 \\ + 2 \\ \hline 7 \end{array} \qquad \begin{array}{r} 4 \\ + 5 \\ \hline 9 \end{array} \qquad \begin{array}{r} 1 \\ + 2 \\ \hline 3 \end{array} \qquad \begin{array}{r} 5 \\ + 4 \\ \hline 9 \end{array} \qquad \begin{array}{r} 5 \\ + 5 \\ \hline 10 \end{array}$$

**Addition**

Name _____

# Adding Zero

Zero is called the **identity element of addition**. This means that, when zero is added to a number, that number does not change.

**Example:** 3 + 0 = 3

 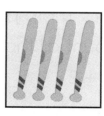

| 4 | + | 0 | = | 4 |

**Sums Through Six**

■ Add.

2 + 0 = 2          3 + 0 = 3

| 1 | 0 | 0 | 3 |
| +0 | +4 | +0 | +0 |
| 1 | 4 | 0 | 3 |

0 + 6 = 6          0 + 4 = 4

| 0 | 6 | 0 | 4 |
| +5 | +0 | +6 | +0 |
| 5 | 6 | 6 | 4 |

0 + 1 = 1          4 + 0 = 4

5 + 0 = 5          0 + 3 = 3

| 0 | 0 | 5 | 2 |
| +2 | +3 | +0 | +0 |

1 + 0 = 1          0 + 2 = 2

0 + 5 = 5          6 + 0 = 6

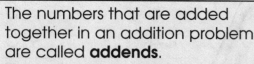

The numbers that are added together in an addition problem are called **addends**.
The answer in an addition problem is called the **sum**.

| 5 | + | 0 | = | 5 |
| addend | | addend | | sum |

| 5 | addend |
| +0 | addend |
| 5 | sum |

Name _____

# Counting On

If one of the addends in an addition fact is a lesser number like 1, 2, or 3, you can find the sum by "counting on" from the other addend.

**Example:** 3 + 2    Start at 3. Count on by moving 2 jumps on the number line. The sum is 5.

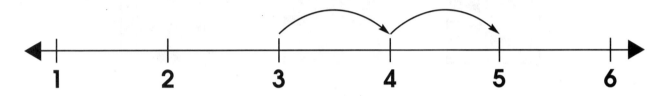

■ Complete each **T** by counting on by the number at the top. Use the number line to help you.

| + 1 | | + 2 | | + 3 | |
|---|---|---|---|---|---|
| 5 | ___ | 4 | ___ | 2 | ___ |
| 3 | ___ | 0 | ___ | 1 | ___ |
| 4 | ___ | 3 | ___ | 0 | ___ |
| 2 | ___ | 1 | ___ | | |
| 0 | ___ | | | | |

**Sums Through Six**

---

**Counting numbers** are all the whole numbers beginning with 1 and going as far as you want. 1, 2, 3, 4, . . .

**Hint:** Always add the smaller addend to the larger one, no matter which comes first.

# Changing the Order of the Addends

The **commutative property of addition** says that the sum is always the same no matter how the addends are arranged.

**Example:** 3 + 2 = 5 is the same as 2 + 3 = 5.

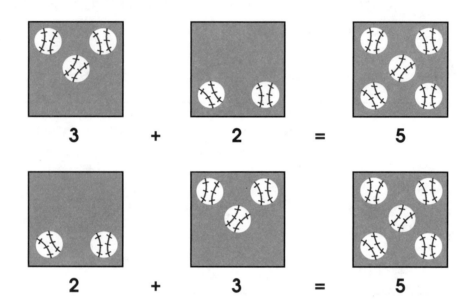

| 3 | + | 2 | = | 5 |

| 2 | + | 3 | = | 5 |

■ Use the commutative property to solve the problems below.

1 + 3 = \_\_\_\_         4 + 2 = \_\_\_\_         2 + 3 = \_\_\_\_

3 + 1 = \_\_\_\_         2 + 4 = \_\_\_\_         3 + 2 = \_\_\_\_

1 + 2 = \_\_\_\_         1 + 4 = \_\_\_\_         5 + 1 = \_\_\_\_

2 + 1 = \_\_\_\_         4 + 1 = \_\_\_\_         1 + 5 = \_\_\_\_

**Sums Through Six**

# Adding Doubles

**Doubles** are basic facts in which the addends are the same number.

**Examples:**  $1 + 1 = 2$

$2 + 2 = 4$

$3 + 3 = 6$

■ Add.

$0 + 0 =$ _____          $2 + 2 =$ _____

$3 + 3 =$ _____          $1 + 1 =$ _____

$$\begin{array}{r} 2 \\ + 2 \\ \hline \end{array} \qquad \begin{array}{r} 1 \\ + 1 \\ \hline \end{array} \qquad \begin{array}{r} 0 \\ + 0 \\ \hline \end{array} \qquad \begin{array}{r} 3 \\ + 3 \\ \hline \end{array}$$

**Sums Through Six**

The sums of doubles are always even numbers, like 0, 2, 4, and 6. This is true even if the addends are odd numbers like 1 and 3.

Name _____

# Practice

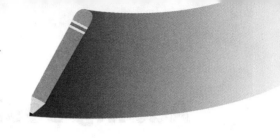

■ Add. Record your score—the number correct—on each Practice page and on page 16.

$3 + 3 =$ _6_    $2 + 1 =$ _3_    $1 + 0 =$ _1_    $0 + 4 =$ _4_

$6 + 0 =$ _6_    $5 + 0 =$ _5_    $4 + 1 =$ _5_    $1 + 1 =$ _2_

$1 + 5 =$ _6_    $2 + 4 =$ _6_    $0 + 2 =$ _2_    $3 + 0 =$ _3_

$2 + 3 =$ _5_    $0 + 0 =$ _0_    $3 + 2 =$ _5_    $1 + 4 =$ _5_

$3 + 1 =$ _4_    $0 + 1 =$ _1_    $4 + 0 =$ _4_    $5 + 1 =$ _6_

$0 + 5 =$ _5_    $1 + 1 =$ _2_    $1 + 3 =$ _4_    $0 + 6 =$ _6_

$1 + 4 =$ _5_    $0 + 3 =$ _3_    $2 + 0 =$ _2_    $1 + 2 =$ _3_

$4 + 2 =$ _6_    $2 + 2 =$ _4_    $3 + 2 =$ _5_    $3 + 1 =$ _4_

$5 + 0 =$ _5_    $3 + 3 =$ _6_    $4 + 1 =$ _5_    $0 + 4 =$ _4_

Score: _____

START

## Practice

■ Add.

| 1<br>+ 4<br>**5** | 0<br>+ 6<br>**6** | 2<br>+ 1<br>**3** | 2<br>+ 4<br>**6** | 0<br>+ 5<br>**5** | 1<br>+ 2<br>**3** | 3<br>+ 3<br>**6** | 0<br>+ 4<br>**4** | 0<br>+ 1<br>**1** |

| 0<br>+ 0<br>**0** | 2<br>+ 2<br>**4** | 0<br>+ 2<br>**2** | 3<br>+ 2<br>**5** | 1<br>+ 0<br>**1** | 0<br>+ 3<br>**3** | 1<br>+ 4<br>**5** | 5<br>+ 0<br>**5** | 3<br>+ 2<br>**5** |

| 2<br>+ 3<br>**5** | 4<br>+ 0<br>**4** | 3<br>+ 3<br>**6** | 1<br>+ 3<br>**4** | 1<br>+ 4<br>**5** | 4<br>+ 2<br>**6** | 0<br>+ 3<br>**3** | 4<br>+ 1<br>**5** | 2<br>+ 0<br>**2** |

| 3<br>+ 0<br>**3** | 1<br>+ 5<br>**6** | 1<br>+ 1<br>**2** | 2<br>+ 2<br>**4** | 6<br>+ 0<br>**6** | 1<br>+ 3<br>**4** | 2<br>+ 3<br>**5** | 3<br>+ 1<br>**4** | 5<br>+ 1<br>**6** |

Score: _____

13

Name _____

# Practice

■ Add.

|  |  |  |  |
|---|---|---|---|
| 6 | 1 | 2 | 1 |
| + 0 | + 3 | + 2 | + 2 |

|  |  |  |  |
|---|---|---|---|
| 1 | 2 | 0 | 3 |
| + 4 | + 4 | + 2 | + 0 |

|  |  |  |  |
|---|---|---|---|
| 0 | 0 | 4 | 2 |
| + 3 | + 6 | + 2 | + 3 |

|  |  |  |  |
|---|---|---|---|
| 3 | 4 | 3 | 1 |
| + 1 | + 1 | + 3 | + 5 |

|  |  |  |  |
|---|---|---|---|
| 6 | 3 | 2 | 2 |
| + 0 | + 2 | + 1 | + 2 |

2 + 0 = ____      1 + 0 = ____

0 + 4 = ____      0 + 5 = ____

4 + 0 = ____      2 + 1 = ____

1 + 5 = ____      0 + 1 = ____

5 + 0 = ____      3 + 3 = ____

0 + 0 = ____      1 + 1 = ____

3 + 2 = ____      5 + 1 = ____

4 + 2 = ____      2 + 2 = ____

Score: _____

# Practice

■ Add.

| | | | |
|---|---|---|---|
| 3<br>+ 3 | 2<br>+ 4 | 2<br>+ 1 | 4<br>+ 2 |

0 + 0 = ___     1 + 1 = ___

2 + 3 = ___     2 + 0 = ___

| | | | |
|---|---|---|---|
| 0<br>+ 1 | 1<br>+ 2 | 5<br>+ 0 | 0<br>+ 3 |

1 + 5 = ___     5 + 1 = ___

4 + 0 = ___     0 + 6 = ___

| | | | |
|---|---|---|---|
| 1<br>+ 0 | 3<br>+ 2 | 1<br>+ 3 | 2<br>+ 2 |

0 + 5 = ___     3 + 1 = ___

3 + 0 = ___     1 + 4 = ___

| | | | |
|---|---|---|---|
| 0<br>+ 2 | 0<br>+ 4 | 5<br>+ 1 | 3<br>+ 1 |

4 + 1 = ___     6 + 0 = ___

3 + 2 = ___     2 + 2 = ___

| | | | |
|---|---|---|---|
| 2<br>+ 1 | 3<br>+ 3 | 0<br>+ 5 | 1<br>+ 4 |

Score: _____

**Sums Through Six**

Circle any problems that you still find difficult to remember. Make your own flash cards to help you master these problems.

FINISH

15

Name _____

# Practice

■ Add.

**Sums Through Six**

| | | | | |
|---|---|---|---|---|
| 0<br>+2 | 3<br>+2 | 5<br>+0 | 2<br>+4 | |

3 + 1 = _____     1 + 0 = _____

0 + 5 = _____     2 + 2 = _____

| | | | |
|---|---|---|---|
| 1<br>+3 | 1<br>+1 | 2<br>+1 | 1<br>+2 |

3 + 0 = _____     1 + 4 = _____

2 + 1 = _____     0 + 0 = _____

| | | | |
|---|---|---|---|
| 2<br>+2 | 2<br>+3 | 2<br>+0 | 4<br>+2 |

5 + 1 = _____     4 + 1 = _____

0 + 3 = _____     1 + 5 = _____

| | | | |
|---|---|---|---|
| 0<br>+6 | 0<br>+1 | 3<br>+2 | 2<br>+1 |

3 + 3 = _____     0 + 4 = _____

2 + 4 = _____     1 + 2 = _____

| | | | |
|---|---|---|---|
| 5<br>+1 | 3<br>+3 | 1<br>+4 | 4<br>+1 |

Record your scores below.

**Page 12** Score: _____     **Page 15** Score: _____

**Page 13** Score: _____     **Page 16** Score: _____

**Page 14** Score: _____

Name _____

# Timed Test

■ Improve your speed on these basic facts. Ask someone to time you.
  Record your time and score on each Timed Test page and on page 28.

0 + 5 = _____     1 + 1 = _____     0 + 2 = _____     2 + 1 = _____

1 + 4 = _____     5 + 0 = _____     3 + 2 = _____     6 + 0 = _____

2 + 0 = _____     2 + 3 = _____     1 + 0 = _____     1 + 5 = _____

3 + 3 = _____     4 + 2 = _____     2 + 4 = _____     5 + 1 = _____

0 + 1 = _____     0 + 3 = _____     1 + 2 = _____     2 + 2 = _____

4 + 1 = _____     1 + 3 = _____     4 + 0 = _____     3 + 1 = _____

3 + 0 = _____     0 + 6 = _____     0 + 4 = _____     0 + 0 = _____

2 + 4 = _____     3 + 3 = _____     1 + 5 = _____     3 + 2 = _____

1 + 4 = _____     5 + 0 = _____     4 + 2 = _____     2 + 2 = _____

3 + 1 = _____     1 + 1 = _____     2 + 0 = _____     1 + 2 = _____

Score: _____     Time: _____ minutes _____ seconds

**Sums Through Six**

Name _____

# Timed Test

■ Complete these facts as accurately and as quickly as you can.

**Sums Through Six**

| | | | | | | | |
|---|---|---|---|---|---|---|---|
| 6<br>+ 0 | 5<br>+ 1 | 5<br>+ 0 | 3<br>+ 1 | 4<br>+ 0 | 2<br>+ 1 | 0<br>+ 3 | 1<br>+ 4 |
| 1<br>+ 3 | 2<br>+ 3 | 0<br>+ 1 | 4<br>+ 2 | 0<br>+ 2 | 0<br>+ 6 | 2<br>+ 0 | 2<br>+ 4 |
| 3<br>+ 3 | 3<br>+ 0 | 2<br>+ 4 | 2<br>+ 2 | 1<br>+ 1 | 1<br>+ 5 | 3<br>+ 2 | 1<br>+ 3 |
| 1<br>+ 2 | 0<br>+ 0 | 0<br>+ 4 | 1<br>+ 4 | 0<br>+ 5 | 4<br>+ 1 | 1<br>+ 0 | 3<br>+ 3 |
| 5<br>+ 1 | 2<br>+ 3 | 4<br>+ 2 | 0<br>+ 6 | 1<br>+ 3 | 2<br>+ 1 | 2<br>+ 2 | 0<br>+ 3 |

Score: _____     Time: _____ minutes _____ seconds

# Timed Test

1 + 4 = ____    2 + 3 = ____

$$\begin{array}{r} 0 \\ +5 \\ \hline \end{array} \quad \begin{array}{r} 3 \\ +1 \\ \hline \end{array} \quad \begin{array}{r} 3 \\ +0 \\ \hline \end{array} \quad \begin{array}{r} 1 \\ +2 \\ \hline \end{array}$$

5 + 1 = ____    1 + 3 = ____

0 + 6 = ____    4 + 0 = ____

$$\begin{array}{r} 4 \\ +2 \\ \hline \end{array} \quad \begin{array}{r} 0 \\ +0 \\ \hline \end{array} \quad \begin{array}{r} 3 \\ +3 \\ \hline \end{array} \quad \begin{array}{r} 3 \\ +2 \\ \hline \end{array}$$

2 + 4 = ____    0 + 3 = ____

2 + 0 = ____    2 + 1 = ____

$$\begin{array}{r} 1 \\ +0 \\ \hline \end{array} \quad \begin{array}{r} 4 \\ +1 \\ \hline \end{array} \quad \begin{array}{r} 2 \\ +0 \\ \hline \end{array} \quad \begin{array}{r} 0 \\ +1 \\ \hline \end{array}$$

6 + 0 = ____    1 + 5 = ____

0 + 4 = ____    5 + 0 = ____

$$\begin{array}{r} 0 \\ +2 \\ \hline \end{array} \quad \begin{array}{r} 1 \\ +1 \\ \hline \end{array} \quad \begin{array}{r} 2 \\ +2 \\ \hline \end{array} \quad \begin{array}{r} 5 \\ +1 \\ \hline \end{array}$$

3 + 3 = ____    4 + 1 = ____

2 + 1 = ____    3 + 2 = ____

$$\begin{array}{r} 1 \\ +2 \\ \hline \end{array} \quad \begin{array}{r} 1 \\ +0 \\ \hline \end{array} \quad \begin{array}{r} 0 \\ +4 \\ \hline \end{array} \quad \begin{array}{r} 2 \\ +4 \\ \hline \end{array}$$

1 + 1 = ____    6 + 0 = ____

**Sums Through Six**

Score: _____    Time: _____ minutes _____ seconds

Name _____

# Timed Test

5 + 0 = ____    0 + 5 = ____

| 0 | 2 | 1 | 3 |
| +3 | +3 | +2 | +3 |

4 + 2 = ____    1 + 1 = ____

0 + 1 = ____    3 + 0 = ____

| 1 | 0 | 5 | 4 |
| +4 | +4 | +1 | +0 |

1 + 0 = ____    4 + 1 = ____

2 + 1 = ____    6 + 0 = ____

| 0 | 2 | 0 | 0 |
| +2 | +4 | +0 | +6 |

3 + 1 = ____    2 + 2 = ____

2 + 0 = ____    5 + 1 = ____

| 1 | 3 | 1 | 4 |
| +3 | +2 | +5 | +2 |

1 + 4 = ____    2 + 4 = ____

0 + 3 = ____    3 + 3 = ____

| 5 | 3 | 2 | 2 |
| +0 | +3 | +1 | +2 |

2 + 3 = ____    4 + 1 = ____

Score: _____    Time: _____ minutes _____ seconds

**Sums Through Six**

Name _____

# Timed Test

$0 + 5 =$ ___     $5 + 0 =$ ___

$$\begin{array}{r} 4 \\ +0 \\ \hline \end{array} \quad \begin{array}{r} 2 \\ +1 \\ \hline \end{array} \quad \begin{array}{r} 3 \\ +2 \\ \hline \end{array} \quad \begin{array}{r} 5 \\ +1 \\ \hline \end{array}$$

$3 + 1 =$ ___     $2 + 4 =$ ___

$3 + 0 =$ ___     $4 + 2 =$ ___

$$\begin{array}{r} 0 \\ +2 \\ \hline \end{array} \quad \begin{array}{r} 0 \\ +6 \\ \hline \end{array} \quad \begin{array}{r} 0 \\ +3 \\ \hline \end{array} \quad \begin{array}{r} 6 \\ +0 \\ \hline \end{array}$$

$2 + 0 =$ ___     $0 + 0 =$ ___

$0 + 1 =$ ___     $1 + 0 =$ ___

$$\begin{array}{r} 3 \\ +3 \\ \hline \end{array} \quad \begin{array}{r} 2 \\ +3 \\ \hline \end{array} \quad \begin{array}{r} 4 \\ +1 \\ \hline \end{array} \quad \begin{array}{r} 1 \\ +5 \\ \hline \end{array}$$

$2 + 2 =$ ___     $0 + 4 =$ ___

$1 + 1 =$ ___     $1 + 4 =$ ___

$$\begin{array}{r} 1 \\ +2 \\ \hline \end{array} \quad \begin{array}{r} 1 \\ +3 \\ \hline \end{array} \quad \begin{array}{r} 1 \\ +1 \\ \hline \end{array} \quad \begin{array}{r} 4 \\ +2 \\ \hline \end{array}$$

$3 + 3 =$ ___     $5 + 1 =$ ___

$2 + 1 =$ ___     $3 + 2 =$ ___

$$\begin{array}{r} 6 \\ +0 \\ \hline \end{array} \quad \begin{array}{r} 2 \\ +4 \\ \hline \end{array} \quad \begin{array}{r} 3 \\ +1 \\ \hline \end{array} \quad \begin{array}{r} 2 \\ +2 \\ \hline \end{array}$$

$1 + 3 =$ ___     $4 + 1 =$ ___

Score: _____     Time: _____ minutes _____ seconds

# Timed Test

**Sums Through Six**

1 + 4 = ____     2 + 2 = ____

$$\begin{array}{r} 3 \\ +\,3 \\ \hline \end{array} \quad \begin{array}{r} 4 \\ +\,0 \\ \hline \end{array} \quad \begin{array}{r} 5 \\ +\,0 \\ \hline \end{array} \quad \begin{array}{r} 2 \\ +\,1 \\ \hline \end{array}$$

0 + 3 = ____     3 + 0 = ____

2 + 3 = ____     0 + 6 = ____

$$\begin{array}{r} 1 \\ +\,1 \\ \hline \end{array} \quad \begin{array}{r} 0 \\ +\,2 \\ \hline \end{array} \quad \begin{array}{r} 1 \\ +\,0 \\ \hline \end{array} \quad \begin{array}{r} 6 \\ +\,0 \\ \hline \end{array}$$

1 + 2 = ____     4 + 1 = ____

2 + 4 = ____     1 + 3 = ____

$$\begin{array}{r} 3 \\ +\,2 \\ \hline \end{array} \quad \begin{array}{r} 5 \\ +\,1 \\ \hline \end{array} \quad \begin{array}{r} 3 \\ +\,1 \\ \hline \end{array} \quad \begin{array}{r} 0 \\ +\,0 \\ \hline \end{array}$$

0 + 4 = ____     0 + 3 = ____

4 + 2 = ____     0 + 1 = ____

$$\begin{array}{r} 1 \\ +\,5 \\ \hline \end{array} \quad \begin{array}{r} 2 \\ +\,0 \\ \hline \end{array} \quad \begin{array}{r} 1 \\ +\,2 \\ \hline \end{array} \quad \begin{array}{r} 0 \\ +\,5 \\ \hline \end{array}$$

3 + 1 = ____     3 + 2 = ____

2 + 0 = ____     1 + 2 = ____

$$\begin{array}{r} 4 \\ +\,2 \\ \hline \end{array} \quad \begin{array}{r} 0 \\ +\,6 \\ \hline \end{array} \quad \begin{array}{r} 2 \\ +\,2 \\ \hline \end{array} \quad \begin{array}{r} 1 \\ +\,4 \\ \hline \end{array}$$

2 + 2 = ____     4 + 1 = ____

Score: _____     Time: _____ minutes _____ seconds

Name _____

# Timed Test

3 + 0 = ____      0 + 5 = ____

| 2 | 5 | 4 | 2 |
| + 4 | + 1 | + 2 | + 3 |

1 + 0 = ____      2 + 0 = ____

3 + 2 = ____      2 + 2 = ____

| 0 | 0 | 0 | 1 |
| + 4 | + 0 | + 2 | + 1 |

0 + 1 = ____      4 + 1 = ____

6 + 0 = ____      0 + 3 = ____

| 3 | 2 | 3 | 0 |
| + 1 | + 1 | + 3 | + 6 |

1 + 5 = ____      5 + 0 = ____

4 + 0 = ____      1 + 3 = ____

| 1 | 1 | 2 | 2 |
| + 4 | + 2 | + 2 | + 3 |

2 + 4 = ____      1 + 4 = ____

3 + 3 = ____      1 + 2 = ____

| 1 | 3 | 4 | 2 |
| + 3 | + 2 | + 1 | + 0 |

1 + 1 = ____      0 + 3 = ____

Score: _____      Time: _____ minutes _____ seconds

23

Name _____

# Timed Test

**Sums Through Six**

1 + 4 = ____     4 + 1 = ____

$$\begin{array}{r}0\\+6\\\hline\end{array}\quad\begin{array}{r}3\\+0\\\hline\end{array}\quad\begin{array}{r}4\\+0\\\hline\end{array}\quad\begin{array}{r}2\\+3\\\hline\end{array}$$

6 + 0 = ____     0 + 5 = ____

0 + 1 = ____     3 + 1 = ____

$$\begin{array}{r}1\\+5\\\hline\end{array}\quad\begin{array}{r}1\\+0\\\hline\end{array}\quad\begin{array}{r}2\\+1\\\hline\end{array}\quad\begin{array}{r}0\\+2\\\hline\end{array}$$

2 + 4 = ____     1 + 1 = ____

1 + 2 = ____     2 + 2 = ____

$$\begin{array}{r}5\\+1\\\hline\end{array}\quad\begin{array}{r}4\\+2\\\hline\end{array}\quad\begin{array}{r}1\\+3\\\hline\end{array}\quad\begin{array}{r}3\\+2\\\hline\end{array}$$

5 + 0 = ____     0 + 3 = ____

2 + 0 = ____     3 + 3 = ____

$$\begin{array}{r}4\\+0\\\hline\end{array}\quad\begin{array}{r}0\\+0\\\hline\end{array}\quad\begin{array}{r}1\\+1\\\hline\end{array}\quad\begin{array}{r}3\\+1\\\hline\end{array}$$

4 + 2 = ____     2 + 3 = ____

1 + 3 = ____     0 + 4 = ____

$$\begin{array}{r}1\\+4\\\hline\end{array}\quad\begin{array}{r}3\\+3\\\hline\end{array}\quad\begin{array}{r}2\\+4\\\hline\end{array}\quad\begin{array}{r}0\\+3\\\hline\end{array}$$

5 + 1 = ____     2 + 1 = ____

Score: _____     Time: _____ minutes _____ seconds

24

# Timed Test

1 + 0 = ____        0 + 3 = ____

$$\begin{array}{r}4\\+2\\\hline\end{array}\qquad\begin{array}{r}3\\+1\\\hline\end{array}\qquad\begin{array}{r}1\\+5\\\hline\end{array}\qquad\begin{array}{r}0\\+4\\\hline\end{array}$$

4 + 1 = ____        5 + 1 = ____

0 + 1 = ____        0 + 5 = ____

$$\begin{array}{r}5\\+0\\\hline\end{array}\qquad\begin{array}{r}0\\+6\\\hline\end{array}\qquad\begin{array}{r}0\\+0\\\hline\end{array}\qquad\begin{array}{r}1\\+3\\\hline\end{array}$$

6 + 0 = ____        1 + 2 = ____

2 + 1 = ____        3 + 3 = ____

$$\begin{array}{r}0\\+2\\\hline\end{array}\qquad\begin{array}{r}2\\+2\\\hline\end{array}\qquad\begin{array}{r}2\\+4\\\hline\end{array}\qquad\begin{array}{r}3\\+0\\\hline\end{array}$$

3 + 2 = ____        1 + 4 = ____

2 + 3 = ____        1 + 1 = ____

$$\begin{array}{r}2\\+0\\\hline\end{array}\qquad\begin{array}{r}4\\+0\\\hline\end{array}\qquad\begin{array}{r}3\\+3\\\hline\end{array}\qquad\begin{array}{r}2\\+1\\\hline\end{array}$$

3 + 1 = ____        4 + 1 = ____

0 + 2 = ____        2 + 4 = ____

$$\begin{array}{r}1\\+1\\\hline\end{array}\qquad\begin{array}{r}1\\+4\\\hline\end{array}\qquad\begin{array}{r}3\\+2\\\hline\end{array}\qquad\begin{array}{r}4\\+2\\\hline\end{array}$$

1 + 5 = ____        2 + 2 = ____

Score: _____        Time: _____ minutes _____ seconds

Name _____

# Timed Test

**Sums Through Six**

1 + 2 = ____    0 + 3 = ____

| 0 | 0 | 5 | 4 |
|---|---|---|---|
| + 0 | + 4 | + 1 | + 2 |

6 + 0 = ____    2 + 4 = ____

3 + 3 = ____    5 + 0 = ____

| 4 | 1 | 2 | 1 |
|---|---|---|---|
| + 0 | + 1 | + 1 | + 5 |

0 + 1 = ____    3 + 1 = ____

2 + 2 = ____    2 + 0 = ____

| 1 | 3 | 0 | 0 |
|---|---|---|---|
| + 3 | + 2 | + 6 | + 2 |

4 + 1 = ____    1 + 4 = ____

0 + 5 = ____    1 + 0 = ____

| 2 | 3 | 3 | 3 |
|---|---|---|---|
| + 3 | + 0 | + 3 | + 1 |

4 + 2 = ____    2 + 1 = ____

3 + 1 = ____    2 + 3 = ____

| 4 | 2 | 1 | 1 |
|---|---|---|---|
| + 1 | + 2 | + 4 | + 2 |

5 + 1 = ____    0 + 2 = ____

Score: _____    Time: _____ minutes _____ seconds

Name _____

# Timed Test

0 + 0 = _____     1 + 3 = _____     0 + 2 = _____     3 + 0 = _____

4 + 2 = _____     2 + 3 = _____     1 + 2 = _____     5 + 1 = _____

1 + 1 = _____     0 + 3 = _____     2 + 1 = _____     0 + 5 = _____

2 + 0 = _____     3 + 3 = _____     0 + 1 = _____     4 + 0 = _____

0 + 4 = _____     1 + 5 = _____     5 + 0 = _____     4 + 1 = _____

2 + 4 = _____     0 + 6 = _____     2 + 2 = _____     1 + 0 = _____

6 + 0 = _____     3 + 2 = _____     1 + 4 = _____     3 + 1 = _____

1 + 3 = _____     2 + 4 = _____     0 + 1 = _____     5 + 1 = _____

1 + 2 = _____     4 + 1 = _____     3 + 3 = _____     2 + 2 = _____

2 + 3 = _____     0 + 2 = _____     5 + 0 = _____     4 + 2 = _____

Sums Through Six

Score: _____     Time: _____ minutes _____ seconds

# Timed Test

**Sums Through Six**

| 1<br>+ 1 | 1<br>+ 2 | 1<br>+ 5 | 2<br>+ 3 | 2<br>+ 1 | 1<br>+ 0 | 1<br>+ 4 | 2<br>+ 2 |
|---|---|---|---|---|---|---|---|

| 6<br>+ 0 | 4<br>+ 0 | 3<br>+ 1 | 0<br>+ 6 | 0<br>+ 0 | 2<br>+ 0 | 5<br>+ 0 | 3<br>+ 2 |
|---|---|---|---|---|---|---|---|

| 0<br>+ 1 | 0<br>+ 5 | 0<br>+ 2 | 0<br>+ 4 | 3<br>+ 0 | 0<br>+ 3 | 3<br>+ 2 | 3<br>+ 3 |
|---|---|---|---|---|---|---|---|

| 1<br>+ 4 | 2<br>+ 1 | 1<br>+ 1 | 3<br>+ 1 | 2<br>+ 4 | 1<br>+ 5 | 4<br>+ 0 | 4<br>+ 1 |
|---|---|---|---|---|---|---|---|

| 2<br>+ 2 | 2<br>+ 4 | 4<br>+ 2 | 1<br>+ 3 | 4<br>+ 1 | 3<br>+ 3 | 5<br>+ 1 | 1<br>+ 2 |
|---|---|---|---|---|---|---|---|

Record your scores and times below.

**Page 17** Score:_____ Time:____min.____sec.    **Page 23** Score:_____ Time:____min.____sec.

**Page 18** Score:_____ Time:____min.____sec.    **Page 24** Score:_____ Time:____min.____sec.

**Page 19** Score:_____ Time:____min.____sec.    **Page 25** Score:_____ Time:____min.____sec.

**Page 20** Score:_____ Time:____min.____sec.    **Page 26** Score:_____ Time:____min.____sec.

**Page 21** Score:_____ Time:____min.____sec.    **Page 27** Score:_____ Time:____min.____sec.

**Page 22** Score:_____ Time:____min.____sec.    **Page 28** Score:_____ Time:____min.____sec.

Name _____

# Adding Zero

**Remember:** Zero is the identity element of addition. When zero is added to a number, that number does not change.

**Example:** 7 + 0 = 7

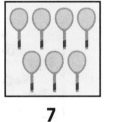    

**7**     **+**     **0**     **=**     **7**

■ Complete the **T** by adding zero to each number on the left. Then, write a number sentence for each problem.

+ 0
_____

7  | _____     _____ + _____ = _____

5  | _____     _____ + _____ = _____

9  | _____     _____ + _____ = _____

4  | _____     _____ + _____ = _____

8  | _____     _____ + _____ = _____

3  | _____     _____ + _____ = _____

0  | _____     _____ + _____ = _____

6  | _____     _____ + _____ = _____

Name _____

# Counting On

**Remember:** If one of the addends is a lesser number like 1, 2, or 3, you can find the sum by counting on from the other addend.

**Example:** 7 + 2    Start at 7 and count on 2 more. Count 7 . . . 8 . . . 9.
The sum is 9.

7    +    2    =    9

■ Count on to find these sums.

6 + 1 = _____        7 + 2 = _____        7 + 1 = _____        6 + 3 = _____

9 + 1 = _____        7 + 3 = _____        8 + 1 = _____        6 + 2 = _____

■ Complete each **T** by counting on.

| + 1 | | + 2 | | + 3 | |
|---|---|---|---|---|---|
| 6 | ___ | 8 | ___ | 6 | ___ |
| 7 | ___ | 5 | ___ | 5 | ___ |
| 9 | ___ | 7 | ___ | 7 | ___ |
| 8 | ___ | 6 | ___ | 4 | ___ |

# Changing the Order of the Addends

**Remember:** The commutative property of addition says that the sum is always the same no matter how the addends are arranged.

**Example:** 6 + 3 = 9 is the same as 3 + 6 = 9.

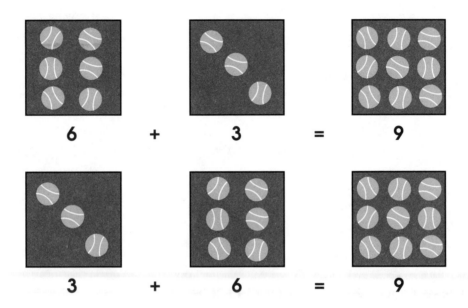

|  |  |  |  |  |
|---|---|---|---|---|
| 6 | + | 3 | = | 9 |

| | | | | |
|---|---|---|---|---|
| 3 | + | 6 | = | 9 |

■ Write another addition fact using the numbers in each fact below.

| 7 + 1 = 8 | 6 + 4 = 10 | 9 + 0 = 9 |
|---|---|---|
| ___ + ___ = ___ | ___ + ___ = ___ | ___ + ___ = ___ |
| 6 + 1 = 7 | 6 + 2 = 8 | 9 + 1 = 10 |
| ___ + ___ = ___ | ___ + ___ = ___ | ___ + ___ = ___ |
| 7 + 2 = 9 | 8 + 1 = 9 | 8 + 2 = 10 |
| ___ + ___ = ___ | ___ + ___ = ___ | ___ + ___ = ___ |

**Sums Through Ten**

# Adding Doubles

**Remember:** Two addends that are the same number are called doubles.

**Example:** 2 + 2 = 4

■ Add.

3 + 3 = ___          5 + 5 = ___          4 + 4 = ___

2 + 2 = ___          1 + 1 = ___          0 + 0 = ___

■ Add these doubles down and across.

| 1 | 1 |   |
|---|---|---|
| 1 | 1 |   |
|   |   |   |

| 2 | 2 |   |
|---|---|---|
| 2 | 2 |   |
|   |   |   |

**Sums Through Ten**

Name _____

# Practice

■ Add. Record your score—the number correct—on each Practice
page and on page 38.

1 + 6 = ____    8 + 0 = ____    3 + 4 = ____    6 + 4 = ____

6 + 1 = ____    2 + 6 = ____    4 + 3 = ____    3 + 6 = ____

4 + 5 = ____    6 + 2 = ____    0 + 7 = ____    6 + 3 = ____

5 + 4 = ____    1 + 8 = ____    7 + 0 = ____    0 + 9 = ____

9 + 1 = ____    8 + 1 - ____    2 + 5 = ____    9 + 0 = ____

1 + 9 = ____    2 + 8 = ____    5 + 2 = ____    2 + 7 = ____

3 + 5 = ____    8 + 2 = ____    1 + 7 = ____    7 + 2 = ____

5 + 3 = ____    4 + 4 = ____    7 + 1 = ____    3 + 7 = ____

0 + 8 = ____    5 + 5 = ____    4 + 6 = ____    7 + 3 = ____

**Sums Through Ten**

Score: _____

# Practice

■ Add.

| | | | | | | | | |
|---|---|---|---|---|---|---|---|---|
| 6<br>+3 | 3<br>+6 | 9<br>+0 | 0<br>+9 | 2<br>+6 | 6<br>+2 | 4<br>+4 | 3<br>+5 | 5<br>+3 |
| 9<br>+1 | 1<br>+9 | 4<br>+5 | 5<br>+4 | 8<br>+0 | 0<br>+8 | 8<br>+2 | 2<br>+8 | 1<br>+6 |
| 6<br>+1 | 3<br>+4 | 4<br>+3 | 3<br>+7 | 7<br>+3 | 8<br>+1 | 1<br>+8 | 5<br>+2 | 2<br>+5 |
| 5<br>+5 | 7<br>+2 | 2<br>+7 | 6<br>+4 | 4<br>+6 | 0<br>+7 | 7<br>+0 | 7<br>+1 | 1<br>+7 |

Score: _____

START

34

Name _____

# Practice

■ Add.

| | | | |
|---|---|---|---|
| 3 | 8 | 1 | 2 |
| + 6 | + 1 | + 7 | + 6 |

| | | | |
|---|---|---|---|
| 4 | 0 | 7 | 6 |
| + 5 | + 7 | + 3 | + 1 |

| | | | |
|---|---|---|---|
| 7 | 2 | 6 | 9 |
| + 0 | + 5 | + 2 | + 0 |

| | | | |
|---|---|---|---|
| 3 | 4 | 0 | 3 |
| + 5 | + 6 | + 9 | + 7 |

| | | | |
|---|---|---|---|
| 8 | 5 | 9 | 6 |
| + 2 | + 5 | + 1 | + 3 |

1 + 6 = ____    8 + 0 = ____

4 + 3 = ____    0 + 8 = ____

4 + 4 = ____    2 + 7 = ____

5 + 4 = ____    7 + 1 = ____

1 + 9 = ____    5 + 2 = ____

2 + 8 = ____    6 + 4 = ____

7 + 2 = ____    1 + 8 = ____

5 + 3 = ____    3 + 4 = ____

Score: _____

Name _____

# Practice

■ Add.

| | | | |
|---|---|---|---|
| 7<br>+ 0 | 1<br>+ 7 | 5<br>+ 5 | 3<br>+ 7 |
| 5<br>+ 2 | 7<br>+ 1 | 5<br>+ 3 | 1<br>+ 9 |
| 9<br>+ 0 | 4<br>+ 4 | 6<br>+ 4 | 1<br>+ 8 |
| 3<br>+ 4 | 2<br>+ 7 | 7<br>+ 3 | 3<br>+ 6 |
| 6<br>+ 1 | 0<br>+ 8 | 4<br>+ 5 | 3<br>+ 6 |

9 + 1 = _____        5 + 4 = _____

7 + 2 = _____        2 + 6 = _____

2 + 5 = _____        8 + 2 = _____

8 + 1 = _____        3 + 5 = _____

4 + 3 = _____        6 + 2 = _____

0 + 9 = _____        2 + 8 = _____

6 + 3 = _____        0 + 7 = _____

4 + 4 = _____        8 + 0 = _____

Score: _____

Name _____

# Practice

■ Add.

| | | | | | |
|---|---|---|---|---|---|
| 6 +4 | 4 +5 | 6 +2 | 1 +8 | 9 + 1 = ___ | 4 + 6 = ___ |

$$2 + 5 = \underline{\quad} \qquad 7 + 0 = \underline{\quad}$$

| 4 +4 | 2 +6 | 3 +7 | 8 +1 |
|---|---|---|---|

$$6 + 3 = \underline{\quad} \qquad 0 + 8 = \underline{\quad}$$

$$0 + 9 = \underline{\quad} \qquad 5 + 5 = \underline{\quad}$$

| 0 +7 | 7 +3 | 3 +6 | 8 +2 |
|---|---|---|---|

$$8 + 0 = \underline{\quad} \qquad 1 + 9 = \underline{\quad}$$

$$4 + 3 = \underline{\quad} \qquad 1 + 6 = \underline{\quad}$$

| 2 +8 | 5 +2 | 1 +7 | 5 +3 |
|---|---|---|---|

$$6 + 1 = \underline{\quad} \qquad 9 + 0 = \underline{\quad}$$

$$2 + 7 = \underline{\quad} \qquad 3 + 4 = \underline{\quad}$$

| 5 +4 | 7 +2 | 7 +3 | 6 +4 |
|---|---|---|---|

Score: _____

 Circle any problems that you still find difficult to remember. Make your own flash cards to help you master these problems.

FINISH

37

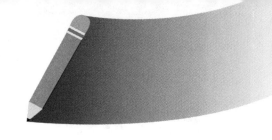

# Practice

■ Add.

3 + 5 = ____     2 + 8 = ____

$$\begin{array}{r} 2 \\ + 5 \\ \hline \end{array}$$ $$\begin{array}{r} 5 \\ + 4 \\ \hline \end{array}$$ $$\begin{array}{r} 3 \\ + 4 \\ \hline \end{array}$$ $$\begin{array}{r} 3 \\ + 7 \\ \hline \end{array}$$

5 + 3 = ____     5 + 5 = ____

0 + 9 = ____     9 + 1 = ____

$$\begin{array}{r} 7 \\ + 1 \\ \hline \end{array}$$ $$\begin{array}{r} 0 \\ + 8 \\ \hline \end{array}$$ $$\begin{array}{r} 9 \\ + 0 \\ \hline \end{array}$$ $$\begin{array}{r} 4 \\ + 4 \\ \hline \end{array}$$

2 + 6 = ____     0 + 7 = ____

7 + 0 = ____     4 + 5 = ____

$$\begin{array}{r} 7 \\ + 2 \\ \hline \end{array}$$ $$\begin{array}{r} 5 \\ + 2 \\ \hline \end{array}$$ $$\begin{array}{r} 6 \\ + 4 \\ \hline \end{array}$$ $$\begin{array}{r} 1 \\ + 6 \\ \hline \end{array}$$

3 + 6 = ____     7 + 3 = ____

8 + 2 = ____     1 + 8 = ____

$$\begin{array}{r} 6 \\ + 1 \\ \hline \end{array}$$ $$\begin{array}{r} 2 \\ + 7 \\ \hline \end{array}$$ $$\begin{array}{r} 4 \\ + 6 \\ \hline \end{array}$$ $$\begin{array}{r} 1 \\ + 9 \\ \hline \end{array}$$

1 + 7 = ____     6 + 3 = ____

$$\begin{array}{r} 4 \\ + 3 \\ \hline \end{array}$$ $$\begin{array}{r} 8 \\ + 0 \\ \hline \end{array}$$ $$\begin{array}{r} 6 \\ + 2 \\ \hline \end{array}$$ $$\begin{array}{r} 8 \\ + 1 \\ \hline \end{array}$$

Record your scores below.

**Page 33** Score: _____     **Page 36** Score: _____

**Page 34** Score: _____     **Page 37** Score: _____

**Page 35** Score: _____     **Page 38** Score: _____

Name _____

# Timed Test

■ Improve your speed on these basic facts. Ask someone to time you.
  Record your time and score on each Timed Test page and on page 50.

Record your time and score on each Timed Test page and on page 50.

0 + 8 = ____    5 + 3 = ____    5 + 4 = ____    2 + 6 = ____

2 + 5 = ____    2 + 8 = ____    0 + 7 = ____    7 + 0 = ____

7 + 3 = ____    8 + 0 = ____    5 + 2 = ____    3 + 7 = ____

1 + 6 = ____    3 + 6 = ____    3 + 5 = ____    8 + 1 = ____

7 + 1 = ____    6 + 4 = ____    4 + 6 = ____    0 + 9 = ____

3 + 4 = ____    1 + 8 = ____    2 + 7 = ____    6 + 2 = ____

6 + 1 = ____    4 + 5 = ____    1 + 7 = ____    4 + 3 = ____

6 + 3 = ____    8 + 2 = ____    4 + 4 = ____    5 + 5 = ____

1 + 9 = ____    7 + 2 = ____    9 + 1 = ____    9 + 0 = ____

3 + 7 = ____    2 + 8 = ____    5 + 4 = ____    4 + 6 = ____

**Sums Through Ten**

Score: _____    Time: _____ minutes _____ seconds

# Timed Test

■ Complete these facts as accurately and as quickly as you can.

| | | | | | | | |
|---|---|---|---|---|---|---|---|
| 6 | 0 | 4 | 7 | 2 | 8 | 3 | 5 |
| + 1 | + 9 | + 3 | + 0 | + 5 | + 1 | + 4 | + 4 |

| | | | | | | | |
|---|---|---|---|---|---|---|---|
| 7 | 3 | 6 | 9 | 1 | 7 | 2 | 8 |
| + 1 | + 6 | + 3 | + 0 | + 6 | + 2 | + 7 | + 0 |

| | | | | | | | |
|---|---|---|---|---|---|---|---|
| 4 | 4 | 2 | 3 | 5 | 1 | 5 | 3 |
| + 6 | + 4 | + 6 | + 7 | + 5 | + 7 | + 2 | + 5 |

| | | | | | | | |
|---|---|---|---|---|---|---|---|
| 4 | 9 | 7 | 0 | 6 | 2 | 5 | 1 |
| + 5 | + 1 | + 3 | + 7 | + 2 | + 8 | + 3 | + 8 |

| | | | | | | | |
|---|---|---|---|---|---|---|---|
| 0 | 1 | 8 | 6 | 5 | 6 | 7 | 4 |
| + 8 | + 9 | + 2 | + 4 | + 4 | + 3 | + 2 | + 4 |

**Sums Through Ten**

Score: _____    Time: _____ minutes _____ seconds

# Timed Test

3 + 5 = ____        6 + 1 = ____

9 + 1 = ____        3 + 7 = ____

6 + 3 = ____        7 + 1 = ____

1 + 9 = ____        0 + 8 = ____

7 + 2 = ____        5 + 3 = ____

2 + 8 = ____        1 + 7 = ____

4 + 5 = ____        6 + 4 = ____

8 + 2 = ____        0 + 7 = ____

5 + 5 = ____        7 + 3 = ____

2 + 5 = ____        1 + 8 = ____

$$\begin{array}{cccc} 9 & 3 & 6 & 1 \\ +0 & +6 & +2 & +6 \\ \hline \end{array}$$

$$\begin{array}{cccc} 7 & 4 & 3 & 4 \\ +3 & +6 & +4 & +4 \\ \hline \end{array}$$

$$\begin{array}{cccc} 0 & 8 & 5 & 2 \\ +9 & +0 & +2 & +7 \\ \hline \end{array}$$

$$\begin{array}{cccc} 5 & 1 & 7 & 4 \\ +4 & +8 & +0 & +3 \\ \hline \end{array}$$

$$\begin{array}{cccc} 5 & 8 & 2 & 2 \\ +5 & +1 & +6 & +5 \\ \hline \end{array}$$

**Sums Through Ten**

Score: ____        Time: ____ minutes ____ seconds

# Timed Test

**Sums Through Ten**

6 + 4 = ____     0 + 7 = ____

$$\begin{array}{cccc} 5 & 8 & 3 & 0 \\ +4 & +1 & +6 & +9 \\ \hline \end{array}$$

7 + 2 = ____     7 + 1 = ____

5 + 3 = ____     2 + 8 = ____

$$\begin{array}{cccc} 1 & 7 & 3 & 5 \\ +6 & +0 & +4 & +5 \\ \hline \end{array}$$

9 + 1 = ____     6 + 1 = ____

0 + 8 = ____     1 + 9 = ____

$$\begin{array}{cccc} 2 & 4 & 8 & 6 \\ +5 & +3 & +0 & +2 \\ \hline \end{array}$$

4 + 5 = ____     3 + 7 = ____

2 + 6 = ____     8 + 2 = ____

$$\begin{array}{cccc} 1 & 4 & 9 & 5 \\ +8 & +4 & +0 & +2 \\ \hline \end{array}$$

6 + 3 = ____     1 + 7 = ____

2 + 7 = ____     4 + 4 = ____

$$\begin{array}{cccc} 4 & 2 & 3 & 7 \\ +6 & +7 & +5 & +3 \\ \hline \end{array}$$

3 + 4 = ____     1 + 8 = ____

Score: _____     Time: _____ minutes _____ seconds

Name _____

# Timed Test

0 + 8 = ____     7 + 0 = ____     8     1     6     4
                                 + 0   + 9   + 3   + 3

8 + 1 = ____     0 + 9 = ____

4 + 4 = ____     4 + 6 = ____     6     0     3     8
                                 + 1   + 7   + 7   + 2

2 + 5 = ____     3 + 4 = ____

6 + 2 = ____     5 + 2 = ____     2     5     1     9
                                 + 7   + 5   + 6   + 1

1 + 8 = ____     1 + 7 = ____

3 + 6 = ____     5 + 3 = ____     5     7     2     6
                                 + 4   + 2   + 8   + 4

9 + 0 = ____     7 + 1 = ____

6 + 4 = ____     7 + 3 = ____     3     7     2     4
                                 + 5   + 3   + 6   + 5

2 + 6 = ____     5 + 4 = ____

Score: _____     Time: _____ minutes _____ seconds

# Timed Test

**Sums Through Ten**

5 + 4 = ____     5 + 5 = ____

$$\begin{array}{r} 3 \\ +5 \\ \hline \end{array} \quad \begin{array}{r} 1 \\ +7 \\ \hline \end{array} \quad \begin{array}{r} 1 \\ +8 \\ \hline \end{array} \quad \begin{array}{r} 5 \\ +2 \\ \hline \end{array}$$

4 + 3 = ____     1 + 9 = ____

9 + 1 = ____     7 + 2 = ____

$$\begin{array}{r} 7 \\ +0 \\ \hline \end{array} \quad \begin{array}{r} 3 \\ +4 \\ \hline \end{array} \quad \begin{array}{r} 4 \\ +4 \\ \hline \end{array} \quad \begin{array}{r} 0 \\ +9 \\ \hline \end{array}$$

8 + 0 = ____     3 + 7 = ____

2 + 7 = ____     6 + 4 = ____

$$\begin{array}{r} 6 \\ +2 \\ \hline \end{array} \quad \begin{array}{r} 3 \\ +6 \\ \hline \end{array} \quad \begin{array}{r} 8 \\ +1 \\ \hline \end{array} \quad \begin{array}{r} 4 \\ +6 \\ \hline \end{array}$$

7 + 3 = ____     6 + 3 = ____

4 + 5 = ____     2 + 8 = ____

$$\begin{array}{r} 9 \\ +0 \\ \hline \end{array} \quad \begin{array}{r} 5 \\ +2 \\ \hline \end{array} \quad \begin{array}{r} 5 \\ +3 \\ \hline \end{array} \quad \begin{array}{r} 2 \\ +6 \\ \hline \end{array}$$

8 + 2 = ____     0 + 7 = ____

5 + 3 = ____     8 + 1 = ____

$$\begin{array}{r} 7 \\ +1 \\ \hline \end{array} \quad \begin{array}{r} 0 \\ +8 \\ \hline \end{array} \quad \begin{array}{r} 6 \\ +1 \\ \hline \end{array} \quad \begin{array}{r} 1 \\ +6 \\ \hline \end{array}$$

4 + 4 = ____     6 + 2 = ____

Score: _____     Time: _____ minutes _____ seconds

Name _____

# Timed Test

The rest of the Timed Tests in this section will include some of the sums through 6 to help you remember what you have already learned.

3 + 6 = ____     1 + 5 = ____

$$\begin{array}{cccc} 5 & 1 & 7 & 3 \\ +5 & +6 & +0 & +7 \\ \hline \end{array}$$

5 + 1 = ____     5 + 2 = ____

0 + 9 = ____     7 + 2 = ____

$$\begin{array}{cccc} 5 & 2 & 3 & 5 \\ +4 & +8 & +0 & +3 \\ \hline \end{array}$$

7 + 1 = ____     4 + 4 = ____

3 + 4 = ____     4 + 6 = ____

$$\begin{array}{cccc} 4 & 8 & 7 & 0 \\ +5 & +2 & +3 & +7 \\ \hline \end{array}$$

9 + 0 = ____     0 + 4 = ____

2 + 5 = ____     2 + 7 = ____

$$\begin{array}{cccc} 4 & 6 & 7 & 2 \\ +2 & +3 & +0 & +6 \\ \hline \end{array}$$

6 + 4 = ____     6 + 1 = ____

4 + 3 = ____     0 + 8 = ____

$$\begin{array}{cccc} 1 & 6 & 0 & 1 \\ +1 & +2 & +0 & +8 \\ \hline \end{array}$$

3 + 3 = ____     4 + 5 = ____

**Sums Through Ten**

Score: _____     Time: _____ minutes _____ seconds

Name _____

# Timed Test

7 + 3 = ____     7 + 0 = ____

$$\begin{array}{r} 6 \\ +\ 2 \\ \hline \end{array} \quad \begin{array}{r} 3 \\ +\ 7 \\ \hline \end{array} \quad \begin{array}{r} 2 \\ +\ 6 \\ \hline \end{array} \quad \begin{array}{r} 7 \\ +\ 2 \\ \hline \end{array}$$

1 + 8 = ____     1 + 6 = ____

7 + 1 = ____     2 + 1 = ____

$$\begin{array}{r} 5 \\ +\ 2 \\ \hline \end{array} \quad \begin{array}{r} 5 \\ +\ 0 \\ \hline \end{array} \quad \begin{array}{r} 1 \\ +\ 7 \\ \hline \end{array} \quad \begin{array}{r} 9 \\ +\ 0 \\ \hline \end{array}$$

0 + 8 = ____     5 + 3 = ____

9 + 1 = ____     3 + 3 = ____

$$\begin{array}{r} 4 \\ +\ 3 \\ \hline \end{array} \quad \begin{array}{r} 2 \\ +\ 4 \\ \hline \end{array} \quad \begin{array}{r} 0 \\ +\ 9 \\ \hline \end{array} \quad \begin{array}{r} 8 \\ +\ 2 \\ \hline \end{array}$$

3 + 4 = ____     2 + 7 = ____

6 + 1 = ____     6 + 3 = ____

$$\begin{array}{r} 5 \\ +\ 4 \\ \hline \end{array} \quad \begin{array}{r} 3 \\ +\ 5 \\ \hline \end{array} \quad \begin{array}{r} 6 \\ +\ 4 \\ \hline \end{array} \quad \begin{array}{r} 1 \\ +\ 9 \\ \hline \end{array}$$

2 + 5 = ____     3 + 6 = ____

8 + 2 = ____     8 + 0 = ____

$$\begin{array}{r} 6 \\ +\ 0 \\ \hline \end{array} \quad \begin{array}{r} 5 \\ +\ 5 \\ \hline \end{array} \quad \begin{array}{r} 4 \\ +\ 1 \\ \hline \end{array} \quad \begin{array}{r} 2 \\ +\ 8 \\ \hline \end{array}$$

4 + 4 = ____     4 + 6 = ____

Score: _____     Time: _____ minutes _____ seconds

# Timed Test

3 + 4 = ____     2 + 6 = ____

$$\begin{array}{r} 9 \\ +\,1 \\ \hline \end{array} \quad \begin{array}{r} 3 \\ +\,2 \\ \hline \end{array} \quad \begin{array}{r} 8 \\ +\,1 \\ \hline \end{array} \quad \begin{array}{r} 6 \\ +\,2 \\ \hline \end{array}$$

8 + 0 = ____     5 + 2 = ____

6 + 3 = ____     7 + 0 = ____

$$\begin{array}{r} 3 \\ +\,5 \\ \hline \end{array} \quad \begin{array}{r} 1 \\ +\,2 \\ \hline \end{array} \quad \begin{array}{r} 2 \\ +\,5 \\ \hline \end{array} \quad \begin{array}{r} 4 \\ +\,4 \\ \hline \end{array}$$

4 + 5 = ____     2 + 4 = ____

5 + 1 = ____     1 + 7 = ____

$$\begin{array}{r} 2 \\ +\,7 \\ \hline \end{array} \quad \begin{array}{r} 0 \\ +\,8 \\ \hline \end{array} \quad \begin{array}{r} 7 \\ +\,3 \\ \hline \end{array} \quad \begin{array}{r} 5 \\ +\,5 \\ \hline \end{array}$$

1 + 9 = ____     3 + 6 = ____

4 + 3 = ____     2 + 8 = ____

$$\begin{array}{r} 4 \\ +\,6 \\ \hline \end{array} \quad \begin{array}{r} 2 \\ +\,3 \\ \hline \end{array} \quad \begin{array}{r} 1 \\ +\,6 \\ \hline \end{array} \quad \begin{array}{r} 3 \\ +\,7 \\ \hline \end{array}$$

6 + 1 = ____     5 + 4 = ____

8 + 2 = ____     0 + 9 = ____

$$\begin{array}{r} 7 \\ +\,1 \\ \hline \end{array} \quad \begin{array}{r} 9 \\ +\,0 \\ \hline \end{array} \quad \begin{array}{r} 4 \\ +\,2 \\ \hline \end{array} \quad \begin{array}{r} 6 \\ +\,4 \\ \hline \end{array}$$

0 + 7 = ____     3 + 3 = ____

Score: _____     Time: _____ minutes _____ seconds

# Timed Test

8 + 2 = ____    9 + 0 = ____

| 2 | 0 | 1 | 5 |
| +1 | +7 | +9 | +3 |

3 + 4 = ____    7 + 2 = ____

4 + 5 = ____    6 + 3 = ____

| 7 | 5 | 9 | 4 |
| +1 | +0 | +1 | +6 |

5 + 2 = ____    0 + 8 = ____

6 + 1 = ____    3 + 6 = ____

| 2 | 1 | 3 | 5 |
| +8 | +5 | +5 | +5 |

8 + 0 = ____    6 + 0 = ____

3 + 1 = ____    4 + 3 = ____

| 6 | 8 | 7 | 4 |
| +2 | +1 | +3 | +4 |

1 + 8 = ____    2 + 5 = ____

2 + 7 = ____    1 + 6 = ____

| 1 | 4 | 3 | 2 |
| +7 | +1 | +7 | +6 |

5 + 4 = ____    7 + 0 = ____

**Sums Through Ten**

Score: _____    Time: _____ minutes _____ seconds

Name _____

# Timed Test

1 + 8 = ____     7 + 0 = ____     5 + 5 = ____     1 + 7 = ____

0 + 6 = ____     1 + 6 = ____     0 + 9 = ____     0 + 8 = ____

6 + 3 = ____     8 + 2 = ____     6 + 1 = ____     2 + 7 = ____

9 + 0 = ____     4 + 5 = ____     6 + 4 = ____     5 + 3 = ____

4 + 3 = ____     1 + 3 = ____     1 + 4 = ____     1 + 9 = ____

4 + 0 = ____     5 + 2 = ____     4 + 4 = ____     3 + 5 = ____

2 + 8 = ____     2 + 6 = ____     7 + 1 = ____     8 + 0 = ____

5 + 4 = ____     3 + 4 = ____     3 + 7 = ____     2 + 3 = ____

0 + 7 = ____     7 + 3 = ____     0 + 2 = ____     9 + 1 = ____

3 + 6 = ____     3 + 2 = ____     7 + 2 = ____     6 + 2 = ____

**Sums Through Ten**

Score: _____     Time: _____ minutes _____ seconds

# Timed Test

Sums Through Ten

| | | | | | | | |
|---|---|---|---|---|---|---|---|
| 4<br>+ 4 | 1<br>+ 7 | 8<br>+ 0 | 3<br>+ 4 | 5<br>+ 3 | 2<br>+ 0 | 2<br>+ 5 | 6<br>+ 4 |
| 7<br>+ 2 | 1<br>+ 6 | 0<br>+ 3 | 6<br>+ 2 | 2<br>+ 7 | 5<br>+ 4 | 2<br>+ 2 | 7<br>+ 0 |
| 6<br>+ 1 | 1<br>+ 0 | 0<br>+ 9 | 8<br>+ 2 | 5<br>+ 2 | 1<br>+ 8 | 4<br>+ 6 | 1<br>+ 2 |
| 3<br>+ 5 | 2<br>+ 6 | 8<br>+ 1 | 4<br>+ 3 | 9<br>+ 1 | 0<br>+ 5 | 2<br>+ 8 | 7<br>+ 1 |
| 0<br>+ 7 | 3<br>+ 7 | 5<br>+ 3 | 4<br>+ 5 | 7<br>+ 3 | 0<br>+ 8 | 5<br>+ 5 | 3<br>+ 2 |

Record your scores and times below.

**Page 39** Score:_____ Time:___min.___sec.    **Page 45** Score:_____ Time:___min.___sec.

**Page 40** Score:_____ Time:___min.___sec.    **Page 46** Score:_____ Time:___min.___sec.

**Page 41** Score:_____ Time:___min.___sec.    **Page 47** Score:_____ Time:___min.___sec.

**Page 42** Score:_____ Time:___min.___sec.    **Page 48** Score:_____ Time:___min.___sec.

**Page 43** Score:_____ Time:___min.___sec.    **Page 49** Score:_____ Time:___min.___sec.

**Page 44** Score:_____ Time:___min.___sec.    **Page 50** Score:_____ Time:___min.___sec.

Name _____

# Counting On

**Remember:** If one of the addends is a lesser number like 1, 2, or 3, you can find the sum by counting on from the other addend.

**Example:** 9 + 2   Start at 9 and count on 2 more.
Count 9 . . . 10 . . . 11. The sum is 11.

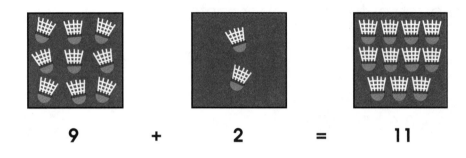

| 9 | + | 2 | = | 11 |
|---|---|---|---|----|

■ Count on to find these sums.

8 + 3 = ____     9 + 3 = ____

7 + 4 = ____     3 + 7 = ____

3 + 9 = ____     9 + 2 = ____

9 + 4 = ____     2 + 7 = ____

2 + 9 = ____     3 + 8 = ____

7 + 3 = ____     1 + 9 = ____

|  9 |  2 |  8 |  3 |
|----|----|----|----|
| + 2 | + 7 | + 3 | + 8 |

|  9 |  7 |  3 |  3 |
|----|----|----|----|
| + 2 | + 3 | + 9 | + 7 |

|  9 |  2 |  1 |  7 |
|----|----|----|----|
| + 3 | + 9 | + 9 | + 4 |

**Sums Through Eighteen**

51

# Thinking of Tens

Another way to remember certain sums is to think about tens.

**Example:** 8 + 6 = 14

**Think:** How much of 6 would be added to 8 to equal 10?
The answer is 8 + 2 = 10, with 4 left over. Therefore, 8 + 6 = 14.

■ Complete each of these number sentences.

9 + 4 is 9 + _____ (or 10), with _____ left over. Therefore, 9 + 4 = _____.

5 + 8 is _____ + 8 (or 10), with _____ left over. Therefore, 5 + 8 = _____.

9 + 7 is 9 + _____ (or 10), with _____ left over. Therefore, 9 + 7 = _____.

5 + 9 is _____ + 9 (or 10), with _____ left over. Therefore, 5 + 9 = _____.

4 + 7 is _____ + 7 (or 10), with _____ left over. Therefore, 4 + 7 = _____.

■ Think about tens as you complete these facts.

6 + 7 = ____     8 + 5 = ____     9 + 6 = ____     6 + 8 = ____

9 + 8 = ____     4 + 9 = ____     4 + 7 = ____     9 + 5 = ____

8 + 7 = ____     5 + 8 = ____     5 + 7 = ____     7 + 9 = ____

5 + 6 = ____     8 + 4 = ____     5 + 9 = ____     6 + 9 = ____

**Sums Through Eighteen**

Name _____

# Changing the Order of the Addends

**Remember:** The commutative property of addition says that the sum is always the same no matter how the addends are arranged.

**Example:** 9 + 4 = 13 is the same as 4 + 9 = 13.

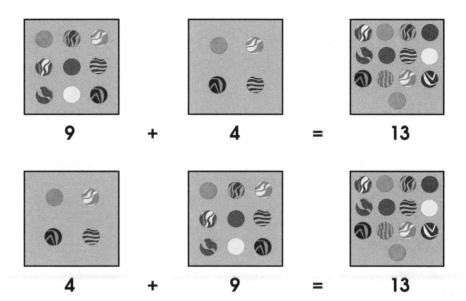

9    +    4    =    13

4    +    9    =    13

■ Write another addition fact using the numbers in each fact below.

| 8 + 4 = 12 | 3 + 9 = 12 | 5 + 6 = 11 |
|---|---|---|
| ___ + ___ = ___ | ___ + ___ = ___ | ___ + ___ = ___ |
| 8 + 6 = 14 | 8 + 7 = 15 | 9 + 5 = 14 |
| ___ + ___ = ___ | ___ + ___ = ___ | ___ + ___ = ___ |
| 6 + 9 = 15 | 8 + 3 = 11 | 5 + 7 = 12 |
| ___ + ___ = ___ | ___ + ___ = ___ | ___ + ___ = ___ |

Sums Through Eighteen

Name _____

# Adding Doubles

**Remember:** Two addends that are the same number are called doubles.

**Example:** 6 + 6 = 12

■ Add.

9 + 9 = ____     7 + 7 = ____     8 + 8 = ____     6 + 6 = ____

$$\begin{array}{r} 8 \\ + 8 \\ \hline \end{array} \qquad \begin{array}{r} 6 \\ + 6 \\ \hline \end{array} \qquad \begin{array}{r} 7 \\ + 7 \\ \hline \end{array} \qquad \begin{array}{r} 9 \\ + 9 \\ \hline \end{array}$$

■ Add these doubles down and across.

| 3 | 3 | |
|---|---|---|
| 3 | 3 | |
| | | |

| 4 | 4 | |
|---|---|---|
| 4 | 4 | |
| | | |

**Remember:** The sums of doubles are always even numbers, like 10, 12, and 14. This is true even if the addends are odd numbers like 7 and 9.

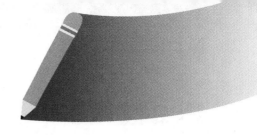

# Practice

■ Add. Record your score—the number correct—on each Practice page and on page 60.

5 + 7 = 12     9 + 5 = ____     6 + 9 = ____     7 + 9 = ____

9 + 7 = ____     7 + 7 = ____     9 + 9 = ____     3 + 8 = ____

2 + 9 = ____     8 + 9 = ____     3 + 9 = ____     9 + 6 = ____

7 + 8 = ____     5 + 8 = ____     9 + 8 = ____     7 + 4 = ____

5 + 6 = ____     8 + 7 = ____     6 + 6 = ____     4 + 9 = ____

9 + 3 = ____     8 + 3 = ____     9 + 2 = ____     8 + 8 = ____

6 + 8 = ____     7 + 6 = ____     4 + 8 = ____     7 + 5 = ____

8 + 5 = ____     6 + 7 = ____     8 + 6 = ____     8 + 4 = ____

4 + 7 = ____     5 + 9 = ____     6 + 5 = ____     5 + 5 = ____

**Sums Through Eighteen**

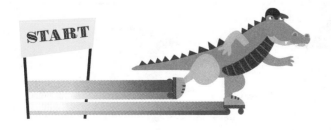
START

Score: _____

Name _____

# Practice

■ Add.

| 3 | 8 | 5 | 8 | 2 | 6 | 9 | 5 | 9 |
|---|---|---|---|---|---|---|---|---|
| + 9 | + 7 | + 8 | + 4 | + 9 | + 7 | + 2 | + 6 | + 5 |

| 6 | 8 | 4 | 7 | 9 | 6 | 7 | 4 | 7 |
|---|---|---|---|---|---|---|---|---|
| + 9 | + 9 | + 8 | + 6 | + 7 | + 5 | + 9 | + 9 | + 7 |

| 7 | 8 | 5 | 8 | 6 | 9 | 3 | 7 | 9 |
|---|---|---|---|---|---|---|---|---|
| + 5 | + 8 | + 9 | + 6 | + 8 | + 6 | + 8 | + 4 | + 3 |

| 5 | 8 | 9 | 4 | 9 | 7 | 9 | 6 | 8 |
|---|---|---|---|---|---|---|---|---|
| + 7 | + 3 | + 8 | + 7 | + 9 | + 8 | + 4 | + 6 | + 5 |

Score: _____

START

## Name _____

# Practice

■ Add.

| | | | |
|---|---|---|---|
| 8<br>+ 9 | 7<br>+ 6 | 4<br>+ 7 | 6<br>+ 5 |
| 8<br>+ 7 | 8<br>+ 5 | 9<br>+ 8 | 6<br>+ 7 |
| 3<br>+ 8 | 5<br>+ 8 | 9<br>+ 7 | 8<br>+ 3 |
| 6<br>+ 9 | 7<br>+ 8 | 9<br>+ 4 | 5<br>+ 6 |
| 7<br>+ 7 | 9<br>+ 6 | 4<br>+ 9 | 9<br>+ 3 |

7 + 4 = ____    9 + 2 = ____

8 + 8 = ____    6 + 8 = ____

6 + 6 = ____    5 + 9 = ____

3 + 9 = ____    4 + 8 = ____

8 + 4 = ____    7 + 9 = ____

7 + 5 = ____    9 + 5 = ____

9 + 9 = ____    5 + 7 = ____

8 + 6 = ____    2 + 9 = ____

**Sums Through Eighteen**

Score: _____

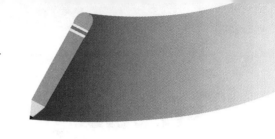

## Name _____

# Practice

■ Add.

| | | | |
|---|---|---|---|
| 7 | 8 | 8 | 4 |
| + 5 | + 6 | + 8 | + 8 |

7 + 8 = ____        5 + 6 = ____

9 + 8 = ____        9 + 7 = ____

| | | | |
|---|---|---|---|
| 9 | 9 | 9 | 7 |
| + 6 | + 9 | + 5 | + 4 |

6 + 9 = ____        4 + 9 = ____

4 + 7 = ____        6 + 5 = ____

| | | | |
|---|---|---|---|
| 7 | 3 | 6 | 7 |
| + 9 | + 9 | + 8 | + 7 |

8 + 3 = ____        3 + 8 = ____

8 + 5 = ____        7 + 6 = ____

| | | | |
|---|---|---|---|
| 5 | 6 | 5 | 9 |
| + 7 | + 6 | + 9 | + 2 |

9 + 3 = ____        5 + 8 = ____

6 + 7 = ____        8 + 7 = ____

| | | | |
|---|---|---|---|
| 8 | 9 | 2 | 8 |
| + 9 | + 4 | + 9 | + 4 |

Score: _____

# Practice

■ Add.

| | | | | | |
|---|---|---|---|---|---|
| 9<br>+ 8 | 6<br>+ 7 | 5<br>+ 6 | 8<br>+ 3 | 9 + 7 = ____ | 5 + 7 = ____ |
| | | | | 4 + 8 = ____ | 8 + 9 = ____ |
| 3<br>+ 8 | 7<br>+ 8 | 6<br>+ 5 | 9<br>+ 6 | 9 + 5 = ____ | 7 + 5 = ____ |
| | | | | 6 + 8 = ____ | 8 + 7 = ____ |
| 7<br>+ 6 | 9<br>+ 9 | 3<br>+ 9 | 8<br>+ 5 | 7 + 9 = ____ | 4 + 9 = ____ |
| | | | | 4 + 7 = ____ | 8 + 4 = ____ |
| 8<br>+ 6 | 5<br>+ 8 | 9<br>+ 4 | 6<br>+ 9 | 7 + 7 = ____ | 7 + 4 = ____ |
| | | | | 6 + 6 = ____ | 5 + 9 = ____ |
| 8<br>+ 8 | 9<br>+ 2 | 8<br>+ 7 | 9<br>+ 3 | | |

**Sums Through Eighteen**

Score: _____

Circle any problems that you still find difficult to remember. Make your own flash cards to help you master these problems.

FINISH

Name _____

# Practice

■ Add.

$9 + 9 =$ _____     $6 + 9 =$ _____

| 7 | 8 | 6 | 9 |
|---|---|---|---|
| + 5 | + 8 | + 8 | + 2 |

$8 + 3 =$ _____     $5 + 6 =$ _____

$2 + 9 =$ _____     $3 + 9 =$ _____

| 6 | 7 | 5 | 5 |
|---|---|---|---|
| + 6 | + 9 | + 9 | + 7 |

$9 + 6 =$ _____     $7 + 6 =$ _____

$9 + 3 =$ _____     $5 + 8 =$ _____

| 4 | 8 | 8 | 9 |
|---|---|---|---|
| + 7 | + 7 | + 4 | + 5 |

$6 + 7 =$ _____     $3 + 8 =$ _____

$7 + 8 =$ _____     $8 + 5 =$ _____

| 7 | 8 | 4 | 7 |
|---|---|---|---|
| + 4 | + 9 | + 9 | + 7 |

$8 + 6 =$ _____     $6 + 5 =$ _____

| 9 | 9 | 7 | 8 |
|---|---|---|---|
| + 8 | + 4 | + 6 | + 5 |

---

Record your scores below.

**Page 55** Score: _____     **Page 58** Score: _____

**Page 56** Score: _____     **Page 59** Score: _____

**Page 57** Score: _____     **Page 60** Score: _____

# Timed Test

■ Improve your speed on these basic facts. Ask someone to time you. Record your time and score on each Timed Test page and on page 72.

| | | | |
|---|---|---|---|
| 9 + 6 = ___ | 9 + 8 = ___ | 8 + 6 = ___ | 5 + 7 = ___ |
| 5 + 8 = ___ | 5 + 9 = ___ | 4 + 7 = ___ | 9 + 2 = ___ |
| 2 + 9 = ___ | 7 + 6 = ___ | 9 + 4 = ___ | 7 + 8 = ___ |
| 9 + 5 = ___ | 3 + 9 = ___ | 6 + 8 = ___ | 8 + 8 = ___ |
| 7 + 4 = ___ | 8 + 3 = ___ | 8 + 5 = ___ | 6 + 5 = ___ |
| 9 + 3 = ___ | 6 + 7 = ___ | 3 + 8 = ___ | 4 + 6 = ___ |
| 5 + 6 = ___ | 8 + 7 = ___ | 9 + 7 = ___ | 7 + 9 = ___ |
| 8 + 9 = ___ | 4 + 8 = ___ | 7 + 5 = ___ | 4 + 9 = ___ |
| 8 + 4 = ___ | 6 + 9 = ___ | 9 + 9 = ___ | 6 + 6 = ___ |
| 7 + 8 = ___ | 8 + 6 = ___ | 7 + 7 = ___ | 3 + 9 = ___ |

**Sums Through Eighteen**

Score: _____     Time: _____ minutes _____ seconds

Name _____

# Timed Test

■ Complete these facts as accurately and as quickly as you can.

**Sums Through Eighteen**

|  |  |  |  |  |  |  |  |
|---|---|---|---|---|---|---|---|
| 7<br>+ 5 | 4<br>+ 9 | 6<br>+ 6 | 7<br>+ 6 | 9<br>+ 4 | 3<br>+ 8 | 5<br>+ 6 | 7<br>+ 7 |
| 6<br>+ 9 | 8<br>+ 6 | 8<br>+ 9 | 4<br>+ 7 | 5<br>+ 7 | 6<br>+ 8 | 7<br>+ 9 | 9<br>+ 7 |
| 9<br>+ 9 | 8<br>+ 5 | 9<br>+ 5 | 4<br>+ 8 | 6<br>+ 5 | 7<br>+ 4 | 9<br>+ 3 | 7<br>+ 8 |
| 2<br>+ 9 | 5<br>+ 8 | 9<br>+ 8 | 8<br>+ 4 | 8<br>+ 8 | 9<br>+ 6 | 3<br>+ 9 | 5<br>+ 9 |
| 8<br>+ 3 | 6<br>+ 7 | 9<br>+ 2 | 8<br>+ 7 | 6<br>+ 6 | 9<br>+ 3 | 6<br>+ 8 | 9<br>+ 7 |

Score: _____     Time: _____ minutes _____ seconds

# Timed Test

3 + 8 = _____    8 + 8 = _____

| 4 | 9 | 2 | 9 |
|---|---|---|---|
| + 7 | + 4 | + 9 | + 5 |

8 + 4 = _____    6 + 5 = _____

9 + 7 = _____    7 + 6 = _____

| 7 | 8 | 6 | 8 |
|---|---|---|---|
| + 4 | + 7 | + 6 | + 3 |

5 + 6 = _____    8 + 9 = _____

7 + 9 = _____    5 + 7 = _____

| 7 | 9 | 4 | 7 |
|---|---|---|---|
| + 5 | + 2 | + 9 | + 8 |

9 + 6 = _____    8 + 6 = _____

4 + 8 = _____    6 + 7 = _____

| 9 | 5 | 3 | 8 |
|---|---|---|---|
| + 8 | + 8 | + 9 | + 5 |

9 + 3 = _____    9 + 9 = _____

6 + 9 = _____    5 + 9 = _____

| 6 | 7 | 7 | 8 |
|---|---|---|---|
| + 8 | + 7 | + 9 | + 4 |

8 + 7 = _____    2 + 9 = _____

**Sums Through Eighteen**

Score: _____    Time: _____ minutes _____ seconds

# Timed Test

**Sums Through Eighteen**

$9 + 2 =$ _____     $4 + 9 =$ _____

$7 + 4 =$ _____     $4 + 7 =$ _____

$3 + 9 =$ _____     $5 + 8 =$ _____

$7 + 5 =$ _____     $6 + 6 =$ _____

$2 + 9 =$ _____     $7 + 8 =$ _____

$6 + 8 =$ _____     $9 + 4 =$ _____

$8 + 3 =$ _____     $7 + 7 =$ _____

$9 + 8 =$ _____     $8 + 7 =$ _____

$9 + 5 =$ _____     $8 + 5 =$ _____

$4 + 8 =$ _____     $7 + 6 =$ _____

$$
\begin{array}{cccc}
5 & 8 & 3 & 6 \\
+6 & +8 & +8 & +7 \\
\hline
\end{array}
$$

$$
\begin{array}{cccc}
5 & 7 & 9 & 9 \\
+7 & +9 & +3 & +9 \\
\hline
\end{array}
$$

$$
\begin{array}{cccc}
9 & 8 & 6 & 5 \\
+7 & +9 & +9 & +9 \\
\hline
\end{array}
$$

$$
\begin{array}{cccc}
9 & 6 & 8 & 8 \\
+6 & +5 & +6 & +4 \\
\hline
\end{array}
$$

$$
\begin{array}{cccc}
7 & 4 & 9 & 8 \\
+6 & +8 & +8 & +7 \\
\hline
\end{array}
$$

Score: _____     Time: _____ minutes _____ seconds

# Timed Test

5 + 7 = ____        6 + 7 = ____

$$\begin{array}{r} 7 \\ +6 \\ \hline \end{array} \quad \begin{array}{r} 9 \\ +2 \\ \hline \end{array} \quad \begin{array}{r} 5 \\ +6 \\ \hline \end{array} \quad \begin{array}{r} 4 \\ +7 \\ \hline \end{array}$$

8 + 9 = ____        8 + 8 = ____

4 + 8 = ____        6 + 9 = ____

$$\begin{array}{r} 9 \\ +6 \\ \hline \end{array} \quad \begin{array}{r} 7 \\ +4 \\ \hline \end{array} \quad \begin{array}{r} 8 \\ +5 \\ \hline \end{array} \quad \begin{array}{r} 2 \\ +9 \\ \hline \end{array}$$

9 + 9 = ____        9 + 7 = ____

7 + 5 = ____        6 + 5 = ____

$$\begin{array}{r} 9 \\ +8 \\ \hline \end{array} \quad \begin{array}{r} 6 \\ +6 \\ \hline \end{array} \quad \begin{array}{r} 6 \\ +8 \\ \hline \end{array} \quad \begin{array}{r} 8 \\ +7 \\ \hline \end{array}$$

8 + 6 = ____        8 + 3 = ____

7 + 7 = ____        5 + 8 = ____

$$\begin{array}{r} 3 \\ +9 \\ \hline \end{array} \quad \begin{array}{r} 8 \\ +4 \\ \hline \end{array} \quad \begin{array}{r} 4 \\ +9 \\ \hline \end{array} \quad \begin{array}{r} 9 \\ +4 \\ \hline \end{array}$$

3 + 8 = ____        9 + 3 = ____

9 + 5 = ____        7 + 9 = ____

$$\begin{array}{r} 5 \\ +9 \\ \hline \end{array} \quad \begin{array}{r} 7 \\ +8 \\ \hline \end{array} \quad \begin{array}{r} 6 \\ +9 \\ \hline \end{array} \quad \begin{array}{r} 8 \\ +3 \\ \hline \end{array}$$

8 + 7 = ____        7 + 4 = ____

**Sums Through Eighteen**

Score: _____        Time: _____ minutes _____ seconds

Name _____

# Timed Test

4 + 7 = _____    7 + 4 = _____

8 + 7 = _____    8 + 4 = _____

7 + 6 = _____    9 + 6 = _____

7 + 8 = _____    6 + 8 = _____

3 + 9 = _____    9 + 4 = _____

5 + 9 = _____    8 + 5 = _____

5 + 6 = _____    9 + 2 = _____

4 + 9 = _____    9 + 8 = _____

6 + 6 = _____    2 + 9 = _____

6 + 7 = _____    6 + 9 = _____

| 9 | 3 | 7 | 9 |
|---|---|---|---|
| + 9 | + 8 | + 9 | + 3 |

| 8 | 4 | 5 | 7 |
|---|---|---|---|
| + 8 | + 8 | + 8 | + 7 |

| 8 | 5 | 9 | 7 |
|---|---|---|---|
| + 3 | + 7 | + 5 | + 5 |

| 6 | 6 | 9 | 8 |
|---|---|---|---|
| + 9 | + 7 | + 7 | + 9 |

| 6 | 8 | 8 | 9 |
|---|---|---|---|
| + 5 | + 6 | + 4 | + 9 |

Score: _____    Time: _____ minutes _____ seconds

# Timed Test

The rest of the Timed Tests in this section will also include some of the sums through 10 to help you remember what you have already learned.

7 + 6 = _____     5 + 7 = _____

$$\begin{array}{cccc} 7 & 3 & 7 & 9 \\ +1 & +9 & +7 & +2 \\ \hline \end{array}$$

4 + 7 = _____     7 + 8 = _____

8 + 9 = _____     0 + 7 = _____

$$\begin{array}{cccc} 8 & 6 & 5 & 8 \\ +0 & +7 & +8 & +6 \\ \hline \end{array}$$

6 + 8 = _____     9 + 8 = _____

9 + 1 = _____     6 + 6 = _____

$$\begin{array}{cccc} 9 & 2 & 7 & 5 \\ +7 & +9 & +9 & +6 \\ \hline \end{array}$$

9 + 5 = _____     1 + 9 = _____

3 + 8 = _____     9 + 3 = _____

$$\begin{array}{cccc} 7 & 9 & 5 & 8 \\ +5 & +6 & +3 & +8 \\ \hline \end{array}$$

3 + 6 = _____     5 + 9 = _____

8 + 5 = _____     8 + 3 = _____

$$\begin{array}{cccc} 4 & 9 & 2 & 8 \\ +8 & +4 & +7 & +4 \\ \hline \end{array}$$

4 + 3 = _____     8 + 6 = _____

**Sums Through Eighteen**

Score: _____     Time: _____ minutes _____ seconds

Name _____

# Timed Test

6 + 8 = ____     7 + 5 = ____

$$\begin{array}{r} 7 \\ + 4 \\ \hline \end{array} \quad \begin{array}{r} 8 \\ + 6 \\ \hline \end{array} \quad \begin{array}{r} 7 \\ + 2 \\ \hline \end{array} \quad \begin{array}{r} 6 \\ + 9 \\ \hline \end{array}$$

4 + 3 = ____     8 + 4 = ____

8 + 5 = ____     0 + 9 = ____

$$\begin{array}{r} 4 \\ + 7 \\ \hline \end{array} \quad \begin{array}{r} 9 \\ + 6 \\ \hline \end{array} \quad \begin{array}{r} 7 \\ + 9 \\ \hline \end{array} \quad \begin{array}{r} 6 \\ + 7 \\ \hline \end{array}$$

9 + 7 = ____     2 + 9 = ____

4 + 8 = ____     8 + 7 = ____

$$\begin{array}{r} 9 \\ + 4 \\ \hline \end{array} \quad \begin{array}{r} 9 \\ + 0 \\ \hline \end{array} \quad \begin{array}{r} 8 \\ + 3 \\ \hline \end{array} \quad \begin{array}{r} 5 \\ + 7 \\ \hline \end{array}$$

8 + 2 = ____     2 + 6 = ____

9 + 5 = ____     9 + 9 = ____

$$\begin{array}{r} 8 \\ + 8 \\ \hline \end{array} \quad \begin{array}{r} 4 \\ + 9 \\ \hline \end{array} \quad \begin{array}{r} 6 \\ + 5 \\ \hline \end{array} \quad \begin{array}{r} 5 \\ + 9 \\ \hline \end{array}$$

6 + 6 = ____     5 + 8 = ____

8 + 9 = ____     9 + 3 = ____

$$\begin{array}{r} 9 \\ + 2 \\ \hline \end{array} \quad \begin{array}{r} 6 \\ + 3 \\ \hline \end{array} \quad \begin{array}{r} 7 \\ + 7 \\ \hline \end{array} \quad \begin{array}{r} 3 \\ + 8 \\ \hline \end{array}$$

5 + 6 = ____     5 + 5 = ____

Score: _____     Time: _____ minutes _____ seconds

# Timed Test

6 + 4 = ____     5 + 8 = ____     9 + 4 = ____     8 + 9 = ____

8 + 4 = ____     9 + 2 = ____     6 + 2 = ____     3 + 8 = ____

7 + 9 = ____     7 + 7 = ____     5 + 9 = ____     8 + 5 = ____

6 + 5 = ____     2 + 9 = ____     9 + 3 = ____     6 + 8 = ____

2 + 8 = ____     8 + 6 = ____     5 + 5 = ____     3 + 7 = ____

4 + 8 = ____     9 + 8 = ____     8 + 3 = ____     7 + 6 = ____

7 + 5 = ____     6 + 7 = ____     9 + 9 = ____     4 + 9 = ____

6 + 9 = ____     3 + 4 = ____     7 + 4 = ____     6 + 1 = ____

3 + 9 = ____     5 + 6 = ____     9 + 1 = ____     9 + 7 = ____

9 + 6 = ____     8 + 8 = ____     5 + 7 = ____     7 + 8 = ____

**Sums Through Eighteen**

Score: _____     Time: _____ minutes _____ seconds

Name _____

# Timed Test

9 + 3 = ____     7 + 4 = ____

| | | | |
|---|---|---|---|
| 8 | 3 | 4 | 5 |
| + 4 | + 9 | + 5 | + 6 |

4 + 7 = ____     8 + 5 = ____

8 + 7 = ____     5 + 4 = ____

| | | | |
|---|---|---|---|
| 7 | 8 | 7 | 6 |
| + 5 | + 6 | + 3 | + 7 |

7 + 2 = ____     6 + 8 = ____

9 + 7 = ____     8 + 9 = ____

| | | | |
|---|---|---|---|
| 9 | 6 | 8 | 3 |
| + 2 | + 9 | + 8 | + 6 |

5 + 9 = ____     7 + 6 = ____

7 + 8 = ____     9 + 5 = ____

| | | | |
|---|---|---|---|
| 2 | 5 | 6 | 7 |
| + 9 | + 8 | + 5 | + 9 |

3 + 8 = ____     8 + 3 = ____

8 + 2 = ____     4 + 6 = ____

| | | | |
|---|---|---|---|
| 5 | 9 | 9 | 3 |
| + 3 | + 8 | + 4 | + 5 |

9 + 9 = ____     6 + 6 = ____

Score: _____     Time: _____ minutes _____ seconds

Name _____

# Timed Test

4 + 5 = _____     1 + 6 = _____     7 + 9 = _____     8 + 3 = _____

5 + 9 = _____     8 + 4 = _____     8 + 6 = _____     0 + 8 = _____

9 + 2 = _____     6 + 8 = _____     9 + 5 = _____     9 + 3 = _____

2 + 5 = _____     3 + 9 = _____     8 + 9 = _____     5 + 8 = _____

8 + 8 = _____     7 + 4 = _____     4 + 7 = _____     9 + 4 = _____

6 + 6 = _____     3 + 4 = _____     8 + 5 = _____     3 + 5 = _____

2 + 9 = _____     7 + 7 = _____     2 + 8 = _____     8 + 7 = _____

9 + 7 = _____     5 + 6 = _____     6 + 5 = _____     4 + 9 = _____

4 + 8 = _____     7 + 5 = _____     3 + 8 = _____     7 + 6 = _____

9 + 9 = _____     3 + 7 = _____     9 + 8 = _____     1 + 8 = _____

**Sums Through Eighteen**

Score: _____     Time: _____ minutes _____ seconds

Name _____

# Timed Test

**Sums Through Eighteen**

| | | | | | | | |
|---|---|---|---|---|---|---|---|
| 7<br>+5 | 5<br>+9 | 9<br>+6 | 7<br>+3 | 8<br>+9 | 4<br>+7 | 8<br>+5 | 8<br>+1 |
| 3<br>+9 | 7<br>+7 | 5<br>+4 | 5<br>+7 | 2<br>+9 | 6<br>+6 | 9<br>+5 | 6<br>+1 |
| 4<br>+9 | 9<br>+3 | 6<br>+4 | 7<br>+9 | 8<br>+7 | 7<br>+6 | 9<br>+8 | 7<br>+0 |
| 7<br>+4 | 4<br>+8 | 9<br>+2 | 5<br>+8 | 9<br>+4 | 5<br>+2 | 8<br>+3 | 6<br>+9 |
| 6<br>+8 | 9<br>+7 | 3<br>+8 | 5<br>+6 | 8<br>+6 | 8<br>+8 | 5<br>+9 | 2<br>+8 |

Record your scores and times below.

| | |
|---|---|
| **Page 61** Score:_____ Time:___min.___sec. | **Page 67** Score:_____ Time:___min.___sec. |
| **Page 62** Score:_____ Time:___min.___sec. | **Page 68** Score:_____ Time:___min.___sec. |
| **Page 63** Score:_____ Time:___min.___sec. | **Page 69** Score:_____ Time:___min.___sec. |
| **Page 64** Score:_____ Time:___min.___sec. | **Page 70** Score:_____ Time:___min.___sec. |
| **Page 65** Score:_____ Time:___min.___sec. | **Page 71** Score:_____ Time:___min.___sec. |
| **Page 66** Score:_____ Time:___min.___sec. | **Page 72** Score:_____ Time:___min.___sec. |

# SUBTRACTION

# What Is Subtraction?

You subtract to find how many are left. The answer is called the **difference**.

5 birds take away 2 birds equals 3 birds.

There are two ways to show the subtraction.

5 – 2 = 3
$$\begin{array}{r} 5 \\ -\,2 \\ \hline 3 \end{array}$$

You can draw a picture to find how many are left.

**Example:** Find the difference.   6 – 2 = _____

**Step 1:** Draw 6 dots. ———→  ● ● ● ● ● ●

**Step 2:** Cross out 2 dots.  ——→  ✗ ✗ ● ● ● ●

**Step 3:** Count the remaining dots.

**Answer:** 6 – 2 = __4__

■ Draw a picture to find the difference.

4 – 1 = ___

4 – 2 = ___

6 – 2 = ___

6 – 5 = ___

5 – 3 = ___

6 – 3 = ___

**Subtraction**

# What Is Subtraction?

You can use counters to find the difference. You will need some pennies.

**Example:** Find the difference.  5 – 2 = _____

**Step 1:** Put 5 pennies in the box. ————→

**Step 2:** Take out 2 pennies. ————→

**Step 3:** Count the pennies that are left. —→

**Answer:** 5 – 2 =  __3__

■ Use counters to find the difference.

6 – 3 = ___          6 – 4 = ___          7 – 4 = ___

$$\begin{array}{r} 5 \\ -\ 4 \\ \hline \end{array} \qquad \begin{array}{r} 4 \\ -\ 1 \\ \hline \end{array} \qquad \begin{array}{r} 7 \\ -\ 5 \\ \hline \end{array} \qquad \begin{array}{r} 3 \\ -\ 1 \\ \hline \end{array} \qquad \begin{array}{r} 5 \\ -\ 2 \\ \hline \end{array}$$

You can use a number line to find the difference.

**Example:** Find the answer.  8 – 3 = _____

**Step 1:** Put your finger on 8.

**Step 2:** Move your finger 3 spaces to the left.

**Step 3:** Read the number your finger is on.

**Answer:** 8 – 3 =  __5__

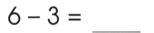

1  2  3  4  5  6  7  8  9  10

■ Use the number line to find the difference.

4 – 1 = ___          5 – 3 = ___          8 – 5 = ___

$$\begin{array}{r} 4 \\ -\ 2 \\ \hline \end{array} \qquad \begin{array}{r} 7 \\ -\ 5 \\ \hline \end{array} \qquad \begin{array}{r} 3 \\ -\ 2 \\ \hline \end{array} \qquad \begin{array}{r} 6 \\ -\ 4 \\ \hline \end{array} \qquad \begin{array}{r} 6 \\ -\ 5 \\ \hline \end{array}$$

**Subtraction**

# Subtracting Zero

Just as it is in addition, zero is the **identity element of subtraction**. This means that, when zero is subtracted from a number, the difference is that number.

**Example:** 3 – 0 = 3

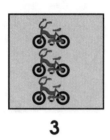    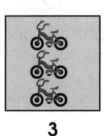

**3**      **–**      **0**      **=**      **3**

■ Complete this **T** by subtracting zero from each number.

■ Write the difference for each fact.

$$\begin{array}{r} -\ 0 \\ \hline \end{array}$$

1 | _____

3 | _____

2 | _____

0 | _____

2 – 0 = _____     0 – 0 = _____

1 – 0 = _____     3 – 0 = _____

$$\begin{array}{r} 1 \\ -\ 0 \\ \hline \end{array} \quad \begin{array}{r} 3 \\ -\ 0 \\ \hline \end{array} \quad \begin{array}{r} 2 \\ -\ 0 \\ \hline \end{array} \quad \begin{array}{r} 0 \\ -\ 0 \\ \hline \end{array}$$

The answer in a subtraction problem is called the **difference**. The number from which the other is subtracted is called the **minuend**. The number being taken away is called the **subtrahend**.

**Differences Through Three**

# Subtracting Doubles

When the subtrahend is the same as the minuend, the difference is always zero.

**Example:** $2 - 2 = 0$

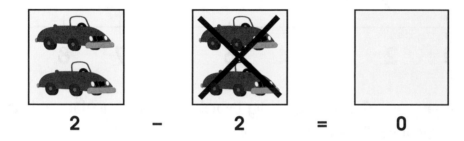

| 2 | – | 2 | = | 0 |

**Remember:** If the difference is zero, the minuend and the subtrahend are the same number.

**Example:** If $6 - ? = 0$, then $6 - 6 = 0$.

■ Complete these facts by writing the missing numbers.

$5 - 5 =$ _____     $8 - 8 =$ _____

$$\begin{array}{r} 6 \\ -\,6 \\ \hline \end{array} \quad \begin{array}{r} 1 \\ -\,\square \\ \hline 0 \end{array} \quad \begin{array}{r} \square \\ -\,9 \\ \hline 0 \end{array} \quad \begin{array}{r} 2 \\ -\,\square \\ \hline 0 \end{array}$$

$6 -$ _____ $= 0$     $7 -$ _____ $= 0$

$$\begin{array}{r} \square \\ -\,4 \\ \hline 0 \end{array} \quad \begin{array}{r} 8 \\ -\,8 \\ \hline \end{array} \quad \begin{array}{r} 5 \\ -\,\square \\ \hline 0 \end{array} \quad \begin{array}{r} \square \\ -\,3 \\ \hline 0 \end{array}$$

_____ $- 4 = 0$     _____ $- 9 = 0$

$1 - 1 =$ _____     _____ $- 3 = 0$

**Differences Through Three**

Name _____

# Counting Back

When the subtrahend is a lesser number like 1, 2, or 3, you can "count back" to find the difference.

**Example:** 3 − 1 = 2

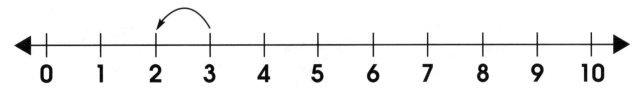

$$0 \quad 1 \quad 2 \quad 3 \quad 4 \quad 5 \quad 6 \quad 7 \quad 8 \quad 9 \quad 10$$

■ Complete each **T** by counting back by the number at the top. Use the number line to help you.

| − 1 | | − 2 | | − 3 | |
|---|---|---|---|---|---|
| 3 | ___ | 2 | ___ | 4 | ___ |
| 2 | ___ | 5 | ___ | 6 | ___ |
| 1 | ___ | 4 | ___ | 5 | ___ |
| 4 | ___ | 3 | ___ | 3 | ___ |

■ Subtract.

6 − 3 = ___        3 − 2 = ___

$$\begin{array}{r} 5 \\ -3 \\ \hline \end{array} \qquad \begin{array}{r} 4 \\ -1 \\ \hline \end{array} \qquad \begin{array}{r} 5 \\ -2 \\ \hline \end{array}$$

4 − 1 = ___        4 − 3 = ___

$$\begin{array}{r} 2 \\ -1 \\ \hline \end{array} \qquad \begin{array}{r} 6 \\ -3 \\ \hline \end{array} \qquad \begin{array}{r} 3 \\ -2 \\ \hline \end{array}$$

5 − 2 = ___        4 − 2 = ___

**Differences Through Three**

Name _____

# Using Addition

You can use addition facts to help you learn subtraction facts. This is because addition and subtraction are inverse operations.

**Example:** You already know that 3 + 2 = 5.

Then, 5 − 2 = 3.

And, 5 − 3 = 2.

■ Write two different subtraction facts using the numbers in each addition sentence.

| 3 + 1 = 4 | 2 + 0 = 2 | 1 + 0 = 1 |
|---|---|---|
| ___ − ___ = ___ | ___ − ___ = ___ | ___ − ___ = ___ |
| ___ − ___ = ___ | ___ − ___ = ___ | ___ − ___ = ___ |
| 1 + 2 = 3 | 3 + 0 = 3 | 2 + 3 = 5 |
| ___ − ___ = ___ | ___ − ___ = ___ | ___ − ___ = ___ |
| ___ − ___ = ___ | ___ − ___ = ___ | ___ − ___ = ___ |

■ Write an addition fact using the numbers in each subtraction sentence.

| 3 − 2 = 1 | 4 − 1 = 3 | 5 − 3 = 2 |
|---|---|---|
| ___ + ___ = ___ | ___ + ___ = ___ | ___ + ___ = ___ |
| 2 − 0 = 2 | 3 − 3 = 0 | 4 − 2 = 2 |
| ___ + ___ = ___ | ___ + ___ = ___ | ___ + ___ = ___ |

# Practice

■ Subtract. Record your score on each Practice page and again
  on page 84.

$10 - 9 =$ _____     $8 - 8 =$ _____     $8 - 7 =$ _____     $4 - 2 =$ _____

$9 - 8 =$ _____     $6 - 5 =$ _____     $4 - 3 =$ _____     $8 - 5 =$ _____

$2 - 2 =$ _____     $4 - 1 =$ _____     $5 - 5 =$ _____     $9 - 7 =$ _____

$5 - 3 =$ _____     $6 - 3 =$ _____     $12 - 9 =$ _____     $3 - 0 =$ _____

$5 - 4 =$ _____     $7 - 6 =$ _____     $10 - 8 =$ _____     $7 - 7 =$ _____

$10 - 8 =$ _____     $1 - 1 =$ _____     $2 - 1 =$ _____     $3 - 1 =$ _____

$0 - 0 =$ _____     $7 - 5 =$ _____     $9 - 6 =$ _____     $7 - 4 =$ _____

$8 - 6 =$ _____     $5 - 2 =$ _____     $11 - 9 =$ _____     $1 - 0 =$ _____

$2 - 0 =$ _____     $9 - 9 =$ _____     $4 - 4 =$ _____     $6 - 4 =$ _____

**Differences Through Three**

Score: _____

Name _____

# Practice

■ Subtract.

| | | | | | | | | |
|---|---|---|---|---|---|---|---|---|
| 0 | 8 | 9 | 7 | 8 | 5 | 3 | 1 | 4 |
| −0 | −7 | −8 | −6 | −8 | −4 | −2 | −1 | −3 |

| | | | | | | | | |
|---|---|---|---|---|---|---|---|---|
| 10 | 7 | 7 | 3 | 9 | 2 | 8 | 1 | 5 |
| −9 | −7 | −5 | −3 | −6 | −2 | −5 | −0 | −2 |

| | | | | | | | | |
|---|---|---|---|---|---|---|---|---|
| 9 | 5 | 4 | 11 | 12 | 9 | 11 | 8 | 2 |
| −7 | −3 | −2 | −8 | −9 | −9 | −9 | −6 | −1 |

| | | | | | | | | |
|---|---|---|---|---|---|---|---|---|
| 3 | 6 | 3 | 2 | 10 | 7 | 6 | 6 | 10 |
| −0 | −3 | −1 | −0 | −8 | −4 | −5 | −4 | −7 |

Score: _____

FINISH

Differences Through Three

# Practice

■ Subtract.

3 − 3 = _____    7 − 5 = _____    12 − 9 = _____    9 − 6 = _____

4 − 2 = _____    7 − 7 = _____    6 − 6 = _____    8 − 8 = _____

7 − 6 = _____    7 − 4 = _____    6 − 4 = _____    2 − 0 = _____

3 − 0 = _____    6 − 5 = _____    5 − 3 = _____    4 − 3 = _____

1 − 1 = _____    5 − 2 = _____    8 − 7 = _____    5 − 4 = _____

3 − 1 = _____    9 − 7 = _____    11 − 9 = _____    2 − 2 = _____

8 − 5 = _____    10 − 7 = _____    0 − 0 = _____    8 − 6 = _____

9 − 9 = _____    3 − 2 = _____    4 − 1 = _____    5 − 5 = _____

1 − 0 = _____    10 − 9 = _____    9 − 8 = _____    2 − 1 = _____

Score: _____

**Differences Through Three**

START

82

Name _____

# Practice

■ Subtract.

| | | | |
|---|---|---|---|
| 8 | 11 | 4 | 6 |
| −6 | −9 | −3 | −6 |

| | | | |
|---|---|---|---|
| 10 | 5 | 2 | 3 |
| −9 | −3 | −2 | −2 |

| | | | |
|---|---|---|---|
| 7 | 9 | 11 | 6 |
| −6 | −9 | −8 | −4 |

| | | | |
|---|---|---|---|
| 8 | 0 | 5 | 7 |
| −5 | −0 | −4 | −5 |

| | | | |
|---|---|---|---|
| 3 | 8 | 6 | 5 |
| −1 | −8 | −5 | −2 |

9 − 8 = ____      4 − 1 = ____

1 − 0 = ____      2 − 0 = ____

4 − 2 = ____      6 − 3 = ____

5 − 5 = ____      7 − 7 = ____

8 − 7 = ____      10 − 7 = ____

2 − 1 = ____      7 − 4 = ____

3 − 0 = ____      12 − 9 = ____

1 − 1 = ____      9 − 7 = ____

Score: _____

 Circle any problems that you still find difficult to remember. Make your own flash cards to help you master these problems.

Name _____

# Practice

■ Subtract.

|  |  |  |  |
|---|---|---|---|
| 9 | 5 | 10 | 7 |
| − 6 | − 5 | − 7 | − 7 |

| 3 | 3 | 6 | 4 |
|---|---|---|---|
| − 1 | − 3 | − 3 | − 2 |

| 2 | 3 | 6 | 7 |
|---|---|---|---|
| − 0 | − 0 | − 5 | − 4 |

| 8 | 1 | 9 | 4 |
|---|---|---|---|
| − 7 | − 0 | − 7 | − 1 |

| 10 | 6 | 8 | 10 |
|---|---|---|---|
| − 8 | − 4 | − 5 | − 9 |

3 − 2 = _____      5 − 3 = _____

11 − 9 = _____      7 − 5 = _____

2 − 2 = _____      4 − 3 = _____

6 − 6 = _____      5 − 4 = _____

10 − 8 = _____      7 − 6 = _____

8 − 5 = _____      0 − 0 = _____

4 − 4 = _____      8 − 8 = _____

8 − 6 = _____      5 − 2 = _____

| Record your scores below. | |
|---|---|
| **Page 80** Score: _____ | **Page 83** Score: _____ |
| **Page 81** Score: _____ | **Page 84** Score: _____ |
| **Page 82** Score: _____ | |

# Timed Test

■ Improve your speed on these basic facts. Ask someone to time you. Record your time and score on each Timed Test page and on page 96.

| | | | |
|---|---|---|---|
| 10 – 9 = ___ | 2 – 2 = ___ | 3 – 0 = ___ | 6 – 3 = ___ |
| 3 – 2 = ___ | 6 – 5 = ___ | 6 – 6 = ___ | 9 – 6 = ___ |
| 7 – 5 = ___ | 2 – 0 = ___ | 11 – 9 = ___ | 1 – 1 = ___ |
| 3 – 3 = ___ | 5 – 3 = ___ | 9 – 8 = ___ | 3 – 1 = ___ |
| 5 – 2 = ___ | 4 – 1 = ___ | 4 – 4 = ___ | 5 – 4 = ___ |
| 7 – 6 = ___ | 9 – 7 = ___ | 12 – 9 = ___ | 8 – 5 = ___ |
| 9 – 9 = ___ | 7 – 7 = ___ | 8 – 7 = ___ | 11 – 8 = ___ |
| 1 – 0 = ___ | 8 – 6 = ___ | 10 – 7 = ___ | 8 – 8 = ___ |
| 6 – 4 = ___ | 4 – 3 = ___ | 2 – 1 = ___ | 4 – 2 = ___ |
| 5 – 3 = ___ | 9 – 6 = ___ | 5 – 5 = ___ | 10 – 8 = ___ |

**Differences Through Three**

Score: _____     Time: _____ minutes _____ seconds

# Timed Test

| | | | | | | | |
|---|---|---|---|---|---|---|---|
| 3<br>− 1 | 6<br>− 6 | 11<br>− 8 | 2<br>− 0 | 11<br>− 9 | 4<br>− 3 | 3<br>− 0 | 6<br>− 5 |
| 6<br>− 3 | 2<br>− 2 | 5<br>− 3 | 6<br>− 4 | 10<br>− 8 | 1<br>− 0 | 5<br>− 2 | 9<br>− 8 |
| 9<br>− 6 | 0<br>− 0 | 4<br>− 4 | 9<br>− 9 | 12<br>− 9 | 5<br>− 5 | 4<br>− 2 | 10<br>− 9 |
| 7<br>− 5 | 3<br>− 2 | 8<br>− 6 | 8<br>− 7 | 4<br>− 1 | 7<br>− 7 | 7<br>− 4 | 2<br>− 1 |
| 5<br>− 4 | 8<br>− 5 | 3<br>− 3 | 9<br>− 7 | 8<br>− 8 | 10<br>− 7 | 1<br>− 1 | 7<br>− 6 |

Score: _____     Time: _____ minutes _____ seconds

Name _____

# Timed Test

8 − 7 = ____    2 − 0 = ____

1 − 0 = ____    3 − 3 = ____

7 − 4 = ____    6 − 4 = ____

5 − 4 = ____    10 − 9 = ____

1 − 1 = ____    4 − 2 = ____

7 − 5 = ____    5 − 5 = ____

3 − 0 = ____    9 − 7 = ____

11 − 9 = ____    8 − 5 = ____

3 − 2 = ____    10 − 7 = ____

12 − 9 = ____    7 − 7 = ____

| 11 | 7 | 4 | 6 |
|----|----|----|----|
| − 8 | − 6 | − 4 | − 3 |

| 6 | 4 | 8 | 5 |
|----|----|----|----|
| − 5 | − 1 | − 8 | − 2 |

| 2 | 8 | 0 | 9 |
|----|----|----|----|
| − 1 | − 6 | − 0 | − 6 |

| 3 | 9 | 10 | 2 |
|----|----|----|----|
| − 1 | − 9 | − 8 | − 2 |

| 5 | 4 | 9 | 6 |
|----|----|----|----|
| − 3 | − 3 | − 8 | − 6 |

Score: _____    Time: _____ minutes _____ seconds

# Timed Test

**Differences Through Three**

$6 - 3 =$ _____     $9 - 9 =$ _____

$9 - 6 =$ _____     $0 - 0 =$ _____

$5 - 2 =$ _____     $10 - 8 =$ _____

$3 - 1 =$ _____     $4 - 1 =$ _____

$7 - 6 =$ _____     $2 - 2 =$ _____

$8 - 8 =$ _____     $2 - 1 =$ _____

$6 - 6 =$ _____     $5 - 3 =$ _____

$6 - 5 =$ _____     $8 - 6 =$ _____

$9 - 8 =$ _____     $4 - 4 =$ _____

$11 - 8 =$ _____    $4 - 3 =$ _____

$$\begin{array}{cccc} 7 & 10 & 2 & 8 \\ -5 & -7 & -0 & -5 \\ \hline \end{array}$$

$$\begin{array}{cccc} 1 & 3 & 3 & 9 \\ -1 & -3 & -0 & -7 \\ \hline \end{array}$$

$$\begin{array}{cccc} 1 & 12 & 5 & 6 \\ -0 & -9 & -4 & -4 \\ \hline \end{array}$$

$$\begin{array}{cccc} 7 & 10 & 8 & 5 \\ -7 & -9 & -7 & -5 \\ \hline \end{array}$$

$$\begin{array}{cccc} 11 & 4 & 7 & 3 \\ -9 & -2 & -4 & -2 \\ \hline \end{array}$$

Score: _____     Time: _____ minutes _____ seconds

# Timed Test

1 – 0 = ____     4 – 2 = ____

$$\begin{array}{r} 8 \\ -5 \\ \hline \end{array} \quad \begin{array}{r} 5 \\ -4 \\ \hline \end{array} \quad \begin{array}{r} 9 \\ -7 \\ \hline \end{array} \quad \begin{array}{r} 1 \\ -1 \\ \hline \end{array}$$

6 – 6 = ____     7 – 7 = ____

2 – 1 = ____     3 – 0 = ____

$$\begin{array}{r} 10 \\ -9 \\ \hline \end{array} \quad \begin{array}{r} 4 \\ -3 \\ \hline \end{array} \quad \begin{array}{r} 3 \\ -1 \\ \hline \end{array} \quad \begin{array}{r} 3 \\ -3 \\ \hline \end{array}$$

9 – 9 = ____     3 – 2 = ____

8 – 6 = ____     11 – 9 = ____

$$\begin{array}{r} 7 \\ -5 \\ \hline \end{array} \quad \begin{array}{r} 8 \\ -8 \\ \hline \end{array} \quad \begin{array}{r} 5 \\ -3 \\ \hline \end{array} \quad \begin{array}{r} 4 \\ -1 \\ \hline \end{array}$$

2 – 0 = ____     7 – 6 = ____

9 – 6 = ____     6 – 3 = ____

$$\begin{array}{r} 0 \\ -0 \\ \hline \end{array} \quad \begin{array}{r} 12 \\ -9 \\ \hline \end{array} \quad \begin{array}{r} 10 \\ -8 \\ \hline \end{array} \quad \begin{array}{r} 6 \\ -5 \\ \hline \end{array}$$

5 – 5 = ____     4 – 4 = ____

6 – 4 = ____     7 – 4 = ____

$$\begin{array}{r} 5 \\ -2 \\ \hline \end{array} \quad \begin{array}{r} 2 \\ -2 \\ \hline \end{array} \quad \begin{array}{r} 8 \\ -7 \\ \hline \end{array} \quad \begin{array}{r} 10 \\ -7 \\ \hline \end{array}$$

9 – 8 = ____     11 – 8 = ____

Score: _____     Time: _____ minutes _____ seconds

# Timed Test

$10 - 8 =$ _____     $8 - 5 =$ _____

$$\begin{array}{r} 8 \\ -6 \\ \hline \end{array} \quad \begin{array}{r} 7 \\ -7 \\ \hline \end{array} \quad \begin{array}{r} 9 \\ -9 \\ \hline \end{array} \quad \begin{array}{r} 4 \\ -2 \\ \hline \end{array}$$

$1 - 1 =$ _____     $6 - 5 =$ _____

$12 - 9 =$ _____     $3 - 1 =$ _____

$$\begin{array}{r} 11 \\ -8 \\ \hline \end{array} \quad \begin{array}{r} 9 \\ -8 \\ \hline \end{array} \quad \begin{array}{r} 3 \\ -0 \\ \hline \end{array} \quad \begin{array}{r} 11 \\ -9 \\ \hline \end{array}$$

$0 - 0 =$ _____     $2 - 2 =$ _____

$4 - 3 =$ _____     $10 - 9 =$ _____

$$\begin{array}{r} 6 \\ -6 \\ \hline \end{array} \quad \begin{array}{r} 7 \\ -4 \\ \hline \end{array} \quad \begin{array}{r} 6 \\ -4 \\ \hline \end{array} \quad \begin{array}{r} 7 \\ -6 \\ \hline \end{array}$$

$4 - 1 =$ _____     $5 - 2 =$ _____

$5 - 3 =$ _____     $3 - 3 =$ _____

$$\begin{array}{r} 2 \\ -0 \\ \hline \end{array} \quad \begin{array}{r} 3 \\ -2 \\ \hline \end{array} \quad \begin{array}{r} 4 \\ -4 \\ \hline \end{array} \quad \begin{array}{r} 2 \\ -1 \\ \hline \end{array}$$

$5 - 4 =$ _____     $8 - 7 =$ _____

$8 - 8 =$ _____     $9 - 7 =$ _____

$$\begin{array}{r} 6 \\ -3 \\ \hline \end{array} \quad \begin{array}{r} 9 \\ -6 \\ \hline \end{array} \quad \begin{array}{r} 5 \\ -5 \\ \hline \end{array} \quad \begin{array}{r} 1 \\ -0 \\ \hline \end{array}$$

$10 - 7 =$ _____     $7 - 5 =$ _____

Score: _____     Time: _____ minutes _____ seconds

Name _____

# Timed Test

8 – 8 = ____    11 – 9 = ____

$$\begin{array}{r}0\\-0\\\hline\end{array}\quad\begin{array}{r}4\\-3\\\hline\end{array}\quad\begin{array}{r}2\\-0\\\hline\end{array}\quad\begin{array}{r}8\\-5\\\hline\end{array}$$

3 – 1 = ____    3 – 3 = ____

7 – 4 = ____    1 – 0 = ____

$$\begin{array}{r}4\\-4\\\hline\end{array}\quad\begin{array}{r}2\\-1\\\hline\end{array}\quad\begin{array}{r}9\\-7\\\hline\end{array}\quad\begin{array}{r}10\\-9\\\hline\end{array}$$

1 – 1 = ____    6 – 4 = ____

3 – 2 = ____    8 – 7 = ____

$$\begin{array}{r}8\\-6\\\hline\end{array}\quad\begin{array}{r}9\\-9\\\hline\end{array}\quad\begin{array}{r}2\\-2\\\hline\end{array}\quad\begin{array}{r}12\\-9\\\hline\end{array}$$

10 – 8 = ____    5 – 3 = ____

6 – 3 = ____    6 – 5 = ____

$$\begin{array}{r}4\\-2\\\hline\end{array}\quad\begin{array}{r}9\\-8\\\hline\end{array}\quad\begin{array}{r}7\\-5\\\hline\end{array}\quad\begin{array}{r}3\\-0\\\hline\end{array}$$

7 – 7 = ____    5 – 5 = ____

$$\begin{array}{r}5\\-4\\\hline\end{array}\quad\begin{array}{r}6\\-6\\\hline\end{array}\quad\begin{array}{r}4\\-1\\\hline\end{array}\quad\begin{array}{r}11\\-8\\\hline\end{array}$$

5 – 2 = ____    9 – 6 = ____

7 – 6 = ____    10 – 7 = ____

**Differences Through Three**

Score: _____    Time: _____ minutes _____ seconds

# Timed Test

$2 - 0 =$ _____     $4 - 1 =$ _____

| 1 | 3 | 8 | 6 |
|---|---|---|---|
| $-1$ | $-3$ | $-8$ | $-3$ |

$9 - 9 =$ _____     $12 - 9 =$ _____

$10 - 9 =$ _____     $11 - 8 =$ _____

| 7 | 10 | 3 | 5 |
|---|---|---|---|
| $-7$ | $-8$ | $-2$ | $-5$ |

$7 - 5 =$ _____     $5 - 4 =$ _____

$9 - 7 =$ _____     $0 - 0 =$ _____

| 1 | 6 | 6 | 11 |
|---|---|---|---|
| $-0$ | $-5$ | $-4$ | $-9$ |

$2 - 2 =$ _____     $4 - 2 =$ _____

$9 - 8 =$ _____     $8 - 6 =$ _____

| 7 | 7 | 5 | 3 |
|---|---|---|---|
| $-4$ | $-6$ | $-2$ | $-1$ |

$3 - 0 =$ _____     $4 - 4 =$ _____

$4 - 3 =$ _____     $8 - 5 =$ _____

| 10 | 9 | 5 | 8 |
|---|---|---|---|
| $-7$ | $-6$ | $-3$ | $-7$ |

$2 - 1 =$ _____     $6 - 6 =$ _____

Score: _____     Time: _____ minutes _____ seconds

Name _____

# Timed Test

11 – 9 = _____     3 – 2 = _____     7 – 4 = _____     9 – 6 = _____

4 – 2 = _____     7 – 5 = _____     10 – 8 = _____     10 – 9 = _____

1 – 1 = _____     3 – 3 = _____     2 – 2 = _____     6 – 5 = _____

1 – 0 = _____     9 – 9 = _____     2 – 1 = _____     4 – 1 = _____

12 – 9 = _____     9 – 8 = _____     11 – 8 = _____     5 – 3 = _____

3 – 1 = _____     5 – 4 = _____     9 – 7 = _____     4 – 4 = _____

10 – 7 = _____     3 – 0 = _____     2 – 0 = _____     8 – 8 = _____

6 – 6 = _____     5 – 5 = _____     8 – 6 = _____     5 – 2 = _____

7 – 7 = _____     6 – 4 = _____     0 – 0 = _____     8 – 7 = _____

6 – 3 = _____     7 – 6 = _____     4 – 3 = _____     8 – 5 = _____

**Differences Through Three**

Score: _____     Time: _____ minutes _____ seconds

# Timed Test

**Differences Through Three**

| | | | | | | | |
|---|---|---|---|---|---|---|---|
| 5<br>− 3 | 12<br>− 9 | 4<br>− 3 | 5<br>− 5 | 2<br>− 1 | 11<br>− 9 | 3<br>− 3 | 4<br>− 1 |
| 10<br>− 9 | 9<br>− 7 | 6<br>− 5 | 9<br>− 9 | 7<br>− 5 | 8<br>− 7 | 3<br>− 1 | 7<br>− 7 |
| 6<br>− 3 | 10<br>− 7 | 1<br>− 1 | 8<br>− 5 | 8<br>− 8 | 5<br>− 4 | 5<br>− 2 | 0<br>− 0 |
| 2<br>− 0 | 10<br>− 8 | 6<br>− 6 | 1<br>− 0 | 7<br>− 4 | 9<br>− 8 | 3<br>− 0 | 2<br>− 2 |
| 7<br>− 6 | 8<br>− 6 | 4<br>− 2 | 9<br>− 6 | 4<br>− 4 | 3<br>− 2 | 6<br>− 4 | 11<br>− 8 |

Score: _____    Time: _____ minutes _____ seconds

# Timed Test

$12 - 9 =$ ____    $7 - 5 =$ ____    $5 - 2 =$ ____    $2 - 2 =$ ____

$1 - 1 =$ ____    $6 - 5 =$ ____    $6 - 4 =$ ____    $7 - 4 =$ ____

$9 - 7 =$ ____    $6 - 3 =$ ____    $4 - 2 =$ ____    $3 - 0 =$ ____

$3 - 3 =$ ____    $3 - 1 =$ ____    $9 - 6 =$ ____    $5 - 4 =$ ____

$7 - 7 =$ ____    $4 - 3 =$ ____    $0 - 0 =$ ____    $3 - 2 =$ ____

$4 - 1 =$ ____    $11 - 9 =$ ____    $8 - 6 =$ ____    $4 - 4 =$ ____

$8 - 5 =$ ____    $10 - 9 =$ ____    $6 - 6 =$ ____    $8 - 8 =$ ____

$8 - 7 =$ ____    $2 - 1 =$ ____    $10 - 8 =$ ____    $11 - 8 =$ ____

$5 - 3 =$ ____    $10 - 7 =$ ____    $2 - 0 =$ ____    $1 - 0 =$ ____

$9 - 9 =$ ____    $5 - 5 =$ ____    $7 - 6 =$ ____    $9 - 8 =$ ____

**Differences Through Three**

Score: _____    Time: _____ minutes _____ seconds

# Timed Test

**Differences Through Three**

| | | | | | | | |
|---|---|---|---|---|---|---|---|
| 8<br>−7 | 5<br>−3 | 5<br>−5 | 1<br>−0 | 5<br>−2 | 7<br>−6 | 9<br>−6 | 1<br>−1 |
| 2<br>−0 | 6<br>−3 | 10<br>−9 | 3<br>−1 | 12<br>−9 | 2<br>−2 | 8<br>−8 | 3<br>−2 |
| 7<br>−5 | 9<br>−8 | 6<br>−4 | 0<br>−0 | 4<br>−4 | 4<br>−1 | 10<br>−7 | 6<br>−5 |
| 8<br>−5 | 4<br>−2 | 6<br>−6 | 9<br>−9 | 2<br>−1 | 11<br>−9 | 5<br>−4 | 8<br>−6 |
| 4<br>−3 | 10<br>−8 | 3<br>−0 | 7<br>−4 | 11<br>−8 | 3<br>−3 | 9<br>−7 | 7<br>−7 |

Record your scores and times below.

| | |
|---|---|
| **Page 85** Score:_____ Time:___min.___sec. | **Page 91** Score:_____ Time:___min.___sec. |
| **Page 86** Score:_____ Time:___min.___sec. | **Page 92** Score:_____ Time:___min.___sec. |
| **Page 87** Score:_____ Time:___min.___sec. | **Page 93** Score:_____ Time:___min.___sec. |
| **Page 88** Score:_____ Time:___min.___sec. | **Page 94** Score:_____ Time:___min.___sec. |
| **Page 89** Score:_____ Time:___min.___sec. | **Page 95** Score:_____ Time:___min.___sec. |
| **Page 90** Score:_____ Time:___min.___sec. | **Page 96** Score:_____ Time:___min.___sec. |

Name _____

# Subtracting Zero

Knowing that zero is the identity element of subtraction helps you to know three of the facts in this new group. Just remember that zero subtracted from any number is that number.

**Example:** $5 - 0 = 5$

■ Draw X's in these boxes to show this is true.

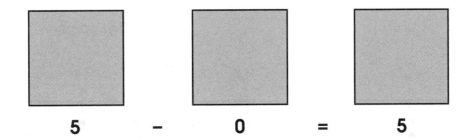

5      −      0      =      5

■ Complete this **T** by subtracting zero from each number.

$$-\,0$$

4 | ____

5 | ____

6 | ____

■ Now, write the answers for these facts.

$6 - 0 =$ _____     $4 - 0 =$ _____

$5 - 0 =$ _____

$$\begin{array}{r} 5 \\ -0 \\ \hline \end{array} \quad \begin{array}{r} 4 \\ -0 \\ \hline \end{array} \quad \begin{array}{r} 6 \\ -0 \\ \hline \end{array}$$

**Differences Through Six**

# Counting Back

**Remember:** When subtracting lesser numbers like 1, 2, or 3, it sometimes helps to count back from the minuend.

**Example:** $7 - 2 = 5$

$$7 \quad - \quad 2 \quad = \quad 5$$

**minuend   subtrahend   difference**

$$\begin{array}{r} 7 \\ -\,2 \\ \hline 5 \end{array}$$ minuend
subtrahend
difference

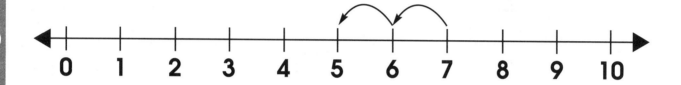

$$\overset{\longleftarrow}{\underset{0 \quad 1 \quad 2 \quad 3 \quad 4 \quad 5 \quad 6 \quad 7 \quad 8 \quad 9 \quad 10}{\mid\quad\mid\quad\mid\quad\mid\quad\mid\quad\mid\quad\mid\quad\mid\quad\mid\quad\mid\quad\mid}}$$

■ Count back to find these differences. Use the number line to help you.

$6 - 2 = $ _____   $5 - 1 = $ _____

$$\begin{array}{r}5\\-\,1\\\hline\end{array} \quad \begin{array}{r}9\\-\,3\\\hline\end{array} \quad \begin{array}{r}7\\-\,2\\\hline\end{array} \quad \begin{array}{r}6\\-\,2\\\hline\end{array} \quad \begin{array}{r}7\\-\,1\\\hline\end{array}$$

$8 - 4 = $ _____   $8 - 2 = $ _____

$9 - 3 = $ _____   $7 - 1 = $ _____

$$\begin{array}{r}8\\-\,2\\\hline\end{array} \quad \begin{array}{r}6\\-\,1\\\hline\end{array} \quad \begin{array}{r}8\\-\,3\\\hline\end{array} \quad \begin{array}{r}8\\-\,4\\\hline\end{array} \quad \begin{array}{r}7\\-\,3\\\hline\end{array}$$

$6 - 1 = $ _____   $8 - 3 = $ _____

$7 - 3 = $ _____   $7 - 2 = $ _____

**Differences Through Six**

Name _____

# Using Addition

You already have learned that addition and subtraction are opposite operations.

**Example:** If $1 + 4 = 5$, then, $5 - 4 = 1$. And, $5 - 1 = 4$.

Notice that the sum in an addition fact becomes the minuend in a related subtraction fact.

**Example:** $1 + 4 = 5 \qquad 5 - 4 = 1$

■ Write two different subtraction facts using the numbers in each addition sentence.

| $6 + 2 = 8$ | $5 + 3 = 8$ | $5 + 1 = 6$ |
|---|---|---|
| ___ − ___ = ___ | ___ − ___ = ___ | ___ − ___ = ___ |
| ___ − ___ = ___ | ___ − ___ = ___ | ___ − ___ = ___ |
| $5 + 2 = 7$ | $3 + 6 = 9$ | $5 + 4 = 9$ |
| ___ − ___ = ___ | ___ − ___ = ___ | ___ − ___ = ___ |
| ___ − ___ = ___ | ___ − ___ = ___ | ___ − ___ = ___ |
| $3 + 4 = 7$ | $4 + 2 = 6$ | $6 + 1 = 7$ |
| ___ − ___ = ___ | ___ − ___ = ___ | ___ − ___ = ___ |
| ___ − ___ = ___ | ___ − ___ = ___ | ___ − ___ = ___ |

Name _____

# Using Addition

You have already learned the higher addition facts like 8 + 3 = 11. Now, use what you learned about opposite operations to discover some of the higher subtraction facts.

**Example:** 8 + 3 = 11    11 − 8 = 3    11 − 3 = 8

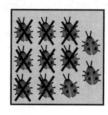

■ Write two different subtraction problems using the numbers in each addition sentence.

$9 + 4 = 13$

____ − ____ = ____

____ − ____ = ____

$7 + 5 = 12$

____ − ____ = ____

____ − ____ = ____

$4 + 6 = 10$

____ − ____ = ____

____ − ____ = ____

$9 + 5 = 14$

____ − ____ = ____

____ − ____ = ____

$7 + 4 = 11$

____ − ____ = ____

____ − ____ = ____

$9 + 6 = 15$

____ − ____ = ____

____ − ____ = ____

$6 + 4 = 10$

____ − ____ = ____

____ − ____ = ____

$8 + 5 = 13$

____ − ____ = ____

____ − ____ = ____

$7 + 6 = 13$

____ − ____ = ____

____ − ____ = ____

**Differences Through Six**

Name _____

# Practice

■ Subtract. Record your score on each Practice page and on page 106.

13 – 8 = _____     7 – 1 = _____     6 – 1 = _____     11 – 5 = _____

5 – 1 = _____     12 – 8 = _____     12 – 6 = _____     10 – 6 = _____

6 – 0 = _____     8 – 2 = _____     11 – 7 = _____     14 – 9 = _____

13 – 9 = _____     10 – 5 = _____     9 – 4 = _____     8 – 4 = _____

5 – 0 = _____     15 – 9 = _____     7 – 3 = _____     13 – 8 = _____

11 – 6 = _____     6 – 2 = _____     9 – 5 = _____     10 – 5 = _____

4 – 0 = _____     9 – 3 = _____     8 – 3 = _____     7 – 1 = _____

14 – 8 = _____     13 – 7 = _____     10 – 4 = _____     12 – 7 = _____

12 – 7 = _____     8 – 4 = _____     7 – 2 = _____     13 – 9 = _____

Score: _____

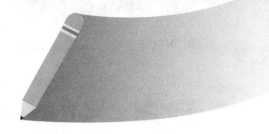

Name _____

# Practice

■ Subtract.

| 5<br>− 0 | 13<br>− 9 | 7<br>− 3 | 15<br>− 9 | 12<br>− 7 | 12<br>− 6 | 6<br>− 2 | 11<br>− 6 | 9<br>− 3 |
|---|---|---|---|---|---|---|---|---|
| 10<br>− 6 | 7<br>− 2 | 6<br>− 0 | 13<br>− 7 | 4<br>− 0 | 9<br>− 4 | 8<br>− 2 | 13<br>− 8 | 5<br>− 1 |
| 12<br>− 8 | 6<br>− 1 | 10<br>− 5 | 14<br>− 9 | 11<br>− 7 | 14<br>− 8 | 10<br>− 4 | 11<br>− 5 | 8<br>− 4 |
| 7<br>− 1 | 9<br>− 5 | 8<br>− 3 | 9<br>− 4 | 7<br>− 0 | 15<br>− 9 | 8<br>− 4 | 13<br>− 9 | 11<br>− 6 |

Score: _____

**Differences Through Six**

START

# Practice

■ Subtract.

| 12 | 10 | 7 | 9 |
|---|---|---|---|
| − 7 | − 6 | − 2 | − 3 |

| 6 | 5 | 7 | 7 |
|---|---|---|---|
| − 2 | − 0 | − 3 | − 1 |

| 11 | 8 | 11 | 12 |
|---|---|---|---|
| − 6 | − 2 | − 7 | − 6 |

| 8 | 14 | 4 | 9 |
|---|---|---|---|
| − 3 | − 8 | − 0 | − 4 |

| 13 | 8 | 9 | 11 |
|---|---|---|---|
| − 7 | − 2 | − 5 | − 5 |

5 − 1 = _____    6 − 1 = _____

13 − 8 = _____    15 − 9 = _____

8 − 4 = _____    10 − 5 = _____

6 − 0 = _____    14 − 9 = _____

10 − 4 = _____    12 − 8 = _____

13 − 9 = _____    14 − 8 = _____

11 − 5 = _____    7 − 1 = _____

9 − 4 = _____    13 − 6 = _____

**Differences Through Six**

Score: _____

FINISH

# Practice

■ Subtract.

| | | | | | |
|---|---|---|---|---|---|
| 8<br>− 4 | 13<br>− 7 | 12<br>− 8 | 10<br>− 4 | 6 − 2 = ____ | 7 − 2 = ____ |
| | | | | 11 − 7 = ____ | 12 − 6 = ____ |
| 15<br>− 9 | 6<br>− 0 | 14<br>− 9 | 9<br>− 5 | 4 − 0 = ____ | 7 − 1 = ____ |
| | | | | 9 − 3 = ____ | 8 − 3 = ____ |
| 13<br>− 9 | 6<br>− 1 | 10<br>− 5 | 5<br>− 1 | 8 − 2 = ____ | 10 − 6 = ____ |
| | | | | 5 − 0 = ____ | 8 − 4 = ____ |
| 11<br>− 5 | 13<br>− 5 | 9<br>− 4 | 12<br>− 6 | 14 − 8 = ____ | 13 − 9 = ____ |
| | | | | 12 − 7 = ____ | 6 − 0 = ____ |
| 7<br>− 3 | 11<br>− 6 | 13<br>− 7 | 6<br>− 2 | | |

**Differences Through Six**

Score: _____

Name _____

# Practice

■ Subtract.

| | | | |
|---|---|---|---|
| 9<br>− 4 | 13<br>− 9 | 8<br>− 2 | 6<br>− 0 |
| 5<br>− 1 | 13<br>− 7 | 8<br>− 3 | 10<br>− 6 |
| 9<br>− 3 | 12<br>− 7 | 14<br>− 8 | 8<br>− 4 |
| 5<br>− 0 | 13<br>− 8 | 11<br>− 5 | 7<br>− 3 |
| 9<br>− 5 | 14<br>− 9 | 12<br>− 8 | 5<br>− 1 |

$15 - 9 =$ _____    $7 - 2 =$ _____

$10 - 5 =$ _____    $10 - 4 =$ _____

$4 - 0 =$ _____    $11 - 7 =$ _____

$7 - 1 =$ _____    $6 - 1 =$ _____

$6 - 2 =$ _____    $7 - 3 =$ _____

$12 - 6 =$ _____    $5 - 0 =$ _____

$12 - 8 =$ _____    $13 - 7 =$ _____

$11 - 6 =$ _____    $8 - 3 =$ _____

Score: _____

**Differences Through Six**

Circle any problems that you still find difficult to remember. Make your own flash cards to help you master these problems.

# Practice

■ Subtract.

Differences Through Six

$$\begin{array}{r} 7 \\ -3 \\ \hline \end{array} \qquad \begin{array}{r} 12 \\ -8 \\ \hline \end{array} \qquad \begin{array}{r} 6 \\ -1 \\ \hline \end{array} \qquad \begin{array}{r} 10 \\ -5 \\ \hline \end{array}$$

$$\begin{array}{r} 11 \\ -7 \\ \hline \end{array} \qquad \begin{array}{r} 7 \\ -1 \\ \hline \end{array} \qquad \begin{array}{r} 7 \\ -2 \\ \hline \end{array} \qquad \begin{array}{r} 15 \\ -9 \\ \hline \end{array}$$

$$\begin{array}{r} 11 \\ -6 \\ \hline \end{array} \qquad \begin{array}{r} 12 \\ -6 \\ \hline \end{array} \qquad \begin{array}{r} 14 \\ -9 \\ \hline \end{array} \qquad \begin{array}{r} 4 \\ -0 \\ \hline \end{array}$$

$$\begin{array}{r} 9 \\ -5 \\ \hline \end{array} \qquad \begin{array}{r} 6 \\ -2 \\ \hline \end{array} \qquad \begin{array}{r} 10 \\ -4 \\ \hline \end{array} \qquad \begin{array}{r} 13 \\ -7 \\ \hline \end{array}$$

$$\begin{array}{r} 10 \\ -6 \\ \hline \end{array} \qquad \begin{array}{r} 8 \\ -4 \\ \hline \end{array} \qquad \begin{array}{r} 9 \\ -3 \\ \hline \end{array} \qquad \begin{array}{r} 5 \\ -0 \\ \hline \end{array}$$

$13 - 7 = $ _____    $5 - 0 = $ _____

$8 - 2 = $ _____    $13 - 9 = $ _____

$12 - 7 = $ _____    $8 - 3 = $ _____

$5 - 1 = $ _____    $6 - 0 = $ _____

$11 - 5 = $ _____    $14 - 8 = $ _____

$9 - 3 = $ _____    $10 - 6 = $ _____

$13 - 8 = $ _____    $8 - 4 = $ _____

$9 - 4 = $ _____    $12 - 8 = $ _____

Record your scores below.

**Page 101** Score: _____    **Page 104** Score: _____

**Page 102** Score: _____    **Page 105** Score: _____

**Page 103** Score: _____    **Page 106** Score: _____

Name _____

# Timed Test

■ Improve your speed on these basic facts. Ask someone to time you.
Record your time and score on each Timed Test page and on page 118.

7 – 2 = _____     5 – 0 = _____     8 – 2 = _____     9 – 4 = _____

12 – 8 = _____     14 – 8 = _____     13 – 8 = _____     10 – 5 = _____

11 – 6 = _____     11 – 7 = _____     9 – 3 = _____     13 – 7 = _____

7 – 3 = _____     6 – 0 = _____     9 – 5 = _____     14 – 9 = _____

6 – 1 = _____     12 – 6 = _____     10 – 6 = _____     8 – 3 = _____

10 – 4 = _____     15 – 9 = _____     7 – 1 = _____     14 – 8 = _____

12 – 7 = _____     13 – 7 = _____     13 – 9 = _____     11 – 7 = _____

11 – 5 = _____     4 – 0 = _____     8 – 4 = _____     12 – 8 = _____

6 – 2 = _____     10 – 5 = _____     14 – 9 = _____     13 – 8 = _____

9 – 4 = _____     5 – 1 = _____     8 – 3 = _____     7 – 3 = _____

Score: _____     Time: _____ minutes _____ seconds

**Differences Through Six**

Name _____

# Timed Test

■ Complete these facts as accurately and as quickly as you can.

| | | | | | | | |
|---|---|---|---|---|---|---|---|
| 5<br>− 1 | 6<br>− 1 | 14<br>− 9 | 9<br>− 5 | 7<br>− 2 | 13<br>− 9 | 6<br>− 0 | 15<br>− 9 |
| 11<br>− 7 | 9<br>− 3 | 10<br>− 5 | 8<br>− 2 | 12<br>− 7 | 10<br>− 6 | 4<br>− 0 | 13<br>− 7 |
| 9<br>− 4 | 7<br>− 3 | 8<br>− 3 | 12<br>− 8 | 11<br>− 5 | 5<br>− 0 | 12<br>− 6 | 6<br>− 2 |
| 8<br>− 4 | 7<br>− 1 | 10<br>− 4 | 11<br>− 6 | 14<br>− 8 | 13<br>− 8 | 6<br>− 1 | 9<br>− 3 |
| 12<br>− 8 | 14<br>− 9 | 11<br>− 7 | 8<br>− 2 | 6<br>− 2 | 5<br>− 0 | 12<br>− 7 | 10<br>− 5 |

Score: _____      Time: _____ minutes _____ seconds

Name _____

# Timed Test

**Differences Through Six**

5 − 0 = _____          7 − 3 = _____

$$\begin{array}{cccc} 13 & 11 & 15 & 11 \\ -\ 8 & -\ 7 & -\ 9 & -\ 6 \\ \hline \end{array}$$

12 − 7 = _____          10 − 4 = _____

6 − 2 = _____          9 − 4 = _____

$$\begin{array}{cccc} 8 & 9 & 6 & 14 \\ -\ 4 & -\ 3 & -\ 1 & -\ 8 \\ \hline \end{array}$$

10 − 5 = _____          13 − 9 = _____

13 − 7 = _____          11 − 5 = _____

$$\begin{array}{cccc} 10 & 6 & 8 & 5 \\ -\ 6 & -\ 0 & -\ 3 & -\ 1 \\ \hline \end{array}$$

12 − 8 = _____          15 − 9 = _____

7 − 1 = _____          12 − 6 = _____

$$\begin{array}{cccc} 8 & 12 & 4 & 13 \\ -\ 2 & -\ 6 & -\ 0 & -\ 9 \\ \hline \end{array}$$

9 − 5 = _____          6 − 0 = _____

7 − 2 = _____          13 − 8 = _____

$$\begin{array}{cccc} 5 & 6 & 10 & 7 \\ -\ 0 & -\ 2 & -\ 5 & -\ 1 \\ \hline \end{array}$$

14 − 9 = _____          9 − 3 = _____

Score: _____          Time: _____ minutes _____ seconds

# Timed Test

6 − 1 = _____     15 − 9 = _____

$$\begin{array}{r} 7 \\ -2 \\ \hline \end{array} \quad \begin{array}{r} 13 \\ -7 \\ \hline \end{array} \quad \begin{array}{r} 14 \\ -9 \\ \hline \end{array} \quad \begin{array}{r} 7 \\ -1 \\ \hline \end{array}$$

8 − 4 = _____     10 − 6 = _____

4 − 0 = _____     8 − 3 = _____

$$\begin{array}{r} 13 \\ -9 \\ \hline \end{array} \quad \begin{array}{r} 9 \\ -5 \\ \hline \end{array} \quad \begin{array}{r} 7 \\ -3 \\ \hline \end{array} \quad \begin{array}{r} 12 \\ -7 \\ \hline \end{array}$$

11 − 6 = _____     11 − 7 = _____

8 − 2 = _____     6 − 0 = _____

$$\begin{array}{r} 9 \\ -4 \\ \hline \end{array} \quad \begin{array}{r} 10 \\ -5 \\ \hline \end{array} \quad \begin{array}{r} 11 \\ -5 \\ \hline \end{array} \quad \begin{array}{r} 5 \\ -0 \\ \hline \end{array}$$

14 − 8 = _____     7 − 2 = _____

12 − 6 = _____     13 − 7 = _____

$$\begin{array}{r} 10 \\ -4 \\ \hline \end{array} \quad \begin{array}{r} 12 \\ -8 \\ \hline \end{array} \quad \begin{array}{r} 6 \\ -2 \\ \hline \end{array} \quad \begin{array}{r} 8 \\ -3 \\ \hline \end{array}$$

13 − 8 = _____     14 − 9 = _____

$$\begin{array}{r} 6 \\ -1 \\ \hline \end{array} \quad \begin{array}{r} 8 \\ -4 \\ \hline \end{array} \quad \begin{array}{r} 11 \\ -6 \\ \hline \end{array} \quad \begin{array}{r} 9 \\ -3 \\ \hline \end{array}$$

5 − 1 = _____     7 − 1 = _____

9 − 3 = _____     13 − 9 = _____

Score: _____     Time: _____ minutes _____ seconds

# Timed Test

9 – 5 = _____        11 – 7 = _____

11 – 5 = _____       14 – 9 = _____

6 – 2 = _____        10 – 5 = _____

13 – 8 = _____       14 – 8 = _____

8 – 3 = _____        5 – 1 = _____

6 – 0 = _____        15 – 9 = _____

12 – 8 = _____       4 – 0 = _____

8 – 2 = _____        7 – 2 = _____

5 – 0 = _____        12 – 7 = _____

9 – 3 = _____        8 – 4 = _____

| 15 | 4 | 7 | 12 |
|---|---|---|---|
| – 9 | – 0 | – 2 | – 7 |

| 8 | 6 | 13 | 11 |
|---|---|---|---|
| – 4 | – 1 | – 9 | – 6 |

| 7 | 7 | 9 | 10 |
|---|---|---|---|
| – 3 | – 1 | – 4 | – 6 |

| 13 | 10 | 12 | 9 |
|---|---|---|---|
| – 7 | – 4 | – 6 | – 5 |

| 6 | 8 | 10 | 11 |
|---|---|---|---|
| – 2 | – 3 | – 5 | – 7 |

Score: _____        Time: _____ minutes _____ seconds

# Timed Test

**Differences Through Six**

8 – 4 = ____      7 – 2 = ____

13 – 9 = ____      9 – 4 = ____

10 – 6 = ____      4 – 0 = ____

6 – 1 = ____      7 – 1 = ____

12 – 6 = ____      12 – 7 = ____

7 – 3 = ____      9 – 5 = ____

13 – 7 = ____      14 – 9 = ____

15 – 9 = ____      6 – 0 = ____

11 – 6 = ____      10 – 5 = ____

10 – 4 = ____      13 – 8 = ____

| 13 | 10 | 6 | 14 |
|----|----|----|----|
| – 8 | – 5 | – 0 | – 9 |

| 9 | 8 | 9 | 8 |
|----|----|----|----|
| – 5 | – 2 | – 3 | – 3 |

| 11 | 5 | 14 | 11 |
|----|----|----|----|
| – 7 | – 0 | – 8 | – 5 |

| 5 | 12 | 6 | 8 |
|----|----|----|----|
| – 1 | – 8 | – 2 | – 4 |

| 7 | 13 | 15 | 6 |
|----|----|----|----|
| – 3 | – 7 | – 9 | – 1 |

Score: _____      Time: _____ minutes _____ seconds

# Timed Test

The rest of the Timed Tests in this section will include some of the differences through 3 to help you remember what you have already learned.

7 – 3 = _____    6 – 1 = _____

11 – 7 = _____    7 – 6 = _____

8 – 2 = _____    9 – 4 = _____

12 – 9 = _____    6 – 4 = _____

10 – 6 = _____    13 – 8 = _____

13 – 7 = _____    1 – 0 = _____

3 – 3 = _____    6 – 2 = _____

5 – 0 = _____    12 – 7 = _____

8 – 7 = _____    7 – 1 = _____

4 – 0 = _____    11 – 9 = _____

| 12 | 6 | 11 | 8 |
|---|---|---|---|
| – 6 | – 0 | – 6 | – 8 |

| 10 | 14 | 5 | 12 |
|---|---|---|---|
| – 5 | – 8 | – 1 | – 8 |

| 6 | 11 | 9 | 14 |
|---|---|---|---|
| – 3 | – 5 | – 5 | – 9 |

| 8 | 9 | 13 | 7 |
|---|---|---|---|
| – 4 | – 3 | – 9 | – 2 |

| 2 | 8 | 10 | 15 |
|---|---|---|---|
| – 0 | – 3 | – 4 | – 9 |

**Differences Through Six**

Score: _____    Time: _____ minutes _____ seconds

# Timed Test

| | | |
|---|---|---|
| 11 − 6 = _____ | 5 − 4 = _____ | |

$$\begin{array}{cccc} 8 & 10 & 9 & 3 \\ -3 & -4 & -4 & -1 \\ \hline \end{array}$$

8 − 4 = _____     14 − 8 = _____

0 − 0 = _____     12 − 6 = _____

$$\begin{array}{cccc} 13 & 4 & 9 & 7 \\ -8 & -0 & -7 & -1 \\ \hline \end{array}$$

14 − 9 = _____     13 − 9 = _____

9 − 3 = _____     3 − 0 = _____

$$\begin{array}{cccc} 11 & 8 & 5 & 7 \\ -7 & -2 & -0 & -5 \\ \hline \end{array}$$

2 − 1 = _____     7 − 2 = _____

9 − 5 = _____     10 − 5 = _____

$$\begin{array}{cccc} 6 & 11 & 13 & 10 \\ -1 & -5 & -7 & -6 \\ \hline \end{array}$$

6 − 0 = _____     12 − 8 = _____

$$\begin{array}{cccc} 9 & 12 & 7 & 6 \\ -6 & -7 & -3 & -2 \\ \hline \end{array}$$

15 − 9 = _____     10 − 7 = _____

5 − 1 = _____     9 − 9 = _____

Score: _____     Time: _____ minutes _____ seconds

Name _____

# Timed Test

11 − 5 = ____     4 − 0 = ____     4 − 2 = ____     5 − 1 = ____

9 − 4 = ____     12 − 7 = ____     10 − 4 = ____     13 − 8 = ____

8 − 4 = ____     6 − 1 = ____     7 − 3 = ____     5 − 2 = ____

3 − 2 = ____     5 − 5 = ____     15 − 9 = ____     11 − 6 = ____

9 − 3 = ____     5 − 0 = ____     10 − 5 = ____     10 − 6 = ____

13 − 7 = ____     9 − 5 = ____     7 − 7 = ____     14 − 9 = ____

8 − 3 = ____     6 − 0 = ____     12 − 8 = ____     7 − 2 = ____

6 − 2 = ____     11 − 8 = ____     13 − 9 = ____     8 − 5 = ____

11 − 7 = ____     12 − 6 = ____     8 − 2 = ____     7 − 1 = ____

10 − 8 = ____     1 − 1 = ____     6 − 5 = ____     14 − 8 = ____

**Differences Through Six**

Score: _____     Time: _____ minutes _____ seconds

# Timed Test

| 5<br>− 0 | 8<br>− 4 | 8<br>− 2 | 12<br>− 5 | 6<br>− 0 | 12<br>− 9 | 11<br>− 6 | 9<br>− 4 |
|---|---|---|---|---|---|---|---|
| 10<br>− 4 | 6<br>− 2 | 9<br>− 9 | 13<br>− 8 | 7<br>− 6 | 7<br>− 2 | 11<br>− 9 | 4<br>− 0 |
| 14<br>− 8 | 10<br>− 6 | 12<br>− 6 | 10<br>− 7 | 10<br>− 8 | 13<br>− 9 | 15<br>− 9 | 8<br>− 6 |
| 10<br>− 5 | 14<br>− 9 | 9<br>− 5 | 7<br>− 1 | 5<br>− 5 | 7<br>− 3 | 13<br>− 7 | 6<br>− 1 |
| 11<br>− 5 | 11<br>− 8 | 5<br>− 1 | 9<br>− 3 | 11<br>− 7 | 5<br>− 4 | 8<br>− 3 | 12<br>− 7 |

Score: _____     Time: _____ minutes _____ seconds

Name _____

# Timed Test

15 − 9 = ____     8 − 5 = ____     7 − 5 = ____     10 − 4 = ____

10 − 5 = ____     12 − 7 = ____     9 − 4 = ____     14 − 8 = ____

14 − 9 = ____     5 − 1 = ____     8 − 4 = ____     9 − 8 = ____

8 − 7 = ____     13 − 7 = ____     9 − 7 = ____     4 − 0 = ____

9 − 5 = ____     7 − 3 = ____     10 − 6 = ____     7 − 2 = ____

9 − 3 = ____     8 − 3 = ____     5 − 0 = ____     12 − 6 = ____

11 − 7 = ____     10 − 9 = ____     13 − 8 = ____     8 − 2 = ____

9 − 6 = ____     13 − 9 = ____     7 − 4 = ____     6 − 2 = ____

6 − 1 = ____     7 − 1 = ____     6 − 0 = ____     6 − 5 = ____

11 − 5 = ____     8 − 8 = ____     11 − 6 = ____     12 − 8 = ____

**Differences Through Six**

Score: _____     Time: _____ minutes _____ seconds

# Timed Test

**Differences Through Six**

| | | | | | | | |
|---|---|---|---|---|---|---|---|
| 4<br>−0 | 12<br>−6 | 5<br>−3 | 9<br>−5 | 11<br>−7 | 10<br>−5 | 4<br>−3 | 9<br>−4 |
| 7<br>−4 | 5<br>−0 | 2<br>−2 | 5<br>−1 | 12<br>−8 | 12<br>−7 | 9<br>−3 | 13<br>−9 |
| 9<br>−8 | 13<br>−8 | 7<br>−1 | 10<br>−4 | 14<br>−8 | 11<br>−5 | 6<br>−6 | 10<br>−6 |
| 6<br>−0 | 14<br>−9 | 11<br>−6 | 8<br>−6 | 4<br>−4 | 6<br>−2 | 8<br>−4 | 13<br>−7 |
| 7<br>−2 | 6<br>−1 | 10<br>−9 | 8<br>−3 | 7<br>−3 | 4<br>−1 | 8<br>−2 | 15<br>−9 |

Record your scores and times below.

**Page 107** Score: _____ Time: ___min. ___sec.   **Page 113** Score: _____ Time: ___min. ___sec.
**Page 108** Score: _____ Time: ___min. ___sec.   **Page 114** Score: _____ Time: ___min. ___sec.
**Page 109** Score: _____ Time: ___min. ___sec.   **Page 115** Score: _____ Time: ___min. ___sec.
**Page 110** Score: _____ Time: ___min. ___sec.   **Page 116** Score: _____ Time: ___min. ___sec.
**Page 111** Score: _____ Time: ___min. ___sec.   **Page 117** Score: _____ Time: ___min. ___sec.
**Page 112** Score: _____ Time: ___min. ___sec.   **Page 118** Score: _____ Time: ___min. ___sec.

# Subtracting Zero

If you remember that zero is the identity element of subtraction, you already know three of the facts in this new group.

**Example:** $8 - 0 = 8$

■ Draw small circles in these boxes to show this is true.

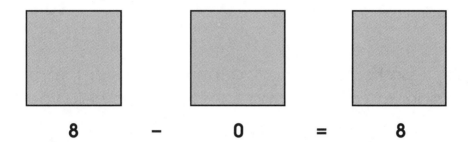

**8**    **–**    **0**    **=**    **8**

■ Complete this **T** by subtracting zero from each number.

■ Write the difference for each fact.

$$-0$$

7 | ____

8 | ____

9 | ____

$9 - 0 = $ ____     $7 - 0 = $ ____

$8 - 0 = $ ____

$$\begin{array}{ccc} 7 & 9 & 8 \\ -0 & -0 & -0 \\ \hline \end{array}$$

**Differences Through Nine**

Name _____

# Counting Back

**Remember:** You can count back to find the difference when the subtrahend is a lesser number like 1, 2, or 3.

**Example:** $10 - 1 = 9$

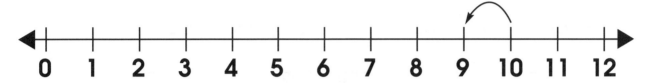

| 0 | 1 | 2 | 3 | 4 | 5 | 6 | 7 | 8 | 9 | 10 | 11 | 12 |

■ Complete these **T**'s by subtracting the numbers at the top from those along the side. You may use the number line to help you count.

|  – 1  |  – 2  |  – 3  |
|-------|-------|-------|
| 10 \_\_\_ | 11 \_\_\_ | 10 \_\_\_ |
| 9 \_\_\_ | 9 \_\_\_ | 12 \_\_\_ |
| 8 \_\_\_ | 10 \_\_\_ | 11 \_\_\_ |

■ Subtract.

$9 - 2 = $ _____       $11 - 3 = $ _____

|   8   |   10  |   11  |
|-------|-------|-------|
| – 1   | – 2   | – 3   |

$10 - 3 = $ _____       $8 - 1 = $ _____

|   10  |   12  |   9   |
|-------|-------|-------|
| – 1   | – 3   | – 1   |

$11 - 2 = $ _____       $12 - 3 = $ _____

**Differences Through Nine**

Name _____

# Using Addition

**Remember:** Addition and subtraction are opposite operations.

**Example:** If $3 + 8 = 11$, then, $11 - 3 = 8$. And, $11 - 8 = 3$.

**Remember:** The sum in an addition fact is the same as the minuend in a related subtraction fact.

**Example:** $3 + 8 = 11$

$11 - 3 = 8$

■ Write two different subtraction facts for each addition sentence.

| $2 + 7 = 9$ | $5 + 7 = 12$ | $3 + 8 = 11$ |
|:---:|:---:|:---:|
| ___ – ___ = ___ | ___ – ___ = ___ | ___ – ___ = ___ |
| ___ – ___ = ___ | ___ – ___ = ___ | ___ – ___ = ___ |
| $8 + 2 = 10$ | $9 + 1 = 10$ | $4 + 7 = 11$ |
| ___ – ___ = ___ | ___ – ___ = ___ | ___ – ___ = ___ |
| ___ – ___ = ___ | ___ – ___ = ___ | ___ – ___ = ___ |
| $1 + 8 = 9$ | $9 + 2 = 11$ | $1 + 7 = 8$ |
| ___ – ___ = ___ | ___ – ___ = ___ | ___ – ___ = ___ |
| ___ – ___ = ___ | ___ – ___ = ___ | ___ – ___ = ___ |

# Using Addition

Use the higher addition facts and what you know about opposite operations to help you discover the higher subtraction facts.

**Example:** If 9 + 6 = 15, then, 15 – 9 = 6. And, 15 – 6 = 9.

■ Write two different subtraction problems for each addition sentence.

| 7 + 6 = 13 | 9 + 4 = 13 | 7 + 8 = 15 |
|---|---|---|
| ____ – ____ = ____ | ____ – ____ = ____ | ____ – ____ = ____ |
| ____ – ____ = ____ | ____ – ____ = ____ | ____ – ____ = ____ |
| 9 + 6 = 15 | 7 + 4 = 11 | 9 + 4 = 13 |
| ____ – ____ = ____ | ____ – ____ = ____ | ____ – ____ = ____ |
| ____ – ____ = ____ | ____ – ____ = ____ | ____ – ____ = ____ |
| 5 + 7 = 12 | 9 + 8 = 17 | 9 + 7 = 16 |
| ____ – ____ = ____ | ____ – ____ = ____ | ____ – ____ = ____ |
| ____ – ____ = ____ | ____ – ____ = ____ | ____ – ____ = ____ |

■ Write one subtraction fact related to each addition sentence.

| 7 + 7 = 14 | 8 + 8 = 16 | 9 + 9 = 18 |
|---|---|---|
| ____ – ____ = ____ | ____ – ____ = ____ | ____ – ____ = ____ |

**Differences Through Nine**

# Practice

■ Subtract. Record your score on each Practice page and again on page 128.

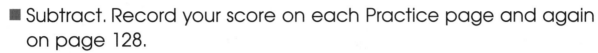

10 – 1 = _____    12 – 3 = _____    10 – 3 = _____    11 – 3 = _____

12 – 4 = _____    14 – 5 = _____    11 – 2 = _____    17 – 8 = _____

13 – 5 = _____    18 – 9 = _____    16 – 8 = _____    16 – 9 = _____

12 – 5 = _____    13 – 4 = _____    10 – 2 = _____    9 – 2 = _____

14 – 6 = _____    15 – 7 = _____    16 – 7 = _____    14 – 7 = _____

9 – 1 = _____    9 – 2 = _____    17 – 9 = _____    13 – 6 = _____

7 – 0 = _____    15 – 8 = _____    8 – 1 = _____    11 – 2 = _____

14 – 7 = _____    13 – 6 = _____    11 – 4 = _____    13 – 5 = _____

8 – 0 = _____    15 – 6 = _____    9 – 0 = _____    12 – 3 = _____

**Differences Through Nine**

Score: _____

Name _____

# Practice

■ Subtract.

| 15 | 7 | 16 | 8 | 14 | 16 | 15 | 10 | 12 |
|---|---|---|---|---|---|---|---|---|
| − 8 | − 0 | − 8 | − 0 | − 7 | − 9 | − 6 | − 1 | − 5 |

| 12 | 14 | 16 | 11 | 9 | 13 | 9 | 15 | 13 |
|---|---|---|---|---|---|---|---|---|
| − 3 | − 6 | − 7 | − 2 | − 2 | − 6 | − 1 | − 7 | − 5 |

| 11 | 14 | 12 | 17 | 11 | 9 | 8 | 18 | 10 |
|---|---|---|---|---|---|---|---|---|
| − 4 | − 5 | − 4 | − 9 | − 3 | − 0 | − 1 | − 9 | − 2 |

| 13 | 10 | 17 | 16 | 12 | 11 | 15 | 10 | 14 |
|---|---|---|---|---|---|---|---|---|
| − 4 | − 3 | − 8 | − 8 | − 5 | − 2 | − 8 | − 1 | − 7 |

Score: _____

START

Name _____

# Practice

■ Subtract.

| | | | |
|---|---|---|---|
| 12 | 15 | 12 | 8 |
| − 5 | − 7 | − 4 | − 1 |

| | | | |
|---|---|---|---|
| 13 | 11 | 16 | 13 |
| − 4 | − 3 | − 7 | − 6 |

| | | | |
|---|---|---|---|
| 16 | 18 | 10 | 9 |
| − 8 | − 9 | − 1 | − 2 |

| | | | |
|---|---|---|---|
| 8 | 12 | 16 | 14 |
| − 0 | − 3 | − 9 | − 6 |

| | | | |
|---|---|---|---|
| 14 | 9 | 15 | 11 |
| − 5 | − 0 | − 8 | − 2 |

14 − 6 = _____     17 − 9 = _____

11 − 4 = _____     10 − 2 = _____

13 − 5 = _____     15 − 8 = _____

15 − 6 = _____     11 − 2 = _____

14 − 7 = _____     17 − 8 = _____

9 − 1 = _____     12 − 5 = _____

7 − 0 = _____     15 − 7 = _____

10 − 3 = _____     8 − 1 = _____

**Differences Through Nine**

Score: _____

FINISH

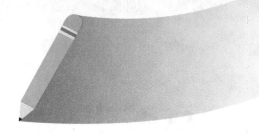

Name _____

# Practice

■ Subtract.

| | | | | | |
|---|---|---|---|---|---|
| 14 <br> − 7 | 10 <br> − 2 | 7 <br> − 0 | 15 <br> − 8 | 11 − 3 = _____ | 8 − 0 = _____ |

$$9 - 2 = \underline{\hspace{1cm}} \qquad 12 - 4 = \underline{\hspace{1cm}}$$

| | | | |
|---|---|---|---|
| 17 <br> − 9 | 13 <br> − 5 | 11 <br> − 2 | 9 <br> − 1 |

$$8 - 1 = \underline{\hspace{1cm}} \qquad 16 - 8 = \underline{\hspace{1cm}}$$

$$16 - 7 = \underline{\hspace{1cm}} \qquad 12 - 5 = \underline{\hspace{1cm}}$$

| | | | |
|---|---|---|---|
| 14 <br> − 6 | 9 <br> − 0 | 10 <br> − 3 | 11 <br> − 4 |

$$10 - 1 = \underline{\hspace{1cm}} \qquad 13 - 4 = \underline{\hspace{1cm}}$$

| | | | |
|---|---|---|---|
| 17 <br> − 8 | 15 <br> − 6 | 14 <br> − 5 | 12 <br> − 3 |

$$12 - 3 = \underline{\hspace{1cm}} \qquad 14 - 7 = \underline{\hspace{1cm}}$$

$$18 - 9 = \underline{\hspace{1cm}} \qquad 17 - 8 = \underline{\hspace{1cm}}$$

$$15 - 7 = \underline{\hspace{1cm}} \qquad 11 - 2 = \underline{\hspace{1cm}}$$

| | | | |
|---|---|---|---|
| 16 <br> − 9 | 13 <br> − 6 | 10 <br> − 1 | 18 <br> − 9 |

Score: _____

 START

# Practice

■ Subtract.

$$
\begin{array}{r} 7 \\ -0 \\ \hline \end{array}
\qquad
\begin{array}{r} 13 \\ -4 \\ \hline \end{array}
\qquad
\begin{array}{r} 12 \\ -4 \\ \hline \end{array}
\qquad
\begin{array}{r} 16 \\ -8 \\ \hline \end{array}
$$

$$
\begin{array}{r} 11 \\ -4 \\ \hline \end{array}
\qquad
\begin{array}{r} 9 \\ -0 \\ \hline \end{array}
\qquad
\begin{array}{r} 16 \\ -9 \\ \hline \end{array}
\qquad
\begin{array}{r} 15 \\ -7 \\ \hline \end{array}
$$

$$
\begin{array}{r} 18 \\ -9 \\ \hline \end{array}
\qquad
\begin{array}{r} 9 \\ -2 \\ \hline \end{array}
\qquad
\begin{array}{r} 12 \\ -3 \\ \hline \end{array}
\qquad
\begin{array}{r} 13 \\ -6 \\ \hline \end{array}
$$

$$
\begin{array}{r} 15 \\ -6 \\ \hline \end{array}
\qquad
\begin{array}{r} 10 \\ -2 \\ \hline \end{array}
\qquad
\begin{array}{r} 14 \\ -6 \\ \hline \end{array}
\qquad
\begin{array}{r} 12 \\ -5 \\ \hline \end{array}
$$

$$
\begin{array}{r} 10 \\ -3 \\ \hline \end{array}
\qquad
\begin{array}{r} 14 \\ -7 \\ \hline \end{array}
\qquad
\begin{array}{r} 11 \\ -2 \\ \hline \end{array}
\qquad
\begin{array}{r} 13 \\ -5 \\ \hline \end{array}
$$

$8 - 1 =$ _____     $11 - 2 =$ _____

$14 - 5 =$ _____     $13 - 5 =$ _____

$11 - 3 =$ _____     $10 - 1 =$ _____

$17 - 8 =$ _____     $15 - 8 =$ _____

$12 - 5 =$ _____     $16 - 7 =$ _____

$8 - 0 =$ _____     $9 - 2 =$ _____

$17 - 9 =$ _____     $11 - 4 =$ _____

$9 - 1 =$ _____     $13 - 6 =$ _____

Score: _____

Circle any problems that you still find difficult to remember. Make your own flash cards to help you master these problems.

# Practice

■ Subtract.

16 – 8 = _____     13 – 6 = _____

$$\begin{array}{r} 17 \\ -8 \\ \hline \end{array} \quad \begin{array}{r} 8 \\ -0 \\ \hline \end{array} \quad \begin{array}{r} 10 \\ -3 \\ \hline \end{array} \quad \begin{array}{r} 15 \\ -8 \\ \hline \end{array}$$

10 – 2 = _____      7 – 0 = _____

$$\begin{array}{r} 10 \\ -1 \\ \hline \end{array} \quad \begin{array}{r} 11 \\ -2 \\ \hline \end{array} \quad \begin{array}{r} 9 \\ -1 \\ \hline \end{array} \quad \begin{array}{r} 14 \\ -5 \\ \hline \end{array}$$

14 – 6 = _____     15 – 6 = _____

12 – 3 = _____     11 – 4 = _____

$$\begin{array}{r} 17 \\ -9 \\ \hline \end{array} \quad \begin{array}{r} 14 \\ -7 \\ \hline \end{array} \quad \begin{array}{r} 11 \\ -3 \\ \hline \end{array} \quad \begin{array}{r} 13 \\ -5 \\ \hline \end{array}$$

16 – 9 = _____     18 – 9 = _____

12 – 4 = _____     13 – 4 = _____

$$\begin{array}{r} 12 \\ -5 \\ \hline \end{array} \quad \begin{array}{r} 16 \\ -7 \\ \hline \end{array} \quad \begin{array}{r} 8 \\ -1 \\ \hline \end{array} \quad \begin{array}{r} 18 \\ -9 \\ \hline \end{array}$$

9 – 0 = _____      9 – 2 = _____

15 – 7 = _____     17 – 9 = _____

$$\begin{array}{r} 10 \\ -2 \\ \hline \end{array} \quad \begin{array}{r} 9 \\ -0 \\ \hline \end{array} \quad \begin{array}{r} 12 \\ -3 \\ \hline \end{array} \quad \begin{array}{r} 15 \\ -6 \\ \hline \end{array}$$

**Differences Through Nine**

| Record your scores below. | |
|---|---|
| **Page 123** Score: _____ | **Page 126** Score: _____ |
| **Page 124** Score: _____ | **Page 127** Score: _____ |
| **Page 125** Score: _____ | **Page 128** Score: _____ |

Name _____

# Timed Test

■ Improve your speed on these basic facts. Ask someone to time you.
Record your time and score on each Timed Test page and on page 140.

9 – 2 = _____    16 – 8 = _____    12 – 4 = _____    13 – 5 = _____

14 – 6 = _____    15 – 6 = _____    18 – 9 = _____    15 – 8 = _____

7 – 0 = _____    13 – 4 = _____    8 – 1 = _____    11 – 4 = _____

13 – 6 = _____    16 – 9 = _____    17 – 9 = _____    12 – 5 = _____

10 – 2 = _____    12 – 3 = _____    11 – 3 = _____    10 – 3 = _____

14 – 5 = _____    9 – 1 = _____    17 – 8 = _____    9 – 0 = _____

10 – 1 = _____    10 – 3 = _____    13 – 5 = _____    14 – 6 = _____

14 – 7 = _____    8 – 0 = _____    11 – 4 = _____    17 – 9 = _____

16 – 7 = _____    11 – 2 = _____    12 – 5 = _____    12 – 3 = _____

9 – 0 = _____    15 – 8 = _____    15 – 7 = _____    14 – 6 = _____

Score: _____    Time: _____ minutes _____ seconds

# Timed Test

| 12 | 13 | 13 | 16 | 14 | 9 | 16 | 18 |
|---|---|---|---|---|---|---|---|
| − 4 | − 6 | − 5 | − 9 | − 5 | − 2 | − 7 | − 9 |

| 9 | 10 | 17 | 15 | 8 | 11 | 17 | 15 |
|---|---|---|---|---|---|---|---|
| − 1 | − 3 | − 8 | − 6 | − 1 | − 4 | − 9 | − 8 |

| 13 | 11 | 16 | 12 | 15 | 14 | 9 | 14 |
|---|---|---|---|---|---|---|---|
| − 4 | − 3 | − 8 | − 5 | − 7 | − 6 | − 0 | − 7 |

| 10 | 12 | 10 | 8 | 7 | 11 | 13 | 15 |
|---|---|---|---|---|---|---|---|
| − 2 | − 3 | − 1 | − 0 | − 0 | − 2 | − 5 | − 7 |

| 16 | 11 | 16 | 8 | 12 | 14 | 9 | 17 |
|---|---|---|---|---|---|---|---|
| − 8 | − 4 | − 9 | − 1 | − 4 | − 6 | − 2 | − 8 |

Score: _____    Time: _____ minutes _____ seconds

# Timed Test

17 – 8 = _____     10 – 2 = _____

$$\begin{array}{r} 16 \\ -\ 7 \\ \hline \end{array}$$  $$\begin{array}{r} 17 \\ -\ 9 \\ \hline \end{array}$$  $$\begin{array}{r} 11 \\ -\ 4 \\ \hline \end{array}$$  $$\begin{array}{r} 8 \\ -\ 0 \\ \hline \end{array}$$

15 – 8 = _____     18 – 9 = _____

7 – 0 = _____     12 – 3 = _____

$$\begin{array}{r} 9 \\ -\ 0 \\ \hline \end{array}$$  $$\begin{array}{r} 16 \\ -\ 9 \\ \hline \end{array}$$  $$\begin{array}{r} 14 \\ -\ 6 \\ \hline \end{array}$$  $$\begin{array}{r} 8 \\ -\ 1 \\ \hline \end{array}$$

9 – 1 = _____     11 – 3 = _____

16 – 8 = _____     13 – 4 = _____

$$\begin{array}{r} 15 \\ -\ 7 \\ \hline \end{array}$$  $$\begin{array}{r} 14 \\ -\ 7 \\ \hline \end{array}$$  $$\begin{array}{r} 13 \\ -\ 6 \\ \hline \end{array}$$  $$\begin{array}{r} 14 \\ -\ 5 \\ \hline \end{array}$$

10 – 3 = _____     16 – 7 = _____

11 – 2 = _____     9 – 0 = _____

$$\begin{array}{r} 12 \\ -\ 4 \\ \hline \end{array}$$  $$\begin{array}{r} 15 \\ -\ 6 \\ \hline \end{array}$$  $$\begin{array}{r} 9 \\ -\ 2 \\ \hline \end{array}$$  $$\begin{array}{r} 17 \\ -\ 8 \\ \hline \end{array}$$

13 – 5 = _____     14 – 7 = _____

10 – 1 = _____     15 – 6 = _____

$$\begin{array}{r} 7 \\ -\ 0 \\ \hline \end{array}$$  $$\begin{array}{r} 18 \\ -\ 9 \\ \hline \end{array}$$  $$\begin{array}{r} 11 \\ -\ 2 \\ \hline \end{array}$$  $$\begin{array}{r} 10 \\ -\ 3 \\ \hline \end{array}$$

12 – 5 = _____     9 – 2 = _____

Score: _____     Time: _____ minutes _____ seconds

# Timed Test

**Differences Through Nine**

| | | | | | |
|---|---|---|---|---|---|
| $12 - 4 =$ ___ | $14 - 7 =$ ___ | $\begin{array}{r} 9 \\ -1 \\ \hline \end{array}$ | $\begin{array}{r} 12 \\ -3 \\ \hline \end{array}$ | $\begin{array}{r} 15 \\ -8 \\ \hline \end{array}$ | $\begin{array}{r} 12 \\ -5 \\ \hline \end{array}$ |

$12 - 4 =$ ___      $14 - 7 =$ ___

$8 - 0 =$ ___      $11 - 4 =$ ___

$8 - 1 =$ ___      $9 - 2 =$ ___

$17 - 9 =$ ___      $15 - 6 =$ ___

$14 - 5 =$ ___      $14 - 6 =$ ___

$9 - 0 =$ ___      $12 - 3 =$ ___

$15 - 7 =$ ___      $10 - 1 =$ ___

$16 - 7 =$ ___      $15 - 8 =$ ___

$13 - 6 =$ ___      $17 - 8 =$ ___

$16 - 9 =$ ___      $10 - 3 =$ ___

$\begin{array}{r} 9 \\ -1 \\ \hline \end{array}$  $\begin{array}{r} 12 \\ -3 \\ \hline \end{array}$  $\begin{array}{r} 15 \\ -8 \\ \hline \end{array}$  $\begin{array}{r} 12 \\ -5 \\ \hline \end{array}$

$\begin{array}{r} 16 \\ -8 \\ \hline \end{array}$  $\begin{array}{r} 11 \\ -3 \\ \hline \end{array}$  $\begin{array}{r} 10 \\ -1 \\ \hline \end{array}$  $\begin{array}{r} 17 \\ -8 \\ \hline \end{array}$

$\begin{array}{r} 13 \\ -5 \\ \hline \end{array}$  $\begin{array}{r} 10 \\ -3 \\ \hline \end{array}$  $\begin{array}{r} 7 \\ -0 \\ \hline \end{array}$  $\begin{array}{r} 13 \\ -4 \\ \hline \end{array}$

$\begin{array}{r} 10 \\ -2 \\ \hline \end{array}$  $\begin{array}{r} 11 \\ -2 \\ \hline \end{array}$  $\begin{array}{r} 18 \\ -9 \\ \hline \end{array}$  $\begin{array}{r} 9 \\ -2 \\ \hline \end{array}$

$\begin{array}{r} 9 \\ -0 \\ \hline \end{array}$  $\begin{array}{r} 17 \\ -9 \\ \hline \end{array}$  $\begin{array}{r} 12 \\ -4 \\ \hline \end{array}$  $\begin{array}{r} 15 \\ -6 \\ \hline \end{array}$

Score: _____      Time: _____ minutes _____ seconds

## Timed Test

Name _____

12 − 5 = ____      14 − 6 = ____

16 − 7 = ____      10 − 1 = ____

9 − 2 = ____      8 − 1 = ____

11 − 2 = ____      7 − 0 = ____

13 − 5 = ____      15 − 8 = ____

9 − 1 = ____      12 − 4 = ____

14 − 5 = ____      11 − 3 = ____

13 − 6 = ____      18 − 9 = ____

9 − 0 = ____      15 − 7 = ____

10 − 2 = ____      16 − 8 = ____

|  |  |  |  |
|---|---|---|---|
| 17<br>− 8 | 12<br>− 4 | 15<br>− 6 | 14<br>− 7 |
| 13<br>− 4 | 11<br>− 3 | 18<br>− 9 | 10<br>− 3 |
| 15<br>− 7 | 8<br>− 0 | 12<br>− 3 | 16<br>− 8 |
| 16<br>− 9 | 11<br>− 4 | 17<br>− 9 | 12<br>− 5 |
| 14<br>− 5 | 8<br>− 1 | 10<br>− 2 | 13<br>− 6 |

**Differences Through Nine**

Score: _____      Time: _____ minutes _____ seconds

Name _____

# Timed Test

18 − 9 = ____     12 − 3 = ____

| 14 | 11 | 14 | 9 |
|---|---|---|---|
| − 5 | − 2 | − 6 | − 0 |

11 − 3 = ____     16 − 9 = ____

17 − 9 = ____     15 − 6 = ____

| 12 | 9 | 10 | 13 |
|---|---|---|---|
| − 5 | − 1 | − 2 | − 5 |

15 − 7 = ____     16 − 8 = ____

12 − 4 = ____     13 − 4 = ____

| 7 | 10 | 16 | 8 |
|---|---|---|---|
| − 0 | − 1 | − 7 | − 1 |

10 − 3 = ____     11 − 2 = ____

14 − 7 = ____     9 − 1 = ____

| 13 | 15 | 9 | 11 |
|---|---|---|---|
| − 6 | − 8 | − 2 | − 3 |

11 − 4 = ____     16 − 7 = ____

8 − 0 = ____     14 − 5 = ____

| 17 | 15 | 11 | 8 |
|---|---|---|---|
| − 8 | − 7 | − 4 | − 0 |

17 − 8 = ____     9 − 0 = ____

Score: _____     Time: _____ minutes _____ seconds

# Timed Test

The rest of the Timed Tests in this section will include some of the differences through 6 to help you remember what you have already learned.

11 − 3 = _____    12 − 6 = _____

$$\begin{array}{cccc} 11 & 12 & 9 & 13 \\ -2 & -4 & -3 & -5 \\ \hline \end{array}$$

14 − 7 = _____    7 − 0 = _____

4 − 0 = _____    9 − 1 = _____

$$\begin{array}{cccc} 13 & 10 & 12 & 9 \\ -6 & -2 & -7 & -0 \\ \hline \end{array}$$

11 − 4 = _____    14 − 9 = _____

9 − 4 = _____    15 − 7 = _____

$$\begin{array}{cccc} 10 & 17 & 14 & 9 \\ -3 & -8 & -5 & -5 \\ \hline \end{array}$$

10 − 1 = _____    11 − 5 = _____

14 − 6 = _____    12 − 3 = _____

$$\begin{array}{cccc} 8 & 17 & 16 & 8 \\ -1 & -9 & -9 & -0 \\ \hline \end{array}$$

6 − 1 = _____    18 − 9 = _____

15 − 8 = _____    15 − 6 = _____

$$\begin{array}{cccc} 9 & 15 & 16 & 13 \\ -2 & -9 & -8 & -4 \\ \hline \end{array}$$

16 − 7 = _____    12 − 5 = _____

Score: _____    Time: _____ minutes _____ seconds

# Timed Test

$14 - 5 =$ _____    $6 - 2 =$ _____

| 15 | 7 | 16 | 11 |
|----|----|----|----|
| − 6 | − 3 | − 7 | − 3 |

$17 - 8 =$ _____    $11 - 6 =$ _____

$12 - 8 =$ _____    $17 - 9 =$ _____

| 15 | 18 | 12 | 11 |
|----|----|----|----|
| − 8 | − 9 | − 5 | − 7 |

$10 - 2 =$ _____    $10 - 3 =$ _____

$13 - 4 =$ _____    $6 - 0 =$ _____

| 14 | 5 | 11 | 13 |
|----|----|----|----|
| − 6 | − 0 | − 4 | − 7 |

$8 - 1 =$ _____    $16 - 9 =$ _____

$14 - 8 =$ _____    $12 - 4 =$ _____

| 7 | 15 | 11 | 9 |
|----|----|----|----|
| − 0 | − 7 | − 2 | − 1 |

$13 - 5 =$ _____    $9 - 2 =$ _____

$16 - 8 =$ _____    $13 - 6 =$ _____

| 12 | 10 | 14 | 7 |
|----|----|----|----|
| − 3 | − 1 | − 7 | − 1 |

$9 - 0 =$ _____    $8 - 0 =$ _____

Score: _____    Time: _____ minutes _____ seconds

# Timed Test

$7 - 2 =$ ___     $15 - 6 =$ ___

$\begin{array}{r} 17 \\ -8 \\ \hline \end{array}$     $\begin{array}{r} 10 \\ -4 \\ \hline \end{array}$     $\begin{array}{r} 17 \\ -9 \\ \hline \end{array}$     $\begin{array}{r} 13 \\ -4 \\ \hline \end{array}$

$8 - 0 =$ ___     $8 - 1 =$ ___

$18 - 9 =$ ___     $12 - 5 =$ ___

$\begin{array}{r} 12 \\ -4 \\ \hline \end{array}$     $\begin{array}{r} 13 \\ -6 \\ \hline \end{array}$     $\begin{array}{r} 12 \\ -3 \\ \hline \end{array}$     $\begin{array}{r} 13 \\ -5 \\ \hline \end{array}$

$9 - 2 =$ ___     $10 - 2 =$ ___

$14 - 5 =$ ___     $8 - 3 =$ ___

$\begin{array}{r} 10 \\ -6 \\ \hline \end{array}$     $\begin{array}{r} 11 \\ -2 \\ \hline \end{array}$     $\begin{array}{r} 9 \\ -0 \\ \hline \end{array}$     $\begin{array}{r} 13 \\ -9 \\ \hline \end{array}$

$16 - 8 =$ ___     $16 - 7 =$ ___

$5 - 1 =$ ___     $13 - 8 =$ ___

$\begin{array}{r} 10 \\ -3 \\ \hline \end{array}$     $\begin{array}{r} 15 \\ -7 \\ \hline \end{array}$     $\begin{array}{r} 8 \\ -2 \\ \hline \end{array}$     $\begin{array}{r} 11 \\ -4 \\ \hline \end{array}$

$16 - 9 =$ ___     $11 - 3 =$ ___

$10 - 5 =$ ___     $14 - 7 =$ ___

$\begin{array}{r} 14 \\ -6 \\ \hline \end{array}$     $\begin{array}{r} 10 \\ -1 \\ \hline \end{array}$     $\begin{array}{r} 15 \\ -8 \\ \hline \end{array}$     $\begin{array}{r} 7 \\ -0 \\ \hline \end{array}$

$9 - 1 =$ ___     $8 - 4 =$ ___

**Differences Through Nine**

Score: _____     Time: _____ minutes _____ seconds

# Timed Test

**Differences Through Nine**

| 7 | 10 | 17 | 13 | 14 | 12 | 16 | 11 |
|---|----|----|----|----|----|----|----|
| − 0 | − 4 | − 9 | − 5 | − 5 | − 6 | − 9 | − 4 |

| 12 | 9 | 9 | 15 | 11 | 16 | 9 | 10 |
|----|---|---|----|----|----|---|----|
| − 3 | − 1 | − 4 | − 8 | − 3 | − 7 | − 2 | − 6 |

| 15 | 13 | 10 | 6 | 18 | 9 | 9 | 7 |
|----|----|----|---|----|---|---|---|
| − 7 | − 6 | − 1 | − 6 | − 9 | − 5 | − 0 | − 7 |

| 12 | 15 | 13 | 8 | 12 | 8 | 16 | 14 |
|----|----|----|---|----|---|----|----|
| − 5 | − 6 | − 4 | − 4 | − 4 | − 1 | − 8 | − 6 |

| 11 | 8 | 10 | 14 | 10 | 11 | 17 | 10 |
|----|---|----|----|----|----|----|----|
| − 2 | − 0 | − 3 | − 7 | − 2 | − 5 | − 8 | − 5 |

Score: _____     Time: _____ minutes _____ seconds

Name _____

# Timed Test

15 – 6 = _____     9 – 1 = _____     14 – 5 = _____     15 – 8 = _____

8 – 1 = _____     10 – 7 = _____     6 – 2 = _____     18 – 9 = _____

14 – 6 = _____     16 – 8 = _____     9 – 3 = _____     9 – 2 = _____

17 – 8 = _____     14 – 7 = _____     16 – 7 = _____     8 – 3 = _____

7 – 3 = _____     13 – 5 = _____     7 – 0 = _____     8 – 0 = _____

16 – 9 = _____     4 – 3 = _____     15 – 7 = _____     10 – 2 = _____

9 – 0 = _____     11 – 3 = _____     13 – 6 = _____     6 – 3 = _____

3 – 2 = _____     13 – 4 = _____     17 – 9 = _____     12 – 3 = _____

11 – 2 = _____     12 – 5 = _____     10 – 1 = _____     11 – 4 = _____

4 – 4 = _____     5 – 3 = _____     6 – 4 = _____     12 – 4 = _____

Score: _____     Time: _____ minutes _____ seconds

# Timed Test

**Differences Through Nine**

| 12 | 14 | 12 | 8 | 11 | 13 | 11 | 13 |
|----|----|----|----|----|----|----|----|
| − 8 | − 6 | − 4 | − 1 | − 3 | − 7 | − 4 | − 8 |

| 15 | 10 | 15 | 14 | 9 | 10 | 14 | 7 |
|----|----|----|----|----|----|----|----|
| − 7 | − 1 | − 8 | − 7 | − 0 | − 2 | − 8 | − 0 |

| 12 | 11 | 16 | 13 | 11 | 14 | 13 | 15 |
|----|----|----|----|----|----|----|----|
| − 7 | − 2 | − 7 | − 9 | − 7 | − 5 | − 6 | − 6 |

| 13 | 15 | 12 | 13 | 9 | 17 | 8 | 12 |
|----|----|----|----|----|----|----|----|
| − 5 | − 9 | − 5 | − 4 | − 1 | − 8 | − 0 | − 3 |

| 11 | 16 | 18 | 10 | 16 | 14 | 9 | 17 |
|----|----|----|----|----|----|----|----|
| − 6 | − 8 | − 9 | − 3 | − 9 | − 9 | − 2 | − 9 |

Record your scores and times below.

**Page 129** Score: _____ Time: ____ min. ____ sec.  **Page 135** Score: _____ Time: ____ min. ____ sec.

**Page 130** Score: _____ Time: ____ min. ____ sec.  **Page 136** Score: _____ Time: ____ min. ____ sec.

**Page 131** Score: _____ Time: ____ min. ____ sec.  **Page 137** Score: _____ Time: ____ min. ____ sec.

**Page 132** Score: _____ Time: ____ min. ____ sec.  **Page 138** Score: _____ Time: ____ min. ____ sec.

**Page 133** Score: _____ Time: ____ min. ____ sec.  **Page 139** Score: _____ Time: ____ min. ____ sec.

**Page 134** Score: _____ Time: ____ min. ____ sec.  **Page 140** Score: _____ Time: ____ min. ____ sec.

# All-Addition Review

■ Here are 60 addition facts. Prove to yourself that you are an expert
in addition. Concentrate on accuracy.

| | | | |
|---|---|---|---|
| 8 + 2 = ___ | 1 + 8 = ___ | 4 + 1 = ___ | 7 + 8 = ___ |
| 6 + 8 = ___ | 5 + 9 = ___ | 8 + 0 = ___ | 3 + 9 = ___ |
| 0 + 7 = ___ | 7 + 4 = ___ | 2 + 5 = ___ | 4 + 9 = ___ |
| 4 + 5 = ___ | 9 + 6 = ___ | 5 + 7 = ___ | 7 + 1 = ___ |
| 7 + 2 = ___ | 9 + 5 = ___ | 6 + 3 = ___ | 4 + 4 = ___ |
| 3 + 6 = ___ | 1 + 7 = ___ | 8 + 7 = ___ | 3 + 5 = ___ |
| 6 + 7 = ___ | 5 + 2 = ___ | 6 + 9 = ___ | 5 + 0 = ___ |
| 2 + 4 = ___ | 9 + 8 = ___ | 4 + 7 = ___ | 1 + 2 = ___ |
| 4 + 0 = ___ | 5 + 8 = ___ | 6 + 2 = ___ | 4 + 8 = ___ |
| 1 + 5 = ___ | 5 + 6 = ___ | 2 + 8 = ___ | 2 + 7 = ___ |
| 9 + 0 = ___ | 2 + 6 = ___ | 7 + 5 = ___ | 5 + 3 = ___ |
| 3 + 2 = ___ | 2 + 3 = ___ | 8 + 9 = ___ | 7 + 6 = ___ |
| 8 + 8 = ___ | 7 + 7 = ___ | 9 + 7 = ___ | 8 + 1 = ___ |
| 7 + 3 = ___ | 3 + 4 = ___ | 9 + 9 = ___ | 4 + 2 = ___ |
| 4 + 6 = ___ | 1 + 6 = ___ | 8 + 3 = ___ | 9 + 1 = ___ |

**Addition Review**

# All-Subtraction Review

■ Here are 60 subtraction facts. Prove to yourself that you are also an expert in subtraction. Concentrate on accuracy.

Subtraction Review

| | | | |
|---|---|---|---|
| $4 - 0 =$ ___ | $16 - 9 =$ ___ | $13 - 6 =$ ___ | $7 - 3 =$ ___ |
| $11 - 4 =$ ___ | $17 - 9 =$ ___ | $15 - 9 =$ ___ | $2 - 1 =$ ___ |
| $9 - 3 =$ ___ | $2 - 2 =$ ___ | $16 - 7 =$ ___ | $13 - 4 =$ ___ |
| $4 - 3 =$ ___ | $14 - 5 =$ ___ | $9 - 5 =$ ___ | $6 - 2 =$ ___ |
| $8 - 2 =$ ___ | $10 - 7 =$ ___ | $5 - 3 =$ ___ | $9 - 6 =$ ___ |
| $10 - 5 =$ ___ | $5 - 5 =$ ___ | $9 - 4 =$ ___ | $11 - 3 =$ ___ |
| $14 - 9 =$ ___ | $9 - 2 =$ ___ | $6 - 5 =$ ___ | $12 - 7 =$ ___ |
| $5 - 4 =$ ___ | $13 - 5 =$ ___ | $8 - 3 =$ ___ | $9 - 7 =$ ___ |
| $11 - 5 =$ ___ | $12 - 6 =$ ___ | $14 - 6 =$ ___ | $12 - 3 =$ ___ |
| $12 - 9 =$ ___ | $15 - 6 =$ ___ | $18 - 9 =$ ___ | $12 - 8 =$ ___ |
| $4 - 2 =$ ___ | $12 - 4 =$ ___ | $5 - 2 =$ ___ | $11 - 2 =$ ___ |
| $6 - 6 =$ ___ | $16 - 8 =$ ___ | $13 - 8 =$ ___ | $5 - 1 =$ ___ |
| $8 - 4 =$ ___ | $14 - 7 =$ ___ | $15 - 7 =$ ___ | $14 - 8 =$ ___ |
| $11 - 7 =$ ___ | $13 - 9 =$ ___ | $10 - 8 =$ ___ | $12 - 5 =$ ___ |
| $9 - 8 =$ ___ | $11 - 6 =$ ___ | $11 - 9 =$ ___ | $13 - 7 =$ ___ |

MULTIPLICATION

# What Is Multiplication?

You multiply to find how many there are in all in groups that are equal. The answer is called the **product**.

**5 plums** + **5 plums** + **5 plums**

Here are two ways to show the multiplication. You read the problem this way: **3 times 5 equals 15**.

$$3 \times 5 = 15$$

$$\begin{array}{r} 3 \\ \times 5 \\ \hline 15 \end{array}$$

You can draw a picture to find a product.

**Example:** Find the answer.  $4 \times 2 =$ _____

**Step 1:** Draw 4 sets of 2 dots.    ● ●    ● ●    ● ●    ● ●

**Step 2:** Count all the dots.

**Answer:** $4 \times 2 = \underline{\phantom{8}8\phantom{8}}$

■ Draw a picture to find the product.

| | | |
|---|---|---|

$3 \times 2 = $ ____        $2 \times 4 = $ ____        $5 \times 2 = $ ____

| | | |
|---|---|---|

$2 \times 3 = $ ____        $4 \times 3 = $ ____        $3 \times 4 = $ ____

**Multiplication**

Name _____

# What Is Multiplication?

You can use grid paper to find the product.

**Example:** Find the product.  4 x 5 = _____

**Step 1:** Draw a rectangle 5 units long and 4 units wide.

**Step 2:** Count the squares inside the rectangle.

**Answer:** 4 x 5 = __20__

■ Use grid paper to find the product.

3 x 3 = ____          2 x 5 = ____                    4 x 4 = ____

$$\begin{array}{r} 3 \\ \times 5 \\ \hline \end{array}$$    $$\begin{array}{r} 2 \\ \times 2 \\ \hline \end{array}$$    $$\begin{array}{r} 6 \\ \times 2 \\ \hline \end{array}$$    $$\begin{array}{r} 3 \\ \times 4 \\ \hline \end{array}$$    $$\begin{array}{r} 6 \\ \times 3 \\ \hline \end{array}$$

You can use a number line to find the product.

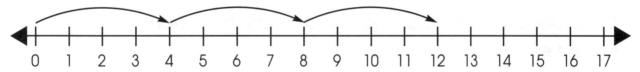

**Example:** Find the product.  3 x 4 = _____

**Step 1:** Put your finger on 0.

**Step 2:** Make 3 moves to the right of 4 spaces each.

**Step 3:** Read the number your finger is on.

**Answer:** 3 x 4 = __12__

■ Use the number line to find the product.

3 x 3 = ____          2 x 5 = ____                    4 x 4 = ____

$$\begin{array}{r} 4 \\ \times 2 \\ \hline \end{array}$$    $$\begin{array}{r} 3 \\ \times 4 \\ \hline \end{array}$$    $$\begin{array}{r} 3 \\ \times 2 \\ \hline \end{array}$$    $$\begin{array}{r} 2 \\ \times 6 \\ \hline \end{array}$$    $$\begin{array}{r} 3 \\ \times 5 \\ \hline \end{array}$$

**Multiplication**

# Products Through Nine

The answer in multiplication is called the **product**. The numbers multiplied together are called **factors**.

**Example:** 0 x 4 = 0.

| 0 | x | 4 | = | 0 |
|---|---|---|---|---|
| factor | | factor | | product |

$$\begin{array}{r} 0 \text{ factor} \\ \times 4 \text{ factor} \\ \hline 0 \text{ product} \end{array}$$

There are three important things to remember about the multiplication facts on this page.

- When one of the factors is 0, the product is always 0.
  **Example:** 6 x 0 = 0

- When one of the factors is 1, the product is the same as the other factor. One is the **identity element of multiplication**.
  **Example:** 5 x 1 = 5

- The order of the factors does not change the product.
  **Example:** 3 x 1 = 3 and 1 x 3 = 3

■ Find the products for these basic facts.

| | | | |
|---|---|---|---|
| 0 x 3 = ____ | 0 x 5 = ____ | 7 x 0 = ____ | 1 x 7 = ____ |
| 6 x 0 = ____ | 9 x 1 = ____ | 4 x 1 = ____ | 0 x 9 = ____ |
| 0 x 7 = ____ | 1 x 0 = ____ | 0 x 4 = ____ | 0 x 8 = ____ |
| 4 x 1 = ____ | 3 x 0 = ____ | 1 x 3 = ____ | 1 x 2 = ____ |
| 7 x 1 = ____ | 5 x 1 = ____ | 9 x 0 = ____ | 2 x 0 = ____ |

**Zero and One as Factors**

Name _____

# Practice

■ Multiply. Record your score—the number correct—on each Practice page and again on page 150.

0 x 6 = ____     2 x 0 = ____     4 x 1 = ____     1 x 4 = ____

1 x 9 = ____     0 x 4 = ____     0 x 3 = ____     5 x 1 = ____

3 x 0 = ____     6 x 0 = ____     1 x 2 = ____     6 x 1 = ____

4 x 0 = ____     1 x 6 = ____     7 x 1 = ____     9 x 1 = ____

1 x 8 = ____     1 x 0 = ____     9 x 0 = ____     3 x 1 = ____

1 x 1 = ____     0 x 9 = ____     5 x 0 = ____     0 x 1 = ____

0 x 0 = ____     0 x 2 = ____     2 x 1 = ____     8 x 0 = ____

0 x 5 = ____     8 x 1 = ____     1 x 3 = ____     1 x 5 = ____

1 x 7 = ____     7 x 0 = ____     0 x 7 = ____     0 x 8 = ____

Score: _____

START

Name _____

# Practice

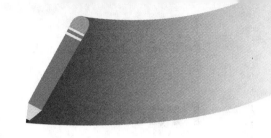

■ Multiply.

| | | | | | | | | |
|---|---|---|---|---|---|---|---|---|
| 0 | 1 | 2 | 4 | 9 | 5 | 0 | 1 | 0 |
| x 0 | x 2 | x 0 | x 1 | x 0 | x 1 | x 3 | x 9 | x 5 |

| | | | | | | | | |
|---|---|---|---|---|---|---|---|---|
| 1 | 5 | 1 | 0 | 9 | 7 | 1 | 0 | 0 |
| x 1 | x 0 | x 8 | x 7 | x 1 | x 1 | x 7 | x 9 | x 8 |

| | | | | | | | | |
|---|---|---|---|---|---|---|---|---|
| 4 | 8 | 1 | 1 | 3 | 1 | 3 | 0 | 0 |
| x 0 | x 0 | x 4 | x 0 | x 1 | x 3 | x 0 | x 1 | x 4 |

| | | | | | | | | |
|---|---|---|---|---|---|---|---|---|
| 2 | 6 | 8 | 1 | 0 | 6 | 7 | 0 | 1 |
| x 1 | x 0 | x 1 | x 5 | x 6 | x 1 | x 0 | x 2 | x 6 |

Score: _____

Circle any problems that you still find difficult to remember. Make your own flash cards to help you master these problems.

Name _____

# Timed Test

■ Improve your speed on these basic multiplication facts. Ask someone to time you. Record your time and score below and on page 150.

1 x 0 = ____        2 x 1 = ____

$$\begin{array}{cccc} 0 & 1 & 4 & 8 \\ \underline{\times 3} & \underline{\times 5} & \underline{\times 1} & \underline{\times 1} \end{array}$$

1 x 4 = ____        0 x 4 = ____

0 x 2 = ____        7 x 1 = ____

$$\begin{array}{cccc} 6 & 1 & 9 & 3 \\ \underline{\times 1} & \underline{\times 6} & \underline{\times 1} & \underline{\times 0} \end{array}$$

6 x 0 = ____        9 x 0 = ____

1 x 9 = ____        0 x 5 = ____

$$\begin{array}{cccc} 1 & 0 & 0 & 5 \\ \underline{\times 1} & \underline{\times 6} & \underline{\times 0} & \underline{\times 1} \end{array}$$

2 x 0 = ____        7 x 0 = ____

0 x 9 = ____        1 x 7 = ____

$$\begin{array}{cccc} 1 & 3 & 0 & 1 \\ \underline{\times 8} & \underline{\times 1} & \underline{\times 8} & \underline{\times 2} \end{array}$$

1 x 3 = ____        4 x 0 = ____

5 x 0 = ____        1 x 5 = ____

$$\begin{array}{cccc} 0 & 8 & 1 & 7 \\ \underline{\times 1} & \underline{\times 0} & \underline{\times 3} & \underline{\times 1} \end{array}$$

0 x 7 = ____        9 x 1 = ____

Score: _____        Time: _____ minutes _____ seconds

Name _____

# Timed Test

■ Complete these facts as accurately and as quickly as you can.

**Zero and One as Factors**

9 x 1 = ____        7 x 1 = ____

| 5 | 1 | 8 | 0 |
|---|---|---|---|
| x 0 | x 5 | x 1 | x 4 |

2 x 0 = ____        8 x 0 = ____

1 x 7 = ____        1 x 4 = ____

| 0 | 1 | 6 | 2 |
|---|---|---|---|
| x 6 | x 0 | x 1 | x 1 |

0 x 1 = ____        3 x 0 = ____

6 x 0 = ____        1 x 3 = ____

| 1 | 1 | 9 | 0 |
|---|---|---|---|
| x 6 | x 2 | x 0 | x 7 |

0 x 2 = ____        5 x 1 = ____

0 x 9 = ____        0 x 0 = ____

| 1 | 4 | 1 | 0 |
|---|---|---|---|
| x 1 | x 1 | x 8 | x 5 |

4 x 0 = ____        0 x 3 = ____

| 7 | 3 | 9 | 1 |
|---|---|---|---|
| x 0 | x 1 | x 1 | x 4 |

1 x 9 = ____        8 x 1 = ____

0 x 8 = ____        1 x 2 = ____

| Record your scores and times below. | |
|---|---|
| **Page 147** Score: _____ | **Page 149** Score: _____ Time: ___min. ___sec. |
| **Page 148** Score: _____ | **Page 150** Score: _____ Time: ___min. ___sec. |

Name _____

# Products Through Eighteen

**Remember:** The answer in multiplication is called the **product**. The numbers that are multiplied together are called **factors**.

Multiplication is like addition in some ways. Like a sum, a product represents how many in all. What makes multiplication different is that one of the factors represents the number of things in a group and the other factor represents the number of groups.

**Example:** 2 x 4 = ?

  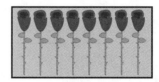

There are 2 groups of 4 roses each. Therefore, there are 8 roses in all.

2 x 4 = 8

Notice that the product is the same if you think of the problem as 4 groups of 2 roses each.

    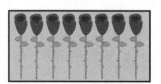

Notice that the product of 2 and another factor is always an even number, such as 0, 2, 4, 6, 8, 10, 12, 14, 16, or 18. These numbers are the first ten multiples of 2. They are the same as the products of 2 times any number from 0 through 9.

■ Complete these **T**'s by multiplying the numbers by 2.

| x 2 | x 2 | x 2 | x 2 | x 2 |
|------|------|------|------|------|
| 4 ___ | 5 ___ | 9 ___ | 0 ___ | 2 ___ |
| 1 ___ | 3 ___ | 7 ___ | 6 ___ | 8 ___ |

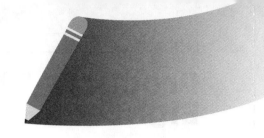

Name _____

# Practice

■ Multiply. Record your score—the number correct—on each Practice page and again on page 156.

$$
\begin{array}{cccc}
1 & 2 & 6 & 4 \\
\times 2 & \times 3 & \times 2 & \times 2 \\
\hline
\end{array}
$$

$$
\begin{array}{cccc}
2 & 7 & 2 & 5 \\
\times 7 & \times 2 & \times 0 & \times 2 \\
\hline
\end{array}
$$

$$
\begin{array}{cccc}
0 & 2 & 2 & 2 \\
\times 2 & \times 5 & \times 4 & \times 2 \\
\hline
\end{array}
$$

$$
\begin{array}{cccc}
2 & 2 & 2 & 3 \\
\times 9 & \times 7 & \times 8 & \times 2 \\
\hline
\end{array}
$$

$$
\begin{array}{cccc}
2 & 2 & 7 & 2 \\
\times 8 & \times 3 & \times 2 & \times 1 \\
\hline
\end{array}
$$

2 x 9 = _____     5 x 2 = _____

0 x 2 = _____     2 x 2 = _____

6 x 2 = _____     8 x 2 = _____

2 x 1 = _____     2 x 6 = _____

2 x 4 = _____     4 x 2 = _____

2 x 0 = _____     2 x 7 = _____

1 x 2 = _____     3 x 2 = _____

9 x 2 = _____     2 x 5 = _____

Score: _____

**Two as a Factor**

START

Name _____

# Practice

■ Multiply.

<table>
<tr><td>2<br>x 3</td><td>4<br>x 2</td><td>2<br>x 0</td><td>6<br>x 2</td></tr>
<tr><td>2<br>x 1</td><td>2<br>x 6</td><td>2<br>x 4</td><td>7<br>x 2</td></tr>
<tr><td>2<br>x 7</td><td>0<br>x 2</td><td>9<br>x 2</td><td>1<br>x 2</td></tr>
<tr><td>5<br>x 2</td><td>2<br>x 9</td><td>2<br>x 8</td><td>2<br>x 3</td></tr>
<tr><td>1<br>x 2</td><td>2<br>x 6</td><td>3<br>x 2</td><td>2<br>x 9</td></tr>
</table>

2 x 5 = _____     4 x 2 = _____

9 x 2 = _____     2 x 0 = _____

3 x 2 = _____     6 x 2 = _____

0 x 2 = _____     2 x 7 = _____

2 x 1 = _____     5 x 2 = _____

2 x 9 = _____     2 x 4 = _____

8 x 2 = _____     7 x 2 = _____

2 x 3 = _____     2 x 8 = _____

**Two as a Factor**

Score: _____

Circle any problems that you still find difficult to remember. Make your own flash cards to help you master these problems.

Name _____

# Timed Test

■ Improve your speed on these facts of 2. Ask someone to time you.
Record your time and score on each Timed Test page and on page 156.

9 x 2 = ____       2 x 5 = ____

$$\begin{array}{cccc} 5 & 7 & 2 & 9 \\ \underline{\times 2} & \underline{\times 2} & \underline{\times 3} & \underline{\times 2} \end{array}$$

2 x 0 = ____       0 x 2 = ____

2 x 7 = ____       8 x 2 = ____

$$\begin{array}{cccc} 2 & 8 & 2 & 0 \\ \underline{\times 8} & \underline{\times 2} & \underline{\times 4} & \underline{\times 2} \end{array}$$

2 x 2 = ____       5 x 2 = ____

3 x 2 = ____       2 x 9 = ____

$$\begin{array}{cccc} 2 & 4 & 2 & 3 \\ \underline{\times 2} & \underline{\times 2} & \underline{\times 7} & \underline{\times 2} \end{array}$$

1 x 2 = ____       7 x 2 = ____

4 x 2 = ____       2 x 1 = ____

$$\begin{array}{cccc} 2 & 2 & 2 & 2 \\ \underline{\times 0} & \underline{\times 6} & \underline{\times 9} & \underline{\times 5} \end{array}$$

2 x 8 = ____       2 x 2 = ____

5 x 2 = ____       2 x 4 = ____

$$\begin{array}{cccc} 2 & 9 & 6 & 1 \\ \underline{\times 1} & \underline{\times 2} & \underline{\times 2} & \underline{\times 2} \end{array}$$

2 x 6 = ____       8 x 2 = ____

Score: _____       Time: _____ minutes _____ seconds

# Timed Test

■ Complete these facts as accurately and as quickly as you can.

2 x 7 = ____        3 x 2 = ____

$$\begin{array}{cccc} 2 & 0 & 7 & 2 \\ \underline{\times 0} & \underline{\times 2} & \underline{\times 2} & \underline{\times 3} \end{array}$$

2 x 5 = ____        9 x 2 = ____

0 x 2 = ____        2 x 0 = ____

$$\begin{array}{cccc} 6 & 1 & 2 & 2 \\ \underline{\times 2} & \underline{\times 2} & \underline{\times 9} & \underline{\times 5} \end{array}$$

2 x 1 = ____        5 x 2 = ____

6 x 2 = ____        2 x 3 = ____

$$\begin{array}{cccc} 2 & 2 & 3 & 2 \\ \underline{\times 4} & \underline{\times 8} & \underline{\times 2} & \underline{\times 1} \end{array}$$

2 x 6 = ____        2 x 8 = ____

3 x 2 = ____        9 x 2 = ____

$$\begin{array}{cccc} 9 & 5 & 2 & 4 \\ \underline{\times 2} & \underline{\times 2} & \underline{\times 6} & \underline{\times 2} \end{array}$$

7 x 2 = ____        4 x 2 = ____

1 x 2 = ____        2 x 2 = ____

$$\begin{array}{cccc} 2 & 2 & 7 & 2 \\ \underline{\times 7} & \underline{\times 5} & \underline{\times 2} & \underline{\times 2} \end{array}$$

2 x 4 = ____        2 x 9 = ____

**Two as a Factor**

Score: _____        Time: _____ minutes _____ seconds

# Timed Test

## Two as a Factor

$2 \times 9 =$ _____     $2 \times 8 =$ _____

$$\begin{array}{cccc} 8 & 2 & 2 & 7 \\ \underline{\times 2} & \underline{\times 5} & \underline{\times 2} & \underline{\times 2} \end{array}$$

$2 \times 7 =$ _____     $4 \times 2 =$ _____

$6 \times 2 =$ _____     $8 \times 2 =$ _____

$$\begin{array}{cccc} 2 & 0 & 2 & 5 \\ \underline{\times 8} & \underline{\times 2} & \underline{\times 6} & \underline{\times 2} \end{array}$$

$2 \times 0 =$ _____     $2 \times 5 =$ _____

$1 \times 2 =$ _____     $2 \times 6 =$ _____

$$\begin{array}{cccc} 2 & 6 & 2 & 8 \\ \underline{\times 9} & \underline{\times 2} & \underline{\times 1} & \underline{\times 2} \end{array}$$

$9 \times 2 =$ _____     $3 \times 2 =$ _____

$2 \times 2 =$ _____     $7 \times 2 =$ _____

$$\begin{array}{cccc} 2 & 9 & 2 & 1 \\ \underline{\times 0} & \underline{\times 2} & \underline{\times 5} & \underline{\times 2} \end{array}$$

$5 \times 2 =$ _____     $2 \times 4 =$ _____

$2 \times 3 =$ _____     $9 \times 2 =$ _____

$$\begin{array}{cccc} 3 & 2 & 2 & 2 \\ \underline{\times 2} & \underline{\times 4} & \underline{\times 7} & \underline{\times 3} \end{array}$$

$0 \times 2 =$ _____     $2 \times 1 =$ _____

---

Record your scores and times below.

**Page 152** Score: _____

**Page 153** Score: _____

**Page 154** Score: _____ Time: ____min. ____sec.

**Page 155** Score: _____ Time: ____min. ____sec.

**Page 156** Score: _____ Time: ____min. ____sec.

Name _____

# Products Through Twenty-Seven

When you multiply a number by 3, you triple that number. It is the same as adding that number three times.

**Example:** 3 x 4 = ?

Therefore, 3 x 4 = 12.

Notice that the product is the same if you multiply 4 by 3. In this case, it would be 4 groups of 3 each. Therefore, 4 x 3 = 12.

The first ten multiples of 3 are 0, 3, 6, 9, 12, 15, 18, 21, 24, 27. They are the same as the products of 3 times any number from 0 through 9.

■ Complete this circle by multiplying each of the numbers by 3.

■ Now, complete these facts.

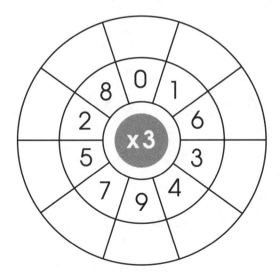

| | | | |
|---|---|---|---|
| 5 | 9 | 3 | 3 |
| x 3 | x 3 | x 1 | x 8 |

| | | | |
|---|---|---|---|
| 6 | 3 | 0 | 3 |
| x 3 | x 2 | x 3 | x 5 |

| | | | |
|---|---|---|---|
| 2 | 3 | 8 | 3 |
| x 3 | x 4 | x 3 | x 9 |

Three as a Factor

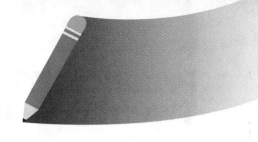

Name _____

# Practice

■ Multiply. Record your score—the number correct—on each Practice page and again on page 162.

$$
\begin{array}{cccc}
3 & 3 & 2 & 3 \\
\times 8 & \times 4 & \times 3 & \times 2 \\
\hline
\end{array}
$$

$$
\begin{array}{cccc}
3 & 1 & 9 & 3 \\
\times 9 & \times 3 & \times 3 & \times 3 \\
\hline
\end{array}
$$

$$
\begin{array}{cccc}
8 & 0 & 4 & 3 \\
\times 3 & \times 3 & \times 3 & \times 6 \\
\hline
\end{array}
$$

$$
\begin{array}{cccc}
3 & 5 & 7 & 3 \\
\times 1 & \times 3 & \times 3 & \times 5 \\
\hline
\end{array}
$$

$$
\begin{array}{cccc}
9 & 3 & 3 & 6 \\
\times 3 & \times 0 & \times 9 & \times 3 \\
\hline
\end{array}
$$

3 x 5 = _____     3 x 8 = _____

8 x 3 = _____     3 x 1 = _____

0 x 3 = _____     2 x 3 = _____

3 x 2 = _____     3 x 6 = _____

7 x 3 = _____     6 x 3 = _____

3 x 0 = _____     3 x 3 = _____

1 x 3 = _____     3 x 7 = _____

3 x 4 = _____     5 x 3 = _____

Score: _____

# Practice

■ Multiply.

| 3 | 3 | 5 | 3 |
|---|---|---|---|
| x 3 | x 0 | x 3 | x 2 |

| 9 | 3 | 2 | 3 |
|---|---|---|---|
| x 3 | x 6 | x 3 | x 7 |

| 3 | 8 | 1 | 3 |
|---|---|---|---|
| x 4 | x 3 | x 3 | x 9 |

| 6 | 4 | 3 | 7 |
|---|---|---|---|
| x 3 | x 3 | x 5 | x 3 |

| 0 | 2 | 3 | 3 |
|---|---|---|---|
| x 3 | x 3 | x 1 | x 8 |

3 x 0 = _____          6 x 3 = _____

0 x 3 = _____          3 x 1 = _____

3 x 8 = _____          3 x 5 = _____

3 x 7 = _____          4 x 3 = _____

8 x 3 = _____          9 x 3 = _____

3 x 4 = _____          3 x 2 = _____

1 x 3 = _____          5 x 3 = _____

7 x 3 = _____          3 x 3 = _____

**Three as a Factor**

Score: _____

Circle any problems that you still find difficult to remember. Make your own flash cards to help you master these problems.

# Timed Test

■ Improve your speed on these facts of 3. Ask someone to time you.
Record your time and score on each Timed Test page and on page 162.

**Three as a Factor**

3 x 5 = ____     3 x 0 = ____

$\begin{array}{r} 9 \\ \times 3 \\ \hline \end{array}$  $\begin{array}{r} 3 \\ \times 0 \\ \hline \end{array}$  $\begin{array}{r} 2 \\ \times 3 \\ \hline \end{array}$  $\begin{array}{r} 3 \\ \times 8 \\ \hline \end{array}$

3 x 4 = ____     3 x 9 = ____

0 x 3 = ____     8 x 3 = ____

$\begin{array}{r} 6 \\ \times 3 \\ \hline \end{array}$  $\begin{array}{r} 3 \\ \times 4 \\ \hline \end{array}$  $\begin{array}{r} 3 \\ \times 7 \\ \hline \end{array}$  $\begin{array}{r} 5 \\ \times 3 \\ \hline \end{array}$

5 x 3 = ____     3 x 2 = ____

3 x 3 = ____     3 x 8 = ____

$\begin{array}{r} 3 \\ \times 1 \\ \hline \end{array}$  $\begin{array}{r} 3 \\ \times 6 \\ \hline \end{array}$  $\begin{array}{r} 7 \\ \times 3 \\ \hline \end{array}$  $\begin{array}{r} 3 \\ \times 2 \\ \hline \end{array}$

9 x 3 = ____     2 x 3 = ____

6 x 3 = ____     7 x 3 = ____

$\begin{array}{r} 3 \\ \times 5 \\ \hline \end{array}$  $\begin{array}{r} 0 \\ \times 3 \\ \hline \end{array}$  $\begin{array}{r} 3 \\ \times 9 \\ \hline \end{array}$  $\begin{array}{r} 5 \\ \times 3 \\ \hline \end{array}$

3 x 6 = ____     3 x 1 = ____

$\begin{array}{r} 3 \\ \times 3 \\ \hline \end{array}$  $\begin{array}{r} 8 \\ \times 3 \\ \hline \end{array}$  $\begin{array}{r} 1 \\ \times 3 \\ \hline \end{array}$  $\begin{array}{r} 4 \\ \times 3 \\ \hline \end{array}$

1 x 3 = ____     8 x 3 = ____

4 x 3 = ____     3 x 7 = ____

Score: _____     Time: _____ minutes _____ seconds

# Timed Test

■ Complete these facts as accurately and as quickly as you can.

| | | | | | |
|---|---|---|---|---|---|
| 3 x 6 = ____ | 3 x 3 = ____ | 3<br>x 8 | 5<br>x 3 | 4<br>x 3 | 0<br>x 3 |
| 3 x 5 = ____ | 3 x 1 = ____ | | | | |
| 0 x 3 = ____ | 3 x 4 = ____ | 3<br>x 1 | 1<br>x 3 | 3<br>x 4 | 6<br>x 3 |
| 3 x 2 = ____ | 1 x 3 = ____ | | | | |
| 3 x 0 = ____ | 3 x 9 = ____ | 3<br>x 6 | 7<br>x 3 | 3<br>x 0 | 9<br>x 3 |
| 6 x 3 = ____ | 2 x 3 = ____ | | | | |
| 3 x 8 = ____ | 3 x 3 = ____ | 2<br>x 3 | 3<br>x 3 | 8<br>x 3 | 3<br>x 7 |
| 9 x 3 = ____ | 8 x 3 = ____ | | | | |
| 3 x 7 = ____ | 4 x 3 = ____ | 3<br>x 5 | 3<br>x 2 | 3<br>x 9 | 3<br>x 6 |
| 5 x 3 = ____ | 3 x 1 = ____ | | | | |

Three as a Factor

Score: _____     Time: _____ minutes _____ seconds

# Timed Test

**Three as a Factor**

3 x 4 = ____     3 x 9 = ____

| 9 | 3 | 3 | 3 |
|---|---|---|---|
| x 3 | x 8 | x 5 | x 0 |

4 x 3 = ____     5 x 3 = ____

8 x 3 = ____     3 x 0 = ____

| 2 | 1 | 3 | 3 |
|---|---|---|---|
| x 3 | x 3 | x 6 | x 4 |

3 x 5 = ____     6 x 3 = ____

9 x 3 = ____     3 x 7 = ____

| 8 | 0 | 2 | 6 |
|---|---|---|---|
| x 3 | x 3 | x 3 | x 3 |

2 x 3 = ____     1 x 3 = ____

3 x 1 = ____     3 x 8 = ____

| 3 | 3 | 4 | 7 |
|---|---|---|---|
| x 1 | x 3 | x 3 | x 3 |

3 x 3 = ____     7 x 3 = ____

3 x 6 = ____     3 x 2 = ____

| 3 | 3 | 5 | 3 |
|---|---|---|---|
| x 2 | x 7 | x 3 | x 9 |

0 x 3 = ____     6 x 3 = ____

---

Record your scores and times below.

**Page 158** Score: _____          **Page 161** Score: _____ Time: ____min. ____sec.

**Page 159** Score: _____          **Page 162** Score: _____ Time: ____min. ____sec.

**Page 160** Score: _____ Time: ____min. ____sec.

# Products Through Thirty-Six

The first ten multiples of 4 are 0, 4, 8, 12, 16, 20, 24, 28, 32, and 36. They are the same as the products of 4 times any number from 0 through 9.

**Example:** 4 x 5 = ?

Remember to think of one of the factors as the number of groups in all and the other as the number of objects in one group.

    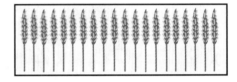

Therefore, 4 x 5 = 20.

■ Complete these **T**'s by multiplying each of the numbers by 4.

| x 4 | |
|---|---|
| 6 | ___ |
| 9 | ___ |
| 0 | ___ |
| 8 | ___ |
| 4 | ___ |

| x 4 | |
|---|---|
| 2 | ___ |
| 7 | ___ |
| 1 | ___ |
| 3 | ___ |
| 5 | ___ |

■ Now, complete these facts.

4 x 9 = ___        4 x 7 = ___

3 x 4 = ___        2 x 4 = ___

4 x 2 = ___        4 x 3 = ___

8 x 4 = ___        4 x 0 = ___

1 x 4 = ___        5 x 4 = ___

6 x 4 = ___        0 x 4 = ___

4 x 1 = ___        4 x 6 = ___

**Four as a Factor**

# Practice

■ Multiply. Record your score—the number correct—on each Practice page and again on page 168.

**Four as a Factor**

| | | | |
|---|---|---|---|
| 0<br>x 4 | 7<br>x 4 | 4<br>x 0 | 3<br>x 4 |
| 4<br>x 9 | 4<br>x 7 | 6<br>x 4 | 4<br>x 1 |
| 4<br>x 6 | 4<br>x 3 | 8<br>x 4 | 5<br>x 4 |
| 4<br>x 2 | 4<br>x 5 | 1<br>x 4 | 4<br>x 4 |
| 9<br>x 4 | 2<br>x 4 | 4<br>x 8 | 4<br>x 7 |

4 x 6 = ____        4 x 9 = ____

7 x 4 = ____        4 x 3 = ____

4 x 0 = ____        5 x 4 = ____

0 x 4 = ____        4 x 7 = ____

4 x 4 = ____        9 x 4 = ____

2 x 4 = ____        4 x 1 = ____

4 x 5 = ____        6 x 4 = ____

3 x 4 = ____        4 x 8 = ____

Score: _____

START

# Practice

■ Multiply.

| | | | |
|---|---|---|---|
| 4 | 4 | 4 | 9 |
| x 2 | x 6 | x 0 | x 4 |

| | | | |
|---|---|---|---|
| 3 | 4 | 8 | 4 |
| x 4 | x 5 | x 4 | x 3 |

| | | | |
|---|---|---|---|
| 0 | 5 | 7 | 1 |
| x 4 | x 4 | x 4 | x 4 |

| | | | |
|---|---|---|---|
| 4 | 4 | 6 | 2 |
| x 8 | x 1 | x 4 | x 4 |

| | | | |
|---|---|---|---|
| 9 | 4 | 4 | 4 |
| x 4 | x 6 | x 7 | x 4 |

4 x 1 = _____     0 x 4 = _____

5 x 4 = _____     4 x 3 = _____

4 x 6 = _____     7 x 4 = _____

3 x 4 = _____     1 x 4 = _____

4 x 4 = _____     4 x 5 = _____

6 x 4 = _____     4 x 8 = _____

9 x 4 = _____     8 x 4 = _____

2 x 4 = _____     4 x 0 = _____

**Four as a Factor**

Score: _____

Circle any problems that you still find difficult to remember. Make your own flash cards to help you master these problems.

# Timed Test

■ Improve your speed on these facts of 4. Ask someone to time you. Record your time and score on each Timed Test page and on page 168.

4 x 3 = _____     4 x 8 = _____

$$\begin{array}{cccc} 4 & 4 & 9 & 0 \\ \underline{\times 1} & \underline{\times 4} & \underline{\times 4} & \underline{\times 4} \end{array}$$

7 x 4 = _____     5 x 4 = _____

4 x 2 = _____     4 x 0 = _____

$$\begin{array}{cccc} 4 & 7 & 3 & 1 \\ \underline{\times 8} & \underline{\times 4} & \underline{\times 4} & \underline{\times 4} \end{array}$$

0 x 4 = _____     8 x 4 = _____

3 x 4 = _____     4 x 7 = _____

$$\begin{array}{cccc} 4 & 6 & 4 & 8 \\ \underline{\times 7} & \underline{\times 4} & \underline{\times 3} & \underline{\times 4} \end{array}$$

6 x 4 = _____     1 x 4 = _____

9 x 4 = _____     4 x 5 = _____

$$\begin{array}{cccc} 4 & 4 & 4 & 4 \\ \underline{\times 9} & \underline{\times 0} & \underline{\times 2} & \underline{\times 6} \end{array}$$

4 x 4 = _____     3 x 4 = _____

4 x 9 = _____     4 x 6 = _____

$$\begin{array}{cccc} 2 & 5 & 4 & 4 \\ \underline{\times 4} & \underline{\times 4} & \underline{\times 8} & \underline{\times 5} \end{array}$$

2 x 4 = _____     4 x 1 = _____

Score: _____     Time: _____ minutes _____ seconds

# Timed Test

■ Complete these facts as accurately and as quickly as you can.

4 x 4 = ____    4 x 5 = ____

$$\begin{array}{cccc} 4 & 8 & 9 & 4 \\ \underline{x\,5} & \underline{x\,4} & \underline{x\,4} & \underline{x\,3} \end{array}$$

2 x 4 = ____    5 x 4 = ____

4 x 8 = ____    8 x 4 = ____

$$\begin{array}{cccc} 4 & 7 & 0 & 4 \\ \underline{x\,4} & \underline{x\,4} & \underline{x\,4} & \underline{x\,1} \end{array}$$

0 x 4 = ____    4 x 0 = ____

4 x 3 = ____    4 x 2 = ____

$$\begin{array}{cccc} 4 & 4 & 4 & 5 \\ \underline{x\,6} & \underline{x\,0} & \underline{x\,9} & \underline{x\,4} \end{array}$$

3 x 4 = ____    4 x 6 = ____

6 x 4 = ____    7 x 4 = ____

$$\begin{array}{cccc} 4 & 4 & 1 & 6 \\ \underline{x\,2} & \underline{x\,8} & \underline{x\,4} & \underline{x\,4} \end{array}$$

1 x 4 = ____    9 x 4 = ____

4 x 7 = ____    4 x 5 = ____

$$\begin{array}{cccc} 9 & 3 & 4 & 2 \\ \underline{x\,4} & \underline{x\,4} & \underline{x\,7} & \underline{x\,4} \end{array}$$

4 x 9 = ____    4 x 1 = ____

**Four as a Factor**

Score: _____    Time: _____ minutes _____ seconds

# Timed Test

Name _____

Four as a Factor

4 x 4 = ____     4 x 5 = ____

$$\begin{array}{cccc} 4 & 0 & 7 & 4 \\ \underline{\times 6} & \underline{\times 4} & \underline{\times 4} & \underline{\times 3} \end{array}$$

0 x 4 = ____     1 x 4 = ____

4 x 9 = ____     6 x 4 = ____

$$\begin{array}{cccc} 6 & 2 & 4 & 4 \\ \underline{\times 4} & \underline{\times 4} & \underline{\times 4} & \underline{\times 1} \end{array}$$

4 x 1 = ____     4 x 2 = ____

4 x 0 = ____     4 x 6 = ____

$$\begin{array}{cccc} 4 & 1 & 4 & 4 \\ \underline{\times 7} & \underline{\times 4} & \underline{\times 8} & \underline{\times 5} \end{array}$$

9 x 4 = ____     3 x 4 = ____

4 x 8 = ____     7 x 4 = ____

$$\begin{array}{cccc} 4 & 3 & 8 & 4 \\ \underline{\times 9} & \underline{\times 4} & \underline{\times 4} & \underline{\times 2} \end{array}$$

8 x 4 = ____     5 x 4 = ____

4 x 3 = ____     4 x 7 = ____

$$\begin{array}{cccc} 5 & 4 & 4 & 9 \\ \underline{\times 4} & \underline{\times 8} & \underline{\times 0} & \underline{\times 4} \end{array}$$

2 x 4 = ____     4 x 6 = ____

Record your scores and times below.

**Page 164** Score: _____

**Page 165** Score: _____

**Page 166** Score: _____ Time: ___min. ___sec.

**Page 167** Score: _____ Time: ___min. ___sec.

**Page 168** Score: _____ Time: ___min. ___sec.

Name _____

# Products Through Forty-Five

The first ten multiples of 5 are 0, 5, 10, 15, 20, 25, 30, 35, 40, and 45. They are the same as the products of 5 times any number from 0 through 9.

**Example:** 5 x 3 = ?

Therefore, 5 x 3 = 15.

Remember, 3 x 5 is also 15.

Notice that when one of the factors is 5, the product always ends in a 5 or 0.

■ Complete this circle by multiplying each of the numbers by 5.

■ Now, complete these facts.

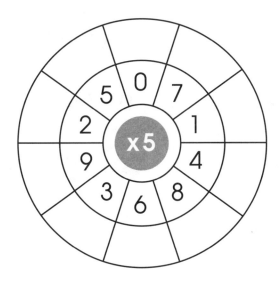

|  |  |  |  |
|---|---|---|---|
| 5<br>x 8 | 5<br>x 4 | 5<br>x 2 | 7<br>x 5 |
| 5<br>x 7 | 1<br>x 5 | 5<br>x 0 | 6<br>x 5 |
| 5<br>x 9 | 3<br>x 5 | 8<br>x 5 | 5<br>x 5 |

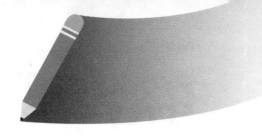

Name _____

# Practice

■ Multiply. Record your score—the number correct—on each Practice page and again on page 174.

**Five as a Factor**

$$
\begin{array}{cccc}
5 & 5 & 4 & 5 \\
\times 1 & \times 5 & \times 5 & \times 6 \\
\hline
\end{array}
$$

$$
\begin{array}{cccc}
2 & 5 & 7 & 5 \\
\times 5 & \times 9 & \times 5 & \times 0 \\
\hline
\end{array}
$$

$$
\begin{array}{cccc}
5 & 1 & 5 & 8 \\
\times 7 & \times 5 & \times 4 & \times 5 \\
\hline
\end{array}
$$

$$
\begin{array}{cccc}
3 & 6 & 5 & 0 \\
\times 5 & \times 5 & \times 3 & \times 5 \\
\hline
\end{array}
$$

$$
\begin{array}{cccc}
5 & 9 & 5 & 5 \\
\times 0 & \times 5 & \times 2 & \times 8 \\
\hline
\end{array}
$$

6 x 5 = _____      7 x 5 = _____

3 x 5 = _____      1 x 5 = _____

5 x 8 = _____      5 x 7 = _____

5 x 0 = _____      8 x 5 = _____

4 x 5 = _____      5 x 4 = _____

2 x 5 = _____      9 x 5 = _____

5 x 3 = _____      5 x 2 = _____

5 x 6 = _____      0 x 5 = _____

Score: _____

# Practice

■ Multiply.

| | | | |
|---|---|---|---|
| 5<br>x 5 | 8<br>x 5 | 6<br>x 5 | 5<br>x 4 |
| 3<br>x 5 | 5<br>x 8 | 1<br>x 5 | 5<br>x 3 |
| 5<br>x 2 | 9<br>x 5 | 7<br>x 5 | 5<br>x 6 |
| 0<br>x 5 | 5<br>x 1 | 4<br>x 5 | 5<br>x 9 |
| 5<br>x 7 | 2<br>x 5 | 5<br>x 3 | 5<br>x 0 |

5 x 0 = ____     5 x 6 = ____

5 x 9 = ____     2 x 5 = ____

0 x 5 = ____     7 x 5 = ____

5 x 3 = ____     9 x 5 = ____

8 x 5 = ____     4 x 5 = ____

5 x 5 = ____     5 x 7 = ____

6 x 5 = ____     5 x 2 = ____

5 x 8 = ____     3 x 5 = ____

**Five as a Factor**

Score: _____

Circle any problems that you still find difficult to remember. Make your own flash cards to help you master these problems.

# Timed Test

■ Improve your speed on these facts of 5. Ask someone to time you.
Record your time and score on each Timed Test page and on page 174.

**Five as a Factor**

| | | | | |
|---|---|---|---|---|
| 5 x 6 = ____ | 3 x 5 = ____ | 5<br>x 2 | 1<br>x 5 | 5<br>x 6 | 5<br>x 8 |

5 x 6 = ____      3 x 5 = ____      5      1      5      5
                                    x 2    x 5    x 6    x 8

9 x 5 = ____      5 x 7 = ____

5 x 3 = ____      6 x 5 = ____      5      5      3      0
                                    x 0    x 1    x 5    x 5

5 x 9 = ____      4 x 5 = ____

8 x 5 = ____      5 x 0 = ____      5      2      4      9
                                    x 4    x 5    x 5    x 5

1 x 5 = ____      5 x 8 = ____

2 x 5 = ____      5 x 5 = ____      8      5      2      5
                                    x 5    x 5    x 5    x 3

5 x 4 = ____      0 x 5 = ____

7 x 5 = ____      9 x 5 = ____      5      6      5      7
                                    x 7    x 5    x 9    x 5

5 x 1 = ____      5 x 2 = ____

Score: _____      Time: _____ minutes _____ seconds

# Timed Test

■ Complete these facts as accurately and as quickly as you can.

| | | |
|---|---|---|
| 5 x 8 = ____ | 5 x 5 = ____ | |
| 7 x 5 = ____ | 1 x 5 = ____ | |
| 2 x 5 = ____ | 3 x 5 = ____ | |
| 5 x 7 = ____ | 6 x 5 = ____ | |
| 4 x 5 = ____ | 5 x 1 = ____ | |
| 5 x 0 = ____ | 9 x 5 = ____ | |
| 8 x 5 = ____ | 5 x 3 = ____ | |
| 5 x 6 = ____ | 5 x 4 = ____ | |
| 0 x 5 = ____ | 5 x 9 = ____ | |
| 5 x 2 = ____ | 4 x 5 = ____ | |

```
  5      7      5      6
x 3    x 5    x 1    x 5
____   ____   ____   ____

  4      5      5      9
x 5    x 2    x 0    x 5
____   ____   ____   ____

  3      8      5      5
x 5    x 5    x 5    x 4
____   ____   ____   ____

  2      9      1      5
x 5    x 5    x 5    x 7
____   ____   ____   ____

  5      5      5      0
x 8    x 6    x 9    x 5
____   ____   ____   ____
```

Score: _____     Time: _____ minutes _____ seconds

# Timed Test

**Five as a Factor**

| | | |
|---|---|---|
| 5 x 9 = ____ | 0 x 5 = ____ | $\begin{array}{r} 5 \\ \times 5 \\ \hline \end{array}$  $\begin{array}{r} 2 \\ \times 5 \\ \hline \end{array}$  $\begin{array}{r} 5 \\ \times 6 \\ \hline \end{array}$  $\begin{array}{r} 7 \\ \times 5 \\ \hline \end{array}$ |
| 7 x 5 = ____ | 5 x 0 = ____ | |
| 5 x 3 = ____ | 8 x 5 = ____ | $\begin{array}{r} 5 \\ \times 4 \\ \hline \end{array}$  $\begin{array}{r} 1 \\ \times 5 \\ \hline \end{array}$  $\begin{array}{r} 5 \\ \times 2 \\ \hline \end{array}$  $\begin{array}{r} 9 \\ \times 5 \\ \hline \end{array}$ |
| 4 x 5 = ____ | 5 x 7 = ____ | |
| 1 x 5 = ____ | 5 x 6 = ____ | $\begin{array}{r} 0 \\ \times 5 \\ \hline \end{array}$  $\begin{array}{r} 5 \\ \times 7 \\ \hline \end{array}$  $\begin{array}{r} 8 \\ \times 5 \\ \hline \end{array}$  $\begin{array}{r} 3 \\ \times 5 \\ \hline \end{array}$ |
| 2 x 5 = ____ | 5 x 1 = ____ | |
| 5 x 8 = ____ | 2 x 5 = ____ | $\begin{array}{r} 5 \\ \times 3 \\ \hline \end{array}$  $\begin{array}{r} 5 \\ \times 8 \\ \hline \end{array}$  $\begin{array}{r} 4 \\ \times 5 \\ \hline \end{array}$  $\begin{array}{r} 5 \\ \times 9 \\ \hline \end{array}$ |
| 3 x 5 = ____ | 5 x 5 = ____ | |
| 9 x 5 = ____ | 3 x 5 = ____ | $\begin{array}{r} 7 \\ \times 5 \\ \hline \end{array}$  $\begin{array}{r} 5 \\ \times 1 \\ \hline \end{array}$  $\begin{array}{r} 5 \\ \times 0 \\ \hline \end{array}$  $\begin{array}{r} 6 \\ \times 5 \\ \hline \end{array}$ |
| 5 x 4 = ____ | 6 x 5 = ____ | |

| Record your scores and times below. | |
|---|---|
| **Page 170** Score: _____ | **Page 173** Score: _____ Time: ___min. ___sec. |
| **Page 171** Score: _____ | **Page 174** Score: _____ Time: ___min. ___sec. |
| **Page 172** Score: _____ Time: ___min. ___sec. | |

_____

# Products Through Fifty-Four

The first ten multiples of 6 are 0, 6, 12, 18, 24, 30, 36, 42, 48, and 54. They are the same as the products of 6 times any number from 0 through 9.

**Example:** 6 x 4 = ?

6 groups of 4 each

Therefore, 6 x 4 = 24.

Remember, 4 x 6 is also 24.

Notice that when you learn each set of facts, you are actually learning facts from other sets. For example, when you learned that 3 x 6 = 18, you also learned 6 x 3 = 18. This cuts down on the number of new facts you actually have to learn.

■ Complete these facts that you have already learned in which 6 is a factor.

```
  6        6        6
x 4      x 0      x 5
____     ____     ____


  6        6        6
x 2      x 3      x 1
____     ____     ____
```

■ Complete these **T**'s by multiplying each of the numbers by 6.

| x 6 | |   | x 6 | |
|-----|---|---|-----|---|
| 3 | ___ |   | 9 | ___ |
| 0 | ___ |   | 4 | ___ |
| 5 | ___ |   | 6 | ___ |
| 2 | ___ |   | 1 | ___ |
| 7 | ___ |   | 8 | ___ |

**Six as a Factor**

Name _____

# Practice

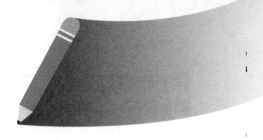

■ Multiply. Record your score—the number correct—on each Practice page and again on page 180.

**Six as a Factor**

|  |  |  |  |
|---|---|---|---|
| 6<br>x 7 | 0<br>x 6 | 6<br>x 5 | 6<br>x 0 |
| 8<br>x 6 | 6<br>x 6 | 2<br>x 6 | 9<br>x 6 |
| 6<br>x 1 | 3<br>x 6 | 7<br>x 6 | 6<br>x 4 |
| 1<br>x 6 | 6<br>x 2 | 4<br>x 6 | 6<br>x 8 |
| 5<br>x 6 | 3<br>x 6 | 9<br>x 6 | 8<br>x 6 |

6 x 4 = _____     4 x 6 = _____

6 x 9 = _____     6 x 5 = _____

6 x 3 = _____     7 x 6 = _____

3 x 6 = _____     1 x 6 = _____

6 x 6 = _____     6 x 2 = _____

9 x 6 = _____     0 x 6 = _____

6 x 0 = _____     6 x 7 = _____

8 x 6 = _____     5 x 6 = _____

Score: _____

START

Name _____

# Practice

■ Multiply.

```
    0        9        6        6
  x 6      x 6      x 6      x 3
  ___      ___      ___      ___


    6        4        2        6
  x 0      x 6      x 6      x 7
  ___      ___      ___      ___


    6        3        6        1
  x 1      x 6      x 8      x 6
  ___      ___      ___      ___


    7        6        6        6
  x 6      x 9      x 5      x 2
  ___      ___      ___      ___


    8        4        6        5
  x 6      x 6      x 3      x 6
  ___      ___      ___      ___
```

6 x 6 = _____       6 x 8 = _____

3 x 6 = _____       0 x 6 = _____

6 x 3 = _____       6 x 2 = _____

2 x 6 = _____       4 x 6 = _____

6 x 9 = _____       6 x 4 = _____

8 x 6 = _____       5 x 6 = _____

1 x 6 = _____       6 x 7 = _____

6 x 5 = _____       6 x 0 = _____

**Six as a Factor**

Score: _____

 Circle any problems that you still find difficult to remember. Make your own flash cards to help you master these problems.

Name _____

# Timed Test

■ Improve your speed on these facts of 6. Ask someone to time you. Record your time and score on each Timed Test page and on page 180.

**Six as a Factor**

6 x 9 = ____      3 x 6 = ____

| 6 | 0 | 6 | 5 |
|---|---|---|---|
| x 2 | x 6 | x 9 | x 6 |

6 x 8 = ____      6 x 4 = ____

6 x 3 = ____      6 x 0 = ____

| 7 | 6 | 6 | 6 |
|---|---|---|---|
| x 6 | x 3 | x 8 | x 1 |

7 x 6 = ____      1 x 6 = ____

4 x 6 = ____      9 x 6 = ____

| 9 | 1 | 8 | 4 |
|---|---|---|---|
| x 6 | x 6 | x 6 | x 6 |

6 x 7 = ____      6 x 5 = ____

6 x 1 = ____      2 x 6 = ____

| 6 | 6 | 6 | 2 |
|---|---|---|---|
| x 7 | x 0 | x 5 | x 6 |

8 x 6 = ____      4 x 6 = ____

6 x 2 = ____      6 x 6 = ____

| 6 | 7 | 3 | 6 |
|---|---|---|---|
| x 4 | x 6 | x 6 | x 6 |

0 x 6 = ____      5 x 6 = ____

Score: _____      Time: _____ minutes _____ seconds

Name _____

# Timed Test

■ Complete these facts as accurately and as quickly as you can.

6 x 3 = _____    7 x 6 = _____

$$\begin{array}{r} 6 \\ \times\, 1 \\ \hline \end{array}\qquad \begin{array}{r} 6 \\ \times\, 3 \\ \hline \end{array}\qquad \begin{array}{r} 4 \\ \times\, 6 \\ \hline \end{array}\qquad \begin{array}{r} 6 \\ \times\, 5 \\ \hline \end{array}$$

1 x 6 = _____    2 x 6 = _____

0 x 6 = _____    8 x 6 = _____

$$\begin{array}{r} 6 \\ \times\, 8 \\ \hline \end{array}\qquad \begin{array}{r} 3 \\ \times\, 6 \\ \hline \end{array}\qquad \begin{array}{r} 9 \\ \times\, 6 \\ \hline \end{array}\qquad \begin{array}{r} 6 \\ \times\, 6 \\ \hline \end{array}$$

6 x 9 = _____    6 x 6 = _____

6 x 2 = _____    4 x 6 = _____

$$\begin{array}{r} 2 \\ \times\, 6 \\ \hline \end{array}\qquad \begin{array}{r} 6 \\ \times\, 0 \\ \hline \end{array}\qquad \begin{array}{r} 6 \\ \times\, 7 \\ \hline \end{array}\qquad \begin{array}{r} 1 \\ \times\, 6 \\ \hline \end{array}$$

6 x 5 = _____    6 x 0 = _____

6 x 7 = _____    6 x 3 = _____

$$\begin{array}{r} 6 \\ \times\, 4 \\ \hline \end{array}\qquad \begin{array}{r} 6 \\ \times\, 9 \\ \hline \end{array}\qquad \begin{array}{r} 0 \\ \times\, 6 \\ \hline \end{array}\qquad \begin{array}{r} 6 \\ \times\, 2 \\ \hline \end{array}$$

9 x 6 = _____    5 x 6 = _____

6 x 4 = _____    7 x 6 = _____

$$\begin{array}{r} 5 \\ \times\, 6 \\ \hline \end{array}\qquad \begin{array}{r} 8 \\ \times\, 6 \\ \hline \end{array}\qquad \begin{array}{r} 3 \\ \times\, 6 \\ \hline \end{array}\qquad \begin{array}{r} 7 \\ \times\, 6 \\ \hline \end{array}$$

6 x 8 = _____    6 x 1 = _____

**Six as a Factor**

Score: _____    Time: _____ minutes _____ seconds

179

Name _____

# Timed Test

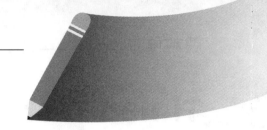

6 x 3 = _____        6 x 8 = _____

$$\begin{array}{cccc} 6 & 7 & 6 & 4 \\ \underline{\times 4} & \underline{\times 6} & \underline{\times 0} & \underline{\times 6} \end{array}$$

7 x 6 = _____        9 x 6 = _____

5 x 6 = _____        6 x 0 = _____

$$\begin{array}{cccc} 6 & 6 & 5 & 3 \\ \underline{\times 6} & \underline{\times 1} & \underline{\times 6} & \underline{\times 6} \end{array}$$

2 x 6 = _____        6 x 5 = _____

0 x 6 = _____        3 x 6 = _____

$$\begin{array}{cccc} 6 & 6 & 2 & 6 \\ \underline{\times 5} & \underline{\times 9} & \underline{\times 6} & \underline{\times 3} \end{array}$$

6 x 6 = _____        8 x 6 = _____

6 x 4 = _____        6 x 7 = _____

$$\begin{array}{cccc} 4 & 8 & 1 & 6 \\ \underline{\times 6} & \underline{\times 6} & \underline{\times 6} & \underline{\times 7} \end{array}$$

6 x 9 = _____        4 x 6 = _____

1 x 6 = _____        6 x 1 = _____

$$\begin{array}{cccc} 9 & 6 & 6 & 0 \\ \underline{\times 6} & \underline{\times 8} & \underline{\times 2} & \underline{\times 6} \end{array}$$

6 x 2 = _____        9 x 6 = _____

**Six as a Factor**

---

Record your scores and times below.

**Page 176** Score: _____

**Page 177** Score: _____

**Page 178** Score: _____ Time: ____min. ____sec.

**Page 179** Score: _____ Time: ____min. ____sec.

**Page 180** Score: _____ Time: ____min. ____sec.

180

# Products Through Sixty-Three

The first ten multiples of 7 are 0, 7, 14, 21, 28, 35, 42, 49, 56, and 63. They are the same as the products of 7 times any number from 0 through 9.

**Example:** 7 x 5 = ?

7 groups of 5 each

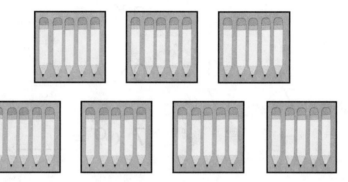

Therefore, 7 x 5 = 35.

Remember, 5 x 7 is also 35.

■ Complete these facts that you have already learned in which 7 is a factor.

$$
\begin{array}{cccc}
3 & 1 & 5 & 2 \\
\times 7 & \times 7 & \times 7 & \times 7 \\
\hline
\end{array}
$$

$$
\begin{array}{ccc}
0 & 4 & 6 \\
\times 7 & \times 7 & \times 7 \\
\hline
\end{array}
$$

■ Complete this circle by multiplying each of the numbers by 7.

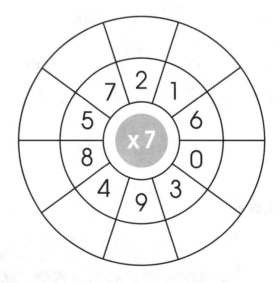

Name _____

# Practice

■ Multiply. Record your score—the number correct—on each
  Practice page and again on page 188.

again on page 188.

**Seven as a Factor**

| | | | |
|---|---|---|---|
| 6<br>x 7 | 7<br>x 0 | 7<br>x 8 | 4<br>x 7 |
| 7<br>x 7 | 7<br>x 3 | 8<br>x 7 | 3<br>x 7 |
| 7<br>x 6 | 7<br>x 9 | 7<br>x 4 | 5<br>x 7 |
| 7<br>x 2 | 0<br>x 7 | 7<br>x 1 | 7<br>x 5 |
| 1<br>x 7 | 9<br>x 7 | 8<br>x 7 | 2<br>x 7 |

7 x 2 = _____   1 x 7 = _____

5 x 7 = _____   7 x 3 = _____

0 x 7 = _____   7 x 7 = _____

7 x 9 = _____   8 x 7 = _____

7 x 5 = _____   7 x 1 = _____

6 x 7 = _____   9 x 7 = _____

4 x 7 = _____   7 x 8 = _____

7 x 0 = _____   2 x 7 = _____

Score: _____

# Practice

■ Multiply.

| | | | |
|---|---|---|---|
| 7 | 5 | 7 | 9 |
| x 7 | x 7 | x 4 | x 7 |

| | | | |
|---|---|---|---|
| 7 | 3 | 7 | 4 |
| x 0 | x 7 | x 8 | x 7 |

| | | | |
|---|---|---|---|
| 7 | 6 | 1 | 7 |
| x 3 | x 7 | x 7 | x 9 |

| | | | |
|---|---|---|---|
| 7 | 8 | 7 | 0 |
| x 5 | x 7 | x 2 | x 7 |

| | | | |
|---|---|---|---|
| 2 | 7 | 7 | 7 |
| x 7 | x 6 | x 8 | x 1 |

7 x 4 = _____     7 x 5 = _____

2 x 7 = _____     3 x 7 = _____

7 x 1 = _____     9 x 7 = _____

7 x 7 = _____     7 x 2 = _____

7 x 8 = _____     5 x 7 = _____

1 x 7 = _____     0 x 7 = _____

7 x 3 = _____     7 x 6 = _____

8 x 7 = _____     4 x 7 = _____

Score: _____

**Seven as a Factor**

Circle any problems that you still find difficult to remember. Make your own flash cards to help you master these problems.

# Timed Test

■ Improve your speed on these facts of 7. Ask someone to time you.
  Record your time and score on each Timed Test page and on page 188.

**Seven as a Factor**

| | | |
|---|---|---|
| 7 x 3 = \_\_\_\_ | 7 x 6 = \_\_\_\_ | $\begin{array}{r}7\\ \times 3\\ \hline\end{array}$ $\begin{array}{r}9\\ \times 7\\ \hline\end{array}$ $\begin{array}{r}3\\ \times 7\\ \hline\end{array}$ $\begin{array}{r}7\\ \times 8\\ \hline\end{array}$ |

7 x 3 = \_\_\_\_       7 x 6 = \_\_\_\_        7        9        3        7
                                            x 3      x 7      x 7      x 8

5 x 7 = \_\_\_\_       2 x 7 = \_\_\_\_

7 x 8 = \_\_\_\_       7 x 1 = \_\_\_\_        7        7        7        6
                                            x 1      x 6      x 9      x 7

7 x 5 = \_\_\_\_       7 x 9 = \_\_\_\_

0 x 7 = \_\_\_\_       7 x 7 = \_\_\_\_        2        7        7        0
                                            x 7      x 4      x 1      x 7

6 x 7 = \_\_\_\_       7 x 2 = \_\_\_\_

7 x 4 = \_\_\_\_       8 x 7 = \_\_\_\_        7        7        8        7
                                            x 7      x 0      x 7      x 2

3 x 7 = \_\_\_\_       7 x 8 = \_\_\_\_

7 x 0 = \_\_\_\_       1 x 7 = \_\_\_\_        4        7        5        1
                                            x 7      x 5      x 7      x 7

9 x 7 = \_\_\_\_       4 x 7 = \_\_\_\_

Score: _____       Time: _____ minutes _____ seconds

# Timed Test

■ Complete these facts as accurately and as quickly as you can.

| 7 x 6 = ____ | 1 x 7 = ____ | 0<br>x 7 | 7<br>x 3 | 7<br>x 8 | 7<br>x 6 |

| 8 x 7 = ____ | 7 x 9 = ____ |

| 2 x 7 = ____ | 3 x 7 = ____ | 7<br>x 2 | 6<br>x 7 | 7<br>x 5 | 7<br>x 4 |

| 5 x 7 = ____ | 7 x 1 = ____ |

| 0 x 7 = ____ | 6 x 7 = ____ | 7<br>x 9 | 5<br>x 7 | 1<br>x 7 | 4<br>x 7 |

| 7 x 2 = ____ | 7 x 8 = ____ |

| 7 x 0 = ____ | 9 x 7 = ____ | 7<br>x 1 | 9<br>x 7 | 2<br>x 7 | 3<br>x 7 |

| 4 x 7 = ____ | 7 x 4 = ____ |

| 7 x 7 = ____ | 2 x 7 = ____ | 8<br>x 7 | 7<br>x 5 | 7<br>x 7 | 7<br>x 0 |

| 7 x 5 = ____ | 7 x 3 = ____ |

**Seven as a Factor**

Score: _____     Time: _____ minutes _____ seconds

# Timed Test

**Seven as a Factor**

7 x 8 = _____    7 x 4 = _____

7 x 2 = _____    7 x 1 = _____

5 x 7 = _____    7 x 9 = _____

1 x 7 = _____    7 x 2 = _____

3 x 7 = _____    7 x 3 = _____

7 x 0 = _____    7 x 5 = _____

6 x 7 = _____    0 x 7 = _____

7 x 7 = _____    4 x 7 = _____

2 x 7 = _____    9 x 7 = _____

8 x 7 = _____    7 x 6 = _____

```
  7      0      7      4
x 6    x 7    x 1    x 7
____   ____   ____   ____


  7      9      7      2
x 8    x 7    x 3    x 7
____   ____   ____   ____


  6      7      3      5
x 7    x 7    x 7    x 7
____   ____   ____   ____


  7      4      1      7
x 2    x 7    x 7    x 5
____   ____   ____   ____


  7      8      7      7
x 9    x 7    x 4    x 0
____   ____   ____   ____
```

Score: _____    Time: _____ minutes _____ seconds

# Timed Test

7 x 2 = ____    7 x 4 = ____    7        2        7        5
                                x 0      x 7      x 7      x 7
                                ___      ___      ___      ___

4 x 7 = ____    7 x 0 = ____

7 x 9 = ____    2 x 7 = ____     0        7        7        7
                                x 7      x 3      x 9      x 5
                                ___      ___      ___      ___

7 x 6 = ____    7 x 7 = ____

7 x 5 = ____    7 x 1 = ____     7        7        1        9
                                x 1      x 6      x 7      x 7
                                ___      ___      ___      ___

3 x 7 = ____    8 x 7 = ____

5 x 7 = ____    1 x 7 = ____     4        7        3        8
                                x 7      x 8      x 7      x 7
                                ___      ___      ___      ___

7 x 8 = ____    7 x 3 = ____

                                7        6        7        2
0 x 7 = ____    9 x 7 = ____     x 2      x 7      x 4      x 7
                                ___      ___      ___      ___

6 x 7 = ____    7 x 6 = ____

**Seven as a Factor**

Score: _____    Time: _____ minutes _____ seconds

# Timed Test

7 x 0 = ____    7 x 9 = ____

| 7 | 4 | 7 | 7 |
|---|---|---|---|
| x 3 | x 7 | x 1 | x 4 |

2 x 7 = ____    8 x 7 = ____

7 x 5 = ____    7 x 7 = ____

| 5 | 3 | 7 | 6 |
|---|---|---|---|
| x 7 | x 7 | x 0 | x 7 |

1 x 7 = ____    5 x 7 = ____

7 x 9 = ____    7 x 3 = ____

| 7 | 2 | 8 | 1 |
|---|---|---|---|
| x 7 | x 7 | x 7 | x 7 |

4 x 7 = ____    6 x 7 = ____

0 x 7 = ____    7 x 8 = ____

| 7 | 9 | 7 | 0 |
|---|---|---|---|
| x 5 | x 7 | x 8 | x 7 |

7 x 4 = ____    3 x 7 = ____

| 7 | 7 | 7 | 7 |
|---|---|---|---|
| x 4 | x 2 | x 9 | x 6 |

9 x 7 = ____    7 x 1 = ____

7 x 6 = ____    7 x 2 = ____

---

### Record your scores and times below.

**Page 182** Score: _____

**Page 183** Score: _____

**Page 184** Score: _____ Time: ___min. ___sec.

**Page 185** Score: _____ Time: ___min. ___sec.

**Page 186** Score: _____ Time: ___min. ___sec.

**Page 187** Score: _____ Time: ___min. ___sec.

**Page 188** Score: _____ Time: ___min. ___sec.

# Products Through Seventy-Two

The first ten multiples of 8 are 0, 8, 16, 24, 32, 40, 48, 56, 64, and 72. They are the same as the products of 8 times any number from 0 through 9.

**Example:** 8 x 6 = ?

8 groups of 6 each

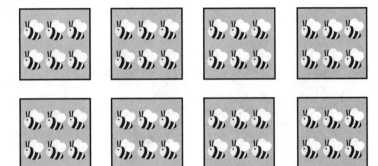

Therefore, 8 x 6 = 48.

Remember, 6 x 8 is also 48.

■ Complete these facts that you have already learned in which 8 is a factor.

| 6 | 1 | 4 | 0 |
|------|------|------|------|
| x 8 | x 8 | x 8 | x 8 |

| 2 | 5 | 7 | 3 |
|------|------|------|------|
| x 8 | x 8 | x 8 | x 8 |

■ Complete these **T**'s by multiplying each of the numbers by 8.

| x 8 | | x 8 | |
|-----|-----|-----|-----|
| 5 | ___ | 6 | ___ |
| 1 | ___ | 3 | ___ |
| 4 | ___ | 7 | ___ |
| 9 | ___ | 2 | ___ |
| 0 | ___ | 8 | ___ |

**Eight as a Factor**

Name _____

# Practice

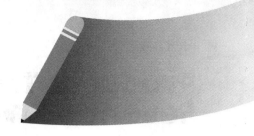

■ Multiply. Record your score—the number correct—on each Practice page and again on page 196.

| | | | |
|---|---|---|---|
| 8<br>x 6 | 5<br>x 8 | 4<br>x 8 | 8<br>x 7 |
| 8<br>x 2 | 6<br>x 8 | 3<br>x 8 | 8<br>x 4 |
| 8<br>x 8 | 7<br>x 8 | 9<br>x 8 | 8<br>x 1 |
| 8<br>x 3 | 8<br>x 9 | 0<br>x 8 | 8<br>x 5 |
| 8<br>x 0 | 2<br>x 8 | 8<br>x 6 | 1<br>x 8 |

8 x 1 = _____     1 x 8 = _____

5 x 8 = _____     8 x 6 = _____

8 x 7 = _____     2 x 8 = _____

4 x 8 = _____     9 x 8 = _____

8 x 3 = _____     8 x 0 = _____

8 x 5 = _____     8 x 8 = _____

8 x 4 = _____     8 x 2 = _____

3 x 8 = _____     0 x 8 = _____

Score: _____

**Eight as a Factor**

START

# Practice

■ Multiply.

| 8 | 8 | 0 | 9 |
|---|---|---|---|
| x 0 | x 6 | x 8 | x 8 |

| 8 | 5 | 8 | 1 |
|---|---|---|---|
| x 4 | x 8 | x 9 | x 8 |

| 8 | 8 | 6 | 8 |
|---|---|---|---|
| x 5 | x 3 | x 8 | x 8 |

| 3 | 8 | 7 | 4 |
|---|---|---|---|
| x 8 | x 2 | x 8 | x 8 |

| 8 | 8 | 2 | 5 |
|---|---|---|---|
| x 1 | x 7 | x 8 | x 8 |

8 x 9 = _____     2 x 8 = _____

8 x 3 = _____     8 x 8 = _____

9 x 8 = _____     0 x 8 = _____

4 x 8 = _____     8 x 2 = _____

8 x 1 = _____     8 x 7 = _____

8 x 4 = _____     1 x 8 = _____

8 x 6 = _____     6 x 8 = _____

7 x 8 = _____     5 x 8 = _____

**Eight as a Factor**

Score: _____

 Circle any problems that you still find difficult to remember. Make your own flash cards to help you master these problems.

# Timed Test

■ Improve your speed on these facts of 8. Ask someone to time you. Record your time and score on each Timed Test page and on page 196.

**Eight as a Factor**

8 x 5 = ____     8 x 2 = ____

8 2 = ____       8 x 6 = ____

| 8 | 0 | 8 | 7 |
|---|---|---|---|
| x 6 | x 8 | x 2 | x 8 |

2 x 8 = ____     8 x 6 = ____

7 x 8 = ____     5 x 8 = ____

| 3 | 8 | 8 | 1 |
|---|---|---|---|
| x 8 | x 9 | x 7 | x 8 |

8 x 9 = ____     8 x 0 = ____

4 x 8 = ____     9 x 8 = ____

| 4 | 8 | 8 | 5 |
|---|---|---|---|
| x 8 | x 3 | x 0 | x 8 |

6 x 8 = ____     1 x 8 = ____

3 x 8 = ____     8 x 6 = ____

| 9 | 8 | 8 | 6 |
|---|---|---|---|
| x 8 | x 2 | x 1 | x 8 |

8 x 3 = ____     8 x 1 = ____

8 x 8 = ____     8 x 7 = ____

| 8 | 8 | 2 | 8 |
|---|---|---|---|
| x 8 | x 4 | x 8 | x 5 |

0 x 8 = ____     8 x 4 = ____

Score: _____     Time: _____ minutes _____ seconds

Name _____

# Timed Test

■ Complete these facts as accurately and as quickly as you can.

8 x 4 = ____        6 x 8 = ____

8 x 0 = ____        0 x 8 = ____

7 x 8 = ____        3 x 8 = ____

5 x 8 = ____        8 x 3 = ____

8 x 6 = ____        8 x 9 = ____

9 x 8 = ____        2 x 8 = ____

4 x 8 = ____        8 x 7 = ____

1 x 8 = ____        8 x 2 = ____

8 x 8 = ____        8 x 1 = ____

8 x 5 = ____        3 x 8 = ____

| 8 | 2 | 0 | 5 |
|---|---|---|---|
| x 3 | x 8 | x 8 | x 8 |

| 3 | 8 | 8 | 6 |
|---|---|---|---|
| x 8 | x 8 | x 0 | x 8 |

| 8 | 1 | 8 | 9 |
|---|---|---|---|
| x 7 | x 8 | x 2 | x 8 |

| 8 | 8 | 8 | 8 |
|---|---|---|---|
| x 4 | x 6 | x 1 | x 9 |

| 8 | 2 | 4 | 7 |
|---|---|---|---|
| x 5 | x 8 | x 8 | x 8 |

Score: _____        Time: _____ minutes _____ seconds

# Timed Test

**Eight as a Factor**

8 x 9 = _____     8 x 6 = _____

$$\begin{array}{r}8\\ \times 4\\ \hline\end{array}\qquad\begin{array}{r}3\\ \times 8\\ \hline\end{array}\qquad\begin{array}{r}8\\ \times 0\\ \hline\end{array}\qquad\begin{array}{r}1\\ \times 8\\ \hline\end{array}$$

6 x 8 = _____     1 x 8 = _____

8 x 2 = _____     4 x 8 = _____

$$\begin{array}{r}9\\ \times 8\\ \hline\end{array}\qquad\begin{array}{r}4\\ \times 8\\ \hline\end{array}\qquad\begin{array}{r}8\\ \times 3\\ \hline\end{array}\qquad\begin{array}{r}8\\ \times 6\\ \hline\end{array}$$

0 x 8 = _____     8 x 3 = _____

7 x 8 = _____     9 x 8 = _____

$$\begin{array}{r}2\\ \times 8\\ \hline\end{array}\qquad\begin{array}{r}8\\ \times 9\\ \hline\end{array}\qquad\begin{array}{r}5\\ \times 8\\ \hline\end{array}\qquad\begin{array}{r}7\\ \times 8\\ \hline\end{array}$$

8 x 5 = _____     8 x 8 = _____

5 x 8 = _____     2 x 8 = _____

$$\begin{array}{r}8\\ \times 5\\ \hline\end{array}\qquad\begin{array}{r}0\\ \times 8\\ \hline\end{array}\qquad\begin{array}{r}8\\ \times 4\\ \hline\end{array}\qquad\begin{array}{r}8\\ \times 7\\ \hline\end{array}$$

8 x 7 = _____     8 x 1 = _____

8 x 0 = _____     8 x 4 = _____

$$\begin{array}{r}8\\ \times 1\\ \hline\end{array}\qquad\begin{array}{r}6\\ \times 8\\ \hline\end{array}\qquad\begin{array}{r}2\\ \times 8\\ \hline\end{array}\qquad\begin{array}{r}8\\ \times 8\\ \hline\end{array}$$

9 x 8 = _____     3 x 8 = _____

Score: _____     Time: _____ minutes _____ seconds

# Timed Test

8 x 3 = ____     8 x 2 = ____

$$\begin{array}{r} 8 \\ \times\ 5 \\ \hline \end{array} \quad \begin{array}{r} 3 \\ \times\ 8 \\ \hline \end{array} \quad \begin{array}{r} 8 \\ \times\ 1 \\ \hline \end{array} \quad \begin{array}{r} 8 \\ \times\ 4 \\ \hline \end{array}$$

8 x 7 = ____     8 x 6 = ____

0 x 8 = ____     9 x 8 = ____

$$\begin{array}{r} 2 \\ \times\ 8 \\ \hline \end{array} \quad \begin{array}{r} 9 \\ \times\ 8 \\ \hline \end{array} \quad \begin{array}{r} 8 \\ \times\ 2 \\ \hline \end{array} \quad \begin{array}{r} 8 \\ \times\ 6 \\ \hline \end{array}$$

8 x 1 = ____     8 x 4 = ____

8 x 9 = ____     2 x 8 = ____

$$\begin{array}{r} 5 \\ \times\ 8 \\ \hline \end{array} \quad \begin{array}{r} 1 \\ \times\ 8 \\ \hline \end{array} \quad \begin{array}{r} 8 \\ \times\ 0 \\ \hline \end{array} \quad \begin{array}{r} 8 \\ \times\ 9 \\ \hline \end{array}$$

8 x 3 = ____     5 x 8 = ____

6 x 8 = ____     7 x 8 = ____

$$\begin{array}{r} 4 \\ \times\ 8 \\ \hline \end{array} \quad \begin{array}{r} 8 \\ \times\ 2 \\ \hline \end{array} \quad \begin{array}{r} 8 \\ \times\ 7 \\ \hline \end{array} \quad \begin{array}{r} 6 \\ \times\ 8 \\ \hline \end{array}$$

4 x 8 = ____     8 x 0 = ____

8 x 8 = ____     8 x 5 = ____

$$\begin{array}{r} 0 \\ \times\ 8 \\ \hline \end{array} \quad \begin{array}{r} 8 \\ \times\ 8 \\ \hline \end{array} \quad \begin{array}{r} 7 \\ \times\ 8 \\ \hline \end{array} \quad \begin{array}{r} 8 \\ \times\ 3 \\ \hline \end{array}$$

8 x 6 = ____     1 x 8 = ____

**Eight as a Factor**

Score: _____     Time: _____ minutes _____ seconds

# Timed Test

**Eight as a Factor**

6 x 8 = _____     9 x 8 = _____

8 x 3 = _____     5 x 8 = _____

8 x 8 = _____     8 x 1 = _____

3 x 8 = _____     8 x 6 = _____

7 x 8 = _____     0 x 8 = _____

1 x 8 = _____     4 x 8 = _____

8 x 9 = _____     8 x 5 = _____

8 x 4 = _____     2 x 8 = _____

8 x 0 = _____     8 x 6 = _____

8 x 7 = _____     8 x 2 = _____

| 2 | 0 | 8 | 3 |
|---|---|---|---|
| x 8 | x 8 | x 9 | x 8 |

| 4 | 8 | 8 | 8 |
|---|---|---|---|
| x 8 | x 5 | x 8 | x 3 |

| 9 | 6 | 8 | 8 |
|---|---|---|---|
| x 8 | x 8 | x 0 | x 6 |

| 1 | 8 | 5 | 8 |
|---|---|---|---|
| x 8 | x 7 | x 8 | x 9 |

| 8 | 8 | 7 | 8 |
|---|---|---|---|
| x 4 | x 1 | x 8 | x 2 |

| Record your scores and times below. | |
|---|---|
| **Page 190** Score: _____ | **Page 194** Score: _____ Time: ___min. ___sec. |
| **Page 191** Score: _____ | **Page 195** Score: _____ Time: ___min. ___sec. |
| **Page 192** Score: _____ Time: ___min. ___sec. | **Page 196** Score: _____ Time: ___min. ___sec. |
| **Page 193** Score: _____ Time: ___min. ___sec. | |

Name _____

# Products Through Eighty-One

The first ten multiples of 9 are 0, 9, 18, 27, 36, 45, 54, 63, 72, and 81. They are the same as the products of 9 times any number from 0 through 9.

**Example:** $9 \times 4 = ?$

9 groups of 4 each

Therefore, $9 \times 4 = 36$. Remember, $4 \times 9$ is also 36.

Nine as a Factor

■ Complete these facts that you have already learned in which 9 is a factor.

| 2 | 0 | 5 | 6 |
|---|---|---|---|
| x 9 | x 9 | x 9 | x 9 |

| 4 | 7 | 1 | 8 | 3 |
|---|---|---|---|---|
| x 9 | x 9 | x 9 | x 9 | x 9 |

Here is the only new fact in this set in which 9 is a factor:

$9 \times 9 =$ _____

■ Complete these **T**'s by multiplying all the numbers by 9.

| x 9 | |
|-----|---|
| 4 | ___ |
| 3 | ___ |
| 6 | ___ |
| 7 | ___ |
| 2 | ___ |

| x 9 | |
|-----|---|
| 1 | ___ |
| 5 | ___ |
| 9 | ___ |
| 0 | ___ |
| 8 | ___ |

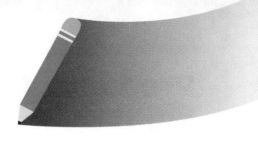

# Practice

■ Multiply. Record your score—the number correct—on this page and again on page 204.

**Nine as a Factor**

| | | | |
|---|---|---|---|
| 9 <br> x 3 | 2 <br> x 9 | 0 <br> x 9 | 5 <br> x 9 |
| 3 <br> x 9 | 9 <br> x 9 | 9 <br> x 0 | 6 <br> x 9 |
| 9 <br> x 7 | 1 <br> x 9 | 9 <br> x 2 | 9 <br> x 8 |
| 9 <br> x 4 | 9 <br> x 6 | 9 <br> x 1 | 8 <br> x 9 |
| 9 <br> x 5 | 2 <br> x 9 | 4 <br> x 9 | 7 <br> x 9 |

9 x 4 = _____         6 x 9 = _____

9 x 0 = _____         0 x 9 = _____

7 x 9 = _____         3 x 9 = _____

5 x 9 = _____         9 x 3 = _____

9 x 6 = _____         8 x 9 = _____

9 x 8 = _____         2 x 9 = _____

4 x 9 = _____         9 x 7 = _____

1 x 9 = _____         9 x 2 = _____

Score: _____

START

# Practice

■ Complete these facts as accurately and as quickly as you can.

| | | | |
|---|---|---|---|
| 8 x 9 | 9 x 5 | 9 x 9 | 1 x 9 |
| 9 x 4 | 9 x 8 | 3 x 9 | 0 x 9 |
| 9 x 6 | 9 x 7 | 7 x 9 | 2 x 9 |
| 9 x 1 | 9 x 3 | 5 x 9 | 9 x 0 |
| 4 x 9 | 9 x 2 | 9 x 8 | 6 x 9 |

9 x 4 = _____     9 x 9 = _____

5 x 9 = _____     1 x 9 = _____

0 x 9 = _____     7 x 9 = _____

9 x 6 = _____     3 x 9 = _____

9 x 7 = _____     9 x 2 = _____

4 x 9 = _____     9 x 8 = _____

9 x 0 = _____     2 x 9 = _____

6 x 9 = _____     9 x 3 = _____

**Nine as a Factor**

Score: _____

Circle any problems that you still find difficult to remember. Make your own flash cards to help you master these problems.

# Timed Test

■ Improve your speed on these facts of 9. Ask someone to time you. Record your time and score on each Timed Test page and on page 204.

$9 \times 6 =$ _____     $9 \times 3 =$ _____

$$\begin{matrix} 3 & 9 & 9 & 6 \\ \times 9 & \times 4 & \times 2 & \times 9 \end{matrix}$$

$7 \times 9 =$ _____     $9 \times 7 =$ _____

$9 \times 4 =$ _____     $0 \times 9 =$ _____

$$\begin{matrix} 9 & 9 & 5 & 9 \\ \times 5 & \times 3 & \times 9 & \times 6 \end{matrix}$$

$6 \times 9 =$ _____     $9 \times 2 =$ _____

$4 \times 9 =$ _____     $9 \times 9 =$ _____

$$\begin{matrix} 7 & 2 & 9 & 9 \\ \times 9 & \times 9 & \times 8 & \times 1 \end{matrix}$$

$9 \times 5 =$ _____     $9 \times 0 =$ _____

$9 \times 8 =$ _____     $3 \times 9 =$ _____

$$\begin{matrix} 9 & 0 & 5 & 8 \\ \times 9 & \times 9 & \times 9 & \times 9 \end{matrix}$$

$5 \times 9 =$ _____     $9 \times 1 =$ _____

$$\begin{matrix} 1 & 9 & 9 & 4 \\ \times 9 & \times 7 & \times 0 & \times 9 \end{matrix}$$

$1 \times 9 =$ _____     $9 \times 9 =$ _____

$8 \times 9 =$ _____     $2 \times 9 =$ _____

Score: _____     Time: _____ minutes _____ seconds

Name _____

# Timed Test

■ Complete these facts as accurately and as quickly as you can.

0 x 9 = _____     5 x 9 = _____

| 9 | 4 | 0 | 1 |
|---|---|---|---|
| x 1 | x 9 | x 9 | x 9 |

7 x 9 = _____     8 x 9 = _____

9 x 0 = _____     4 x 9 = _____

| 8 | 9 | 3 | 9 |
|---|---|---|---|
| x 9 | x 7 | x 9 | x 2 |

6 x 9 = _____     9 x 3 = _____

1 x 9 = _____     9 x 6 = _____

| 7 | 9 | 4 | 9 |
|---|---|---|---|
| x 9 | x 5 | x 9 | x 0 |

9 x 5 = _____     9 x 2 = _____

9 x 9 = _____     9 x 1 = _____

| 5 | 9 | 2 | 9 |
|---|---|---|---|
| x 9 | x 3 | x 9 | x 8 |

9 x 8 = _____     2 x 9 = _____

8 x 9 = _____     9 x 7 = _____

| 6 | 9 | 9 | 9 |
|---|---|---|---|
| x 9 | x 6 | x 9 | x 4 |

9 x 4 = _____     3 x 9 = _____

**Nine as a Factor**

Score: _____     Time: _____ minutes _____ seconds

# Timed Test

**Nine as a Factor**

9 x 1 = ____     4 x 9 = ____

$$\begin{array}{r} 9 \\ \times 4 \\ \hline \end{array} \quad \begin{array}{r} 9 \\ \times 9 \\ \hline \end{array} \quad \begin{array}{r} 9 \\ \times 2 \\ \hline \end{array} \quad \begin{array}{r} 7 \\ \times 9 \\ \hline \end{array}$$

5 x 9 = ____     0 x 9 = ____

3 x 9 = ____     9 x 7 = ____

$$\begin{array}{r} 9 \\ \times 1 \\ \hline \end{array} \quad \begin{array}{r} 9 \\ \times 6 \\ \hline \end{array} \quad \begin{array}{r} 1 \\ \times 9 \\ \hline \end{array} \quad \begin{array}{r} 6 \\ \times 9 \\ \hline \end{array}$$

9 x 5 = ____     7 x 9 = ____

8 x 9 = ____     9 x 9 = ____

$$\begin{array}{r} 9 \\ \times 3 \\ \hline \end{array} \quad \begin{array}{r} 5 \\ \times 9 \\ \hline \end{array} \quad \begin{array}{r} 9 \\ \times 8 \\ \hline \end{array} \quad \begin{array}{r} 9 \\ \times 7 \\ \hline \end{array}$$

1 x 9 = ____     9 x 3 = ____

9 x 6 = ____     9 x 2 = ____

$$\begin{array}{r} 3 \\ \times 9 \\ \hline \end{array} \quad \begin{array}{r} 9 \\ \times 5 \\ \hline \end{array} \quad \begin{array}{r} 0 \\ \times 9 \\ \hline \end{array} \quad \begin{array}{r} 4 \\ \times 9 \\ \hline \end{array}$$

9 x 7 = ____     9 x 8 = ____

9 x 0 = ____     2 x 9 = ____

$$\begin{array}{r} 8 \\ \times 9 \\ \hline \end{array} \quad \begin{array}{r} 9 \\ \times 0 \\ \hline \end{array} \quad \begin{array}{r} 5 \\ \times 9 \\ \hline \end{array} \quad \begin{array}{r} 2 \\ \times 9 \\ \hline \end{array}$$

6 x 9 = ____     9 x 4 = ____

Score: _____     Time: _____ minutes _____ seconds

# Timed Test

3 x 9 = ____   9 x 2 = ____

$$\begin{array}{r} 9 \\ \times 6 \\ \hline \end{array} \quad \begin{array}{r} 9 \\ \times 0 \\ \hline \end{array} \quad \begin{array}{r} 3 \\ \times 9 \\ \hline \end{array} \quad \begin{array}{r} 9 \\ \times 4 \\ \hline \end{array}$$

9 x 9 = ____   7 x 9 = ____

9 x 4 = ____   9 x 8 = ____

$$\begin{array}{r} 9 \\ \times 9 \\ \hline \end{array} \quad \begin{array}{r} 6 \\ \times 9 \\ \hline \end{array} \quad \begin{array}{r} 2 \\ \times 9 \\ \hline \end{array} \quad \begin{array}{r} 9 \\ \times 5 \\ \hline \end{array}$$

6 x 9 = ____   1 x 9 = ____

0 x 9 = ____   9 x 0 = ____

$$\begin{array}{r} 4 \\ \times 9 \\ \hline \end{array} \quad \begin{array}{r} 8 \\ \times 9 \\ \hline \end{array} \quad \begin{array}{r} 9 \\ \times 2 \\ \hline \end{array} \quad \begin{array}{r} 9 \\ \times 8 \\ \hline \end{array}$$

9 x 7 = ____   9 x 6 = ____

8 x 9 = ____   5 x 9 = ____

$$\begin{array}{r} 9 \\ \times 3 \\ \hline \end{array} \quad \begin{array}{r} 7 \\ \times 9 \\ \hline \end{array} \quad \begin{array}{r} 1 \\ \times 9 \\ \hline \end{array} \quad \begin{array}{r} 5 \\ \times 9 \\ \hline \end{array}$$

9 x 2 = ____   9 x 3 = ____

9 x 5 = ____   9 x 1 = ____

$$\begin{array}{r} 9 \\ \times 7 \\ \hline \end{array} \quad \begin{array}{r} 9 \\ \times 1 \\ \hline \end{array} \quad \begin{array}{r} 2 \\ \times 9 \\ \hline \end{array} \quad \begin{array}{r} 0 \\ \times 9 \\ \hline \end{array}$$

2 x 9 = ____   4 x 9 = ____

**Nine as a Factor**

Score: _____   Time: _____ minutes _____ seconds

# Timed Test

9 x 3 = ____        9 x 8 = ____

$$\begin{array}{cccc} 9 & 0 & 7 & 5 \\ \times 3 & \times 9 & \times 9 & \times 9 \\ \hline \end{array}$$

7 x 9 = ____        9 x 0 = ____

2 x 9 = ____        1 x 9 = ____

$$\begin{array}{cccc} 9 & 1 & 9 & 6 \\ \times 4 & \times 9 & \times 8 & \times 9 \\ \hline \end{array}$$

9 x 5 = ____        9 x 7 = ____

6 x 9 = ____        9 x 6 = ____

$$\begin{array}{cccc} 9 & 9 & 4 & 9 \\ \times 2 & \times 6 & \times 9 & \times 7 \\ \hline \end{array}$$

9 x 1 = ____        9 x 2 = ____

3 x 9 = ____        9 x 9 = ____

$$\begin{array}{cccc} 2 & 9 & 9 & 8 \\ \times 9 & \times 4 & \times 0 & \times 9 \\ \hline \end{array}$$

6 x 9 = ____        4 x 9 = ____

9 x 4 = ____        5 x 9 = ____

$$\begin{array}{cccc} 9 & 9 & 9 & 3 \\ \times 9 & \times 5 & \times 1 & \times 9 \\ \hline \end{array}$$

8 x 9 = ____        0 x 9 = ____

---

Record your scores and times below.

**Page 198** Score: _____

**Page 199** Score: _____          **Page 202** Score: _____ Time: ___min. ___sec.

**Page 200** Score: _____ Time: ___min. ___sec.   **Page 203** Score: _____ Time: ___min. ___sec.

**Page 201** Score: _____ Time: ___min. ___sec.   **Page 204** Score: _____ Time: ___min. ___sec.

Name _____

# Practice

■ Multiply. Record your score—the number correct—at the end of each Review and on page 214.

7 x 0 = _____     7 x 9 = _____     3 x 1 = _____     2 x 4 = _____

5 x 1 = _____     0 x 6 = _____     9 x 9 = _____     5 x 0 = _____

1 x 7 = _____     9 x 1 = _____     6 x 6 = _____     4 x 2 = _____

3 x 8 = _____     1 x 1 = _____     8 x 1 = _____     4 x 7 = _____

0 x 3 = _____     7 x 7 = _____     3 x 0 = _____     0 x 7 = _____

4 x 8 = _____     4 x 0 = _____     7 x 1 = _____     5 x 9 = _____

6 x 5 = _____     5 x 8 = _____     6 x 8 = _____     3 x 2 = _____

2 x 3 = _____     9 x 8 = _____     1 x 0 = _____     6 x 7 = _____

9 x 0 = _____     1 x 8 = _____     6 x 4 = _____     2 x 2 = _____

4 x 1 = _____     9 x 7 = _____     3 x 7 = _____     1 x 4 = _____

Continue this Review on the next page.

## Practice

$3 \times 6 =$ _____  $0 \times 8 =$ _____  $0 \times 5 =$ _____  $4 \times 6 =$ _____

$8 \times 6 =$ _____  $6 \times 3 =$ _____  $7 \times 4 =$ _____  $3 \times 4 =$ _____

$2 \times 5 =$ _____  $5 \times 3 =$ _____  $8 \times 2 =$ _____  $1 \times 6 =$ _____

$1 \times 5 =$ _____  $8 \times 4 =$ _____  $8 \times 8 =$ _____  $8 \times 7 =$ _____

$4 \times 9 =$ _____  $1 \times 2 =$ _____  $9 \times 2 =$ _____  $2 \times 7 =$ _____

$3 \times 3 =$ _____  $6 \times 9 =$ _____  $6 \times 1 =$ _____  $1 \times 3 =$ _____

$0 \times 1 =$ _____  $2 \times 8 =$ _____  $9 \times 4 =$ _____  $6 \times 0 =$ _____

$4 \times 5 =$ _____  $6 \times 2 =$ _____  $3 \times 5 =$ _____  $8 \times 5 =$ _____

$7 \times 2 =$ _____  $5 \times 6 =$ _____  $2 \times 6 =$ _____  $4 \times 4 =$ _____

$4 \times 3 =$ _____  $2 \times 1 =$ _____  $0 \times 4 =$ _____  $0 \times 0 =$ _____

Score: _____

Name _____

# Practice

■ Multiply.

| | | | | | | | |
|---|---|---|---|---|---|---|---|
| 5<br>x 6 | 2<br>x 5 | 3<br>x 3 | 4<br>x 4 | 8<br>x 8 | 1<br>x 0 | 7<br>x 2 | 6<br>x 7 |
| 2<br>x 4 | 9<br>x 6 | 5<br>x 5 | 9<br>x 4 | 0<br>x 0 | 6<br>x 3 | 3<br>x 2 | 7<br>x 9 |
| 1<br>x 7 | 8<br>x 0 | 4<br>x 3 | 6<br>x 8 | 0<br>x 4 | 4<br>x 9 | 8<br>x 7 | 1<br>x 8 |
| 9<br>x 5 | 8<br>x 1 | 7<br>x 3 | 2<br>x 2 | 5<br>x 7 | 4<br>x 5 | 8<br>x 9 | 1<br>x 6 |
| 3<br>x 4 | 3<br>x 9 | 6<br>x 6 | 5<br>x 4 | 0<br>x 1 | 7<br>x 8 | 3<br>x 1 | 9<br>x 7 |

**All-Multiplication Review**

START

Continue this Review on the next page.

# Practice

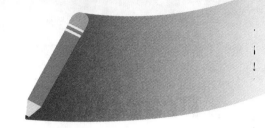

| 9 | 3 | 2 | 4 | 0 | 5 | 1 | 6 |
|---|---|---|---|---|---|---|---|
| x 1 | x 8 | x 3 | x 6 | x 6 | x 8 | x 5 | x 5 |

| 3 | 7 | 0 | 5 | 8 | 3 | 4 | 0 |
|---|---|---|---|---|---|---|---|
| x 0 | x 4 | x 9 | x 2 | x 5 | x 5 | x 1 | x 2 |

| 2 | 6 | 2 | 7 | 1 | 9 | 5 | 7 |
|---|---|---|---|---|---|---|---|
| x 0 | x 1 | x 7 | x 0 | x 2 | x 8 | x 0 | x 7 |

| 8 | 9 | 7 | 1 | 0 | 6 | 4 | 2 |
|---|---|---|---|---|---|---|---|
| x 2 | x 0 | x 5 | x 4 | x 7 | x 4 | x 7 | x 9 |

| 5 | 9 | 5 | 0 | 9 | 3 | 8 | 1 |
|---|---|---|---|---|---|---|---|
| x 9 | x 2 | x 3 | x 3 | x 9 | x 7 | x 4 | x 3 |

FINISH

Circle any problems that you still find difficult to remember. Make your own flash cards to help you master these problems.

Score: _____

# Timed Test

■ Improve your speed on these basic facts. Ask someone to time you. Record your time and score at the end of each Timed Test and on page 214.

3 x 8 = _____    7 x 9 = _____    0 x 9 = _____    0 x 8 = _____

0 x 2 = _____    1 x 6 = _____    6 x 7 = _____    2 x 5 = _____

5 x 9 = _____    4 x 7 = _____    8 x 9 = _____    5 x 0 = _____

3 x 4 = _____    2 x 2 = _____    4 x 0 = _____    6 x 2 = _____

9 x 9 = _____    3 x 0 = _____    9 x 1 = _____    4 x 6 = _____

1 x 7 = _____    6 x 3 = _____    0 x 6 = _____    9 x 8 = _____

5 x 1 = _____    8 x 5 = _____    9 x 0 = _____    0 x 1 = _____

7 x 3 = _____    0 x 7 = _____    5 x 8 = _____    6 x 6 = _____

1 x 2 = _____    5 x 2 = _____    3 x 3 = _____    8 x 4 = _____

2 x 6 = _____    7 x 4 = _____    7 x 8 = _____    3 x 7 = _____

Continue this Timed Test on the next page.

**All-Multiplication Review**

# Timed Test

| | | | |
|---|---|---|---|
| 7 x 6 = ____ | 1 x 0 = ____ | 0 x 5 = ____ | 9 x 6 = ____ |
| 6 x 5 = ____ | 8 x 3 = ____ | 7 x 1 = ____ | 7 x 5 = ____ |
| 5 x 7 = ____ | 6 x 9 = ____ | 2 x 8 = ____ | 6 x 0 = ____ |
| 4 x 4 = ____ | 0 x 0 = ____ | 1 x 4 = ____ | 4 x 5 = ____ |
| 3 x 2 = ____ | 5 x 4 = ____ | 4 x 9 = ____ | 1 x 1 = ____ |
| 8 x 7 = ____ | 3 x 6 = ____ | 1 x 8 = ____ | 2 x 7 = ____ |
| 9 x 7 = ____ | 8 x 2 = ____ | 2 x 3 = ____ | 4 x 8 = ____ |
| 7 x 7 = ____ | 1 x 9 = ____ | 6 x 4 = ____ | 5 x 6 = ____ |
| 6 x 1 = ____ | 9 x 3 = ____ | 0 x 4 = ____ | 8 x 0 = ____ |
| 2 x 4 = ____ | 4 x 2 = ____ | 3 x 9 = ____ | 3 x 5 = ____ |

**All-Multiplication Review**

Score: _____     Time: _____ minutes _____ seconds

# Timed Test

■ Complete these facts as accurately and as quickly as you can.

5 x 4 = _____     2 x 1 = _____     0 x 1 = _____     5 x 5 = _____

1 x 0 = _____     0 x 4 = _____     7 x 3 = _____     4 x 1 = _____

9 x 6 = _____     6 x 3 = _____     8 x 0 = _____     9 x 2 = _____

4 x 4 = _____     9 x 8 = _____     9 x 1 = _____     5 x 3 = _____

9 x 3 = _____     4 x 2 = _____     9 x 7 = _____     4 x 5 = _____

3 x 4 = _____     8 x 3 = _____     2 x 8 = _____     6 x 4 = _____

0 x 9 = _____     2 x 7 = _____     8 x 1 = _____     2 x 0 = _____

3 x 3 = _____     7 x 4 = _____     3 x 5 = _____     3 x 2 = _____

9 x 9 = _____     8 x 4 = _____     1 x 1 = _____     6 x 0 = _____

1 x 3 = _____     6 x 2 = _____     7 x 9 = _____     0 x 2 = _____

All-Multiplication Review

Continue this Timed Test on the next page.

# Timed Test

6 x 9 = ____    6 x 6 = ____    2 x 4 = ____    8 x 6 = ____

4 x 0 = ____    4 x 6 = ____    7 x 1 = ____    5 x 7 = ____

5 x 6 = ____    0 x 3 = ____    1 x 9 = ____    2 x 9 = ____

4 x 9 = ____    5 x 9 = ____    8 x 9 = ____    7 x 7 = ____

1 x 4 = ____    2 x 6 = ____    9 x 5 = ____    4 x 8 = ____

3 x 1 = ____    8 x 5 = ____    8 x 7 = ____    1 x 7 = ____

2 x 2 = ____    5 x 2 = ____    1 x 5 = ____    6 x 8 = ____

7 x 6 = ____    1 x 8 = ____    7 x 8 = ____    3 x 9 = ____

0 x 7 = ____    3 x 7 = ____    3 x 0 = ____    2 x 3 = ____

3 x 6 = ____    5 x 0 = ____    0 x 8 = ____    9 x 0 = ____

Score: _____     Time: _____ minutes _____ seconds

All-Multiplication Review

# Timed Test

| | | | |
|---|---|---|---|
| 0 x 0 = ____ | 5 x 7 = ____ | 8 x 8 = ____ | 0 x 5 = ____ |
| 1 x 7 = ____ | 0 x 9 = ____ | 0 x 4 = ____ | 5 x 8 = ____ |
| 4 x 5 = ____ | 6 x 1 = ____ | 3 x 3 = ____ | 2 x 6 = ____ |
| 2 x 9 = ____ | 8 x 0 = ____ | 4 x 9 = ____ | 8 x 5 = ____ |
| 3 x 7 = ____ | 2 x 5 = ____ | 0 x 7 = ____ | 1 x 8 = ____ |
| 8 x 4 = ____ | 7 x 6 = ____ | 2 x 2 = ____ | 7 x 9 = ____ |
| 2 x 1 = ____ | 9 x 2 = ____ | 1 x 0 = ____ | 9 x 8 = ____ |
| 7 x 0 = ____ | 1 x 3 = ____ | 4 x 6 = ____ | 5 x 4 = ____ |
| 5 x 3 = ____ | 6 x 5 = ____ | 8 x 1 = ____ | 6 x 9 = ____ |
| 9 x 9 = ____ | 4 x 1 = ____ | 6 x 2 = ____ | 0 x 1 = ____ |

**All–Multiplication Review**

Continue this Timed Test on the next page.

Name _____

# Timed Test

4 x 7 = _____        1 x 1 = _____        5 x 1 = _____        5 x 2 = _____

5 x 9 = _____        9 x 7 = _____        1 x 9 = _____        2 x 0 = _____

2 x 3 = _____        7 x 1 = _____        8 x 6 = _____        3 x 6 = _____

0 x 2 = _____        6 x 7 = _____        2 x 7 = _____        0 x 8 = _____

6 x 3 = _____        5 x 5 = _____        9 x 0 = _____        7 x 7 = _____

3 x 5 = _____        1 x 5 = _____        6 x 0 = _____        6 x 4 = _____

7 x 8 = _____        8 x 2 = _____        2 x 8 = _____        9 x 6 = _____

3 x 1 = _____        4 x 3 = _____        4 x 0 = _____        3 x 2 = _____

7 x 4 = _____        9 x 4 = _____        8 x 7 = _____        9 x 5 = _____

3 x 9 = _____        0 x 6 = _____        1 x 2 = _____        4 x 4 = _____

| Record your scores and times below. | |
|---|---|
| **Page 205–206** Score: _____ | **Page 211–212** Score: _____ Time: ___min. ___sec. |
| **Page 207–208** Score: _____ | **Page 213–214** Score: _____ Time: ___min. ___sec. |
| **Page 209–210** Score: _____ Time: ___min. ___sec. | |

All-Multiplication Review

214

# Products Through One Hundred Twenty

Now you will learn about some higher facts.

The first thirteen multiples of 10 are 0, 10, 20, 30, 40, 50, 60, 70, 80, 90, 100, 110, and 120. They are the same as the products of 10 times any number from 0 through 12.

Here are some things to remember about the basic facts in which 10 is one of the factors:

- The product of 10 and another counting number always ends in 0. Here's a shortcut to find a product of 10 and another number: Simply annex (attach) a zero at the end of the other factor.

**Examples:** $10 \times 6 = 60$, $10 \times 3 = 30$, and $10 \times 10 = 100$

- Changing the order of the factors does not change the product. So, $10 \times 7$ is the same as $7 \times 10$.

- As you have learned with other facts, $10 \times 0$ is 0 and $10 \times 1$ is 10.

■ Complete these **T**'s by multiplying each of the numbers by 10.

| $\times 10$ | | $\times 10$ | |
|---|---|---|---|
| 6 | ___ | 5 | ___ |
| 2 | ___ | 3 | ___ |
| 12 | ___ | 11 | ___ |
| 4 | ___ | 0 | ___ |
| 7 | ___ | 8 | ___ |
| 9 | ___ | 10 | ___ |
| 1 | ___ | | |

■ Now, complete these facts.

$10 \times 5 =$ ___     $10 \times 9 =$ ___

$4 \times 10 =$ ___     $10 \times 3 =$ ___

$10 \times 12 =$ ___     $10 \times 7 =$ ___

$10 \times 11 =$ ___     $2 \times 10 =$ ___

$10 \times 10 =$ ___     $10 \times 8 =$ ___

$6 \times 10 =$ ___     $7 \times 10 =$ ___

$10 \times 0 =$ ___     $10 \times 2 =$ ___

$11 \times 10 =$ ___     $1 \times 10 =$ ___

**Ten as a Factor**

# Practice

■ Multiply. Record your score—the number correct—on each Practice page and again on page 220.

**Ten as a Factor**

| 10<br>x 2 | 11<br>x 10 | 10<br>x 10 | 10<br>x 8 |
|---|---|---|---|

10 x 5 = ____          10 x 9 = ____

10 x 6 = ____          4 x 10 = ____

| 10<br>x 0 | 10<br>x 1 | 10<br>x 11 | 10<br>x 7 |
|---|---|---|---|

10 x 1 = ____          10 x 3 = ____

0 x 10 = ____          10 x 7 = ____

| 10<br>x 4 | 10<br>x 6 | 10<br>x 0 | 10<br>x 8 |
|---|---|---|---|

5 x 10 = ____          10 x 10 = ____

6 x 10 = ____          11 x 10 = ____

| 10<br>x 3 | 10<br>x 12 | 10<br>x 4 | 12<br>x 10 |
|---|---|---|---|

10 x 5 = ____          10 x 2 = ____

10 x 12 = ____          3 x 10 = ____

| 10<br>x 6 | 10<br>x 5 | 10<br>x 2 | 10<br>x 1 |
|---|---|---|---|

Score: _____

START

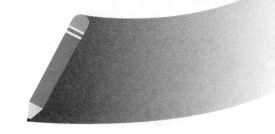

Name _____

# Practice

■ Complete these facts as accurately and as quickly as you can.

Ten as a Factor

| | | | |
|---|---|---|---|
| 10 | 10 | 10 | 10 |
| x 8 | x 5 | x 3 | x 12 |

| | | | |
|---|---|---|---|
| 11 | 10 | 12 | 10 |
| x 10 | x 8 | x 10 | x 4 |

| | | | |
|---|---|---|---|
| 10 | 10 | 10 | 10 |
| x 9 | x 2 | x 4 | x 0 |

| | | | |
|---|---|---|---|
| 10 | 10 | 10 | 10 |
| x 7 | x 6 | x 2 | x 9 |

| | | | |
|---|---|---|---|
| 10 | 10 | 10 | 10 |
| x 5 | x 1 | x 12 | x 7 |

10 x 6 = _____        7 x 10 = _____

0 x 10 = _____        10 x 12 = _____

10 x 2 = _____        10 x 4 = _____

6 x 10 = _____        1 x 10 = _____

3 x 10 = _____        12 x 10 = _____

10 x 7 = _____        10 x 10 = _____

10 x 11 = _____        11 x 10 = _____

10 x 0 = _____        10 x 1 = _____

Score: _____

 Circle any problems that you still find difficult to remember. Make your own flash cards to help you master these problems.

# Timed Test

■ Improve your speed on these basic facts. Ask someone to time you.
Record your time and score on each Timed Test page and on page 220.

**Ten as a Factor**

10 x 0 = ____     10 x 11 = ____     10    10    10    10
                                          x 7   x 8   x 1   x 5

10 x 10 = ____     4 x 10 = ____

10 x 5 = ____     10 x 8 = ____     10    10    10    10
                                          x 10   x 7   x 6   x 3

6 x 10 = ____     7 x 10 = ____

3 x 10 = ____     1 x 10 = ____     11    10    12    10
                                          x 10   x 9   x 10   x 1

10 x 9 = ____     10 x 6 = ____

10 x 1 = ____     10 x 12 = ____     10    10    10    10
                                          x 5   x 2   x 12   x 0

5 x 10 = ____     11 x 10 = ____

                                          10    10    10    10
10 x 4 = ____     8 x 10 = ____     x 8   x 9   x 4   x 11

2 x 10 = ____     0 x 10 = ____

Score: _____     Time: _____ minutes _____ seconds

Name _____

# Timed Test

■ Complete these facts as accurately and as quickly as you can.

10 x 4 = _____    2 x 10 = _____

$$\begin{array}{cccc} 10 & 11 & 10 & 10 \\ \times\ 1 & \times 10 & \times\ 5 & \times\ 9 \\ \hline \end{array}$$

12 x 10 = _____    10 x 8 = _____

10 x 1 = _____    10 x 11 = _____

$$\begin{array}{cccc} 10 & 12 & 10 & 10 \\ \times\ 7 & \times 10 & \times\ 9 & \times\ 8 \\ \hline \end{array}$$

10 x 3 = _____    8 x 10 = _____

5 x 10 = _____    10 x 5 = _____

$$\begin{array}{cccc} 10 & 10 & 10 & 10 \\ \times\ 0 & \times\ 4 & \times 11 & \times\ 5 \\ \hline \end{array}$$

10 x 9 = _____    6 x 10 = _____

3 x 10 = _____    10 x 10 = _____

$$\begin{array}{cccc} 10 & 10 & 10 & 10 \\ \times\ 6 & \times\ 3 & \times 10 & \times\ 7 \\ \hline \end{array}$$

10 x 2 = _____    1 x 10 = _____

10 x 12 = _____    10 x 7 = _____

$$\begin{array}{cccc} 10 & 10 & 10 & 10 \\ \times\ 2 & \times\ 4 & \times 12 & \times\ 1 \\ \hline \end{array}$$

4 x 10 = _____    10 x 6 = _____

Score: _____    Time: _____ minutes _____ seconds

**Ten as a Factor**

# Timed Test

10 x 8 = _____      10 x 2 = _____

$$\begin{array}{cccc} 10 & 12 & 10 & 10 \\ \times\ 4 & \times\ 10 & \times\ 0 & \times\ 9 \\ \hline \end{array}$$

0 x 10 = _____      10 x 12 = _____

10 x 4 = _____      10 x 6 = _____

$$\begin{array}{cccc} 10 & 11 & 10 & 10 \\ \times\ 5 & \times\ 10 & \times\ 8 & \times\ 3 \\ \hline \end{array}$$

8 x 10 = _____      5 x 10 = _____

10 x 11 = _____      10 x 3 = _____

$$\begin{array}{cccc} 10 & 10 & 10 & 10 \\ \times\ 0 & \times\ 8 & \times\ 5 & \times\ 2 \\ \hline \end{array}$$

4 x 10 = _____      9 x 10 = _____

10 x 5 = _____      1 x 10 = _____

$$\begin{array}{cccc} 10 & 10 & 10 & 10 \\ \times\ 10 & \times\ 12 & \times\ 1 & \times\ 4 \\ \hline \end{array}$$

7 x 10 = _____      11 x 10 = _____

10 x 9 = _____      10 x 0 = _____

$$\begin{array}{cccc} 10 & 10 & 10 & 10 \\ \times\ 7 & \times\ 6 & \times\ 2 & \times\ 3 \\ \hline \end{array}$$

3 x 10 = _____      2 x 10 = _____

Record your scores and times below.

**Page 216** Score: _____          **Page 219** Score: _____ Time: ___min. ___sec.

**Page 217** Score: _____          **Page 220** Score: _____ Time: ___min. ___sec.

**Page 218** Score: _____ Time: ___min. ___sec.

220

# Products Through One Hundred Thirty-Two

The first thirteen multiples of 11 are 0, 11, 22, 33, 44, 55, 66, 77, 88, 99, 110, 121, and 132. They are the same as the products of 11 times any number from 0 through 12.

Here are some things to remember about the basic facts in which 11 is one of the factors:

- All of the products from 11 x 2 through 11 x 9 are easy to remember because both digits in each product are the same as the second factor. Thus, 11 x 2 is 22, 11 x 5 is 55, and 11 x 9 is 99.

- That leaves only three other facts to learn. The first of these you already know: 11 x 10 is 110. The other two are new: 11 x 11 is 121 and 11 x 12 is 132.

- Changing the order of the factors does not change the product. So, 11 x 7 is the same as 7 x 11.

- As you have learned with other facts, 11 x 0 is 0 and 11 x 1 is 11.

■ Complete this circle by multiplying each of the numbers by 11.

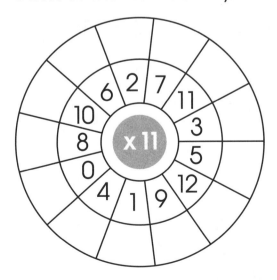

■ Now, complete these facts.

11 x 3 = ____          2 x 11 = ____

8 x 11 = ____          11 x 7 = ____

11 x 6 = ____          4 x 11 = ____

0 x 11 = ____          10 x 11 = ____

11 x 2 = ____          6 x 11 = ____

7 x 11 = ____          11 x 12 = ____

11 x 5 = ____          9 x 11 = ____

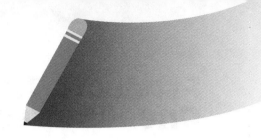

# Practice

■ Multiply. Record your score—the number correct—on each Practice page and again on page 226.

**Eleven as a Factor**

|  |  |  |  |
|---|---|---|---|
| 11 | 11 | 11 | 11 |
| x 7 | x 0 | x 1 | x 8 |

11 x 2 = ____        7 x 11 = ____

9 x 11 = ____        5 x 11 = ____

|  |  |  |  |
|---|---|---|---|
| 11 | 11 | 11 | 10 |
| x 4 | x 12 | x 9 | x 11 |

11 x 10 = ____        12 x 11 = ____

3 x 11 = ____        0 x 11 = ____

|  |  |  |  |
|---|---|---|---|
| 11 | 11 | 11 | 11 |
| x 5 | x 4 | x 3 | x 10 |

11 x 5 = ____        11 x 6 = ____

2 x 11 = ____        11 x 9 = ____

|  |  |  |  |
|---|---|---|---|
| 11 | 11 | 11 | 12 |
| x 2 | x 5 | x 0 | x 11 |

11 x 8 = ____        11 x 12 = ____

1 x 11 = ____        4 x 11 = ____

|  |  |  |  |
|---|---|---|---|
| 11 | 11 | 11 | 11 |
| x 3 | x 11 | x 6 | x 2 |

Score: _____

# Practice

■ Multiply.

```
  12      11      11      11        11 x 1 = ____      11 x 5 = ____
x 11    x 10    x  0    x  4
                                    12 x 11 = ____      1 x 11 = ____

  11      10      11      11         3 x 11 = ____      4 x 11 = ____
x  6    x 11    x  9    x  5
                                    11 x 8 = ____      11 x 10 = ____

  11      11      11      11         2 x 11 = ____      11 x 2 = ____
x  5    x  8    x  3    x  7
                                     9 x 11 = ____      11 x 11 = ____

  11      11      11      11        11 x 0 = ____      11 x 7 = ____
x  1    x  8    x  3    x 12
                                     8 x 11 = ____      5 x 11 = ____

  11      11      11      11
x  4    x  2    x 11    x  5
```

**Eleven as a Factor**

Score: _____

Circle any problems that you still find difficult to remember. Make your own flash cards to help you master these problems.

FINISH

# Timed Test

■ Improve your speed on these facts of 11. Ask someone to time you. Record your time and score on each Timed Test page and on page 226.

**Eleven as a Factor**

11 x 1 = _____    11 x 5 = _____

$$\begin{array}{cccc} 11 & 11 & 11 & 11 \\ \times\ 6 & \times\ 7 & \times\ 0 & \times\ 1 \\ \hline \end{array}$$

11 x 11 = _____    3 x 11 = _____

12 x 11 = _____    6 x 11 = _____

$$\begin{array}{cccc} 11 & 12 & 11 & 11 \\ \times\ 5 & \times\ 11 & \times\ 6 & \times\ 7 \\ \hline \end{array}$$

11 x 7 = _____    11 x 12 = _____

2 x 11 = _____    4 x 11 = _____

$$\begin{array}{cccc} 11 & 11 & 11 & 10 \\ \times\ 10 & \times\ 4 & \times\ 2 & \times\ 11 \\ \hline \end{array}$$

11 x 10 = _____    11 x 2 = _____

1 x 11 = _____    11 x 6 = _____

$$\begin{array}{cccc} 11 & 11 & 11 & 11 \\ \times\ 9 & \times\ 3 & \times\ 9 & \times\ 3 \\ \hline \end{array}$$

11 x 0 = _____    0 x 11 = _____

11 x 8 = _____    11 x 9 = _____

$$\begin{array}{cccc} 11 & 11 & 11 & 11 \\ \times\ 1 & \times\ 8 & \times\ 4 & \times\ 0 \\ \hline \end{array}$$

5 x 11 = _____    7 x 11 = _____

Score: _____    Time: _____ minutes _____ seconds

# Timed Test

■ Complete these facts as accurately and as quickly as you can.

1 x 11 = _____     11 x 5 = _____

$$\begin{array}{cccc} 11 & 11 & 10 & 11 \\ \underline{\times\ 4} & \underline{\times\ 1} & \underline{\times 11} & \underline{\times\ 6} \end{array}$$

5 x 11 = _____     12 x 11 = _____

11 x 6 = _____     11 x 0 = _____

$$\begin{array}{cccc} 11 & 11 & 12 & 11 \\ \underline{\times\ 0} & \underline{\times 10} & \underline{\times 11} & \underline{\times\ 5} \end{array}$$

11 x 4 = _____     11 x 8 = _____

6 x 11 = _____     7 x 11 = _____

$$\begin{array}{cccc} 11 & 11 & 11 & 11 \\ \underline{\times\ 9} & \underline{\times\ 2} & \underline{\times 11} & \underline{\times\ 9} \end{array}$$

11 x 1 = _____     11 x 11 = _____

11 x 7 = _____     10 x 11 = _____

$$\begin{array}{cccc} 11 & 11 & 11 & 11 \\ \underline{\times\ 0} & \underline{\times\ 3} & \underline{\times\ 6} & \underline{\times\ 3} \end{array}$$

11 x 12 = _____     9 x 11 = _____

2 x 11 = _____     11 x 10 = _____

$$\begin{array}{cccc} 11 & 11 & 11 & 11 \\ \underline{\times\ 7} & \underline{\times 12} & \underline{\times\ 5} & \underline{\times\ 1} \end{array}$$

11 x 3 = _____     0 x 11 = _____

**Eleven as a Factor**

Score: _____     Time: _____ minutes _____ seconds

# Timed Test

**Eleven as a Factor**

11 x 7 = _____     11 x 6 = _____

1 x 11 = _____     9 x 11 = _____

11 x 0 = _____     4 x 11 = _____

8 x 11 = _____     11 x 2 = _____

2 x 11 = _____     11 x 8 = _____

0 x 11 = _____     6 x 11 = _____

7 x 11 = _____     3 x 11 = _____

11 x 5 = _____     11 x 11 = _____

11 x 12 = _____     5 x 11 = _____

11 x 10 = _____     11 x 4 = _____

```
  11      11      10      11
x  3    x 11    x 11    x  0
____    ____    ____    ____
```

```
  11      11      11      11
x 12    x  2    x  8    x  8
____    ____    ____    ____
```

```
  11      11      11      11
x  6    x  7    x  5    x  1
____    ____    ____    ____
```

```
  11      11      11      11
x  9    x  1    x  2    x  0
____    ____    ____    ____
```

```
  12      11      11      11
x 11    x 10    x  7    x  4
____    ____    ____    ____
```

Record your scores and times below.

| | |
|---|---|
| **Page 222** Score: _____ | **Page 225** Score: _____ Time: ___min. ___sec. |
| **Page 223** Score: _____ | **Page 226** Score: _____ Time: ___min. ___sec. |
| **Page 224** Score: _____ Time: ___min. ___sec. | |

Name _____

# Products Through
# One Hundred Forty-Four

The first thirteen multiples of 12 are 0, 12, 24, 36, 48, 60, 72, 84, 96, 108, 120, 132, and 144. They are the same as the products of 12 times any number from 0 through 12.

Here are some things to remember about the basic facts in which 12 is one of the factors:

● Changing the order of the factors does not change the product. Therefore, you already know that 12 x 10 is 120 and 10 x 12 is 120.

● As you have learned with other facts, 12 x 0 is 0 and 12 x 1 is 12.

■ Complete these **T**'s by multiplying each of the numbers by 12.

■ Now, complete these facts.

| x 12 | | x 12 | |
|------|------|------|------|
| 6 | ____ | 12 | ____ |
| 10 | ____ | 0 | ____ |
| 8 | ____ | 4 | ____ |
| 1 | ____ | 7 | ____ |
| 5 | ____ | 9 | ____ |
| 3 | ____ | 11 | ____ |
| 2 | ____ | | |

12 x 2 = ____     12 x 0 = ____

12 x 5 = ____     12 x 9 = ____

12 x 4 = ____     12 x 3 = ____

12 x 12 = ____     12 x 8 = ____

12 x 6 = ____     12 x 7 = ____

12 x 1 = ____     12 x 10 = ____

12 x 11 = ____

**Twelve as a Factor**

Name _____

# Practice

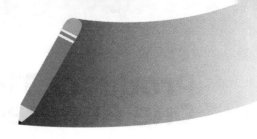

■ Multiply. Record your score—the number correct—on each Practice page and again on page 232.

```
  12      10      12      12
x  1    x 12    x  4    x 11
_____  _____  _____  _____
```

```
  12      12      12      12
x  4    x  8    x  5    x 12
_____  _____  _____  _____
```

```
  12      12      12      11
x  5    x  9    x  0    x 12
_____  _____  _____  _____
```

```
  12      12      12      12
x  7    x  9    x  3    x  6
_____  _____  _____  _____
```

```
  12      12      12      12
x  2    x  6    x  3    x  7
_____  _____  _____  _____
```

12 x 2 = _____          7 x 12 = _____

12 x 6 = _____          3 x 12 = _____

12 x 1 = _____          1 x 12 = _____

0 x 12 = _____          12 x 3 = _____

11 x 12 = _____         12 x 11 = _____

9 x 12 = _____          10 x 12 = _____

12 x 0 = _____          12 x 8 = _____

12 x 10 = _____         2 x 12 = _____

Score: _____

Name _____

# Practice

■ Multiply.

| 12 | 12 | 12 | 12 |
|----|----|----|----|
| x 1 | x 12 | x 9 | x 6 |

12 x 9 = _____     12 x 4 = _____

4 x 12 = _____     2 x 12 = _____

| 12 | 12 | 12 | 12 |
|----|----|----|----|
| x 1 | x 3 | x 8 | x 1 |

12 x 0 = _____     12 x 10 = _____

10 x 12 = _____     6 x 12 = _____

| 12 | 12 | 12 | 12 |
|----|----|----|----|
| x 4 | x 9 | x 8 | x 0 |

3 x 12 = _____     11 x 12 = _____

9 x 12 = _____     1 x 12 = _____

| 12 | 12 | 12 | 10 |
|----|----|----|----|
| x 10 | x 5 | x 7 | x 12 |

12 x 3 = _____     12 x 12 = _____

5 x 12 = _____     12 x 6 = _____

| 12 | 12 | 12 | 12 |
|----|----|----|----|
| x 11 | x 2 | x 6 | x 3 |

Score: _____

 Circle any problems that you still find difficult to remember. Make your own flash cards to help you master these problems.

# Timed Test

■ Improve your speed on these facts of 12. Ask someone to time you. Record your time and score on each Timed Test page and on page 232.

Record your time and score on each Timed Test page and on page 232.

**Twelve as a Factor**

12 x 12 = _____      12 x 0 = _____

10 x 12 = _____      1 x 12 = _____

12 x 2 = _____      12 x 11 = _____

9 x 12 = _____      12 x 5 = _____

12 x 6 = _____      3 x 12 = _____

8 x 12 = _____      11 x 12 = _____

12 x 1 = _____      12 x 7 = _____

7 x 12 = _____      0 x 12 = _____

12 x 3 = _____      12 x 4 = _____

4 x 12 = _____      5 x 12 = _____

```
  12      12      12      10
x  3    x  0    x  1    x 12
____    ____    ____    ____
```

```
  12      12      12      12
x  5    x  8    x  4    x  9
____    ____    ____    ____
```

```
  12      12      12      12
x  4    x  1    x 12    x  2
____    ____    ____    ____
```

```
  11      12      12      12
x 12    x  9    x  2    x  7
____    ____    ____    ____
```

```
  12      12      12      12
x 10    x  3    x  6    x  8
____    ____    ____    ____
```

Score: _____      Time: _____ minutes _____ seconds

Name _____

# Timed Test

■ Complete these facts as accurately and as quickly as you can.

1 x 12 = _____    12 x 2 = _____

|  |  |  |  |
|---|---|---|---|
| 12 | 12 | 12 | 12 |
| x 8 | x 7 | x 0 | x 4 |

6 x 12 = _____    7 x 12 = _____

12 x 1 = _____    12 x 9 = _____

|  |  |  |  |
|---|---|---|---|
| 12 | 12 | 12 | 12 |
| x 6 | x 5 | x 12 | x 3 |

12 x 12 = _____    5 x 12 = _____

12 x 8 = _____    12 x 4 = _____

|  |  |  |  |
|---|---|---|---|
| 12 | 12 | 12 | 10 |
| x 5 | x 6 | x 9 | x 12 |

12 x 5 = _____    0 x 12 = _____

9 x 12 = _____    11 x 12 = _____

|  |  |  |  |
|---|---|---|---|
| 12 | 12 | 12 | 12 |
| x 1 | x 1 | x 8 | x 11 |

12 x 0 = _____    12 x 3 = _____

12 x 6 = _____    8 x 12 = _____

|  |  |  |  |
|---|---|---|---|
| 12 | 12 | 12 | 12 |
| x 7 | x 0 | x 2 | x 10 |

3 x 12 = _____    12 x 7 = _____

Score: _____    Time: _____ minutes _____ seconds

**Twelve as a Factor**

231

# Timed Test

12 x 7 = _____     12 x 6 = _____      12       12       12       12
                                      x  9     x 10     x  0     x 11
                                      _____    _____    _____    _____
3 x 12 = _____     12 x 11 = _____

12 x 1 = _____     11 x 12 = _____      12       12       12       12
                                      x  8     x  9     x  1     x  8
                                      _____    _____    _____    _____
2 x 12 = _____     12 x 0 = _____

12 x 12 = _____    12 x 3 = _____       10       12       12       12
                                      x 12     x  0     x  7     x  2
                                      _____    _____    _____    _____
7 x 12 = _____     4 x 12 = _____

12 x 5 = _____     12 x 10 = _____      12       12       12       11
                                      x  1     x 12     x  7     x 12
                                      _____    _____    _____    _____
1 x 12 = _____     12 x 3 = _____

12 x 8 = _____     4 x 12 = _____       12       12       12       12
                                      x  6     x  5     x  3     x  2
                                      _____    _____    _____    _____

6 x 12 = _____     12 x 10 = _____

| Record your scores and times below. | |
| --- | --- |
| **Page 228** Score: _____ | **Page 231** Score: _____ Time: ___min. ___sec. |
| **Page 229** Score: _____ | **Page 232** Score: _____ Time: ___min. ___sec. |
| **Page 230** Score: _____ Time: ___min. ___sec. | |

232

# Timed Test

■ Improve your speed on these basic facts. Ask someone to time you.
  Record your time and score on page 234.

12 x 10 = _____    1 x 12 = _____    12 x 2 = _____    4 x 10 = _____

10 x 9 = _____    11 x 6 = _____    6 x 11 = _____    11 x 7 = _____

2 x 10 = _____    10 x 12 = _____    11 x 8 = _____    8 x 11 = _____

11 x 9 = _____    5 x 11 = _____    0 x 11 = _____    11 x 0 = _____

10 x 5 = _____    11 x 1 = _____    10 x 4 = _____    10 x 2 = _____

4 x 11 = _____    8 x 12 = _____    12 x 11 = _____    12 x 4 = _____

12 x 1 = _____    10 x 8 = _____    7 x 11 = _____    11 x 5 = _____

6 x 10 = _____    3 x 10 = _____    12 x 5 = _____    10 x 7 = _____

12 x 6 = _____    12 x 3 = _____    7 x 12 = _____    10 x 3 = _____

10 x 1 = _____    3 x 12 = _____    10 x 0 = _____    11 x 9 = _____

Continue this Timed Test on the next page.

**All-Multiplication Review**

# Timed Test

**All-Multiplication Review**

11 x 11 = ____     12 x 8 = ____     1 x 11 = ____     9 x 10 = ____

3 x 11 = ____     2 x 11 = ____     2 x 10 = ____     11 x 5 = ____

10 x 3 = ____     10 x 7 = ____     7 x 10 = ____     9 x 11 = ____

8 x 10 = ____     0 x 12 = ____     11 x 10 = ____     12 x 0 = ____

12 x 12 = ____     11 x 12 = ____     6 x 12 = ____     10 x 10 = ____

5 x 12 = ____     12 x 4 = ____     10 x 6 = ____     11 x 8 = ____

11 x 3 = ____     1 x 10 = ____     0 x 10 = ____     12 x 3 = ____

11 x 4 = ____     12 x 9 = ____     12 x 7 = ____     11 x 5 = ____

5 x 10 = ____     4 x 12 = ____     9 x 12 = ____     10 x 4 = ____

10 x 11 = ____     11 x 2 = ____     10 x 2 = ____     11 x 6 = ____

Score: _____     Time: _____ minutes _____ seconds

DIVISION

# What Is Division?

You divide to answer questions such as how many groups of 3's are there in 12. The answer is called the **quotient**.

12 grapes divided into groups of 3 equals 4 equal groups.

Here are two ways to show the division.

$$12 \div 3 = 4 \qquad 3\,\overline{)12}^{\,4}$$

You read the problem this way: **12 divided by 3 equals 4**.

You can draw a picture to find a quotient.

**Example:** Find the quotient. 8 ÷ 2 = _____

**Step 1:** Draw 8 dots. Group them into 2's.

**Step 2:** Count all the groups.

**Answer:** 8 ÷ 2 = __4__

■ Draw a picture to find the quotient.

| | | |
|---|---|---|
| 6 ÷ 2 = ___ | 8 ÷ 4 = ___ | 10 ÷ 2 = ___ |

| | | |
|---|---|---|
| 6 ÷ 3 = ___ | 12 ÷ 3 = ___ | 12 ÷ 4 = ___ |

**Division**

# What Is Division?

You can use a number line to find a quotient.

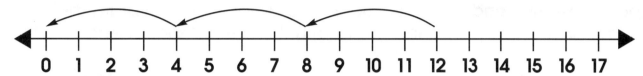

**Example:** Find the quotient. 12 ÷ 4 = _____

**Step 1:** Put your finger on 12.

**Step 2:** Make moves to the left of 4 spaces each, ending on zero.

**Step 3:** Count the number of moves you made.

**Answer:** 12 ÷ 4 = ___3___

■ Use the number line to find the quotient.

8 ÷ 2 = ____          15 ÷ 5 = ____          16 ÷ 4 = ____

2⟌8̄          4⟌12̄          2⟌6̄          6⟌12̄          5⟌15̄

Multiplication and division are **inverse operations.**  10 ÷ 2 = 5   5 x 2 = 10

You can use multiplication facts to find the quotient.

**Example:** Find the quotient. 20 ÷ 5 = _____

**Think:** Some number times 5 equals 20. _____ x 5 = 20

Since 4 x 5 = 20, then 20 ÷ 5 = ___4___

**Answer:** 20 ÷ 5 = ___4___

■ Use a multiplication fact to find the quotient.

9 ÷ 3 = ____          10 ÷ 5 = ____          16 ÷ 2 = ____

5⟌15̄          2⟌4̄          2⟌12̄          6⟌18̄          3⟌18̄

Name _____

# Dividends Through Eighteen

**Division** is the operation in which a number is divided into equal parts. The **dividend** is the number being divided. The **divisor** is the number of equal parts, and the **quotient** is the number in each part.

**Example:**

$$15 \div 3 = 5$$

dividend    divisor    quotient

$$\begin{array}{r} 5 \\ 3\overline{)15} \end{array}$$

divisor           dividend      **quotient**    **dividend**

When you divide a number by 1, the quotient will always be the same as the dividend.

**Example:** $6 \div 1 = 6$

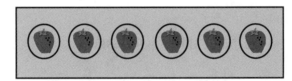

When you divide a number by 2, the quotient is half of the dividend.

**Example:** $6 \div 2 = 3$

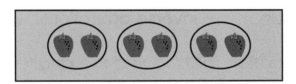

■ Find the quotient for these facts.

$6 \div 1 =$ _____     $18 \div 2 =$ _____     $10 \div 2 =$ _____     $0 \div 1 =$ _____

$7 \div 1 =$ _____     $6 \div 2 =$ _____     $8 \div 1 =$ _____     $5 \div 1 =$ _____

$16 \div 2 =$ _____     $14 \div 2 =$ _____     $8 \div 2 =$ _____     $1 \div 1 =$ _____

$2 \div 1 =$ _____     $9 \div 1 =$ _____     $12 \div 2 =$ _____     $4 \div 2 =$ _____

## Practice

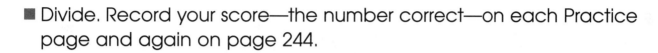

■ Divide. Record your score—the number correct—on each Practice page and again on page 244.

7 ÷ 1 = _____          6 ÷ 2 = _____

2 ÷ 2 = _____          1 ÷ 1 = _____

2 ÷ 1 = _____          4 ÷ 2 = _____

6 ÷ 1 = _____          12 ÷ 2 = _____

4 ÷ 1 = _____          9 ÷ 1 = _____

8 ÷ 1 = _____          3 ÷ 1 = _____

10 ÷ 2 = _____         4 ÷ 1 = _____

16 ÷ 2 = _____         8 ÷ 2 = _____

3 ÷ 1 = _____          5 ÷ 1 = _____

14 ÷ 2 = _____         18 ÷ 2 = _____

$2\overline{)2}$          $1\overline{)4}$

$2\overline{)18}$          $2\overline{)14}$

$1\overline{)5}$          $1\overline{)9}$

$2\overline{)4}$          $1\overline{)1}$

$2\overline{)8}$          $1\overline{)0}$

$1\overline{)8}$          $2\overline{)16}$

$1\overline{)6}$          $1\overline{)3}$

$2\overline{)6}$          $2\overline{)10}$

**One and Two as Divisors**

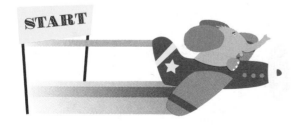

START

Score: _____

239

# Practice

■ Divide.

6 ÷ 2 = _____     2 ÷ 2 = _____

1)3     2)16

2 ÷ 1 = _____     1 ÷ 1 = _____

2)2     1)2

4 ÷ 2 = _____     9 ÷ 1 = _____

2)12     1)9

0 ÷ 2 = _____     7 ÷ 1 = _____

1)7     2)4

18 ÷ 2 = _____     12 ÷ 2 = _____

2)14     1)0

0 ÷ 1 = _____     8 ÷ 2 = _____

2)10     2)18

8 ÷ 1 = _____     3 ÷ 1 = _____

16 ÷ 2 = _____     14 ÷ 2 = _____

1)1     1)6

10 ÷ 2 = _____     6 ÷ 1 = _____

2)6     1)4

5 ÷ 1 = _____     4 ÷ 1 = _____

**One and Two as Divisors**

START

Score: _____

# Practice

■ Divide.

2 ÷ 1 = _____          8 ÷ 2 = _____

6 ÷ 2 = _____          4 ÷ 1 = _____

7 ÷ 1 = _____          14 ÷ 2 = _____

10 ÷ 2 = _____          2 ÷ 2 = _____

9 ÷ 1 = _____          0 ÷ 1 = _____

8 ÷ 1 = _____          18 ÷ 2 = _____

3 ÷ 1 = _____          12 ÷ 2 = _____

0 ÷ 2 = _____          4 ÷ 2 = _____

16 ÷ 2 = _____          5 ÷ 1 = _____

6 ÷ 1 = _____          1 ÷ 1 = _____

2)0̅          1)4̅

2)8̅          2)1̅2̅

2)1̅8̅          1)0̅

1)5̅          1)9̅

2)1̅4̅          2)6̅

1)3̅          2)1̅6̅

1)6̅          2)2̅

1)8̅          1)1̅

Circle any problems that you still find difficult to remember. Make your own flash cards to help you master these problems.

**FINISH**

Score: _____

One and Two as Divisors

241

# Timed Test

■ Improve your speed on these basic facts. Ask someone to time you. Record your time and score on each Timed Test page and on page 244.

$2 \div 1 = $ _____     $18 \div 2 = $ _____

$6 \div 2 = $ _____     $12 \div 2 = $ _____

$16 \div 2 = $ _____     $7 \div 1 = $ _____

$0 \div 2 = $ _____     $10 \div 2 = $ _____

$6 \div 1 = $ _____     $2 \div 2 = $ _____

$5 \div 1 = $ _____     $4 \div 1 = $ _____

$4 \div 2 = $ _____     $8 \div 2 = $ _____

$1 \div 1 = $ _____     $9 \div 1 = $ _____

$0 \div 1 = $ _____     $14 \div 2 = $ _____

$8 \div 1 = $ _____     $3 \div 1 = $ _____

$2\overline{)2}$     $1\overline{)5}$     $1\overline{)4}$

$2\overline{)14}$     $2\overline{)18}$     $1\overline{)9}$

$2\overline{)16}$     $1\overline{)2}$     $1\overline{)3}$

$2\overline{)8}$     $2\overline{)4}$     $1\overline{)6}$

$2\overline{)0}$     $1\overline{)1}$     $1\overline{)8}$

$1\overline{)7}$     $2\overline{)6}$     $2\overline{)10}$

$2\overline{)12}$     $1\overline{)0}$

Score: _____     Time: _____ minutes _____ seconds

# Timed Test

■ Complete these facts as accurately and as quickly as you can.

0 ÷ 1 = _____     1 ÷ 1 = _____

9 ÷ 1 = _____     6 ÷ 1 = _____

6 ÷ 2 = _____     8 ÷ 2 = _____

16 ÷ 2 = _____    4 ÷ 2 = _____

2 ÷ 1 = _____     12 ÷ 2 = _____

8 ÷ 2 = _____     4 ÷ 1 = _____

18 ÷ 2 = _____    2 ÷ 2 = _____

7 ÷ 1 = _____     3 ÷ 1 = _____

14 ÷ 2 = _____    5 ÷ 1 = _____

10 ÷ 2 = _____    0 ÷ 2 = _____

2⟌4     2⟌8     2⟌2

1⟌2     2⟌6     1⟌9

1⟌1     1⟌3     2⟌10

2⟌16    2⟌14    1⟌5

1⟌4     2⟌0     1⟌7

1⟌8     1⟌0     2⟌12

1⟌6     2⟌18

**One and Two as Divisors**

Score: _____     Time: _____ minutes _____ seconds

## Name _____

# Timed Test

**One and Two as Divisors**

$6 \div 1 =$ _____    $8 \div 2 =$ _____

$8 \div 1 =$ _____    $10 \div 2 =$ _____

$2 \div 2 =$ _____    $5 \div 1 =$ _____

$6 \div 2 =$ _____    $14 \div 2 =$ _____

$12 \div 2 =$ _____    $18 \div 2 =$ _____

$0 \div 1 =$ _____    $2 \div 1 =$ _____

$0 \div 2 =$ _____    $16 \div 2 =$ _____

$9 \div 1 =$ _____    $4 \div 2 =$ _____

$4 \div 1 =$ _____    $3 \div 1 =$ _____

$7 \div 1 =$ _____    $1 \div 1 =$ _____

$2\overline{)10}$    $1\overline{)8}$    $1\overline{)4}$

$2\overline{)14}$    $2\overline{)4}$    $1\overline{)3}$

$2\overline{)16}$    $2\overline{)12}$    $1\overline{)7}$

$2\overline{)18}$    $1\overline{)2}$    $1\overline{)9}$

$1\overline{)1}$    $2\overline{)0}$    $2\overline{)6}$

$1\overline{)0}$    $1\overline{)6}$    $2\overline{)8}$

$1\overline{)5}$    $2\overline{)2}$

| Record your scores and times below. | |
|---|---|
| **Page 239** Score: _____ | **Page 242** Score: _____ Time: ____min. ____sec. |
| **Page 240** Score: _____ | **Page 243** Score: _____ Time: ____min. ____sec. |
| **Page 241** Score: _____ | **Page 244** Score: _____ Time: ____min. ____sec. |

# Dividends Through Twenty-Seven

Now, think about what happens when a number is divided by 3.

**Example:** $18 \div 3 = 6$

The dividend is 18. If you put 3 objects in each group, you have 6 equal groups.

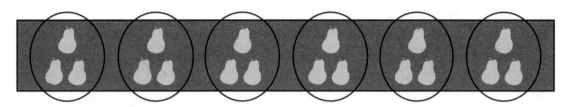

Division and multiplication are **inverse operations**.

**Example:** $6 \times 3 = 18$
$18 \div 3 = 6$

When you divide, you cannot have 0 as a divisor. It doesn't make sense to divide a number into zero groups. However, you could have a 0 as a dividend. But, no matter how many groups you divide 0 into, the quotient will always be 0.

**Examples:** $0 \div 2 = 0$      $0 \div 5 = 0$

Apply what you have learned to the division facts of 3.

**Examples:** $0 \div 3 = 0$      $3 \div 1 = 3$      $3 \div 3 = 1$

■ Complete this circle by dividing each of the numbers by 3.

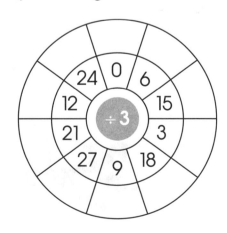

# Practice

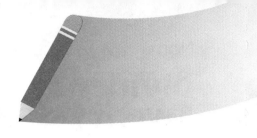

■ Divide. Record your score—the number correct—on each Practice page and again on page 250.

$6 \div 3 =$ _____

$15 \div 3 =$ _____

$3\overline{)12}$     $3\overline{)24}$

$18 \div 3 =$ _____

$24 \div 3 =$ _____

$3\overline{)27}$     $3\overline{)3}$

$9 \div 3 =$ _____

$21 \div 3 =$ _____

$3\overline{)21}$     $3\overline{)15}$

$0 \div 3 =$ _____

$12 \div 3 =$ _____

$27 \div 3 =$ _____

$6 \div 3 =$ _____

$3\overline{)0}$     $3\overline{)9}$

$21 \div 3 =$ _____

$9 \div 3 =$ _____

$3\overline{)18}$     $3\overline{)6}$

$3 \div 3 =$ _____

$18 \div 3 =$ _____

$3\overline{)24}$     $3\overline{)12}$

$15 \div 3 =$ _____

$0 \div 3 =$ _____

$12 \div 3 =$ _____

$27 \div 3 =$ _____

$3\overline{)9}$     $3\overline{)21}$

$24 \div 3 =$ _____

$3 \div 3 =$ _____

$3\overline{)15}$     $3\overline{)27}$

Score: _____

## Practice

■ Divide.

24 ÷ 3 = _____      12 ÷ 3 = _____

3 ÷ 3 = _____      9 ÷ 3 = _____

18 ÷ 3 = _____      0 ÷ 3 = _____

6 ÷ 3 = _____      27 ÷ 3 = _____

15 ÷ 3 = _____      24 ÷ 3 = _____

21 ÷ 3 = _____      18 ÷ 3 = _____

9 ÷ 3 = _____      6 ÷ 3 = _____

0 ÷ 3 = _____      3 ÷ 3 = _____

12 ÷ 3 = _____      15 ÷ 3 = _____

27 ÷ 3 = _____      21 ÷ 3 = _____

$3\overline{)21}$      $3\overline{)12}$

$3\overline{)3}$      $3\overline{)18}$

$3\overline{)27}$      $3\overline{)0}$

$3\overline{)6}$      $3\overline{)24}$

$3\overline{)15}$      $3\overline{)9}$

$3\overline{)27}$      $3\overline{)15}$

$3\overline{)18}$      $3\overline{)21}$

$3\overline{)24}$      $3\overline{)12}$

Circle any problems that you still find difficult to remember. Make your own flash cards to help you master these problems.

**FINISH**

Score: _____

# Timed Test

■ Improve your speed on these basic facts. Ask someone to time you.
Record your time and score on each Timed Test page and on page 250.

$9 \div 3 =$ _____    $0 \div 3 =$ _____

$3\overline{)12}$    $3\overline{)21}$    $3\overline{)24}$

$18 \div 3 =$ _____    $15 \div 3 =$ _____

$3\overline{)27}$    $3\overline{)0}$    $3\overline{)9}$

$24 \div 3 =$ _____    $21 \div 3 =$ _____

$6 \div 3 =$ _____    $12 \div 3 =$ _____

$3\overline{)15}$    $3\overline{)18}$    $3\overline{)21}$

$12 \div 3 =$ _____    $27 \div 3 =$ _____

$3\overline{)9}$    $3\overline{)3}$    $3\overline{)0}$

$15 \div 3 =$ _____    $3 \div 3 =$ _____

$27 \div 3 =$ _____    $6 \div 3 =$ _____

$3\overline{)6}$    $3\overline{)12}$    $3\overline{)27}$

$3 \div 3 =$ _____    $24 \div 3 =$ _____

$3\overline{)24}$    $3\overline{)3}$    $3\overline{)18}$

$18 \div 3 =$ _____    $9 \div 3 =$ _____

$3\overline{)15}$    $3\overline{)6}$

$21 \div 3 =$ _____    $0 \div 3 =$ _____

Score: _____    Time: _____ minutes _____ seconds

## Timed Test

■ Complete these facts as accurately and as quickly as you can.

$15 \div 3 =$ _____     $24 \div 3 =$ _____

$3\overline{)27}$     $3\overline{)21}$     $3\overline{)12}$

$21 \div 3 =$ _____     $9 \div 3 =$ _____

$3\overline{)0}$     $3\overline{)15}$     $3\overline{)6}$

$3 \div 3 =$ _____     $12 \div 3 =$ _____

$24 \div 3 =$ _____     $27 \div 3 =$ _____

$3\overline{)18}$     $3\overline{)9}$     $3\overline{)3}$

$18 \div 3 =$ _____     $0 \div 3 =$ _____

$3\overline{)12}$     $3\overline{)21}$     $3\overline{)6}$

$6 \div 3 =$ _____     $15 \div 3 =$ _____

$12 \div 3 =$ _____     $18 \div 3 =$ _____

$3\overline{)24}$     $3\overline{)9}$     $3\overline{)18}$

$0 \div 3 =$ _____     $3 \div 3 =$ _____

$3\overline{)3}$     $3\overline{)27}$     $3\overline{)15}$

$9 \div 3 =$ _____     $6 \div 3 =$ _____

$3\overline{)21}$     $3\overline{)0}$

$27 \div 3 =$ _____     $21 \div 3 =$ _____

**Three as a Divisor**

Score: _____     Time: _____ minutes _____ seconds

249

# Timed Test

18 ÷ 3 = _____     15 ÷ 3 = _____

27 ÷ 3 = _____     24 ÷ 3 = _____          3)21     3)15     3)27

9 ÷ 3 = _____     3 ÷ 3 = _____            3)24     3)6      3)3

6 ÷ 3 = _____     12 ÷ 3 = _____           3)12     3)18     3)9

0 ÷ 3 = _____     21 ÷ 3 = _____           3)0      3)27     3)12

24 ÷ 3 = _____     6 ÷ 3 = _____

12 ÷ 3 = _____     9 ÷ 3 = _____           3)3      3)15     3)21

21 ÷ 3 = _____     27 ÷ 3 = _____          3)6      3)12     3)24

15 ÷ 3 = _____     18 ÷ 3 = _____          3)18     3)9

3 ÷ 3 = _____     0 ÷ 3 = _____

| Record your scores and times below. | |
|---|---|
| **Page 246** Score: _____ | **Page 249** Score: _____ Time: ___min. ___sec. |
| **Page 247** Score: _____ | **Page 250** Score: _____ Time: ___min. ___sec. |
| **Page 248** Score: _____ Time: ___min. ___sec. | |

# Dividends Through Thirty-Six

Now, think about what happens when a number is divided by 4.

**Example:** 12 ÷ 4 = 3

The dividend is 12. If you put 4 objects in each group, you have 3 equal groups.

**Remember:** Division and multiplication are inverse operations.

**Example:** 4 x 3 = 12
    12 ÷ 4 = 3

Apply what you have learned to the division facts of 4.

**Examples:** 0 ÷ 4 = 0        4 ÷ 1 = 4        4 ÷ 4 = 1

■ Complete these **T**'s by dividing each of the numbers by 4. Then, divide the problems on the right.

| ÷ 4 | | ÷ 4 | |
|---|---|---|---|
| 36 | ___ | 16 | ___ |
| 32 | ___ | 12 | ___ |
| 24 | ___ | 4 | ___ |
| 20 | ___ | 28 | ___ |
| 8 | ___ | 0 | ___ |

4⟌24    4⟌32    4⟌28

4⟌36    4⟌4    4⟌20

4⟌12    4⟌0    4⟌16

4⟌8

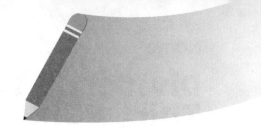

# Practice

■ Divide. Record your score—the number correct—on each Practice page and again on page 256.

page and again on page 256.

$12 \div 4 =$ _____        $36 \div 4 =$ _____

$4 \div 4 =$ _____        $0 \div 4 =$ _____

$28 \div 4 =$ _____        $16 \div 4 =$ _____

$36 \div 4 =$ _____        $24 \div 4 =$ _____

$0 \div 4 =$ _____        $8 \div 4 =$ _____

$16 \div 4 =$ _____        $20 \div 4 =$ _____

$8 \div 4 =$ _____        $32 \div 4 =$ _____

$24 \div 4 =$ _____        $12 \div 4 =$ _____

$32 \div 4 =$ _____        $28 \div 4 =$ _____

$20 \div 4 =$ _____        $4 \div 4 =$ _____

$4\overline{)0}$        $4\overline{)24}$

$4\overline{)32}$        $4\overline{)4}$

$4\overline{)36}$        $4\overline{)28}$

$4\overline{)8}$        $4\overline{)16}$

$4\overline{)20}$        $4\overline{)12}$

$4\overline{)0}$        $4\overline{)4}$

$4\overline{)24}$        $4\overline{)16}$

$4\overline{)36}$        $4\overline{)28}$

Score: _____

**Four as a Divisor**

# Practice

■ Divide.

16 ÷ 4 = _____     12 ÷ 4 = _____

4)20     4)24

0 ÷ 4 = _____     4 ÷ 4 = _____

4)4     4)36

12 ÷ 4 = _____     28 ÷ 4 = _____

4)28     4)0

8 ÷ 4 = _____     20 ÷ 4 = _____

28 ÷ 4 = _____     36 ÷ 4 = _____

4)8     4)16

24 ÷ 4 = _____     4 ÷ 4 = _____

4)32     4)12

32 ÷ 4 = _____     16 ÷ 4 = _____

4)16     4)36

20 ÷ 4 = _____     0 ÷ 4 = _____

4)32     4)20

4 ÷ 4 = _____     24 ÷ 4 = _____

4)24     4)28

36 ÷ 4 = _____     16 ÷ 4 = _____

FINISH

Circle any problems that you still find difficult to remember. Make your own flash cards to help you master these problems.

Score: _____

**Four as a Divisor**

# Timed Test

■ Improve your speed on these basic facts. Ask someone to time you. Record your time and score on each Timed Test page and on page 256.

$8 \div 4 =$ _____    $32 \div 4 =$ _____

$4\overline{)36}$    $4\overline{)28}$    $4\overline{)0}$

$24 \div 4 =$ _____    $16 \div 4 =$ _____

$36 \div 4 =$ _____    $28 \div 4 =$ _____

$4\overline{)32}$    $4\overline{)12}$    $4\overline{)4}$

$20 \div 4 =$ _____    $4 \div 4 =$ _____

$4\overline{)20}$    $4\overline{)8}$    $4\overline{)16}$

$12 \div 4 =$ _____    $0 \div 4 =$ _____

$4\overline{)24}$    $4\overline{)12}$    $4\overline{)36}$

$28 \div 4 =$ _____    $8 \div 4 =$ _____

$4 \div 4 =$ _____    $20 \div 4 =$ _____

$4\overline{)8}$    $4\overline{)16}$    $4\overline{)20}$

$32 \div 4 =$ _____    $36 \div 4 =$ _____

$4\overline{)32}$    $4\overline{)4}$    $4\overline{)28}$

$16 \div 4 =$ _____    $12 \div 4 =$ _____

$4\overline{)24}$    $4\overline{)0}$

$0 \div 4 =$ _____    $24 \div 4 =$ _____

Score: _____    Time: _____ minutes _____ seconds

# Timed Test

■ Complete these facts as accurately and as quickly as you can.

28 ÷ 4 = _____     4 ÷ 4 = _____

4)36     4)0     4)12

16 ÷ 4 = _____     0 ÷ 4 = _____

24 ÷ 4 = _____     36 ÷ 4 = _____

4)4     4)8     4)32

20 ÷ 4 = _____     32 ÷ 4 = _____

4)16     4)36     4)28

4 ÷ 4 = _____     12 ÷ 4 = _____

4)20     4)12     4)8

8 ÷ 4 = _____     28 ÷ 4 = _____

32 ÷ 4 = _____     0 ÷ 4 = _____

4)24     4)0     4)4

12 ÷ 4 = _____     20 ÷ 4 = _____

4)8     4)16     4)20

36 ÷ 4 = _____     8 ÷ 4 = _____

4)32     4)28

16 ÷ 4 = _____     24 ÷ 4 = _____

**Four as a Divisor**

Score: _____     Time: _____ minutes _____ seconds

Name _____

# Timed Test

$32 \div 4 =$ _____     $20 \div 4 =$ _____

$8 \div 4 =$ _____     $0 \div 4 =$ _____

$28 \div 4 =$ _____     $24 \div 4 =$ _____

$12 \div 4 =$ _____     $8 \div 4 =$ _____

$36 \div 4 =$ _____     $4 \div 4 =$ _____

$4 \div 4 =$ _____     $12 \div 4 =$ _____

$16 \div 4 =$ _____     $28 \div 4 =$ _____

$24 \div 4 =$ _____     $32 \div 4 =$ _____

$20 \div 4 =$ _____     $16 \div 4 =$ _____

$36 \div 4 =$ _____     $0 \div 4 =$ _____

$4\overline{)20}$     $4\overline{)8}$     $4\overline{)16}$

$4\overline{)12}$     $4\overline{)0}$     $4\overline{)32}$

$4\overline{)28}$     $4\overline{)24}$     $4\overline{)4}$

$4\overline{)16}$     $4\overline{)36}$     $4\overline{)8}$

$4\overline{)32}$     $4\overline{)0}$     $4\overline{)24}$

$4\overline{)4}$     $4\overline{)28}$     $4\overline{)12}$

$4\overline{)36}$     $4\overline{)20}$

**Four as a Divisor**

Record your scores and times below.

**Page 252** Score: _____

**Page 253** Score: _____

**Page 254** Score: _____ Time: ___min. ___sec.

**Page 255** Score: _____ Time: ___min. ___sec.

**Page 256** Score: _____ Time: ___min. ___sec.

# Dividends Through Forty-Five

Now, think about what happens when a number is divided by 5.

**Example:** 15 ÷ 5 = 3

The dividend is 15. If you put 5 objects in each group, you have 3 equal groups.

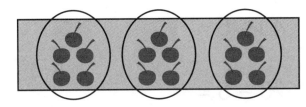

**Remember:** Division and multiplication are inverse operations.

**Example:** 5 x 3 = 15
       15 ÷ 5 = 3

Apply what you have learned to the division facts of 5.

**Examples:** 0 ÷ 5 = 0        5 ÷ 1 = 5        5 ÷ 5 = 1

■ Complete this circle by dividing each of the numbers by 5. Then, divide the problems on the right.

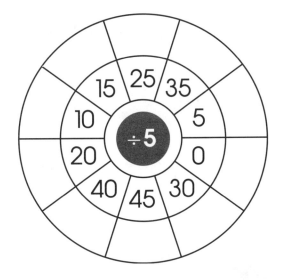

$5\overline{)15}$        $5\overline{)25}$        $5\overline{)0}$

$5\overline{)20}$        $5\overline{)40}$        $5\overline{)10}$

$5\overline{)35}$        $5\overline{)5}$        $5\overline{)30}$

$5\overline{)45}$

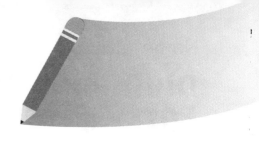

# Practice

■ Divide. Record your score—the number correct—on each Practice page and again on page 262.

**Five as a Divisor**

$5 \div 5 =$ _____     $45 \div 5 =$ _____     $5\overline{)40}$     $5\overline{)10}$

$0 \div 5 =$ _____     $40 \div 5 =$ _____     $5\overline{)45}$     $5\overline{)35}$

$10 \div 5 =$ _____     $25 \div 5 =$ _____     $5\overline{)0}$     $5\overline{)25}$

$20 \div 5 =$ _____     $35 \div 5 =$ _____     $5\overline{)15}$     $5\overline{)5}$

$15 \div 5 =$ _____     $0 \div 5 =$ _____     $5\overline{)30}$     $5\overline{)20}$

$30 \div 5 =$ _____     $20 \div 5 =$ _____     $5\overline{)35}$     $5\overline{)45}$

$45 \div 5 =$ _____     $5 \div 5 =$ _____     $5\overline{)25}$     $5\overline{)30}$

$25 \div 5 =$ _____     $10 \div 5 =$ _____     $5\overline{)20}$     $5\overline{)15}$

$40 \div 5 =$ _____     $30 \div 5 =$ _____

$35 \div 5 =$ _____     $15 \div 5 =$ _____

START

Score: _____

# Practice

■ Divide.

10 ÷ 5 = _____        5 ÷ 5 = _____

5 )‾1‾5‾        5 )‾3‾0‾

35 ÷ 5 = _____        45 ÷ 5 = _____

5 )‾5‾        5 )‾1‾0‾

15 ÷ 5 = _____        20 ÷ 5 = _____

5 )‾4‾5‾        5 )‾2‾5‾

30 ÷ 5 = _____        40 ÷ 5 = _____

5 )‾3‾5‾        5 )‾0‾

5 ÷ 5 = _____        0 ÷ 5 = _____

25 ÷ 5 = _____        15 ÷ 5 = _____

5 )‾4‾0‾        5 )‾2‾0‾

45 ÷ 5 = _____        35 ÷ 5 = _____

5 )‾1‾5‾        5 )‾1‾0‾

20 ÷ 5 = _____        10 ÷ 5 = _____

5 )‾2‾0‾        5 )‾3‾0‾

40 ÷ 5 = _____        30 ÷ 5 = _____

5 )‾4‾5‾        5 )‾4‾0‾

0 ÷ 5 = _____        25 ÷ 5 = _____

**Five as a Divisor**

Circle any problems that you still find difficult to remember. Make your own flash cards to help you master these problems.

FINISH

Score: _____

## Timed Test

■ Improve your speed on these basic facts. Ask someone to time you. Record your time and score on each Timed Test page and on page 262.

$25 \div 5 =$ _____   $45 \div 5 =$ _____

$\phantom{0}5\overline{)30}$   $\phantom{0}5\overline{)0}$   $\phantom{0}5\overline{)25}$

$10 \div 5 =$ _____   $35 \div 5 =$ _____

$\phantom{0}0 \div 5 =$ _____   $\phantom{0}5 \div 5 =$ _____

$\phantom{0}5\overline{)5}$   $\phantom{0}5\overline{)20}$   $\phantom{0}5\overline{)40}$

$40 \div 5 =$ _____   $\phantom{0}0 \div 5 =$ _____

$\phantom{0}5\overline{)35}$   $\phantom{0}5\overline{)10}$   $\phantom{0}5\overline{)45}$

$20 \div 5 =$ _____   $15 \div 5 =$ _____

$\phantom{0}5\overline{)15}$   $\phantom{0}5\overline{)20}$   $\phantom{0}5\overline{)30}$

$45 \div 5 =$ _____   $40 \div 5 =$ _____

$\phantom{0}0 \div 5 =$ _____   $30 \div 5 =$ _____

$\phantom{0}5\overline{)45}$   $\phantom{0}5\overline{)10}$   $\phantom{0}5\overline{)15}$

$15 \div 5 =$ _____   $25 \div 5 =$ _____

$\phantom{0}5\overline{)35}$   $\phantom{0}5\overline{)0}$   $\phantom{0}5\overline{)5}$

$30 \div 5 =$ _____   $10 \div 5 =$ _____

$\phantom{0}5\overline{)45}$   $\phantom{0}5\overline{)40}$

$35 \div 5 =$ _____   $20 \div 5 =$ _____

Score: _____     Time: _____ minutes _____ seconds

## Timed Test

■ Complete these facts as accurately and as quickly as you can.

5 ÷ 5 = _____    20 ÷ 5 = _____

$5\overline{)10}$    $5\overline{)40}$    $5\overline{)45}$

45 ÷ 5 = _____    35 ÷ 5 = _____

$5\overline{)20}$    $5\overline{)35}$    $5\overline{)15}$

30 ÷ 5 = _____    15 ÷ 5 = _____

40 ÷ 5 = _____    10 ÷ 5 = _____

$5\overline{)40}$    $5\overline{)0}$    $5\overline{)30}$

0 ÷ 5 = _____    5 ÷ 5 = _____

$5\overline{)25}$    $5\overline{)45}$    $5\overline{)10}$

15 ÷ 5 = _____    45 ÷ 5 = _____

25 ÷ 5 = _____    40 ÷ 5 = _____

$5\overline{)5}$    $5\overline{)40}$    $5\overline{)30}$

20 ÷ 5 = _____    30 ÷ 5 = _____

$5\overline{)15}$    $5\overline{)0}$    $5\overline{)20}$

10 ÷ 5 = _____    0 ÷ 5 = _____

$5\overline{)5}$    $5\overline{)35}$

35 ÷ 5 = _____    25 ÷ 5 = _____

Five as a Divisor

Score: _____    Time: _____ minutes _____ seconds

# Timed Test

■ Divide.

30 ÷ 5 = _____     45 ÷ 5 = _____

20 ÷ 5 = _____      5 ÷ 5 = _____

40 ÷ 5 = _____     25 ÷ 5 = _____

15 ÷ 5 = _____      0 ÷ 5 = _____

35 ÷ 5 = _____     10 ÷ 5 = _____

10 ÷ 5 = _____     15 ÷ 5 = _____

 0 ÷ 5 = _____     20 ÷ 5 = _____

45 ÷ 5 = _____     40 ÷ 5 = _____

 5 ÷ 5 = _____     30 ÷ 5 = _____

35 ÷ 5 = _____     25 ÷ 5 = _____

5$\overline{)40}$     5$\overline{)15}$     5$\overline{)30}$

5$\overline{)0}$     5$\overline{)25}$     5$\overline{)5}$

5$\overline{)30}$     5$\overline{)20}$     5$\overline{)15}$

5$\overline{)35}$     5$\overline{)45}$     5$\overline{)40}$

5$\overline{)10}$     5$\overline{)30}$     5$\overline{)25}$

5$\overline{)0}$     5$\overline{)5}$     5$\overline{)20}$

5$\overline{)45}$     5$\overline{)35}$

Record your scores and times below.

**Page 258** Score: _____

**Page 259** Score: _____

**Page 260** Score: _____ Time: ____min. ____sec.

**Page 261** Score: _____ Time: ____min. ____sec.

**Page 262** Score: _____ Time: ____min. ____sec.

Name _____

# Dividends Through Fifty-Four

Now, think about what happens when a number is divided by 6.

**Example:** $24 \div 6 = 4$

The dividend is 24. If you put 6 objects in each group, you have 4 equal groups.

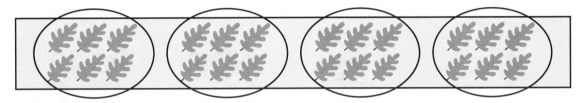

**Remember:** Division and multiplication are inverse operations.

**Example:** $6 \times 4 = 24$
$\phantom{Example: }24 \div 6 = 4$

Apply what you have learned to the division facts of 6.

**Examples:** $0 \div 6 = 0$ $\qquad$ $6 \div 1 = 6$ $\qquad$ $6 \div 6 = 1$

■ Write a division fact related to each of these multiplication facts of 6.

$6 \times 1 = 6$

____ $\div$ ____ = ____

$6 \times 2 = 12$

____ $\div$ ____ = ____

$6 \times 3 = 18$

____ $\div$ ____ = ____

$6 \times 4 = 24$

____ $\div$ ____ = ____

$6 \times 5 = 30$

____ $\div$ ____ = ____

$6 \times 6 = 36$

____ $\div$ ____ = ____

$6 \times 7 = 42$

____ $\div$ ____ = ____

$6 \times 8 = 48$

____ $\div$ ____ = ____

$6 \times 9 = 54$

____ $\div$ ____ = ____

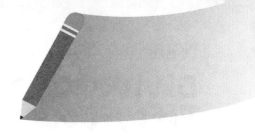

# Practice

■ Divide. Record your score—the number correct—on each Practice page and again on page 268.

**Six as a Divisor**

$0 \div 6 =$ _____     $30 \div 6 =$ _____

$18 \div 6 =$ _____     $24 \div 6 =$ _____

$36 \div 6 =$ _____     $48 \div 6 =$ _____

$6 \div 6 =$ _____     $54 \div 6 =$ _____

$30 \div 6 =$ _____     $42 \div 6 =$ _____

$12 \div 6 =$ _____     $0 \div 6 =$ _____

$24 \div 6 =$ _____     $18 \div 6 =$ _____

$48 \div 6 =$ _____     $36 \div 6 =$ _____

$54 \div 6 =$ _____     $6 \div 6 =$ _____

$42 \div 6 =$ _____     $12 \div 6 =$ _____

$6 \overline{)24}$     $6 \overline{)36}$

$6 \overline{)0}$     $6 \overline{)42}$

$6 \overline{)18}$     $6 \overline{)30}$

$6 \overline{)54}$     $6 \overline{)6}$

$6 \overline{)48}$     $6 \overline{)12}$

$6 \overline{)36}$     $6 \overline{)42}$

$6 \overline{)12}$     $6 \overline{)18}$

$6 \overline{)48}$     $6 \overline{)24}$

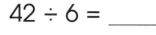

Score: _____

# Practice

■ Divide.

30 ÷ 6 = _____    42 ÷ 6 = _____

$6\overline{)54}$     $6\overline{)18}$

24 ÷ 6 = _____    54 ÷ 6 = _____

$6\overline{)48}$     $6\overline{)24}$

36 ÷ 6 = _____     6 ÷ 6 = _____

$6\overline{)12}$     $6\overline{)0}$

0 ÷ 6 = _____    12 ÷ 6 = _____

$6\overline{)42}$     $6\overline{)30}$

48 ÷ 6 = _____    24 ÷ 6 = _____

$6\overline{)6}$      $6\overline{)36}$

42 ÷ 6 = _____    18 ÷ 6 = _____

$6\overline{)54}$     $6\overline{)12}$

54 ÷ 6 = _____    36 ÷ 6 = _____

$6\overline{)24}$     $6\overline{)48}$

6 ÷ 6 = _____    48 ÷ 6 = _____

$6\overline{)42}$     $6\overline{)36}$

18 ÷ 6 = _____     0 ÷ 6 = _____

12 ÷ 6 = _____    30 ÷ 6 = _____

**Six as a Divisor**

 **FINISH**

Circle any problems that you still find difficult to remember. Make your own flash cards to help you master these problems.

Score: _____

# Timed Test

■ Improve your speed on these basic facts. Ask someone to time you. Record your time and score on each Timed Test page and on page 268.

18 ÷ 6 = _____     12 ÷ 6 = _____

6)42     6)36     6)54

42 ÷ 6 = _____     36 ÷ 6 = _____

6 ÷ 6 = _____     48 ÷ 6 = _____

6)0     6)30     6)24

36 ÷ 6 = _____     0 ÷ 6 = _____

6)48     6)12     6)6

54 ÷ 6 = _____     24 ÷ 6 = _____

6)36     6)54     6)18

30 ÷ 6 = _____     6 ÷ 6 = _____

0 ÷ 6 = _____     42 ÷ 6 = _____

6)24     6)30     6)12

12 ÷ 6 = _____     30 ÷ 6 = _____

6)48     6)6     6)36

24 ÷ 6 = _____     18 ÷ 6 = _____

6)24     6)42

48 ÷ 6 = _____     54 ÷ 6 = _____

Score: _____     Time: _____ minutes _____ seconds

**Six as a Divisor**

# Timed Test

■ Complete these facts as accurately and as quickly as you can.

$6 \div 6 =$ _____    $24 \div 6 =$ _____

$\phantom{xxxxxxx}$ $6\overline{)48}$    $6\overline{)42}$    $6\overline{)54}$

$30 \div 6 =$ _____    $48 \div 6 =$ _____

$\phantom{xxxxxxx}$ $6\overline{)30}$    $6\overline{)0}$    $6\overline{)18}$

$54 \div 6 =$ _____    $0 \div 6 =$ _____

$\phantom{xxxxxxx}$ $6\overline{)6}$    $6\overline{)48}$    $6\overline{)24}$

$42 \div 6 =$ _____    $36 \div 6 =$ _____

$12 \div 6 =$ _____    $18 \div 6 =$ _____

$\phantom{xxxxxxx}$ $6\overline{)12}$    $6\overline{)54}$    $6\overline{)30}$

$0 \div 6 =$ _____    $30 \div 6 =$ _____

$\phantom{xxxxxxx}$ $6\overline{)36}$    $6\overline{)6}$    $6\overline{)18}$

$36 \div 6 =$ _____    $42 \div 6 =$ _____

$18 \div 6 =$ _____    $54 \div 6 =$ _____

$\phantom{xxxxxxx}$ $6\overline{)12}$    $6\overline{)24}$    $6\overline{)36}$

$24 \div 6 =$ _____    $6 \div 6 =$ _____

$\phantom{xxxxxxx}$ $6\overline{)42}$    $6\overline{)0}$

$48 \div 6 =$ _____    $12 \div 6 =$ _____

Score: _____    Time: _____ minutes _____ seconds

267

# Timed Test

24 ÷ 6 = _____     12 ÷ 6 = _____

$6\overline{)36}$     $6\overline{)54}$     $6\overline{)18}$

48 ÷ 6 = _____      6 ÷ 6 = _____

18 ÷ 6 = _____     36 ÷ 6 = _____

$6\overline{)0}$     $6\overline{)42}$     $6\overline{)6}$

54 ÷ 6 = _____     30 ÷ 6 = _____

$6\overline{)24}$     $6\overline{)36}$     $6\overline{)12}$

30 ÷ 6 = _____     48 ÷ 6 = _____

$6\overline{)30}$     $6\overline{)48}$     $6\overline{)54}$

42 ÷ 6 = _____      0 ÷ 6 = _____

 6 ÷ 6 = _____     18 ÷ 6 = _____

$6\overline{)42}$     $6\overline{)6}$     $6\overline{)24}$

 0 ÷ 6 = _____     24 ÷ 6 = _____

$6\overline{)12}$     $6\overline{)18}$     $6\overline{)48}$

12 ÷ 6 = _____     42 ÷ 6 = _____

$6\overline{)30}$     $6\overline{)0}$

54 ÷ 6 = _____     36 ÷ 6 = _____

**Six as a Divisor**

Record your scores and times below.

**Page 264** Score: _____          **Page 267** Score: _____ Time: ___min. ___sec.

**Page 265** Score: _____          **Page 268** Score: _____ Time: ___min. ___sec.

**Page 266** Score: _____ Time: ___min. ___sec.

# Dividends Through Sixty-Three

Name _____

Now, think about what happens when a number is divided by 7.

**Example:** 63 ÷ 7 = 9

The dividend is 63. If you put 7 objects in each group, you have 9 equal groups.

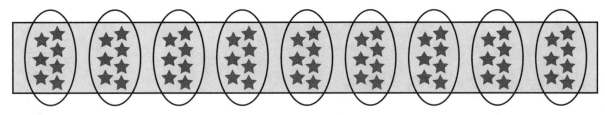

**Remember:** Division and multiplication are inverse operations.

**Example:** 7 x 9 = 63
             63 ÷ 7 = 9

Apply what you have learned to the division facts of 7.

**Examples:** 0 ÷ 7 = 0        7 ÷ 1 = 7        7 ÷ 7 = 1

■ Write a division fact related to each of these multiplication facts of 7.

7 x 1 = 7            7 x 2 = 14           7 x 3 = 21

____ ÷ ____ = ____   ____ ÷ ____ = ____   ____ ÷ ____ = ____


7 x 4 = 28           7 x 5 = 35           7 x 6 = 42

____ ÷ ____ = ____   ____ ÷ ____ = ____   ____ ÷ ____ = ____


7 x 7 = 49           7 x 8 = 56           7 x 9 = 63

____ ÷ ____ = ____   ____ ÷ ____ = ____   ____ ÷ ____ = ____

Name _____

# Practice

■ Divide. Record your score—the number correct—on each Practice page and again on page 276.

$7 \div 7 =$ _____   $56 \div 7 =$ _____

$35 \div 7 =$ _____   $49 \div 7 =$ _____

$0 \div 7 =$ _____   $63 \div 7 =$ _____

$28 \div 7 =$ _____   $42 \div 7 =$ _____

$56 \div 7 =$ _____   $49 \div 7 =$ _____

$14 \div 7 =$ _____   $0 \div 7 =$ _____

$49 \div 7 =$ _____   $35 \div 7 =$ _____

$21 \div 7 =$ _____   $7 \div 7 =$ _____

$63 \div 7 =$ _____   $14 \div 7 =$ _____

$42 \div 7 =$ _____   $28 \div 7 =$ _____

$7\overline{)14}$   $7\overline{)63}$

$7\overline{)7}$   $7\overline{)42}$

$7\overline{)0}$   $7\overline{)35}$

$7\overline{)49}$   $7\overline{)21}$

$7\overline{)56}$   $7\overline{)28}$

$7\overline{)63}$   $7\overline{)7}$

$7\overline{)35}$   $7\overline{)14}$

$7\overline{)21}$   $7\overline{)42}$

**Seven as a Divisor**

Score: _____

# Practice

■ Divide.

14 ÷ 7 = _____      28 ÷ 7 = _____

56 ÷ 7 = _____      63 ÷ 7 = _____

35 ÷ 7 = _____       7 ÷ 7 = _____

 0 ÷ 7 = _____      49 ÷ 7 = _____

42 ÷ 7 = _____      21 ÷ 7 = _____

28 ÷ 7 = _____      35 ÷ 7 = _____

63 ÷ 7 = _____      56 ÷ 7 = _____

 7 ÷ 7 = _____      14 ÷ 7 = _____

49 ÷ 7 = _____       0 ÷ 7 = _____

21 ÷ 7 = _____      42 ÷ 7 = _____

$7\overline{)21}$      $7\overline{)49}$

$7\overline{)14}$      $7\overline{)0}$

$7\overline{)56}$      $7\overline{)28}$

$7\overline{)63}$      $7\overline{)35}$

$7\overline{)42}$      $7\overline{)7}$

$7\overline{)49}$      $7\overline{)63}$

$7\overline{)56}$      $7\overline{)21}$

$7\overline{)14}$      $7\overline{)28}$

**FINISH**

Circle any problems that you still find difficult to remember. Make your own flash cards to help you master these problems.

Score: _____

Seven as a Divisor

# Timed Test

■ Improve your speed on these basic facts. Ask someone to time you. Record your time and score on each Timed Test page and on page 276.

**Seven as a Divisor**

$63 ÷ 7 =$ _____    $14 ÷ 7 =$ _____

$7 ÷ 7 =$ _____    $35 ÷ 7 =$ _____

$21 ÷ 7 =$ _____    $42 ÷ 7 =$ _____

$56 ÷ 7 =$ _____    $49 ÷ 7 =$ _____

$14 ÷ 7 =$ _____    $63 ÷ 7 =$ _____

$0 ÷ 7 =$ _____    $21 ÷ 7 =$ _____

$28 ÷ 7 =$ _____    $7 ÷ 7 =$ _____

$49 ÷ 7 =$ _____    $56 ÷ 7 =$ _____

$42 ÷ 7 =$ _____    $0 ÷ 7 =$ _____

$35 ÷ 7 =$ _____    $28 ÷ 7 =$ _____

$7\overline{)28}$    $7\overline{)7}$    $7\overline{)42}$

$7\overline{)21}$    $7\overline{)0}$    $7\overline{)35}$

$7\overline{)49}$    $7\overline{)42}$    $7\overline{)14}$

$7\overline{)56}$    $7\overline{)28}$    $7\overline{)21}$

$7\overline{)63}$    $7\overline{)14}$    $7\overline{)7}$

$7\overline{)42}$    $7\overline{)7}$    $7\overline{)0}$

$7\overline{)49}$    $7\overline{)35}$

Score: _____    Time: _____ minutes _____ seconds

Name _____

# Timed Test

■ Complete these facts as accurately and as quickly as you can.

35 ÷ 7 = _____     28 ÷ 7 = _____

$7\overline{)7}$      $7\overline{)42}$      $7\overline{)0}$

7 ÷ 7 = _____     49 ÷ 7 = _____

$7\overline{)49}$      $7\overline{)63}$      $7\overline{)35}$

56 ÷ 7 = _____     21 ÷ 7 = _____

42 ÷ 7 = _____     14 ÷ 7 = _____

$7\overline{)0}$      $7\overline{)14}$      $7\overline{)56}$

0 ÷ 7 = _____     7 ÷ 7 = _____

$7\overline{)21}$      $7\overline{)7}$      $7\overline{)63}$

63 ÷ 7 = _____     35 ÷ 7 = _____

21 ÷ 7 = _____     42 ÷ 7 = _____

$7\overline{)28}$      $7\overline{)56}$      $7\overline{)42}$

28 ÷ 7 = _____     63 ÷ 7 = _____

$7\overline{)14}$      $7\overline{)49}$      $7\overline{)21}$

49 ÷ 7 = _____     0 ÷ 7 = _____

$7\overline{)28}$      $7\overline{)35}$

14 ÷ 7 = _____     56 ÷ 7 = _____

Score: _____     Time: _____ minutes _____ seconds

**Seven as a Divisor**

# Timed Test

28 ÷ 7 = _____     49 ÷ 7 = _____

$7\overline{)7}$     $7\overline{)35}$     $7\overline{)28}$

7 ÷ 7 = _____     35 ÷ 7 = _____

42 ÷ 7 = _____     56 ÷ 7 = _____

$7\overline{)21}$     $7\overline{)56}$     $7\overline{)49}$

21 ÷ 7 = _____     0 ÷ 7 = _____

$7\overline{)42}$     $7\overline{)63}$     $7\overline{)14}$

14 ÷ 7 = _____     63 ÷ 7 = _____

$7\overline{)28}$     $7\overline{)49}$     $7\overline{)21}$

35 ÷ 7 = _____     28 ÷ 7 = _____

0 ÷ 7 = _____     42 ÷ 7 = _____

$7\overline{)0}$     $7\overline{)7}$     $7\overline{)35}$

49 ÷ 7 = _____     7 ÷ 7 = _____

$7\overline{)56}$     $7\overline{)49}$     $7\overline{)14}$

63 ÷ 7 = _____     14 ÷ 7 = _____

$7\overline{)63}$     $7\overline{)0}$

21 ÷ 7 = _____     56 ÷ 7 = _____

Score: _____     Time: _____ minutes _____ seconds

# Timed Test

14 ÷ 7 = _____     42 ÷ 7 = _____

7)35     7)63     7)21

49 ÷ 7 = _____     63 ÷ 7 = _____

7)14     7)42     7)56

21 ÷ 7 = _____     35 ÷ 7 = _____

7 ÷ 7 = _____     0 ÷ 7 = _____

7)0     7)35     7)7

56 ÷ 7 = _____     14 ÷ 7 = _____

7)49     7)28     7)35

28 ÷ 7 = _____     35 ÷ 7 = _____

42 ÷ 7 = _____     49 ÷ 7 = _____

7)21     7)63     7)14

0 ÷ 7 = _____     56 ÷ 7 = _____

7)42     7)56     7)0

63 ÷ 7 = _____     28 ÷ 7 = _____

7)49     7)7

21 ÷ 7 = _____     7 ÷ 7 = _____

Score: _____     Time: _____ minutes _____ seconds

## Timed Test

49 ÷ 7 = _____    42 ÷ 7 = _____

7)14    7)0    7)28

7 ÷ 7 = _____    28 ÷ 7 = _____

7)7    7)56    7)42

63 ÷ 7 = _____    0 ÷ 7 = _____

14 ÷ 7 = _____    56 ÷ 7 = _____

7)63    7)21    7)49

35 ÷ 7 = _____    21 ÷ 7 = _____

7)0    7)28    7)63

28 ÷ 7 = _____    7 ÷ 7 = _____

21 ÷ 7 = _____    35 ÷ 7 = _____

7)35    7)42    7)14

49 ÷ 7 = _____    14 ÷ 7 = _____

7)56    7)63    7)7

42 ÷ 7 = _____    63 ÷ 7 = _____

7)21    7)35

56 ÷ 7 = _____    0 ÷ 7 = _____

Record your scores and times below.

**Page 270** Score: _____          **Page 274** Score: _____ Time: ___min. ___sec.

**Page 271** Score: _____          **Page 275** Score: _____ Time: ___min. ___sec.

**Page 272** Score: _____ Time: ___min. ___sec.  **Page 276** Score: _____ Time: ___min. ___sec.

**Page 273** Score: _____ Time: ___min. ___sec.

Seven as a Divisor

# Dividends Through Seventy-Two

Now, think about what happens when a number is divided by 8.

**Example:** 48 ÷ 8 = 6

The dividend is 48. If you put 8 objects in each group, you will have 6 equal groups.

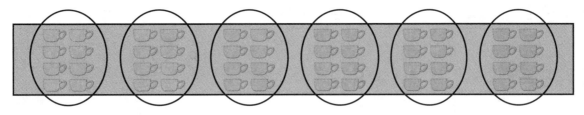

**Remember:** Division and multiplication are inverse operations.

**Example:** 8 x 6 = 48
    48 ÷ 8 = 6

Apply what you have learned to the division facts of 8.

**Examples:** 0 ÷ 8 = 0      8 ÷ 1 = 8      8 ÷ 8 = 1

■ Write a division fact related to each of these multiplication facts of 8.

**Eight as a Divisor**

8 x 1 = 8          8 x 2 = 16          8 x 3 = 24

____ ÷ ____ = ____      ____ ÷ ____ = ____      ____ ÷ ____ = ____

8 x 4 = 32          8 x 5 = 40          8 x 6 = 48

____ ÷ ____ = ____      ____ ÷ ____ = ____      ____ ÷ ____ = ____

8 x 7 = 56          8 x 8 = 64          8 x 9 = 72

____ ÷ ____ = ____      ____ ÷ ____ = ____      ____ ÷ ____ = ____

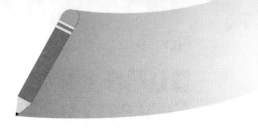

## Name _____

# Practice

■ Divide. Record your score—the number correct—on each Practice page and again on page 284.

page and again on page 284.

$32 \div 8 =$ _____        $56 \div 8 =$ _____

$0 \div 8 =$ _____         $8 \div 8 =$ _____

$64 \div 8 =$ _____        $40 \div 8 =$ _____

$24 \div 8 =$ _____        $16 \div 8 =$ _____

$72 \div 8 =$ _____        $48 \div 8 =$ _____

$56 \div 8 =$ _____        $24 \div 8 =$ _____

$8 \div 8 =$ _____         $64 \div 8 =$ _____

$40 \div 8 =$ _____        $0 \div 8 =$ _____

$16 \div 8 =$ _____        $32 \div 8 =$ _____

$48 \div 8 =$ _____        $72 \div 8 =$ _____

$8\overline{)24}$     $8\overline{)72}$

$8\overline{)32}$     $8\overline{)64}$

$8\overline{)8}$      $8\overline{)56}$

$8\overline{)48}$     $8\overline{)16}$

$8\overline{)0}$      $8\overline{)40}$

$8\overline{)72}$     $8\overline{)32}$

$8\overline{)64}$     $8\overline{)24}$

$8\overline{)56}$     $8\overline{)48}$

Score: _____

**Eight as a Divisor**

# Practice

■ Divide.

0 ÷ 8 = _____        40 ÷ 8 = _____

56 ÷ 8 = _____        72 ÷ 8 = _____

24 ÷ 8 = _____        48 ÷ 8 = _____

64 ÷ 8 = _____        32 ÷ 8 = _____

16 ÷ 8 = _____        8 ÷ 8 = _____

40 ÷ 8 = _____        0 ÷ 8 = _____

72 ÷ 8 = _____        56 ÷ 8 = _____

48 ÷ 8 = _____        24 ÷ 8 = _____

32 ÷ 8 = _____        64 ÷ 8 = _____

8 ÷ 8 = _____        16 ÷ 8 = _____

8 ) 48        8 ) 8

8 ) 56        8 ) 0

8 ) 64        8 ) 16

8 ) 72        8 ) 32

8 ) 40        8 ) 24

8 ) 56        8 ) 48

8 ) 16        8 ) 72

8 ) 32        8 ) 64

Circle any problems that you still find difficult to remember. Make your own flash cards to help you master these problems.

**FINISH**

Score: _____

Eight as a Divisor

# Timed Test

■ Improve your speed on these basic facts. Ask someone to time you. Record your time and score on each Timed Test page and on page 284.

$16 \div 8 =$ _____    $56 \div 8 =$ _____

$8\overline{)24}$    $8\overline{)48}$    $8\overline{)40}$

$72 \div 8 =$ _____    $40 \div 8 =$ _____

$8\overline{)72}$    $8\overline{)16}$    $8\overline{)64}$

$24 \div 8 =$ _____    $8 \div 8 =$ _____

$8\overline{)8}$    $8\overline{)0}$    $8\overline{)56}$

$64 \div 8 =$ _____    $32 \div 8 =$ _____

$0 \div 8 =$ _____    $48 \div 8 =$ _____

$8\overline{)40}$    $8\overline{)24}$    $8\overline{)32}$

$40 \div 8 =$ _____    $16 \div 8 =$ _____

$8\overline{)64}$    $8\overline{)72}$    $8\overline{)8}$

$48 \div 8 =$ _____    $64 \div 8 =$ _____

$32 \div 8 =$ _____    $24 \div 8 =$ _____

$8\overline{)16}$    $8\overline{)48}$    $8\overline{)32}$

$8 \div 8 =$ _____    $72 \div 8 =$ _____

$8\overline{)56}$    $8\overline{)64}$

$56 \div 8 =$ _____    $0 \div 8 =$ _____

Score: _____    Time: _____ minutes _____ seconds

# Timed Test

■ Complete these facts as accurately and as quickly as you can.

56 ÷ 8 = _____    72 ÷ 8 = _____

32 ÷ 8 = _____    24 ÷ 8 = _____

16 ÷ 8 = _____    0 ÷ 8 = _____

40 ÷ 8 = _____    48 ÷ 8 = _____

64 ÷ 8 = _____    32 ÷ 8 = _____

72 ÷ 8 = _____    8 ÷ 8 = _____

8 ÷ 8 = _____    40 ÷ 8 = _____

24 ÷ 8 = _____    16 ÷ 8 = _____

0 ÷ 8 = _____    56 ÷ 8 = _____

48 ÷ 8 = _____    64 ÷ 8 = _____

$8\overline{)40}$    $8\overline{)8}$    $8\overline{)56}$

$8\overline{)32}$    $8\overline{)72}$    $8\overline{)0}$

$8\overline{)48}$    $8\overline{)64}$    $8\overline{)24}$

$8\overline{)16}$    $8\overline{)32}$    $8\overline{)40}$

$8\overline{)24}$    $8\overline{)72}$    $8\overline{)48}$

$8\overline{)8}$    $8\overline{)32}$    $8\overline{)0}$

$8\overline{)64}$    $8\overline{)56}$

**Eight as a Divisor**

Score: _____    Time: _____ minutes _____ seconds

# Timed Test

32 ÷ 8 = _____     56 ÷ 8 = _____

72 ÷ 8 = _____     16 ÷ 8 = _____

8 ÷ 8 = _____     48 ÷ 8 = _____

0 ÷ 8 = _____     40 ÷ 8 = _____

64 ÷ 8 = _____     24 ÷ 8 = _____

40 ÷ 8 = _____     8 ÷ 8 = _____

56 ÷ 8 = _____     0 ÷ 8 = _____

24 ÷ 8 = _____     64 ÷ 8 = _____

16 ÷ 8 = _____     32 ÷ 8 = _____

8 ÷ 8 = _____     48 ÷ 8 = _____

$8\overline{)8}$     $8\overline{)32}$     $8\overline{)64}$

$8\overline{)16}$     $8\overline{)0}$     $8\overline{)56}$

$8\overline{)40}$     $8\overline{)24}$     $8\overline{)72}$

$8\overline{)48}$     $8\overline{)16}$     $8\overline{)8}$

$8\overline{)24}$     $8\overline{)32}$     $8\overline{)0}$

$8\overline{)64}$     $8\overline{)56}$     $8\overline{)72}$

$8\overline{)40}$     $8\overline{)48}$

Score: _____     Time: _____ minutes _____ seconds

Name _____

# Timed Test

$16 \div 8 =$ _____    $24 \div 8 =$ _____

$8\overline{)40}$    $8\overline{)56}$    $8\overline{)8}$

$40 \div 8 =$ _____    $32 \div 8 =$ _____

$8\overline{)72}$    $8\overline{)48}$    $8\overline{)16}$

$72 \div 8 =$ _____    $0 \div 8 =$ _____

$56 \div 8 =$ _____    $64 \div 8 =$ _____

$8\overline{)32}$    $8\overline{)0}$    $8\overline{)24}$

$48 \div 8 =$ _____    $24 \div 8 =$ _____

$8\overline{)56}$    $8\overline{)16}$    $8\overline{)64}$

$8 \div 8 =$ _____    $40 \div 8 =$ _____

$8\overline{)8}$    $8\overline{)72}$    $8\overline{)40}$

$64 \div 8 =$ _____    $72 \div 8 =$ _____

$32 \div 8 =$ _____    $0 \div 8 =$ _____

$8\overline{)32}$    $8\overline{)56}$    $8\overline{)24}$

$16 \div 8 =$ _____    $8 \div 8 =$ _____

$8\overline{)64}$    $8\overline{)8}$

$56 \div 8 =$ _____    $48 \div 8 =$ _____

**Eight as a Divisor**

Score: _____    Time: _____ minutes _____ seconds

# Timed Test

**Eight as a Divisor**

8 ÷ 8 = _____    32 ÷ 8 = _____

64 ÷ 8 = _____    0 ÷ 8 = _____

48 ÷ 8 = _____    24 ÷ 8 = _____

72 ÷ 8 = _____    56 ÷ 8 = _____

16 ÷ 8 = _____    72 ÷ 8 = _____

40 ÷ 8 = _____    48 ÷ 8 = _____

56 ÷ 8 = _____    64 ÷ 8 = _____

0 ÷ 8 = _____    8 ÷ 8 = _____

32 ÷ 8 = _____    40 ÷ 8 = _____

72 ÷ 8 = _____    16 ÷ 8 = _____

$8\overline{)48}$    $8\overline{)8}$    $8\overline{)64}$

$8\overline{)16}$    $8\overline{)0}$    $8\overline{)56}$

$8\overline{)24}$    $8\overline{)40}$    $8\overline{)48}$

$8\overline{)56}$    $8\overline{)32}$    $8\overline{)72}$

$8\overline{)64}$    $8\overline{)0}$    $8\overline{)16}$

$8\overline{)8}$    $8\overline{)24}$    $8\overline{)32}$

$8\overline{)40}$    $8\overline{)72}$

---

Record your scores and times below.

**Page 278** Score: _____

**Page 279** Score: _____

**Page 280** Score: _____ Time: ___min. ___sec.

**Page 281** Score: _____ Time: ___min. ___sec.

**Page 282** Score: _____ Time: ___min. ___sec.

**Page 283** Score: _____ Time: ___min. ___sec.

**Page 284** Score: _____ Time: ___min. ___sec.

# Dividends Through Eighty-One

Now, think about what happens when a number is divided by 9.

**Example:** 72 ÷ 9 = 8

The dividend is 72. If you put 9 objects in each group, you have 8 equal groups.

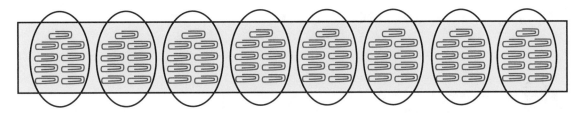

**Remember:** Division and multiplication are inverse operations.

**Example:** 9 x 8 = 72
72 ÷ 9 = 8

Apply what you have learned to the division facts of 9.

**Examples:** 0 ÷ 9 = 0        9 ÷ 1 = 9        9 ÷ 9 = 1

■ Write a division fact related to each multiplication fact of 9.

| 9 x 1 = 9 | 9 x 2 = 18 | 9 x 3 = 27 |
|---|---|---|
| ___ ÷ ___ = ___ | ___ ÷ ___ = ___ | ___ ÷ ___ = ___ |
| 9 x 4 = 36 | 9 x 5 = 45 | 9 x 6 = 54 |
| ___ ÷ ___ = ___ | ___ ÷ ___ = ___ | ___ ÷ ___ = ___ |
| 9 x 7 = 63 | 9 x 8 = 72 | 9 x 9 = 81 |
| ___ ÷ ___ = ___ | ___ ÷ ___ = ___ | ___ ÷ ___ = ___ |

**Nine as a Divisor**

# Practice

■ Divide. Record your score—the number correct—on each Practice page and again on page 292.

$9 \div 9 =$ _____    $81 \div 9 =$ _____

$9\overline{)0}$    $9\overline{)45}$

$36 \div 9 =$ _____    $45 \div 9 =$ _____

$9\overline{)9}$    $9\overline{)81}$

$54 \div 9 =$ _____    $18 \div 9 =$ _____

$9\overline{)18}$    $9\overline{)72}$

$0 \div 9 =$ _____    $72 \div 9 =$ _____

$63 \div 9 =$ _____    $36 \div 9 =$ _____

$9\overline{)36}$    $9\overline{)54}$

$81 \div 9 =$ _____    $9 \div 9 =$ _____

$9\overline{)27}$    $9\overline{)63}$

$45 \div 9 =$ _____    $27 \div 9 =$ _____

$9\overline{)45}$    $9\overline{)0}$

$18 \div 9 =$ _____    $54 \div 9 =$ _____

$9\overline{)36}$    $9\overline{)81}$

$72 \div 9 =$ _____    $0 \div 9 =$ _____

$27 \div 9 =$ _____    $63 \div 9 =$ _____

$9\overline{)72}$    $9\overline{)18}$

**Nine as a Divisor**

Score: _____

## Practice

■ Divide.

27 ÷ 9 = _____       54 ÷ 9 = _____

72 ÷ 9 = _____       45 ÷ 9 = _____

81 ÷ 9 = _____       63 ÷ 9 = _____

36 ÷ 9 = _____       18 ÷ 9 = _____

54 ÷ 9 = _____        0 ÷ 9 = _____

 9 ÷ 9 = _____       27 ÷ 9 = _____

45 ÷ 9 = _____       72 ÷ 9 = _____

63 ÷ 9 = _____       81 ÷ 9 = _____

18 ÷ 9 = _____       36 ÷ 9 = _____

 0 ÷ 9 = _____        9 ÷ 9 = _____

9)81        9)27

9)0         9)63

9)18        9)72

9)9         9)45

9)36        9)54

9)45        9)9

9)63        9)81

9)27        9)0

Circle any problems that you still find difficult to remember. Make your own flash cards to help you master these problems.

**FINISH**

Score: _____

# Timed Test

■ Improve your speed on these basic facts. Ask someone to time you. Record your time and score on each Timed Test page and on page 292.

$18 \div 9 =$ _____    $36 \div 9 =$ _____

$9\overline{)27}$    $9\overline{)72}$    $9\overline{)54}$

$81 \div 9 =$ _____    $45 \div 9 =$ _____

$9\overline{)36}$    $9\overline{)18}$    $9\overline{)45}$

$63 \div 9 =$ _____    $72 \div 9 =$ _____

$27 \div 9 =$ _____    $0 \div 9 =$ _____

$9\overline{)63}$    $9\overline{)81}$    $9\overline{)27}$

$9 \div 9 =$ _____    $36 \div 9 =$ _____

$9\overline{)54}$    $9\overline{)0}$    $9\overline{)9}$

$72 \div 9 =$ _____    $18 \div 9 =$ _____

$0 \div 9 =$ _____    $54 \div 9 =$ _____

$9\overline{)45}$    $9\overline{)63}$    $9\overline{)81}$

$36 \div 9 =$ _____    $81 \div 9 =$ _____

$9\overline{)9}$    $9\overline{)18}$    $9\overline{)72}$

$45 \div 9 =$ _____    $9 \div 9 =$ _____

$9\overline{)0}$    $9\overline{)36}$

$54 \div 9 =$ _____    $27 \div 9 =$ _____

Score: _____    Time: _____ minutes _____ seconds

## Name _____

# Timed Test

■ Complete these facts as accurately and as quickly as you can.

$45 \div 9 =$ _____    $9 \div 9 =$ _____

$18 \div 9 =$ _____    $81 \div 9 =$ _____

$0 \div 9 =$ _____    $36 \div 9 =$ _____

$54 \div 9 =$ _____    $27 \div 9 =$ _____

$9 \div 9 =$ _____    $63 \div 9 =$ _____

$72 \div 9 =$ _____    $18 \div 9 =$ _____

$0 \div 9 =$ _____    $45 \div 9 =$ _____

$81 \div 9 =$ _____    $54 \div 9 =$ _____

$63 \div 9 =$ _____    $72 \div 9 =$ _____

$27 \div 9 =$ _____    $36 \div 9 =$ _____

$9\overline{)81}$    $9\overline{)36}$    $9\overline{)9}$

$9\overline{)18}$    $9\overline{)72}$    $9\overline{)45}$

$9\overline{)27}$    $9\overline{)81}$    $9\overline{)63}$

$9\overline{)9}$    $9\overline{)0}$    $9\overline{)18}$

$9\overline{)54}$    $9\overline{)72}$    $9\overline{)36}$

$9\overline{)45}$    $9\overline{)63}$    $9\overline{)27}$

$9\overline{)0}$    $9\overline{)18}$

**Nine as a Divisor**

Score: _____    Time: _____ minutes _____ seconds

# Timed Test

$27 \div 9 =$ _____     $9 \div 9 =$ _____

$81 \div 9 =$ _____     $72 \div 9 =$ _____

$0 \div 9 =$ _____     $18 \div 9 =$ _____

$45 \div 9 =$ _____     $36 \div 9 =$ _____

$54 \div 9 =$ _____     $63 \div 9 =$ _____

$72 \div 9 =$ _____     $27 \div 9 =$ _____

$36 \div 9 =$ _____     $45 \div 9 =$ _____

$63 \div 9 =$ _____     $81 \div 9 =$ _____

$9 \div 9 =$ _____     $27 \div 9 =$ _____

$54 \div 9 =$ _____     $0 \div 9 =$ _____

$9\overline{)54}$     $9\overline{)72}$     $9\overline{)36}$

$9\overline{)81}$     $9\overline{)45}$     $9\overline{)18}$

$9\overline{)0}$     $9\overline{)27}$     $9\overline{)63}$

$9\overline{)36}$     $9\overline{)18}$     $9\overline{)72}$

$9\overline{)9}$     $9\overline{)45}$     $9\overline{)18}$

$9\overline{)54}$     $9\overline{)27}$     $9\overline{)9}$

$9\overline{)63}$     $9\overline{)81}$

Score: _____     Time: _____ minutes _____ seconds

# Timed Test

18 ÷ 9 = _____    36 ÷ 9 = _____

$9\overline{)63}$    $9\overline{)81}$    $9\overline{)9}$

54 ÷ 9 = _____    63 ÷ 9 = _____

$9\overline{)45}$    $9\overline{)18}$    $9\overline{)54}$

72 ÷ 9 = _____     0 ÷ 9 = _____

45 ÷ 9 = _____    81 ÷ 9 = _____

$9\overline{)9}$    $9\overline{)72}$    $9\overline{)27}$

 9 ÷ 9 = _____    27 ÷ 9 = _____

$9\overline{)54}$    $9\overline{)0}$    $9\overline{)81}$

18 ÷ 9 = _____    63 ÷ 9 = _____

81 ÷ 9 = _____     9 ÷ 9 = _____

$9\overline{)36}$    $9\overline{)63}$    $9\overline{)45}$

27 ÷ 9 = _____    54 ÷ 9 = _____

$9\overline{)9}$    $9\overline{)18}$    $9\overline{)54}$

72 ÷ 9 = _____    45 ÷ 9 = _____

$9\overline{)72}$    $9\overline{)27}$

36 ÷ 9 = _____     0 ÷ 9 = _____

Score: _____    Time: _____ minutes _____ seconds

# Timed Test

**Nine as a Divisor**

$18 \div 9 =$ _____   $45 \div 9 =$ _____

$9\overline{)72}$   $9\overline{)63}$   $9\overline{)81}$

$63 \div 9 =$ _____   $27 \div 9 =$ _____

$81 \div 9 =$ _____   $36 \div 9 =$ _____

$9\overline{)18}$   $9\overline{)27}$   $9\overline{)45}$

$9 \div 9 =$ _____   $0 \div 9 =$ _____

$9\overline{)0}$   $9\overline{)36}$   $9\overline{)72}$

$54 \div 9 =$ _____   $72 \div 9 =$ _____

$9\overline{)45}$   $9\overline{)9}$   $9\overline{)63}$

$0 \div 9 =$ _____   $9 \div 9 =$ _____

$45 \div 9 =$ _____   $63 \div 9 =$ _____

$9\overline{)54}$   $9\overline{)81}$   $9\overline{)18}$

$72 \div 9 =$ _____   $18 \div 9 =$ _____

$9\overline{)27}$   $9\overline{)36}$   $9\overline{)45}$

$81 \div 9 =$ _____   $36 \div 9 =$ _____

$9\overline{)9}$   $9\overline{)0}$

$27 \div 9 =$ _____   $45 \div 9 =$ _____

Record your scores and times below.

| | |
|---|---|
| **Page 286** Score: _____ | **Page 290** Score: _____ Time: ___min. ___sec. |
| **Page 287** Score: _____ | **Page 291** Score: _____ Time: ___min. ___sec. |
| **Page 288** Score: _____ Time: ___min. ___sec. | **Page 292** Score: _____ Time: ___min. ___sec. |
| **Page 289** Score: _____ Time: ___min. ___sec. | |

# Practice

■ Divide. Record your score—the number correct—at the end of each Review and on page 302.

64 ÷ 8 = _____    25 ÷ 5 = _____    10 ÷ 2 = _____    81 ÷ 9 = _____

4 ÷ 2 = _____    9 ÷ 9 = _____    8 ÷ 8 = _____    36 ÷ 6 = _____

5 ÷ 5 = _____    0 ÷ 1 = _____    6 ÷ 1 = _____    18 ÷ 2 = _____

4 ÷ 1 = _____    24 ÷ 6 = _____    18 ÷ 6 = _____    24 ÷ 3 = _____

0 ÷ 3 = _____    20 ÷ 4 = _____    30 ÷ 5 = _____    16 ÷ 2 = _____

54 ÷ 9 = _____    42 ÷ 6 = _____    0 ÷ 8 = _____    6 ÷ 6 = _____

21 ÷ 3 = _____    9 ÷ 3 = _____    4 ÷ 4 = _____    63 ÷ 9 = _____

28 ÷ 7 = _____    12 ÷ 2 = _____    32 ÷ 8 = _____    36 ÷ 4 = _____

9 ÷ 1 = _____    3 ÷ 1 = _____    42 ÷ 7 = _____    7 ÷ 7 = _____

45 ÷ 5 = _____    12 ÷ 3 = _____    28 ÷ 4 = _____    12 ÷ 4 = _____

Continue this Practice on the next page.

All-Division Review

# Practice

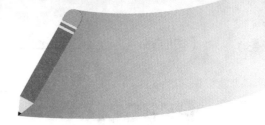

0 ÷ 5 = ____     5 ÷ 1 = ____     7 ÷ 1 = ____     12 ÷ 6 = ____

8 ÷ 1 = ____     56 ÷ 7 = ____     2 ÷ 2 = ____     0 ÷ 7 = ____

45 ÷ 9 = ____     3 ÷ 3 = ____     0 ÷ 6 = ____     24 ÷ 4 = ____

48 ÷ 6 = ____     8 ÷ 4 = ____     14 ÷ 2 = ____     49 ÷ 7 = ____

2 ÷ 1 = ____     15 ÷ 3 = ____     36 ÷ 9 = ____     20 ÷ 5 = ____

6 ÷ 2 = ____     10 ÷ 5 = ____     63 ÷ 7 = ____     40 ÷ 8 = ____

40 ÷ 5 = ____     6 ÷ 3 = ____     54 ÷ 6 = ____     21 ÷ 7 = ____

18 ÷ 3 = ____     0 ÷ 2 = ____     27 ÷ 3 = ____     0 ÷ 4 = ____

0 ÷ 9 = ____     16 ÷ 4 = ____     24 ÷ 8 = ____     56 ÷ 8 = ____

8 ÷ 2 = ____     18 ÷ 9 = ____     35 ÷ 5 = ____     32 ÷ 4 = ____

Score: _____

# Practice

■ Divide.

$8\overline{)56}$    $1\overline{)9}$    $6\overline{)48}$    $6\overline{)0}$    $5\overline{)30}$    $4\overline{)28}$

$3\overline{)6}$    $1\overline{)7}$    $7\overline{)21}$    $8\overline{)0}$    $2\overline{)6}$    $7\overline{)42}$

$4\overline{)8}$    $6\overline{)54}$    $2\overline{)2}$    $3\overline{)18}$    $5\overline{)35}$    $5\overline{)0}$

$9\overline{)18}$    $4\overline{)20}$    $1\overline{)2}$    $8\overline{)32}$    $6\overline{)24}$    $2\overline{)12}$

$3\overline{)24}$    $5\overline{)15}$    $3\overline{)0}$    $9\overline{)63}$    $6\overline{)36}$    $3\overline{)27}$

$7\overline{)35}$    $4\overline{)12}$    $9\overline{)54}$    $1\overline{)0}$    $8\overline{)8}$    $8\overline{)48}$

$7\overline{)7}$    $2\overline{)8}$    $6\overline{)30}$    $9\overline{)27}$    $1\overline{)4}$    $9\overline{)45}$

 FINISH

Circle any problems that you still find difficult to remember. Make your own flash cards to help you master these problems.

Continue this Practice on the next page.

# Practice

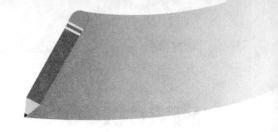

| | | | | | |
|---|---|---|---|---|---|
| 4⟌32 | 4⟌4 | 1⟌3 | 3⟌21 | 8⟌40 | 6⟌12 |
| 2⟌18 | 7⟌49 | 5⟌40 | 4⟌16 | 1⟌1 | 3⟌15 |
| 9⟌9 | 7⟌63 | 5⟌25 | 4⟌0 | 4⟌24 | 9⟌0 |
| 2⟌10 | 9⟌81 | 8⟌24 | 7⟌0 | 9⟌72 | 6⟌6 |
| 6⟌42 | 1⟌8 | 4⟌36 | 7⟌28 | 2⟌0 | 5⟌5 |
| 3⟌3 | 8⟌16 | 1⟌5 | 5⟌45 | 7⟌14 | 6⟌18 |
| 1⟌6 | 7⟌56 | 2⟌14 | 9⟌36 | 5⟌10 | 2⟌4 |

Score: _____

Name _____

# Timed Test

■ Increase your speed on the basic facts of division. Record your time
  and score at the end of each Timed Test and on page 302.

$0 \div 8 =$ _____   $4 \div 4 =$ _____   $0 \div 3 =$ _____   $7 \div 7 =$ _____

$21 \div 7 =$ _____   $3 \div 1 =$ _____   $32 \div 4 =$ _____   $27 \div 9 =$ _____

$18 \div 2 =$ _____   $30 \div 5 =$ _____   $63 \div 9 =$ _____   $2 \div 2 =$ _____

$35 \div 5 =$ _____   $63 \div 7 =$ _____   $72 \div 9 =$ _____   $36 \div 9 =$ _____

$5 \div 1 =$ _____   $24 \div 3 =$ _____   $0 \div 5 =$ _____   $64 \div 8 =$ _____

$24 \div 4 =$ _____   $8 \div 8 =$ _____   $3 \div 3 =$ _____   $28 \div 7 =$ _____

$9 \div 3 =$ _____   $6 \div 6 =$ _____   $45 \div 9 =$ _____   $48 \div 6 =$ _____

$54 \div 6 =$ _____   $56 \div 8 =$ _____   $12 \div 6 =$ _____   $8 \div 4 =$ _____

$10 \div 2 =$ _____   $36 \div 6 =$ _____   $0 \div 1 =$ _____   $2 \div 1 =$ _____

$14 \div 7 =$ _____   $28 \div 4 =$ _____   $27 \div 3 =$ _____   $12 \div 3 =$ _____

Continue this Timed Test on the next page.

**All-Division Review**

Name _____

# Timed Test

$30 \div 6 =$ _____     $42 \div 7 =$ _____     $24 \div 8 =$ _____     $1 \div 1 =$ _____

$6 \div 1 =$ _____     $18 \div 3 =$ _____     $7 \div 1 =$ _____     $48 \div 8 =$ _____

$3 \div 1 =$ _____     $4 \div 1 =$ _____     $4 \div 2 =$ _____     $15 \div 3 =$ _____

$20 \div 4 =$ _____     $16 \div 4 =$ _____     $45 \div 5 =$ _____     $16 \div 8 =$ _____

$0 \div 7 =$ _____     $25 \div 5 =$ _____     $18 \div 9 =$ _____     $8 \div 2 =$ _____

$49 \div 7 =$ _____     $0 \div 9 =$ _____     $20 \div 5 =$ _____     $5 \div 5 =$ _____

$24 \div 6 =$ _____     $32 \div 8 =$ _____     $6 \div 3 =$ _____     $0 \div 6 =$ _____

$16 \div 2 =$ _____     $18 \div 9 =$ _____     $54 \div 9 =$ _____     $40 \div 5 =$ _____

$40 \div 8 =$ _____     $9 \div 1 =$ _____     $72 \div 8 =$ _____     $14 \div 2 =$ _____

$9 \div 9 =$ _____     $56 \div 7 =$ _____     $35 \div 7 =$ _____     $36 \div 4 =$ _____

**All-Division Review**

Score: _____          Time: _____ minutes _____ seconds

# Timed Test

$5\overline{)5}$     $2\overline{)10}$     $6\overline{)12}$     $4\overline{)20}$     $1\overline{)1}$     $3\overline{)27}$

$9\overline{)81}$     $5\overline{)40}$     $4\overline{)20}$     $2\overline{)2}$     $7\overline{)42}$     $6\overline{)6}$

$8\overline{)48}$     $1\overline{)3}$     $3\overline{)3}$     $5\overline{)10}$     $4\overline{)16}$     $7\overline{)56}$

$7\overline{)0}$     $1\overline{)7}$     $3\overline{)9}$     $9\overline{)36}$     $4\overline{)28}$     $1\overline{)2}$

$1\overline{)8}$     $4\overline{)0}$     $8\overline{)64}$     $7\overline{)7}$     $5\overline{)45}$     $9\overline{)63}$

$2\overline{)18}$     $9\overline{)45}$     $8\overline{)56}$     $5\overline{)20}$     $7\overline{)63}$     $6\overline{)54}$

$2\overline{)0}$     $3\overline{)6}$     $5\overline{)15}$     $9\overline{)54}$     $6\overline{)42}$     $4\overline{)36}$

Continue this Timed Test on the next page.

**All-Division Review**

# Timed Test

| | | | | | |
|---|---|---|---|---|---|
| 1)0 | 3)18 | 7)35 | 9)0 | 8)24 | 2)8 |
| 8)32 | 5)35 | 6)36 | 1)6 | 4)36 | 9)27 |
| 2)16 | 4)8 | 7)21 | 9)18 | 5)30 | 6)42 |
| 2)12 | 9)72 | 6)0 | 3)21 | 1)4 | 9)9 |
| 8)16 | 5)0 | 6)24 | 7)28 | 9)1 | 6)30 |
| 8)8 | 3)15 | 2)14 | 3)24 | 5)25 | 7)14 |
| 1)5 | 4)4 | 4)32 | 8)40 | 2)2 | 8)40 |

**All-Division Review**

Score: _____     Time: _____ minutes _____ seconds

# Timed Test

| | | | | | |
|---|---|---|---|---|---|
| 1⟌1 | 6⟌48 | 5⟌45 | 4⟌20 | 6⟌6 | 3⟌0 |
| 7⟌49 | 5⟌35 | 3⟌24 | 9⟌0 | 4⟌28 | 8⟌40 |
| 2⟌0 | 1⟌4 | 9⟌72 | 6⟌18 | 1⟌5 | 7⟌35 |
| 3⟌18 | 5⟌5 | 9⟌45 | 5⟌25 | 2⟌6 | 8⟌56 |
| 3⟌27 | 7⟌0 | 1⟌6 | 8⟌48 | 6⟌54 | 8⟌0 |
| 3⟌21 | 4⟌36 | 6⟌12 | 2⟌8 | 5⟌30 | 8⟌8 |
| 9⟌63 | 4⟌0 | 7⟌42 | 4⟌32 | 2⟌6 | 7⟌28 |

Continue this Timed Test on the next page.

## Timed Test

$9\overline{)27}$  $5\overline{)10}$  $9\overline{)18}$  $7\overline{)14}$  $6\overline{)42}$  $5\overline{)40}$

$2\overline{)14}$  $4\overline{)16}$  $7\overline{)56}$  $1\overline{)2}$  $7\overline{)21}$  $4\overline{)8}$

$6\overline{)36}$  $1\overline{)8}$  $3\overline{)9}$  $6\overline{)30}$  $7\overline{)28}$  $5\overline{)20}$

$2\overline{)18}$  $7\overline{)63}$  $8\overline{)16}$  $9\overline{)36}$  $1\overline{)9}$  $6\overline{)0}$

$8\overline{)64}$  $1\overline{)3}$  $4\overline{)12}$  $7\overline{)7}$  $2\overline{)12}$  $3\overline{)12}$

$4\overline{)24}$  $1\overline{)7}$  $2\overline{)2}$  $8\overline{)48}$  $5\overline{)15}$  $6\overline{)24}$

$2\overline{)16}$  $3\overline{)6}$  $8\overline{)72}$  $9\overline{)9}$  $4\overline{)20}$  $7\overline{)35}$

**All-Division Review**

Record your scores and times below.

**Page 293-294** Score:_____

**Page 295-296** Score:_____

**Page 297-298** Score:_____ Time:___min. ___sec.

**Page 299-300** Score:_____ Time:___min. ___sec.

**Page 301-302** Score:_____ Time:___min. ___sec.

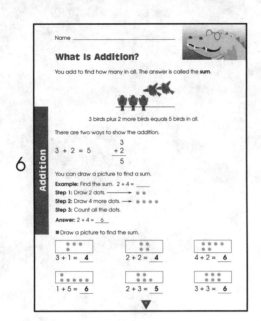

**What Is Addition?**

You add to find how many in all. The answer is called the **sum**.

3 birds plus 2 more birds equals 5 birds in all.

There are two ways to show the addition.

$3 + 2 = 5$     $\begin{array}{r} 3 \\ +2 \\ \hline 5 \end{array}$

You can draw a picture to find a sum.

**Example:** Find the sum. $2 + 4 =$ ____
**Step 1:** Draw 2 dots.
**Step 2:** Draw 4 more dots.
**Step 3:** Count all the dots.
**Answer:** $2 + 4 = \underline{6}$

■ Draw a picture to find the sum.

$3 + 1 = \underline{4}$    $2 + 2 = \underline{4}$    $4 + 2 = \underline{6}$

$1 + 5 = \underline{6}$    $2 + 3 = \underline{5}$    $3 + 3 = \underline{6}$

Addition — 6

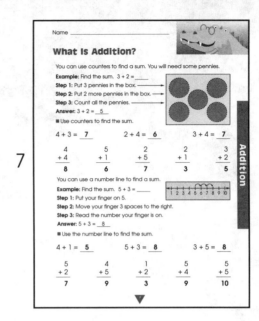

**What Is Addition?**

You can use counters to find a sum. You will need some pennies.

**Example:** Find the sum. $3 + 2 =$ ____
**Step 1:** Put 3 pennies in the box.
**Step 2:** Put 2 more pennies in the box.
**Step 3:** Count all the pennies.
**Answer:** $3 + 2 = \underline{5}$

■ Use counters to find the sum.

$4 + 3 = \underline{7}$    $2 + 4 = \underline{6}$    $3 + 4 = \underline{7}$

$\begin{array}{r} 4 \\ +4 \\ \hline 8 \end{array}$   $\begin{array}{r} 5 \\ +1 \\ \hline 6 \end{array}$   $\begin{array}{r} 2 \\ +5 \\ \hline 7 \end{array}$   $\begin{array}{r} 2 \\ +1 \\ \hline 3 \end{array}$   $\begin{array}{r} 3 \\ +2 \\ \hline 5 \end{array}$

You can use a number line to find a sum.

**Example:** Find the sum. $5 + 3 =$ ____
**Step 1:** Put your finger on 5.
**Step 2:** Move your finger 3 spaces to the right.
**Step 3:** Read the number your finger is on.
**Answer:** $5 + 3 = \underline{8}$

■ Use the number line to find the sum.

$4 + 1 = \underline{5}$    $5 + 3 = \underline{8}$    $3 + 5 = \underline{8}$

$\begin{array}{r} 5 \\ +2 \\ \hline 7 \end{array}$   $\begin{array}{r} 4 \\ +5 \\ \hline 9 \end{array}$   $\begin{array}{r} 1 \\ +2 \\ \hline 3 \end{array}$   $\begin{array}{r} 5 \\ +4 \\ \hline 9 \end{array}$   $\begin{array}{r} 5 \\ +5 \\ \hline 10 \end{array}$

Addition — 7

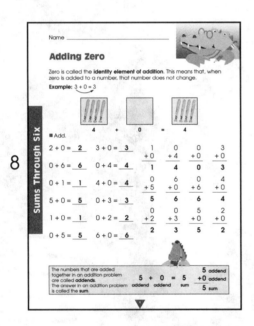

**Adding Zero**

Zero is called the **identity element of addition**. This means that, when zero is added to a number, that number does not change.

**Example:** $3 + 0 = 3$

$4 + 0 = 4$

■ Add.

$2 + 0 = \underline{2}$    $3 + 0 = \underline{3}$

$0 + 6 = \underline{6}$    $0 + 4 = \underline{4}$

$0 + 1 = \underline{1}$    $0 + 4 = \underline{4}$

$5 + 0 = \underline{5}$    $0 + 3 = \underline{3}$

$1 + 0 = \underline{1}$    $0 + 2 = \underline{2}$

$0 + 5 = \underline{5}$    $6 + 0 = \underline{6}$

$\begin{array}{r} 1 \\ +0 \\ \hline 1 \end{array}$ $\begin{array}{r} 0 \\ +4 \\ \hline 4 \end{array}$ $\begin{array}{r} 0 \\ +0 \\ \hline 0 \end{array}$ $\begin{array}{r} 3 \\ +0 \\ \hline 3 \end{array}$

$\begin{array}{r} 0 \\ +5 \\ \hline 5 \end{array}$ $\begin{array}{r} 6 \\ +0 \\ \hline 6 \end{array}$ $\begin{array}{r} 0 \\ +6 \\ \hline 6 \end{array}$ $\begin{array}{r} 4 \\ +0 \\ \hline 4 \end{array}$

$\begin{array}{r} 0 \\ +2 \\ \hline 2 \end{array}$ $\begin{array}{r} 0 \\ +3 \\ \hline 3 \end{array}$ $\begin{array}{r} 5 \\ +0 \\ \hline 5 \end{array}$ $\begin{array}{r} 2 \\ +0 \\ \hline 2 \end{array}$

The numbers that are added together in an addition problem are called **addends**. The answer in an addition problem is called the **sum**.

$5 + 0 = 5$ ... addend, addend, sum → 5 addend, +0 addend, 5 sum

Sums Through Six — 8

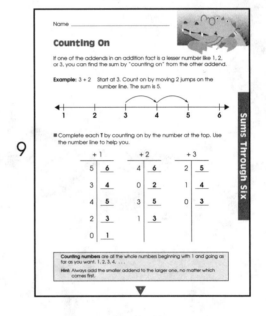

**Counting On**

If one of the addends in an addition fact is a lesser number like 1, 2, or 3, you can find the sum by "counting on" from the other addend.

**Example:** $3 + 2$   Start at 3. Count on by moving 2 jumps on the number line. The sum is 5.

■ Complete each T by counting on by the number at the top. Use the number line to help you.

| $+1$ | | $+2$ | | $+3$ | |
|---|---|---|---|---|---|
| 5 | 6 | 4 | 6 | 2 | 5 |
| 3 | 4 | 0 | 2 | 1 | 4 |
| 4 | 5 | 3 | 5 | 0 | 3 |
| 2 | 3 | 1 | 3 | | |
| 0 | 1 | | | | |

**Counting numbers** are all the whole numbers beginning with 1 and going as far as you want. 1, 2, 3, 4, . . . .

**Hint:** Always add the smaller addend to the larger one, no matter which comes first.

Sums Through Six — 9

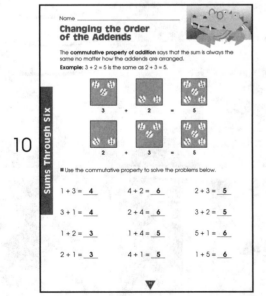

**Changing the Order of the Addends**

The **commutative property of addition** says that the sum is always the same no matter how the addends are arranged.

**Example:** $3 + 2 = 5$ is the same as $2 + 3 = 5$.

$3 + 2 = 5$

$2 + 3 = 5$

■ Use the commutative property to solve the problems below.

$1 + 3 = \underline{4}$    $4 + 2 = \underline{6}$    $2 + 3 = \underline{5}$

$3 + 1 = \underline{4}$    $2 + 4 = \underline{6}$    $3 + 2 = \underline{5}$

$1 + 2 = \underline{3}$    $1 + 4 = \underline{5}$    $5 + 1 = \underline{6}$

$2 + 1 = \underline{3}$    $4 + 1 = \underline{5}$    $1 + 5 = \underline{6}$

Sums Through Six — 10

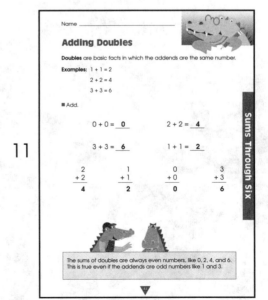

**Adding Doubles**

**Doubles** are basic facts in which the addends are the same number.

**Examples:** $1 + 1 = 2$
$2 + 2 = 4$
$3 + 3 = 6$

■ Add.

$0 + 0 = \underline{0}$    $2 + 2 = \underline{4}$

$3 + 3 = \underline{6}$    $1 + 1 = \underline{2}$

$\begin{array}{r} 2 \\ +2 \\ \hline 4 \end{array}$   $\begin{array}{r} 1 \\ +1 \\ \hline 2 \end{array}$   $\begin{array}{r} 0 \\ +0 \\ \hline 0 \end{array}$   $\begin{array}{r} 3 \\ +3 \\ \hline 6 \end{array}$

The sums of doubles are always even numbers, like 0, 2, 4, and 6. This is true even if the addends are odd numbers like 1 and 3.

Sums Through Six — 11

## Page 12

Name _____

### Practice

■ Add. Record your score—the number correct—on each Practice page and on page 16.

$3+3=6$  $2+1=3$  $1+0=1$  $0+4=4$

$6+0=6$  $5+0=5$  $4+1=5$  $1+1=2$

$1+5=6$  $2+4=6$  $0+2=2$  $3+0=3$

$2+3=5$  $0+0=0$  $3+2=5$  $1+4=5$

$3+1=4$  $0+1=1$  $4+0=4$  $5+1=6$

$0+5=5$  $1+1=2$  $1+3=4$  $0+6=6$

$1+4=5$  $0+3=3$  $2+0=2$  $1+2=3$

$4+2=6$  $2+2=4$  $3+2=5$  $3+1=4$

$5+0=5$  $3+3=6$  $4+1=5$  $0+4=4$

Sums Through Six

Score: _____

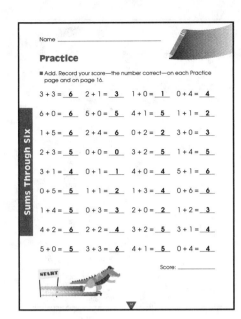

## Page 13

Name _____

### Practice

■ Add.

```
 1   0   2   2   0   1   3   0   0
+4  +6  +1  +4  +5  +2  +3  +4  +1
 5   6   3   6   5   3   6   4   1

 0   2   0   3   1   0   1   5   3
+0  +2  +2  +2  +0  +3  +4  +0  +2
 0   4   2   5   1   3   5   5   5

 2   4   3   1   1   4   0   4   2
+3  +0  +3  +3  +4  +2  +3  +1  +0
 5   4   6   4   5   6   3   5   2

 3   1   1   2   6   1   2   3   5
+0  +5  +1  +2  +0  +3  +3  +1  +1
 3   6   2   4   6   4   5   4   6
```

Score: _____

Sums Through Six

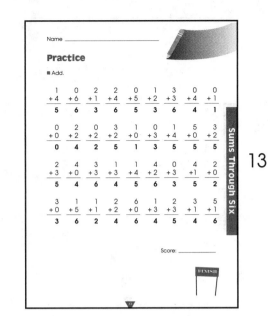

## Page 14

Name _____

### Practice

■ Add.

```
 6   1   2   1       2+0=2   1+0=1
+0  +3  +2  +2
 6   4   4   3       0+4=4   0+5=5

 1   2   0   3       4+0=4   2+1=3
+4  +4  +2  +0
 5   6   2   3       1+5=6   0+1=1

 0   0   4   2       5+0=5   3+3=6
+3  +6  +2  +3
 3   6   6   5       0+0=0   1+1=2

 3   4   3   1       3+2=5   5+1=6
+1  +1  +3  +5
 4   5   6   6

 6   3   2   2       4+2=6   2+2=4
+0  +2  +1  +2
 6   5   3   4       Score: _____
```

Sums Through Six

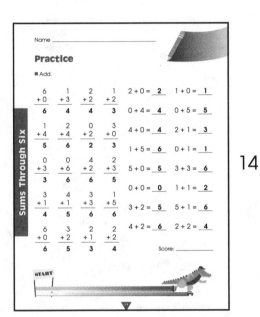

## Page 15

Name _____

### Practice

■ Add.

```
 3   2   2   4       0+0=0   1+1=2
+3  +4  +1  +2
 6   6   3   6       2+3=5   2+0=2

 0   1   5   0       1+5=6   5+1=6
+1  +2  +0  +3
 1   3   5   3       4+0=4   0+6=6

 1   3   1   2       0+5=5   3+1=4
+0  +2  +3  +2
 1   5   4   4       3+0=3   1+4=5

 0   0   5   3       4+1=5   6+0=6
+2  +4  +1  +1
 2   4   6   4       3+2=5   2+2=4

 2   3   0   1
+1  +3  +5  +4
 3   6   5   5       Score: _____
```

Sums Through Six

Circle any problems that you still find difficult to remember. Make your own flash cards to help you master these problems.

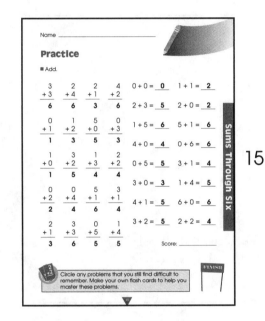

## Page 16

Name _____

### Practice

■ Add.

```
 0   3   5   2       3+1=4   1+0=1
+2  +2  +0  +4
 2   5   5   6       0+5=5   2+2=4

 1   1   2   1       3+0=3   1+4=5
+3  +1  +1  +2
 4   2   3   3       2+1=3   0+0=0

 2   2   2   4       5+1=6   4+1=5
+2  +3  +0  +2
 4   5   2   6       0+3=3   1+5=6

 0   0   3   2       3+3=6   0+4=4
+6  +1  +2  +1
 6   1   5   3       2+4=6   1+2=3

 5   3   1   4
+1  +3  +4  +1
 6   6   5   5
```

Record your scores below.

| Page 12 Score: _____ | Page 15 Score: _____ |
| Page 13 Score: _____ | Page 16 Score: _____ |
| Page 14 Score: _____ | |

Sums Through Six

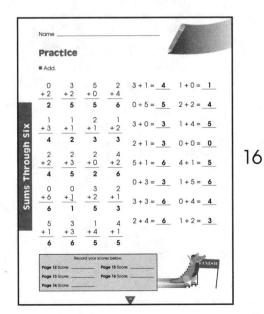

## Page 17

Name _____

### Timed Test

■ Improve your speed on these basic facts. Ask someone to time you. Record your time and score on each Timed Test page and on page 28.

$0+5=5$  $1+1=2$  $0+2=2$  $2+1=3$

$1+4=5$  $5+0=5$  $3+2=5$  $6+0=6$

$2+0=2$  $2+3=5$  $1+0=1$  $1+5=6$

$3+3=6$  $4+2=6$  $2+4=6$  $5+1=6$

$0+1=1$  $0+3=3$  $1+2=3$  $2+2=4$

$4+1=5$  $1+3=4$  $4+0=4$  $3+1=4$

$3+0=3$  $0+6=6$  $0+4=4$  $0+0=0$

$2+4=6$  $3+3=6$  $1+5=6$  $3+2=5$

$1+4=5$  $5+0=5$  $4+2=6$  $2+2=4$

$3+1=4$  $1+1=2$  $2+0=2$  $1+2=3$

Score: _____    Time: _____ minutes _____ seconds

Sums Through Six

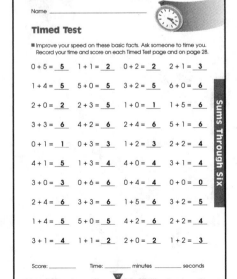

# Timed Test Answer Key

**Sums Through Six**

---

**18**

Name _____

### Timed Test

■ Complete these facts as accurately and as quickly as you can.

```
 6    5    5    3    4    2    0    1
+0   +1   +0   +1   +0   +1   +3   +4
 6    6    5    4    4    3    3    5

 1    2    0    4    0    0    2    2
+3   +3   +1   +2   +2   +6   +0   +4
 4    5    1    6    2    6    2    6

 3    3    2    2    1    1    3    1
+3   +0   +4   +2   +1   +5   +2   +3
 6    3    6    4    2    6    5    4

 1    0    0    1    0    4    1    3
+2   +0   +4   +4   +5   +1   +0   +3
 3    0    4    5    5    5    1    6

 5    2    4    0    1    2    2    0
+1   +3   +2   +6   +3   +1   +2   +3
 6    5    6    6    4    3    4    3
```

Score: _____  Time: _____ minutes _____ seconds

---

**19**

Name _____

### Timed Test

```
1 + 4 = 5    2 + 3 = 5     0    3    3    1
                          +5   +1   +0   +2
5 + 1 = 6    1 + 3 = 4     5    4    3    3

0 + 6 = 6    4 + 0 = 4     4    0    3    3
                          +2   +0   +3   +2
2 + 4 = 6    0 + 3 = 3     6    0    6    5

2 + 0 = 2    2 + 1 = 3     1    4    2    0
                          +0   +1   +0   +1
6 + 0 = 6    1 + 5 = 6     1    5    2    1

0 + 4 = 4    5 + 0 = 5     0    1    2    5
                          +2   +1   +2   +1
3 + 3 = 6    4 + 1 = 5     2    2    4    6

2 + 1 = 3    3 + 2 = 5     1    1    0    2
                          +2   +0   +4   +4
1 + 1 = 2    6 + 0 = 6     3    1    4    6
```

Score: _____  Time: _____ minutes _____ seconds

---

**20**

Name _____

### Timed Test

```
5 + 0 = 5    0 + 5 = 5     0    2    1    3
                          +3   +3   +2   +3
4 + 2 = 6    1 + 1 = 2     3    5    3    6

0 + 1 = 1    3 + 0 = 3     1    0    5    4
                          +4   +4   +1   +0
1 + 0 = 1    4 + 1 = 5     5    4    6    4

2 + 1 = 3    6 + 0 = 6     0    2    0    0
                          +2   +4   +0   +6
3 + 1 = 4    2 + 2 = 4     2    6    0    6

2 + 0 = 2    5 + 1 = 6     1    3    1    4
                          +3   +2   +5   +2
1 + 4 = 5    2 + 4 = 6     4    5    6    6

0 + 3 = 3    3 + 3 = 6     5    3    2    2
                          +0   +3   +1   +2
2 + 3 = 5    4 + 1 = 5     5    6    3    4
```

Score: _____  Time: _____ minutes _____ seconds

---

**21**

Name _____

### Timed Test

```
0 + 5 = 5    5 + 0 = 5     4    2    3    5
                          +0   +1   +2   +1
3 + 1 = 4    2 + 4 = 6     4    3    5    6

3 + 0 = 3    4 + 2 = 6     0    0    0    0
                          +2   +6   +3   +6
2 + 0 = 2    0 + 0 = 0     2    6    3    6

0 + 1 = 1    1 + 0 = 1     3    2    4    1
                          +3   +3   +1   +5
2 + 2 = 4    0 + 4 = 4     6    5    5    6

1 + 1 = 2    1 + 4 = 5     1    1    1    4
                          +2   +3   +1   +2
3 + 3 = 6    5 + 1 = 6     3    4    2    6

2 + 1 = 3    3 + 2 = 5     6    2    3    2
                          +0   +4   +1   +2
1 + 3 = 4    4 + 1 = 5     6    6    4    4
```

Score: _____  Time: _____ minutes _____ seconds

---

**22**

Name _____

### Timed Test

```
1 + 4 = 5    2 + 2 = 4     3    4    5    2
                          +3   +0   +0   +1
0 + 3 = 3    3 + 0 = 3     6    4    5    3

2 + 3 = 5    0 + 6 = 6     1    0    1    6
                          +1   +2   +0   +0
1 + 2 = 3    4 + 1 = 5     2    2    1    6

2 + 4 = 6    1 + 3 = 4     3    5    3    0
                          +2   +1   +1   +4
0 + 4 = 4    0 + 3 = 3     5    6    4    4

4 + 2 = 6    0 + 1 = 1     1    2    1    0
                          +5   +0   +2   +5
3 + 1 = 4    3 + 2 = 5     6    2    3    5

2 + 0 = 2    1 + 2 = 3     4    0    2    1
                          +2   +6   +2   +4
2 + 2 = 4    4 + 1 = 5     6    6    4    5
```

Score: _____  Time: _____ minutes _____ seconds

---

**23**

Name _____

### Timed Test

```
3 + 0 = 3    0 + 5 = 5     2    5    4    2
                          +4   +1   +2   +3
1 + 0 = 1    2 + 0 = 2     6    6    6    5

3 + 2 = 5    2 + 2 = 4     0    0    0    1
                          +4   +0   +2   +1
0 + 1 = 1    4 + 1 = 5     4    0    2    2

6 + 0 = 6    0 + 3 = 3     3    2    3    0
                          +1   +1   +3   +6
1 + 5 = 6    5 + 0 = 5     4    3    6    6

4 + 0 = 4    1 + 3 = 4     1    1    2    2
                          +4   +2   +2   +3
2 + 4 = 6    1 + 4 = 5     5    3    4    5

3 + 3 = 6    1 + 2 = 3     1    3    4    2
                          +3   +2   +1   +0
1 + 1 = 2    0 + 3 = 3     4    5    5    2
```

Score: _____  Time: _____ minutes _____ seconds

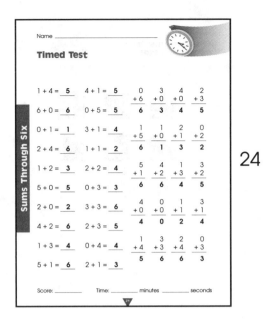

**Timed Test**

Sums Through Six

| | | | | |
|---|---|---|---|---|
| 1 + 4 = **5** | 4 + 1 = **5** | 0<br>+6<br>**6** | 3<br>+0<br>**3** | 4<br>+0<br>**4** | 2<br>+3<br>**5** |
| 6 + 0 = **6** | 0 + 5 = **5** | | | | |
| 0 + 1 = **1** | 3 + 1 = **4** | 1<br>+5<br>**6** | 1<br>+0<br>**1** | 2<br>+1<br>**3** | 0<br>+2<br>**2** |
| 2 + 4 = **6** | 1 + 1 = **2** | | | | |
| 1 + 2 = **3** | 2 + 2 = **4** | 5<br>+1<br>**6** | 4<br>+2<br>**6** | 1<br>+3<br>**4** | 3<br>+2<br>**5** |
| 5 + 0 = **5** | 0 + 3 = **3** | | | | |
| 2 + 0 = **2** | 3 + 3 = **6** | 4<br>+0<br>**4** | 0<br>+0<br>**0** | 1<br>+1<br>**2** | 3<br>+1<br>**4** |
| 4 + 2 = **6** | 2 + 3 = **5** | | | | |
| 1 + 3 = **4** | 0 + 4 = **4** | 1<br>+4<br>**5** | 3<br>+3<br>**6** | 2<br>+4<br>**6** | 0<br>+3<br>**3** |
| 5 + 1 = **6** | 2 + 1 = **3** | | | | |

Score: _____  Time: _____ minutes _____ seconds

**24**

---

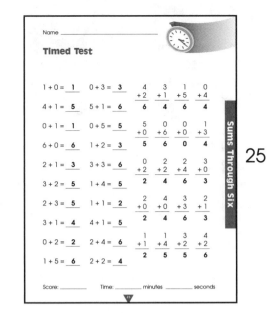

**Timed Test**

Sums Through Six

| | | | | |
|---|---|---|---|---|
| 1 + 0 = **1** | 0 + 3 = **3** | 4<br>+2<br>**6** | 3<br>+1<br>**4** | 1<br>+5<br>**6** | 0<br>+4<br>**4** |
| 4 + 1 = **5** | 5 + 1 = **6** | | | | |
| 0 + 1 = **1** | 0 + 5 = **5** | 5<br>+0<br>**5** | 0<br>+6<br>**6** | 0<br>+0<br>**0** | 1<br>+3<br>**4** |
| 6 + 0 = **6** | 1 + 2 = **3** | | | | |
| 2 + 1 = **3** | 3 + 3 = **6** | 0<br>+2<br>**2** | 2<br>+2<br>**4** | 2<br>+4<br>**6** | 3<br>+0<br>**3** |
| 3 + 2 = **5** | 1 + 4 = **5** | | | | |
| 2 + 3 = **5** | 1 + 1 = **2** | 2<br>+0<br>**2** | 4<br>+0<br>**4** | 3<br>+3<br>**6** | 2<br>+1<br>**3** |
| 3 + 1 = **4** | 4 + 1 = **5** | | | | |
| 0 + 2 = **2** | 2 + 4 = **6** | 1<br>+1<br>**2** | 1<br>+4<br>**5** | 3<br>+2<br>**5** | 4<br>+2<br>**6** |
| 1 + 5 = **6** | 2 + 2 = **4** | | | | |

Score: _____  Time: _____ minutes _____ seconds

**25**

---

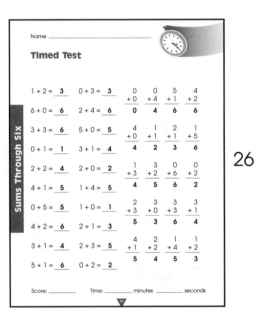

**Timed Test**

Sums Through Six

| | | | | |
|---|---|---|---|---|
| 1 + 2 = **3** | 0 + 3 = **3** | 0<br>+0<br>**0** | 0<br>+4<br>**4** | 5<br>+1<br>**6** | 4<br>+2<br>**6** |
| 6 + 0 = **6** | 2 + 4 = **6** | | | | |
| 3 + 3 = **6** | 5 + 0 = **5** | 4<br>+0<br>**4** | 1<br>+1<br>**2** | 2<br>+1<br>**3** | 1<br>+5<br>**6** |
| 0 + 1 = **1** | 3 + 1 = **4** | | | | |
| 2 + 2 = **4** | 2 + 0 = **2** | 1<br>+3<br>**4** | 3<br>+2<br>**5** | 0<br>+6<br>**6** | 0<br>+2<br>**2** |
| 4 + 1 = **5** | 1 + 4 = **5** | | | | |
| 0 + 5 = **5** | 1 + 0 = **1** | 2<br>+3<br>**5** | 3<br>+0<br>**3** | 3<br>+3<br>**6** | 3<br>+1<br>**4** |
| 4 + 2 = **6** | 2 + 1 = **3** | | | | |
| 3 + 1 = **4** | 2 + 3 = **5** | 4<br>+1<br>**5** | 2<br>+2<br>**4** | 1<br>+4<br>**5** | 1<br>+2<br>**3** |
| 5 + 1 = **6** | 0 + 2 = **2** | | | | |

Score: _____  Time: _____ minutes _____ seconds

**26**

---

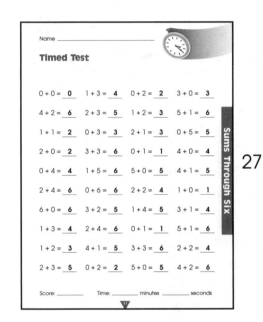

**Timed Test**

Sums Through Six

| | | | |
|---|---|---|---|
| 0 + 0 = **0** | 1 + 3 = **4** | 0 + 2 = **2** | 3 + 0 = **3** |
| 4 + 2 = **6** | 2 + 3 = **5** | 1 + 2 = **3** | 5 + 1 = **6** |
| 1 + 1 = **2** | 0 + 3 = **3** | 2 + 1 = **3** | 0 + 5 = **5** |
| 2 + 0 = **2** | 3 + 3 = **6** | 0 + 1 = **1** | 4 + 0 = **4** |
| 0 + 4 = **4** | 1 + 5 = **6** | 5 + 0 = **5** | 4 + 1 = **5** |
| 2 + 4 = **6** | 0 + 6 = **6** | 2 + 2 = **4** | 1 + 0 = **1** |
| 6 + 0 = **6** | 3 + 2 = **5** | 1 + 4 = **5** | 3 + 1 = **4** |
| 1 + 3 = **4** | 2 + 4 = **6** | 0 + 1 = **1** | 5 + 1 = **6** |
| 1 + 2 = **3** | 4 + 1 = **5** | 3 + 3 = **6** | 2 + 2 = **4** |
| 2 + 3 = **5** | 0 + 2 = **2** | 5 + 0 = **5** | 4 + 2 = **6** |

Score: _____  Time: _____ minutes _____ seconds

**27**

---

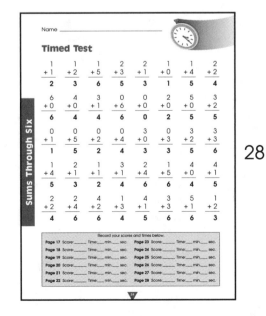

**Timed Test**

Sums Through Six

| | | | | | | | |
|---|---|---|---|---|---|---|---|
| 1<br>+1<br>**2** | 1<br>+2<br>**3** | 1<br>+5<br>**6** | 2<br>+3<br>**5** | 2<br>+1<br>**3** | 1<br>+0<br>**1** | 1<br>+4<br>**5** | 2<br>+2<br>**4** |
| 6<br>+0<br>**6** | 4<br>+0<br>**4** | 3<br>+1<br>**4** | 0<br>+6<br>**6** | 0<br>+0<br>**0** | 2<br>+0<br>**2** | 5<br>+0<br>**5** | 3<br>+2<br>**5** |
| 0<br>+1<br>**1** | 0<br>+5<br>**5** | 0<br>+2<br>**2** | 0<br>+4<br>**4** | 3<br>+0<br>**3** | 0<br>+3<br>**3** | 3<br>+2<br>**5** | 3<br>+3<br>**6** |
| 1<br>+4<br>**5** | 2<br>+1<br>**3** | 1<br>+1<br>**2** | 3<br>+1<br>**4** | 2<br>+4<br>**6** | 1<br>+5<br>**6** | 4<br>+0<br>**4** | 1<br>+4<br>**5** |
| 2<br>+2<br>**4** | 2<br>+4<br>**6** | 4<br>+2<br>**6** | 1<br>+3<br>**4** | 4<br>+1<br>**5** | 3<br>+3<br>**6** | 5<br>+1<br>**6** | 1<br>+2<br>**3** |

Record your scores and times below.

| | |
|---|---|
| Page 17 Score:_____ Time:_____ min.____ sec. | Page 23 Score:_____ Time:_____ min.____ sec. |
| Page 18 Score:_____ Time:_____ min.____ sec. | Page 24 Score:_____ Time:_____ min.____ sec. |
| Page 19 Score:_____ Time:_____ min.____ sec. | Page 25 Score:_____ Time:_____ min.____ sec. |
| Page 20 Score:_____ Time:_____ min.____ sec. | Page 26 Score:_____ Time:_____ min.____ sec. |
| Page 21 Score:_____ Time:_____ min.____ sec. | Page 27 Score:_____ Time:_____ min.____ sec. |
| Page 22 Score:_____ Time:_____ min.____ sec. | Page 28 Score:_____ Time:_____ min.____ sec. |

**28**

---

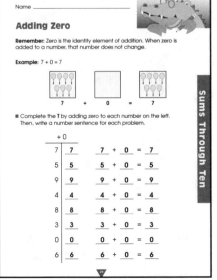

**Adding Zero**

Sums Through Ten

**Remember:** Zero is the identity element of addition. When zero is added to a number, that number does not change.

**Example:** 7 + 0 = 7

7 + 0 = 7

■ Complete the T by adding zero to each number on the left. Then, write a number sentence for each problem.

| +0 | |
|---|---|
| 7 | **7** |
| 5 | **5** |
| 9 | **9** |
| 4 | **4** |
| 8 | **8** |
| 3 | **3** |
| 0 | **0** |
| 6 | **6** |

7 + **0** = **7**
5 + **0** = **5**
9 + **0** = **9**
4 + **0** = **4**
8 + **0** = **8**
3 + **0** = **3**
0 + **0** = **0**
6 + **0** = **6**

**29**

**Timed Test Answer Key**

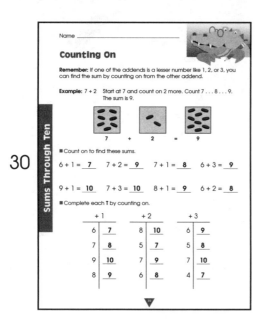

**30**

Name _____

## Counting On

**Remember:** If one of the addends is a lesser number like 1, 2, or 3, you can find the sum by counting on from the other addend.

**Example:** 7 + 2   Start at 7 and count on 2 more. Count 7 . . . 8 . . . 9. The sum is 9.

7 + 2 = 9

■ Count on to find these sums.

6 + 1 = **7**   7 + 2 = **9**   7 + 1 = **8**   6 + 3 = **9**

9 + 1 = **10**   7 + 3 = **10**   8 + 1 = **9**   6 + 2 = **8**

■ Complete each T by counting on.

| +1 | | +2 | | +3 | |
|---|---|---|---|---|---|
| 6 | **7** | 8 | **10** | 6 | **9** |
| 7 | **8** | 5 | **7** | 5 | **8** |
| 9 | **10** | 7 | **9** | 7 | **10** |
| 8 | **9** | 6 | **8** | 4 | **7** |

*Sums Through Ten*

---

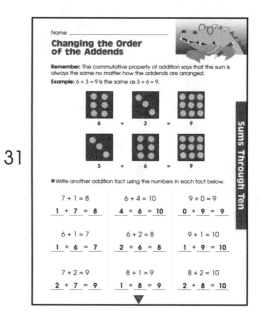

**31**

Name _____

## Changing the Order of the Addends

**Remember:** The commutative property of addition says that the sum is always the same no matter how the addends are arranged.

**Example:** 6 + 3 = 9 is the same as 3 + 6 = 9.

6 + 3 = 9
3 + 6 = 9

■ Write another addition fact using the numbers in each fact below.

| 7 + 1 = 8 | 6 + 4 = 10 | 9 + 0 = 9 |
|---|---|---|
| **1** + **7** = **8** | **4** + **6** = **10** | **0** + **9** = **9** |

| 6 + 1 = 7 | 6 + 2 = 8 | 9 + 1 = 10 |
|---|---|---|
| **1** + **6** = **7** | **2** + **6** = **8** | **1** + **9** = **10** |

| 7 + 2 = 9 | 8 + 1 = 9 | 8 + 2 = 10 |
|---|---|---|
| **2** + **7** = **9** | **1** + **8** = **9** | **2** + **8** = **10** |

*Sums Through Ten*

---

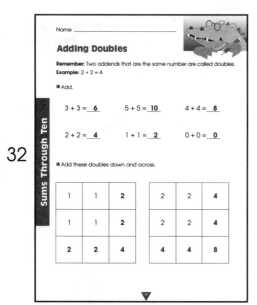

**32**

Name _____

## Adding Doubles

**Remember:** Two addends that are the same number are called doubles.
**Example:** 2 + 2 = 4

■ Add.

3 + 3 = **6**   5 + 5 = **10**   4 + 4 = **8**

2 + 2 = **4**   1 + 1 = **2**   0 + 0 = **0**

■ Add these doubles down and across.

| 1 | 1 | 2 |
|---|---|---|
| 1 | 1 | 2 |
| 2 | 2 | 4 |

| 2 | 2 | 4 |
|---|---|---|
| 2 | 2 | 4 |
| 4 | 4 | 8 |

*Sums Through Ten*

---

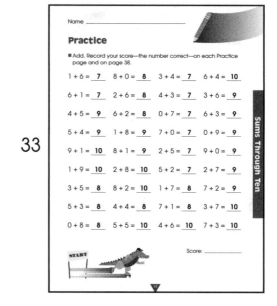

**33**

Name _____

## Practice

■ Add. Record your score—the number correct—on each Practice page and on page 38.

1 + 6 = **7**   8 + 0 = **8**   3 + 4 = **7**   6 + 4 = **10**

6 + 1 = **7**   2 + 6 = **8**   4 + 3 = **7**   3 + 6 = **9**

4 + 5 = **9**   6 + 2 = **8**   0 + 7 = **7**   6 + 3 = **9**

5 + 4 = **9**   1 + 8 = **9**   7 + 0 = **7**   0 + 9 = **9**

9 + 1 = **10**   8 + 1 = **9**   2 + 5 = **7**   9 + 0 = **9**

1 + 9 = **10**   2 + 8 = **10**   5 + 2 = **7**   2 + 7 = **9**

3 + 5 = **8**   8 + 2 = **10**   1 + 7 = **8**   7 + 2 = **9**

5 + 3 = **8**   4 + 4 = **8**   7 + 1 = **8**   3 + 7 = **10**

0 + 8 = **8**   5 + 5 = **10**   4 + 6 = **10**   7 + 3 = **10**

START

Score: _____

*Sums Through Ten*

---

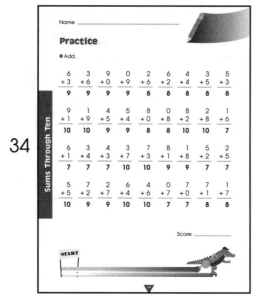

**34**

Name _____

## Practice

■ Add.

| 6 +3 | 3 +6 | 9 +0 | 0 +9 | 2 +6 | 6 +2 | 4 +4 | 3 +5 | 5 +3 |
|---|---|---|---|---|---|---|---|---|
| 9 | 9 | 9 | 9 | 8 | 8 | 8 | 8 | 8 |

| 9 +1 | 1 +9 | 4 +5 | 5 +4 | 8 +0 | 0 +8 | 8 +2 | 2 +8 | 1 +6 |
|---|---|---|---|---|---|---|---|---|
| 10 | 10 | 9 | 9 | 8 | 8 | 10 | 10 | 7 |

| 6 +1 | 3 +4 | 4 +3 | 3 +7 | 7 +3 | 8 +1 | 1 +8 | 5 +2 | 2 +5 |
|---|---|---|---|---|---|---|---|---|
| 7 | 7 | 7 | 10 | 10 | 9 | 9 | 7 | 7 |

| 5 +5 | 7 +2 | 2 +7 | 6 +4 | 4 +6 | 0 +7 | 7 +0 | 7 +1 | 1 +7 |
|---|---|---|---|---|---|---|---|---|
| 10 | 9 | 9 | 10 | 10 | 7 | 7 | 8 | 8 |

Score: _____

START

*Sums Through Ten*

---

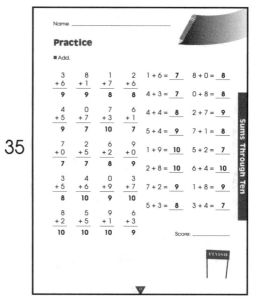

**35**

Name _____

## Practice

■ Add.

| 3 +6 | 8 +1 | 1 +7 | 2 +6 |
|---|---|---|---|
| 9 | 9 | 8 | 8 |

1 + 6 = **7**   8 + 0 = **8**

4 + 3 = **7**   0 + 8 = **8**

| 4 +5 | 0 +7 | 7 +3 | 6 +1 |
|---|---|---|---|
| 9 | 7 | 10 | 7 |

4 + 4 = **8**   2 + 7 = **9**

5 + 4 = **9**   7 + 1 = **8**

| 7 +0 | 2 +5 | 6 +2 | 9 +0 |
|---|---|---|---|
| 7 | 7 | 8 | 9 |

1 + 9 = **10**   5 + 2 = **7**

2 + 8 = **10**   6 + 4 = **10**

| 3 +5 | 4 +6 | 0 +9 | 3 +7 |
|---|---|---|---|
| 8 | 10 | 9 | 10 |

7 + 2 = **9**   1 + 8 = **9**

5 + 3 = **8**   3 + 4 = **7**

| 8 +2 | 5 +5 | 9 +1 | 6 +3 |
|---|---|---|---|
| 10 | 10 | 10 | 9 |

Score: _____

FINISH

*Sums Through Ten*

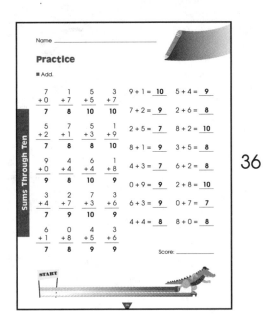

**Practice**

■ Add.

Sums Through Ten

$7+0=7$  $1+7=8$  $5+5=10$  $3+7=10$  $9+1=10$  $5+4=9$
$7+2=9$  $2+6=8$

$5+2=7$  $7+1=8$  $5+3=8$  $1+9=10$  $2+5=7$  $8+2=10$
$8+1=9$  $3+5=8$

$9+0=9$  $4+4=8$  $6+4=10$  $1+8=9$  $4+3=7$  $6+2=8$
$0+9=9$  $2+8=10$

$3+4=7$  $2+7=9$  $7+3=10$  $3+6=9$  $6+3=9$  $0+7=7$
$4+4=8$  $8+0=8$

$6+1=7$  $0+8=8$  $4+5=9$  $3+6=9$

Score: _____

START                    FINISH

36

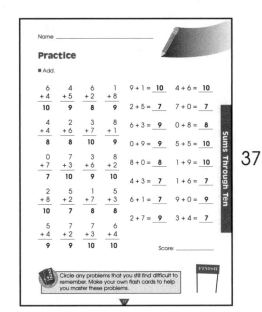

**Practice**

■ Add.

Sums Through Ten

$6+4=10$  $4+5=9$  $6+2=8$  $1+8=9$  $9+1=10$  $4+6=10$
$2+5=7$  $7+0=7$

$4+4=8$  $2+6=8$  $3+7=10$  $8+1=9$  $6+3=9$  $0+8=8$
$0+9=9$  $5+5=10$

$0+7=7$  $7+3=10$  $3+6=9$  $8+2=10$  $8+0=8$  $1+9=10$
$4+3=7$  $1+6=7$

$2+8=10$  $5+2=7$  $1+7=8$  $5+3=8$  $6+1=7$  $9+0=9$
$2+7=9$  $3+4=7$

$5+4=9$  $7+2=9$  $7+3=10$  $6+4=10$

Score: _____

Circle any problems that you still find difficult to remember. Make your own flash cards to help you master these problems.

FINISH

37

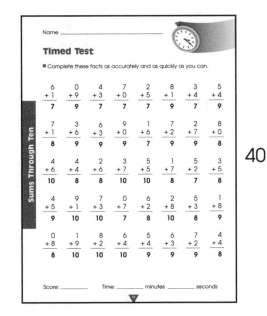

**Practice**

■ Add.

Sums Through Ten

$3+5=8$  $2+8=10$  $2+5=7$  $5+4=9$  $3+4=7$  $3+7=10$
$5+3=8$  $5+5=10$  $7$  $9$  $7$  $10$

$0+9=9$  $9+1=10$  $7+1=8$  $0+8=8$  $9+0=9$  $4+4=8$
$2+6=8$  $0+7=7$  $8$  $8$  $9$  $8$

$7+0=7$  $4+5=9$  $7+2=9$  $5+2=7$  $6+4=10$  $1+6=7$
$3+6=9$  $7+3=10$  $9$  $7$  $10$  $7$

$8+2=10$  $1+8=9$  $6+1=7$  $2+7=9$  $4+6=10$  $1+9=10$
$1+7=8$  $6+3=9$  $7$  $9$  $10$  $10$

$4+3=7$  $8+0=8$  $6+2=8$  $8+1=9$
$7$  $8$  $8$  $9$

Record your scores below.

Page 33 Score: _____   Page 36 Score: _____
Page 34 Score: _____   Page 37 Score: _____
Page 35 Score: _____   Page 38 Score: _____

FINISH

38

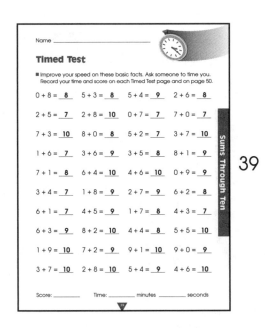

**Timed Test**

■ Improve your speed on these basic facts. Ask someone to time you. Record your time and score on each Timed Test page and on page 50.

Sums Through Ten

$0+8=8$  $5+3=8$  $5+4=9$  $2+6=8$
$2+5=7$  $2+8=10$  $0+7=7$  $7+0=7$
$7+3=10$  $8+0=8$  $5+2=7$  $3+7=10$
$1+6=7$  $3+6=9$  $3+5=8$  $8+1=9$
$7+1=8$  $6+4=10$  $4+6=10$  $0+9=9$
$3+4=7$  $1+8=9$  $2+7=9$  $6+2=8$
$6+1=7$  $4+5=9$  $1+7=8$  $4+3=7$
$6+3=9$  $8+2=10$  $4+4=8$  $5+5=10$
$1+9=10$  $7+2=9$  $9+1=10$  $9+0=9$
$3+7=10$  $2+8=10$  $5+4=9$  $4+6=10$

Score: _____   Time: _____ minutes _____ seconds

39

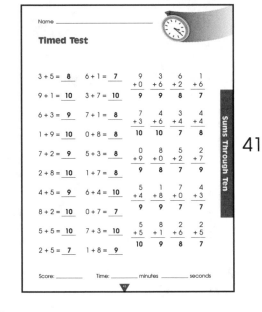

**Timed Test**

■ Complete these facts as accurately and as quickly as you can.

Sums Through Ten

$6+1=7$  $0+9=9$  $4+3=7$  $7+0=7$  $2+5=7$  $8+1=9$  $3+4=7$  $5+4=9$

$7+1=8$  $3+6=9$  $6+3=9$  $9+0=9$  $1+6=7$  $7+2=9$  $2+7=9$  $8+0=8$

$4+6=10$  $4+4=8$  $2+6=8$  $3+7=10$  $5+5=10$  $1+7=8$  $5+2=7$  $3+5=8$

$4+5=9$  $9+1=10$  $7+3=10$  $0+7=7$  $6+2=8$  $2+8=10$  $5+3=8$  $1+8=9$

$0+8=8$  $1+9=10$  $8+2=10$  $6+4=10$  $5+4=9$  $6+3=9$  $7+2=9$  $4+4=8$

Score: _____   Time: _____ minutes _____ seconds

40

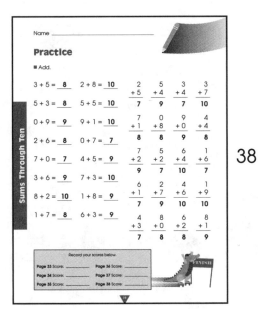

**Timed Test**

Sums Through Ten

$3+5=8$  $6+1=7$  $9+0=9$  $3+6=9$  $6+2=8$  $1+6=7$
$9+1=10$  $3+7=10$  $9$  $9$  $8$  $7$

$6+3=9$  $7+1=8$  $7+3=10$  $4+6=10$  $3+4=7$  $4+4=8$
$1+9=10$  $0+8=8$  $10$  $10$  $7$  $8$

$7+2=9$  $5+3=8$  $0+9=9$  $8+0=8$  $5+2=7$  $2+7=9$
$2+8=10$  $1+7=8$  $9$  $8$  $7$  $9$

$4+5=9$  $6+4=10$  $5+4=9$  $1+8=9$  $7+0=7$  $4+3=7$
$8+2=10$  $0+7=7$  $9$  $9$  $7$  $7$

$5+5=10$  $7+3=10$  $5+5=10$  $8+1=9$  $2+6=8$  $2+5=7$
$2+5=7$  $1+8=9$  $10$  $9$  $8$  $7$

Score: _____   Time: _____ minutes _____ seconds

41

## 42

**Sums Through Ten**

Name _____

### Timed Test

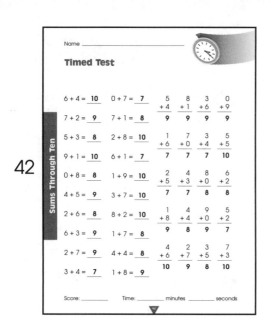

| | |
|---|---|
| 6 + 4 = **10** | 0 + 7 = **7** |
| 7 + 2 = **9** | 7 + 1 = **8** |
| 5 + 3 = **8** | 2 + 8 = **10** |
| 9 + 1 = **10** | 6 + 1 = **7** |
| 0 + 8 = **8** | 1 + 9 = **10** |
| 4 + 5 = **9** | 3 + 7 = **10** |
| 2 + 6 = **8** | 8 + 2 = **10** |
| 6 + 3 = **9** | 1 + 7 = **8** |
| 2 + 7 = **9** | 4 + 4 = **8** |
| 3 + 4 = **7** | 1 + 8 = **9** |

```
 5    8    3    0
+4   +1   +6   +9
 9    9    9    9

 1    7    3    5
+6   +0   +4   +5
 7    7    7    7

 2    4    8    6
+5   +3   +0   +2
 7    7    8    8

 1    4    9    5
+8   +4   +0   +2
 9    8    9    7

 4    2    3    7
+6   +7   +5   +3
10    9    8   10
```

Score: _____  Time: _____ minutes _____ seconds

## 43

**Sums Through Ten**

Name _____

### Timed Test

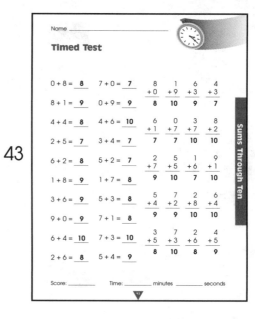

| | |
|---|---|
| 0 + 8 = **8** | 7 + 0 = **7** |
| 8 + 1 = **9** | 0 + 9 = **9** |
| 4 + 4 = **8** | 4 + 6 = **10** |
| 2 + 5 = **7** | 3 + 4 = **7** |
| 6 + 2 = **8** | 5 + 2 = **7** |
| 1 + 8 = **9** | 1 + 7 = **8** |
| 3 + 6 = **9** | 5 + 3 = **8** |
| 9 + 0 = **9** | 7 + 1 = **8** |
| 6 + 4 = **10** | 7 + 3 = **10** |
| 2 + 6 = **8** | 5 + 4 = **9** |

```
 8    1    6    4
+0   +9   +3   +3
 8   10    9    7

 6    0    3    8
+1   +7   +7   +2
 7    7   10   10

 2    5    1    9
+7   +5   +6   +1
 9   10    7   10

 5    7    2    6
+4   +2   +8   +4
 9    9   10   10

 3    7    2    4
+5   +3   +6   +5
 8   10    8    9
```

Score: _____  Time: _____ minutes _____ seconds

## 44

**Sums Through Ten**

Name _____

### Timed Test

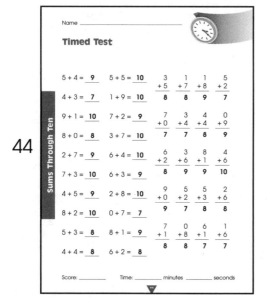

| | |
|---|---|
| 5 + 4 = **9** | 5 + 5 = **10** |
| 4 + 3 = **7** | 1 + 9 = **10** |
| 9 + 1 = **10** | 7 + 2 = **9** |
| 8 + 0 = **8** | 3 + 7 = **10** |
| 2 + 7 = **9** | 6 + 4 = **10** |
| 7 + 3 = **10** | 6 + 3 = **9** |
| 4 + 5 = **9** | 2 + 8 = **10** |
| 8 + 2 = **10** | 0 + 7 = **7** |
| 5 + 3 = **8** | 8 + 1 = **9** |
| 4 + 4 = **8** | 6 + 2 = **8** |

```
 3    1    1    5
+5   +7   +8   +2
 8    8    9    7

 7    3    4    0
+0   +4   +4   +9
 7    7    8    9

 6    3    8    4
+2   +6   +1   +6
 8    9    9   10

 9    5    5    2
+0   +2   +3   +6
 9    7    8    8

 7    0    6    1
+1   +8   +1   +6
 8    8    7    7
```

Score: _____  Time: _____ minutes _____ seconds

## 45

**Sums Through Ten**

Name _____

### Timed Test

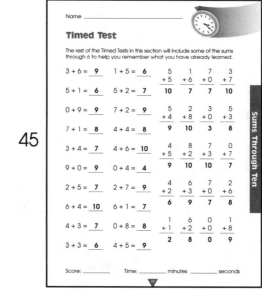

The rest of the Timed Tests in this section will include some of the sums through 6 to help you remember what you have already learned.

| | |
|---|---|
| 3 + 6 = **9** | 1 + 5 = **6** |
| 5 + 1 = **6** | 5 + 2 = **7** |
| 0 + 9 = **9** | 7 + 2 = **9** |
| 7 + 1 = **8** | 4 + 4 = **8** |
| 3 + 4 = **7** | 4 + 6 = **10** |
| 9 + 0 = **9** | 0 + 4 = **4** |
| 2 + 5 = **7** | 2 + 7 = **9** |
| 6 + 4 = **10** | 6 + 1 = **7** |
| 4 + 3 = **7** | 0 + 8 = **8** |
| 3 + 3 = **6** | 4 + 5 = **9** |

```
 5    1    7    3
+5   +6   +0   +7
10    7    7   10

 5    2    3    5
+4   +8   +0   +3
 9   10    3    8

 4    8    7    0
+5   +2   +3   +7
 9   10   10    7

 4    6    7    2
+2   +3   +0   +6
 6    9    7    8

 1    6    0    1
+1   +2   +0   +8
 2    8    0    9
```

Score: _____  Time: _____ minutes _____ seconds

## 46

**Sums Through Ten**

Name _____

### Timed Test

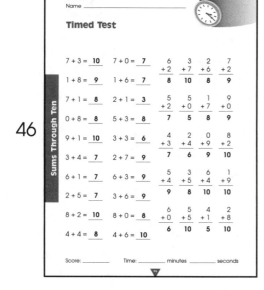

| | |
|---|---|
| 7 + 3 = **10** | 7 + 0 = **7** |
| 1 + 8 = **9** | 1 + 6 = **7** |
| 7 + 1 = **8** | 2 + 1 = **3** |
| 0 + 8 = **8** | 5 + 3 = **8** |
| 9 + 1 = **10** | 3 + 3 = **6** |
| 3 + 4 = **7** | 2 + 7 = **9** |
| 6 + 1 = **7** | 6 + 3 = **9** |
| 2 + 5 = **7** | 3 + 6 = **9** |
| 8 + 2 = **10** | 8 + 0 = **8** |
| 4 + 4 = **8** | 4 + 6 = **10** |

```
 6    3    2    7
+2   +7   +6   +2
 8   10    8    9

 5    5    1    9
+2   +0   +7   +0
 7    5    8    9

 4    2    0    8
+3   +4   +9   +2
 7    6    9   10

 5    3    6    1
+4   +5   +4   +9
 9    8   10   10

 6    5    4    2
+0   +5   +1   +8
 6   10    5   10
```

Score: _____  Time: _____ minutes _____ seconds

## 47

**Sums Through Ten**

Name _____

### Timed Test

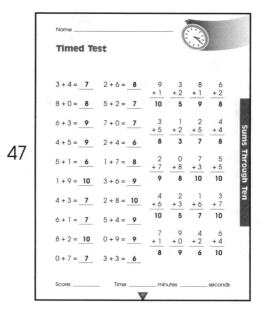

| | |
|---|---|
| 3 + 4 = **7** | 2 + 6 = **8** |
| 8 + 0 = **8** | 5 + 2 = **7** |
| 6 + 3 = **9** | 7 + 0 = **7** |
| 4 + 5 = **9** | 2 + 4 = **6** |
| 5 + 1 = **6** | 1 + 7 = **8** |
| 1 + 9 = **10** | 3 + 6 = **9** |
| 4 + 3 = **7** | 2 + 8 = **10** |
| 6 + 1 = **7** | 5 + 4 = **9** |
| 8 + 2 = **10** | 0 + 9 = **9** |
| 0 + 7 = **7** | 3 + 3 = **6** |

```
 9    3    8    6
+1   +2   +1   +2
10    5    9    8

 3    1    2    4
+5   +2   +5   +4
 8    3    7    8

 2    0    7    5
+7   +8   +3   +5
 9    8   10   10

 1    6    1    3
+6   +3   +6   +7
10    5    7   10

 7    9    4    6
+1   +0   +2   +4
 8    9    6   10
```

Score: _____  Time: _____ minutes _____ seconds

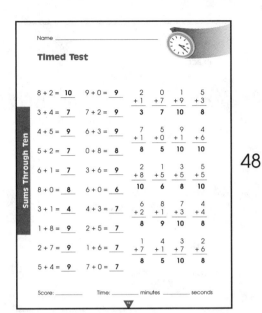

**Timed Test**

Sums Through Ten

| | | | | | |
|---|---|---|---|---|---|
| 8 + 2 = **10** | 9 + 0 = **9** | 2<br>+1<br>**3** | 0<br>+7<br>**7** | 1<br>+9<br>**10** | 5<br>+3<br>**8** |
| 3 + 4 = **7** | 7 + 2 = **9** | | | | |
| 4 + 5 = **9** | 6 + 3 = **9** | 7<br>+1<br>**8** | 5<br>+0<br>**5** | 9<br>+1<br>**10** | 4<br>+6<br>**10** |
| 5 + 2 = **7** | 0 + 8 = **8** | | | | |
| 6 + 1 = **7** | 3 + 6 = **9** | 2<br>+8<br>**10** | 1<br>+5<br>**6** | 3<br>+5<br>**8** | 5<br>+5<br>**10** |
| 8 + 0 = **8** | 6 + 0 = **6** | | | | |
| 3 + 1 = **4** | 4 + 3 = **7** | 6<br>+2<br>**8** | 8<br>+1<br>**9** | 7<br>+3<br>**10** | 4<br>+4<br>**8** |
| 1 + 8 = **9** | 2 + 5 = **7** | | | | |
| 2 + 7 = **9** | 1 + 6 = **7** | 1<br>+7<br>**8** | 4<br>+1<br>**5** | 3<br>+7<br>**10** | 2<br>+6<br>**8** |
| 5 + 4 = **9** | 7 + 0 = **7** | | | | |

Score: _____  Time: _____ minutes _____ seconds

**48**

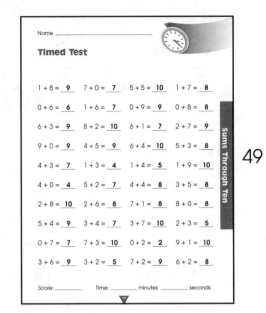

**Timed Test**

Sums Through Ten

| | | | |
|---|---|---|---|
| 1 + 8 = **9** | 7 + 0 = **7** | 5 + 5 = **10** | 1 + 7 = **8** |
| 0 + 6 = **6** | 1 + 6 = **7** | 0 + 9 = **9** | 0 + 8 = **8** |
| 6 + 3 = **9** | 8 + 2 = **10** | 6 + 1 = **7** | 2 + 7 = **9** |
| 9 + 0 = **9** | 4 + 5 = **9** | 6 + 4 = **10** | 5 + 3 = **8** |
| 4 + 3 = **7** | 1 + 3 = **4** | 1 + 4 = **5** | 1 + 9 = **10** |
| 4 + 0 = **4** | 5 + 2 = **7** | 4 + 4 = **8** | 3 + 5 = **8** |
| 2 + 8 = **10** | 2 + 6 = **8** | 7 + 1 = **8** | 8 + 0 = **8** |
| 5 + 4 = **9** | 3 + 4 = **7** | 3 + 7 = **10** | 2 + 3 = **5** |
| 0 + 7 = **7** | 7 + 3 = **10** | 0 + 2 = **2** | 9 + 1 = **10** |
| 3 + 6 = **9** | 3 + 2 = **5** | 7 + 2 = **9** | 6 + 2 = **8** |

Score: _____  Time: _____ minutes _____ seconds

**49**

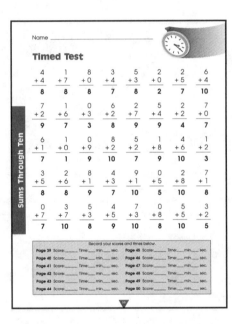

**Timed Test**

Sums Through Ten

| 4<br>+4<br>**8** | 1<br>+7<br>**8** | 8<br>+0<br>**8** | 3<br>+4<br>**7** | 5<br>+3<br>**8** | 2<br>+0<br>**2** | 2<br>+5<br>**7** | 6<br>+4<br>**10** |
|---|---|---|---|---|---|---|---|
| 7<br>+2<br>**9** | 1<br>+6<br>**7** | 0<br>+3<br>**3** | 6<br>+2<br>**8** | 2<br>+7<br>**9** | 5<br>+4<br>**9** | 2<br>+2<br>**4** | 7<br>+0<br>**7** |
| 6<br>+1<br>**7** | 1<br>+0<br>**1** | 0<br>+9<br>**9** | 8<br>+2<br>**10** | 5<br>+2<br>**7** | 1<br>+8<br>**9** | 4<br>+6<br>**10** | 1<br>+2<br>**3** |
| 3<br>+5<br>**8** | 2<br>+6<br>**8** | 8<br>+1<br>**9** | 4<br>+3<br>**7** | 9<br>+1<br>**10** | 0<br>+5<br>**5** | 2<br>+8<br>**10** | 7<br>+1<br>**8** |
| 0<br>+7<br>**7** | 3<br>+7<br>**10** | 5<br>+3<br>**8** | 4<br>+5<br>**9** | 7<br>+3<br>**10** | 0<br>+8<br>**8** | 5<br>+5<br>**10** | 3<br>+2<br>**5** |

**50**

| Record your scores and times below. | |
|---|---|
| Page 39 Score:_____ Time:____ min.____ sec. | Page 45 Score:_____ Time:____ min.____ sec. |
| Page 40 Score:_____ Time:____ min.____ sec. | Page 46 Score:_____ Time:____ min.____ sec. |
| Page 41 Score:_____ Time:____ min.____ sec. | Page 47 Score:_____ Time:____ min.____ sec. |
| Page 42 Score:_____ Time:____ min.____ sec. | Page 48 Score:_____ Time:____ min.____ sec. |
| Page 43 Score:_____ Time:____ min.____ sec. | Page 49 Score:_____ Time:____ min.____ sec. |
| Page 44 Score:_____ Time:____ min.____ sec. | Page 50 Score:_____ Time:____ min.____ sec. |

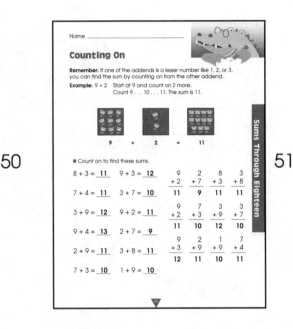

**Counting On**

Sums Through Eighteen

**Remember:** If one of the addends is a lesser number like 1, 2, or 3, you can find the sum by counting on from the other addend.

**Example:** 9 + 2   Start at 9 and count on 2 more.
Count 9 . . . 10 . . . 11. The sum is 11.

9   +   2   =   11

■ Count on to find these sums.

| | | | | | |
|---|---|---|---|---|---|
| 8 + 3 = **11** | 9 + 3 = **12** | 9<br>+2<br>**11** | 2<br>+7<br>**9** | 8<br>+3<br>**11** | 3<br>+8<br>**11** |
| 7 + 4 = **11** | 3 + 7 = **10** | | | | |
| 3 + 9 = **12** | 9 + 2 = **11** | 9<br>+2<br>**11** | 7<br>+3<br>**10** | 3<br>+9<br>**12** | 3<br>+7<br>**10** |
| 9 + 4 = **13** | 2 + 7 = **9** | | | | |
| 2 + 9 = **11** | 3 + 8 = **11** | 9<br>+3<br>**12** | 2<br>+9<br>**11** | 1<br>+9<br>**10** | 7<br>+4<br>**11** |
| 7 + 3 = **10** | 1 + 9 = **10** | | | | |

**51**

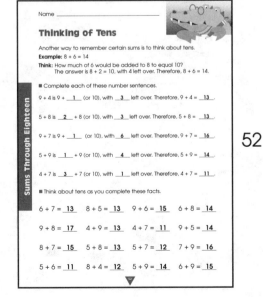

**Thinking of Tens**

Sums Through Eighteen

Another way to remember certain sums is to think about tens.

**Example:** 8 + 6 = 14

**Think:** How much of 6 would be added to 8 to equal 10?
The answer is 8 + 2 = 10, with 4 left over. Therefore, 8 + 6 = 14.

■ Complete each of these number sentences.

9 + 4 is 9 + **1** (or 10), with **3** left over. Therefore, 9 + 4 = **13**.

5 + 8 is **2** + 8 (or 10), with **3** left over. Therefore, 5 + 8 = **13**.

9 + 7 is 9 + **1** (or 10), with **6** left over. Therefore, 9 + 7 = **16**.

5 + 9 is **1** + 9 (or 10), with **4** left over. Therefore, 5 + 9 = **14**.

4 + 7 is **3** + 7 (or 10), with **1** left over. Therefore, 4 + 7 = **11**.

■ Think about tens as you complete these facts.

| | | | |
|---|---|---|---|
| 6 + 7 = **13** | 8 + 5 = **13** | 9 + 6 = **15** | 6 + 8 = **14** |
| 9 + 8 = **17** | 4 + 9 = **13** | 4 + 7 = **11** | 9 + 5 = **14** |
| 8 + 7 = **15** | 5 + 8 = **13** | 5 + 7 = **12** | 7 + 9 = **16** |
| 5 + 6 = **11** | 8 + 4 = **12** | 5 + 9 = **14** | 6 + 9 = **15** |

**52**

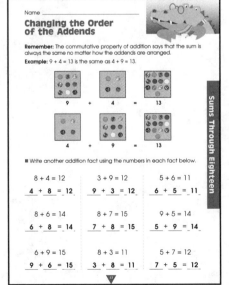

**Changing the Order
of the Addends**

Sums Through Eighteen

**Remember:** The commutative property of addition says that the sum is always the same no matter how the addends are arranged.

**Example:** 9 + 4 = 13 is the same as 4 + 9 = 13.

9   +   4   =   13

4   +   9   =   13

■ Write another addition fact using the numbers in each fact below.

| | | |
|---|---|---|
| 8 + 4 = 12 | 3 + 9 = 12 | 5 + 6 = 11 |
| **4** + **8** = **12** | **9** + **3** = **12** | **6** + **5** = **11** |
| 8 + 6 = 14 | 8 + 7 = 15 | 9 + 5 = 14 |
| **6** + **8** = **14** | **7** + **8** = **15** | **5** + **9** = **14** |
| 6 + 9 = 15 | 8 + 3 = 11 | 5 + 7 = 12 |
| **9** + **6** = **15** | **3** + **8** = **11** | **7** + **5** = **12** |

**53**

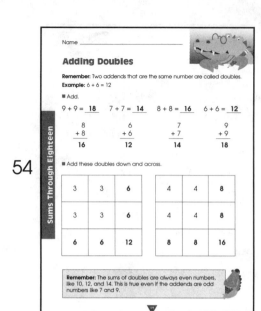

### Page 54

**Sums Through Eighteen**

Name _____

## Adding Doubles

**Remember:** Two addends that are the same number are called doubles.

**Example:** 6 + 6 = 12

■ Add.

9 + 9 = __18__   7 + 7 = __14__   8 + 8 = __16__   6 + 6 = __12__

| 8 | 6 | 7 | 9 |
|---|---|---|---|
| +8 | +6 | +7 | +9 |
| 16 | 12 | 14 | 18 |

■ Add these doubles down and across.

| 3 | 3 | 6 |
|---|---|---|
| 3 | 3 | 6 |
| 6 | 6 | 12 |

| 4 | 4 | 8 |
|---|---|---|
| 4 | 4 | 8 |
| 8 | 8 | 16 |

**Remember:** The sums of doubles are always even numbers, like 10, 12, and 14. This is true even if the addends are odd numbers like 7 and 9.

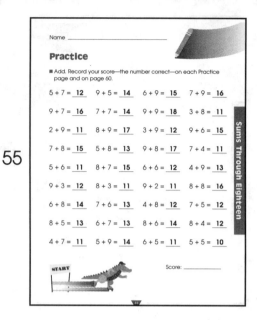

### Page 55

**Sums Through Eighteen**

Name _____

## Practice

■ Add. Record your score—the number correct—on each Practice page and on page 60.

5 + 7 = __12__   9 + 5 = __14__   6 + 9 = __15__   7 + 9 = __16__

9 + 7 = __16__   7 + 7 = __14__   9 + 9 = __18__   3 + 8 = __11__

2 + 9 = __11__   8 + 9 = __17__   3 + 9 = __12__   9 + 6 = __15__

7 + 8 = __15__   5 + 8 = __13__   9 + 8 = __17__   7 + 4 = __11__

5 + 6 = __11__   8 + 7 = __15__   6 + 6 = __12__   4 + 9 = __13__

9 + 3 = __12__   8 + 3 = __11__   9 + 2 = __11__   8 + 8 = __16__

6 + 8 = __14__   7 + 6 = __13__   4 + 8 = __12__   7 + 5 = __12__

8 + 5 = __13__   6 + 7 = __13__   8 + 6 = __14__   8 + 4 = __12__

4 + 7 = __11__   5 + 9 = __14__   6 + 5 = __11__   5 + 5 = __10__

START

Score: _____

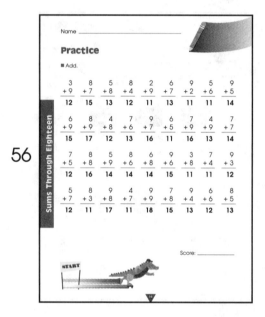

### Page 56

**Sums Through Eighteen**

Name _____

## Practice

■ Add.

| 3 | 8 | 5 | 8 | 2 | 6 | 9 | 5 | 9 |
|---|---|---|---|---|---|---|---|---|
| +9 | +7 | +8 | +4 | +9 | +7 | +2 | +6 | +5 |
| 12 | 15 | 13 | 12 | 11 | 13 | 11 | 11 | 14 |

| 6 | 8 | 4 | 7 | 9 | 6 | 7 | 4 | 7 |
|---|---|---|---|---|---|---|---|---|
| +9 | +9 | +8 | +6 | +7 | +5 | +9 | +9 | +7 |
| 15 | 17 | 12 | 13 | 16 | 11 | 16 | 13 | 14 |

| 7 | 8 | 5 | 8 | 6 | 9 | 3 | 7 | 9 |
|---|---|---|---|---|---|---|---|---|
| +5 | +8 | +9 | +6 | +8 | +6 | +8 | +4 | +3 |
| 12 | 16 | 14 | 14 | 14 | 15 | 11 | 11 | 12 |

| 5 | 8 | 9 | 4 | 9 | 7 | 9 | 6 | 8 |
|---|---|---|---|---|---|---|---|---|
| +7 | +3 | +8 | +7 | +9 | +8 | +4 | +6 | +5 |
| 12 | 11 | 17 | 11 | 18 | 15 | 13 | 12 | 13 |

START

Score: _____

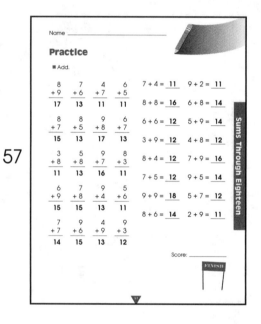

### Page 57

**Sums Through Eighteen**

Name _____

## Practice

■ Add.

| 8 | 7 | 4 | 6 |
|---|---|---|---|
| +9 | +6 | +7 | +5 |
| 17 | 13 | 11 | 11 |

7 + 4 = __11__   9 + 2 = __11__

8 + 8 = __16__   6 + 8 = __14__

| 8 | 8 | 9 | 6 |
|---|---|---|---|
| +7 | +5 | +8 | +7 |
| 15 | 13 | 17 | 13 |

6 + 6 = __12__   5 + 9 = __14__

3 + 9 = __12__   4 + 8 = __12__

| 3 | 5 | 9 | 8 |
|---|---|---|---|
| +8 | +8 | +7 | +3 |
| 11 | 13 | 16 | 11 |

8 + 4 = __12__   7 + 9 = __16__

7 + 5 = __12__   9 + 5 = __14__

| 6 | 7 | 9 | 5 |
|---|---|---|---|
| +9 | +8 | +4 | +6 |
| 15 | 15 | 13 | 11 |

9 + 9 = __18__   5 + 7 = __12__

8 + 6 = __14__   2 + 9 = __11__

| 7 | 9 | 4 | 9 |
|---|---|---|---|
| +7 | +6 | +9 | +3 |
| 14 | 15 | 13 | 12 |

FINISH

Score: _____

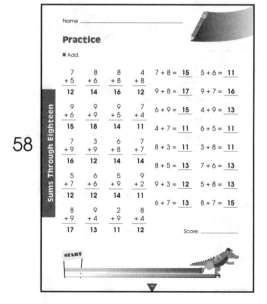

### Page 58

**Sums Through Eighteen**

Name _____

## Practice

■ Add.

| 7 | 8 | 8 | 4 |
|---|---|---|---|
| +5 | +6 | +8 | +8 |
| 12 | 14 | 16 | 12 |

7 + 8 = __15__   5 + 6 = __11__

9 + 8 = __17__   9 + 7 = __16__

| 9 | 9 | 9 | 7 |
|---|---|---|---|
| +6 | +9 | +5 | +4 |
| 15 | 18 | 14 | 11 |

6 + 9 = __15__   4 + 9 = __13__

4 + 7 = __11__   6 + 5 = __11__

| 7 | 3 | 6 | 7 |
|---|---|---|---|
| +9 | +9 | +8 | +7 |
| 16 | 12 | 14 | 14 |

8 + 3 = __11__   3 + 8 = __11__

8 + 5 = __13__   7 + 6 = __13__

| 5 | 6 | 5 | 9 |
|---|---|---|---|
| +7 | +6 | +9 | +2 |
| 12 | 12 | 14 | 11 |

9 + 3 = __12__   5 + 8 = __13__

6 + 7 = __13__   8 + 7 = __15__

| 8 | 9 | 2 | 8 |
|---|---|---|---|
| +9 | +4 | +9 | +4 |
| 17 | 13 | 11 | 12 |

START

Score: _____

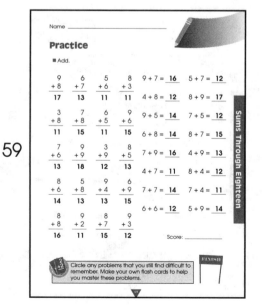

### Page 59

**Sums Through Eighteen**

Name _____

## Practice

■ Add.

| 9 | 6 | 5 | 8 |
|---|---|---|---|
| +8 | +7 | +6 | +3 |
| 17 | 13 | 11 | 11 |

9 + 7 = __16__   5 + 7 = __12__

4 + 8 = __12__   8 + 9 = __17__

| 3 | 7 | 6 | 9 |
|---|---|---|---|
| +8 | +8 | +5 | +6 |
| 11 | 15 | 11 | 15 |

9 + 5 = __14__   7 + 5 = __12__

6 + 8 = __14__   8 + 7 = __15__

| 7 | 9 | 3 | 8 |
|---|---|---|---|
| +6 | +9 | +9 | +5 |
| 13 | 18 | 12 | 13 |

7 + 9 = __16__   4 + 9 = __13__

4 + 7 = __11__   8 + 4 = __12__

| 8 | 5 | 9 | 6 |
|---|---|---|---|
| +6 | +8 | +4 | +9 |
| 14 | 13 | 13 | 15 |

7 + 7 = __14__   7 + 4 = __11__

6 + 6 = __12__   5 + 9 = __14__

| 8 | 9 | 8 | 9 |
|---|---|---|---|
| +8 | +2 | +7 | +3 |
| 16 | 11 | 15 | 12 |

Circle any problems that you still find difficult to remember. Make your own flash cards to help you master these problems.

FINISH

Score: _____

## Page 60 — Practice

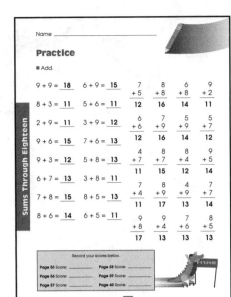

Name _____

**Practice**

■ Add.

Sums Through Eighteen

9 + 9 = **18**  6 + 9 = **15**  7 + 5 = **12**  8 + 8 = **16**  6 + 8 = **14**  9 + 2 = **11**

8 + 3 = **11**  5 + 6 = **11**  6 + 6 = **12**  7 + 9 = **16**  5 + 9 = **14**  5 + 7 = **12**

2 + 9 = **11**  3 + 9 = **12**  4 + 7 = **11**  8 + 7 = **15**  8 + 4 = **12**  9 + 5 = **14**

9 + 6 = **15**  7 + 6 = **13**  7 + 4 = **11**  8 + 9 = **17**  4 + 9 = **13**  7 + 7 = **14**

9 + 3 = **12**  5 + 8 = **13**

6 + 7 = **13**  3 + 8 = **11**  9 + 8 = **17**  9 + 4 = **13**  7 + 6 = **13**  8 + 5 = **13**

7 + 8 = **15**  8 + 5 = **13**

8 + 6 = **14**  6 + 5 = **11**

Record your scores below.

Page 55 Score: _____  Page 58 Score: _____
Page 56 Score: _____  Page 59 Score: _____
Page 57 Score: _____  Page 60 Score: _____

60

## Page 61 — Timed Test

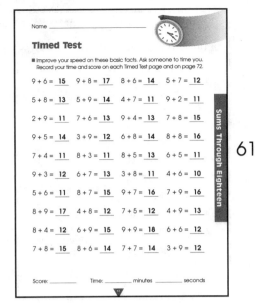

Name _____

**Timed Test**

■ Improve your speed on these basic facts. Ask someone to time you. Record your time and score on each Timed Test page and on page 72.

Sums Through Eighteen

9 + 6 = **15**  9 + 8 = **17**  8 + 6 = **14**  5 + 7 = **12**

5 + 8 = **13**  5 + 9 = **14**  4 + 7 = **11**  9 + 2 = **11**

2 + 9 = **11**  7 + 6 = **13**  9 + 4 = **13**  7 + 8 = **15**

9 + 5 = **14**  3 + 9 = **12**  6 + 8 = **14**  8 + 8 = **16**

7 + 4 = **11**  8 + 3 = **11**  8 + 5 = **13**  6 + 5 = **11**

9 + 3 = **12**  6 + 7 = **13**  3 + 8 = **11**  4 + 6 = **10**

5 + 6 = **11**  8 + 7 = **15**  9 + 7 = **16**  7 + 9 = **16**

8 + 9 = **17**  4 + 8 = **12**  7 + 5 = **12**  4 + 9 = **13**

8 + 4 = **12**  6 + 9 = **15**  9 + 9 = **18**  6 + 6 = **12**

7 + 8 = **15**  8 + 6 = **14**  7 + 7 = **14**  3 + 9 = **12**

Score: _____  Time: _____ minutes _____ seconds

61

## Page 62 — Timed Test

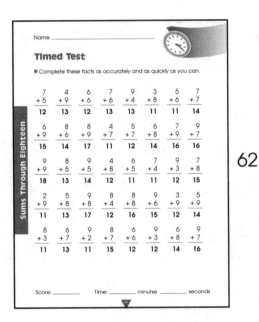

Name _____

**Timed Test**

■ Complete these facts as accurately and as quickly as you can.

Sums Through Eighteen

7 + 5 = **12**  4 + 9 = **13**  6 + 6 = **12**  7 + 6 = **13**  9 + 4 = **13**  3 + 8 = **11**  5 + 6 = **11**  7 + 7 = **14**

6 + 9 = **15**  8 + 6 = **14**  8 + 9 = **17**  4 + 7 = **11**  5 + 7 = **12**  6 + 8 = **14**  7 + 9 = **16**  9 + 7 = **16**

9 + 9 = **18**  8 + 5 = **13**  9 + 5 = **14**  4 + 8 = **12**  6 + 5 = **11**  7 + 4 = **11**  9 + 3 = **12**  7 + 8 = **15**

2 + 9 = **11**  5 + 8 = **13**  9 + 8 = **17**  8 + 4 = **12**  8 + 8 = **16**  9 + 6 = **15**  3 + 9 = **12**  5 + 9 = **14**

8 + 3 = **11**  6 + 7 = **13**  9 + 2 = **11**  8 + 7 = **15**  7 + 6 = **13**  9 + 3 = **12**  6 + 8 = **14**  9 + 7 = **16**

Score: _____  Time: _____ minutes _____ seconds

62

## Page 63 — Timed Test

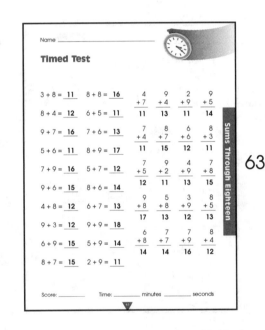

Name _____

**Timed Test**

Sums Through Eighteen

3 + 8 = **11**  8 + 8 = **16**  4 + 7 = **11**  9 + 4 = **13**  2 + 9 = **11**  9 + 5 = **14**

8 + 4 = **12**  6 + 5 = **11**

9 + 7 = **16**  7 + 6 = **13**  7 + 4 = **11**  8 + 7 = **15**  6 + 6 = **12**  8 + 3 = **11**

5 + 6 = **11**  8 + 9 = **17**

7 + 9 = **16**  5 + 7 = **12**  7 + 5 = **12**  9 + 2 = **11**  4 + 9 = **13**  7 + 8 = **15**

9 + 6 = **15**  8 + 6 = **14**

4 + 8 = **12**  6 + 7 = **13**  9 + 8 = **17**  5 + 8 = **13**  3 + 9 = **12**  8 + 5 = **13**

9 + 3 = **12**  9 + 9 = **18**

6 + 9 = **15**  5 + 9 = **14**  6 + 8 = **14**  7 + 7 = **14**  7 + 9 = **16**  8 + 4 = **12**

8 + 7 = **15**  2 + 9 = **11**

Score: _____  Time: _____ minutes _____ seconds

63

## Page 64 — Timed Test

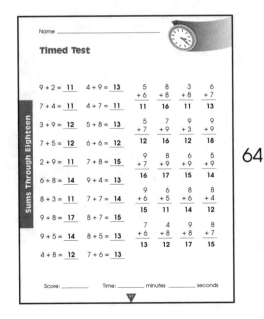

Name _____

**Timed Test**

Sums Through Eighteen

9 + 2 = **11**  4 + 9 = **13**  5 + 6 = **11**  8 + 8 = **16**  3 + 8 = **11**  6 + 7 = **13**

7 + 4 = **11**  4 + 7 = **11**

3 + 9 = **12**  5 + 8 = **13**  5 + 7 = **12**  7 + 9 = **16**  9 + 3 = **12**  9 + 9 = **18**

7 + 5 = **12**  6 + 6 = **12**

2 + 9 = **11**  7 + 8 = **15**  9 + 7 = **16**  8 + 9 = **17**  6 + 9 = **15**  5 + 9 = **14**

6 + 8 = **14**  9 + 4 = **13**

8 + 3 = **11**  7 + 7 = **14**  9 + 6 = **15**  6 + 5 = **11**  8 + 6 = **14**  8 + 4 = **12**

9 + 8 = **17**  8 + 7 = **15**

9 + 5 = **14**  8 + 5 = **13**  7 + 6 = **13**  4 + 8 = **12**  9 + 8 = **17**  8 + 7 = **15**

4 + 8 = **12**  7 + 6 = **13**

Score: _____  Time: _____ minutes _____ seconds

64

## Page 65 — Timed Test

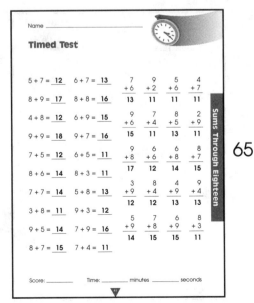

Name _____

**Timed Test**

Sums Through Eighteen

5 + 7 = **12**  6 + 7 = **13**  7 + 6 = **13**  9 + 2 = **11**  5 + 6 = **11**  4 + 7 = **11**

8 + 9 = **17**  8 + 8 = **16**

4 + 8 = **12**  6 + 9 = **15**  9 + 6 = **15**  7 + 4 = **11**  8 + 5 = **13**  2 + 9 = **11**

9 + 9 = **18**  9 + 7 = **16**

7 + 5 = **12**  6 + 5 = **11**  9 + 8 = **17**  6 + 6 = **12**  6 + 8 = **14**  8 + 7 = **15**

8 + 6 = **14**  8 + 3 = **11**

7 + 7 = **14**  5 + 8 = **13**  3 + 9 = **12**  4 + 8 = **12**  9 + 4 = **13**  9 + 4 = **13**

3 + 8 = **11**  9 + 3 = **12**

9 + 5 = **14**  7 + 9 = **16**  5 + 9 = **14**  7 + 8 = **15**  6 + 9 = **15**  8 + 3 = **11**

8 + 7 = **15**  7 + 4 = **11**

Score: _____  Time: _____ minutes _____ seconds

65

# Timed Test Answer Key

## 66

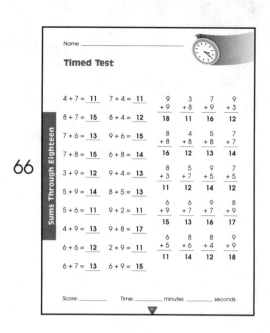

**Timed Test**

Sums Through Eighteen

4 + 7 = __11__    7 + 4 = __11__

8 + 7 = __15__    8 + 4 = __12__

7 + 6 = __13__    9 + 6 = __15__

7 + 8 = __15__    6 + 8 = __14__

3 + 9 = __12__    9 + 4 = __13__

5 + 9 = __14__    8 + 5 = __13__

5 + 6 = __11__    9 + 2 = __11__

4 + 9 = __13__    9 + 8 = __17__

6 + 6 = __12__    2 + 9 = __11__

6 + 7 = __13__    6 + 9 = __15__

| 9 | 3 | 7 | 9 |
|---|---|---|---|
| +9 | +8 | +9 | +3 |
| 18 | 11 | 16 | 12 |
| 8 | 4 | 5 | 7 |
| +8 | +8 | +8 | +7 |
| 16 | 12 | 13 | 14 |
| 8 | 5 | 9 | 7 |
| +3 | +7 | +5 | +5 |
| 11 | 12 | 14 | 12 |
| 6 | 6 | 9 | 8 |
| +9 | +7 | +7 | +9 |
| 15 | 13 | 16 | 17 |
| 6 | 8 | 8 | 9 |
| +5 | +6 | +4 | +9 |
| 11 | 14 | 12 | 18 |

Score: _____    Time: _____ minutes _____ seconds

## 67

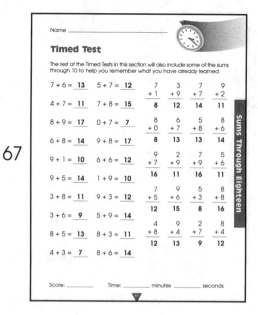

**Timed Test**

The rest of the Timed Tests in this section will also include some of the sums through 10 to help you remember what you have already learned.

Sums Through Eighteen

7 + 6 = __13__    5 + 7 = __12__

4 + 7 = __11__    7 + 8 = __15__

8 + 9 = __17__    0 + 7 = __7__

6 + 8 = __14__    9 + 8 = __17__

9 + 1 = __10__    6 + 6 = __12__

9 + 5 = __14__    1 + 9 = __10__

3 + 8 = __11__    9 + 3 = __12__

3 + 6 = __9__    5 + 9 = __14__

8 + 5 = __13__    8 + 3 = __11__

4 + 3 = __7__    8 + 6 = __14__

| 7 | 3 | 7 | 9 |
|---|---|---|---|
| +1 | +9 | +7 | +2 |
| 8 | 12 | 14 | 11 |
| 8 | 6 | 5 | 8 |
| +0 | +7 | +8 | +6 |
| 8 | 13 | 13 | 14 |
| 9 | 2 | 7 | 5 |
| +7 | +9 | +9 | +6 |
| 16 | 11 | 16 | 11 |
| 7 | 9 | 6 | 8 |
| +5 | +6 | +3 | +8 |
| 12 | 15 | 8 | 16 |
| 4 | 9 | 2 | 8 |
| +8 | +4 | +7 | +4 |
| 12 | 13 | 9 | 12 |

Score: _____    Time: _____ minutes _____ seconds

## 68

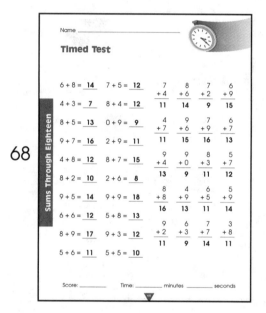

**Timed Test**

Sums Through Eighteen

6 + 8 = __14__    7 + 5 = __12__

4 + 3 = __7__    8 + 4 = __12__

8 + 5 = __13__    0 + 9 = __9__

9 + 7 = __16__    2 + 9 = __11__

4 + 8 = __12__    8 + 7 = __15__

8 + 2 = __10__    2 + 6 = __8__

9 + 5 = __14__    9 + 9 = __18__

6 + 6 = __12__    5 + 8 = __13__

8 + 9 = __17__    9 + 3 = __12__

5 + 6 = __11__    5 + 5 = __10__

| 7 | 8 | 7 | 6 |
|---|---|---|---|
| +4 | +6 | +2 | +9 |
| 11 | 14 | 9 | 15 |
| 4 | 9 | 7 | 6 |
| +7 | +6 | +9 | +7 |
| 11 | 15 | 16 | 13 |
| 9 | 9 | 8 | 5 |
| +4 | +0 | +3 | +7 |
| 13 | 9 | 11 | 12 |
| 8 | 4 | 6 | 5 |
| +8 | +9 | +5 | +9 |
| 16 | 13 | 11 | 14 |
| 9 | 6 | 7 | 3 |
| +2 | +3 | +7 | +8 |
| 11 | 9 | 14 | 11 |

Score: _____    Time: _____ minutes _____ seconds

## 69

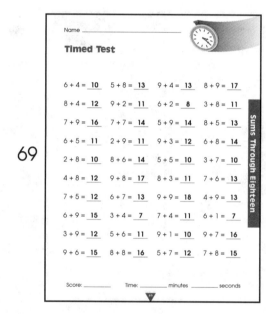

**Timed Test**

Sums Through Eighteen

6 + 4 = __10__    5 + 8 = __13__    9 + 4 = __13__    8 + 9 = __17__

8 + 4 = __12__    9 + 2 = __11__    6 + 2 = __8__    3 + 8 = __11__

7 + 9 = __16__    7 + 7 = __14__    5 + 9 = __14__    8 + 5 = __13__

6 + 5 = __11__    2 + 9 = __11__    9 + 3 = __12__    6 + 8 = __14__

2 + 8 = __10__    8 + 6 = __14__    5 + 5 = __10__    3 + 7 = __10__

4 + 8 = __12__    9 + 8 = __17__    8 + 3 = __11__    7 + 6 = __13__

7 + 5 = __12__    6 + 7 = __13__    9 + 9 = __18__    4 + 9 = __13__

6 + 9 = __15__    3 + 4 = __7__    7 + 4 = __11__    6 + 1 = __7__

3 + 9 = __12__    5 + 6 = __11__    9 + 1 = __10__    9 + 7 = __16__

9 + 6 = __15__    8 + 8 = __16__    5 + 7 = __12__    7 + 8 = __15__

Score: _____    Time: _____ minutes _____ seconds

## 70

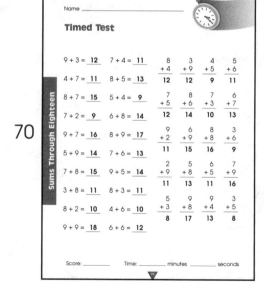

**Timed Test**

Sums Through Eighteen

9 + 3 = __12__    7 + 4 = __11__

4 + 7 = __11__    8 + 5 = __13__

8 + 7 = __15__    5 + 4 = __9__

7 + 2 = __9__    6 + 8 = __14__

9 + 7 = __16__    8 + 9 = __17__

5 + 9 = __14__    7 + 6 = __13__

7 + 8 = __15__    9 + 5 = __14__

3 + 8 = __11__    8 + 3 = __11__

8 + 2 = __10__    4 + 6 = __10__

9 + 9 = __18__    6 + 6 = __12__

| 8 | 3 | 4 | 5 |
|---|---|---|---|
| +4 | +9 | +5 | +6 |
| 12 | 12 | 9 | 11 |
| 7 | 8 | 7 | 6 |
| +5 | +6 | +3 | +7 |
| 12 | 14 | 10 | 13 |
| 9 | 6 | 8 | 3 |
| +2 | +9 | +8 | +6 |
| 11 | 15 | 16 | 9 |
| 2 | 5 | 6 | 7 |
| +9 | +8 | +5 | +9 |
| 11 | 13 | 11 | 16 |
| 5 | 9 | 9 | 3 |
| +3 | +8 | +4 | +5 |
| 8 | 17 | 13 | 8 |

Score: _____    Time: _____ minutes _____ seconds

## 71

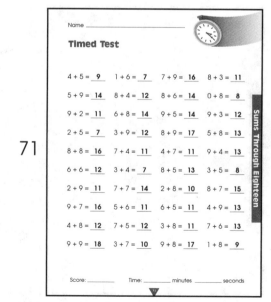

**Timed Test**

Sums Through Eighteen

4 + 5 = __9__    1 + 6 = __7__    7 + 9 = __16__    8 + 3 = __11__

5 + 9 = __14__    8 + 4 = __12__    8 + 6 = __14__    0 + 8 = __8__

9 + 2 = __11__    6 + 8 = __14__    9 + 5 = __14__    9 + 3 = __12__

2 + 5 = __7__    3 + 9 = __12__    8 + 9 = __17__    5 + 8 = __13__

8 + 8 = __16__    7 + 4 = __11__    4 + 7 = __11__    9 + 4 = __13__

6 + 6 = __12__    3 + 4 = __7__    8 + 5 = __13__    3 + 5 = __8__

2 + 9 = __11__    7 + 7 = __14__    2 + 8 = __10__    8 + 7 = __15__

9 + 7 = __16__    5 + 6 = __11__    6 + 5 = __11__    4 + 9 = __13__

4 + 8 = __12__    7 + 5 = __12__    3 + 8 = __11__    7 + 6 = __13__

9 + 9 = __18__    3 + 7 = __10__    9 + 8 = __17__    1 + 8 = __9__

Score: _____    Time: _____ minutes _____ seconds

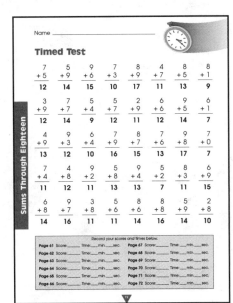

Name _____

## Timed Test

| | | | | | | | |
|---|---|---|---|---|---|---|---|
| 7 | 5 | 7 | 7 | 8 | 4 | 8 | 8 |
| +5 | +9 | +6 | +3 | +9 | +7 | +5 | +1 |
| **12** | **14** | **15** | **10** | **17** | **11** | **13** | **9** |

| | | | | | | | |
|---|---|---|---|---|---|---|---|
| 3 | 7 | 5 | 5 | 2 | 6 | 9 | 6 |
| +9 | +7 | +4 | +7 | +9 | +6 | +5 | +1 |
| **12** | **14** | **9** | **12** | **11** | **12** | **14** | **7** |

| | | | | | | | |
|---|---|---|---|---|---|---|---|
| 4 | 9 | 6 | 7 | 8 | 7 | 9 | 7 |
| +9 | +3 | +4 | +9 | +7 | +6 | +8 | +0 |
| **13** | **12** | **10** | **16** | **15** | **13** | **17** | **7** |

| | | | | | | | |
|---|---|---|---|---|---|---|---|
| 7 | 4 | 9 | 5 | 9 | 5 | 8 | 6 |
| +4 | +8 | +2 | +8 | +4 | +2 | +3 | +9 |
| **11** | **12** | **11** | **13** | **13** | **7** | **11** | **15** |

| | | | | | | | |
|---|---|---|---|---|---|---|---|
| 6 | 9 | 3 | 5 | 8 | 8 | 5 | 2 |
| +8 | +7 | +8 | +6 | +6 | +8 | +9 | +8 |
| **14** | **16** | **11** | **11** | **14** | **16** | **14** | **10** |

Record your scores and times below.

| | | | |
|---|---|---|---|
| Page 61 Score:___ Time:___min.___sec. | Page 67 Score:___ Time:___min.___sec. |
| Page 62 Score:___ Time:___min.___sec. | Page 68 Score:___ Time:___min.___sec. |
| Page 63 Score:___ Time:___min.___sec. | Page 69 Score:___ Time:___min.___sec. |
| Page 64 Score:___ Time:___min.___sec. | Page 70 Score:___ Time:___min.___sec. |
| Page 65 Score:___ Time:___min.___sec. | Page 71 Score:___ Time:___min.___sec. |
| Page 66 Score:___ Time:___min.___sec. | Page 72 Score:___ Time:___min.___sec. |

Sums Through Eighteen

**72**

---

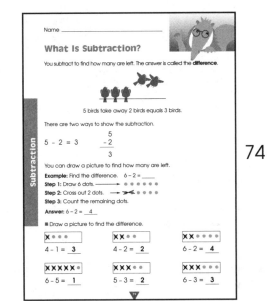

Name _____

## What Is Subtraction?

You subtract to find how many are left. The answer is called the **difference**.

5 birds take away 2 birds equals 3 birds.

There are two ways to show the subtraction.

$5 - 2 = 3$

$$\begin{array}{r} 5 \\ -2 \\ \hline 3 \end{array}$$

You can draw a picture to find how many are left.

**Example:** Find the difference. $6 - 2 =$

**Step 1:** Draw 6 dots. → • • • • • •

**Step 2:** Cross out 2 dots. → ✗✗ • • • •

**Step 3:** Count the remaining dots.

**Answer:** $6 - 2 = $ __4__

■ Draw a picture to find the difference.

| | | |
|---|---|---|
| ✗ • • • | ✗✗ • • | ✗✗ • • • • |
| $4 - 1 = $ **3** | $4 - 2 = $ **2** | $6 - 2 = $ **4** |
| ✗✗✗✗✗ • | ✗✗✗ • • | ✗✗✗ • • • |
| $6 - 5 = $ **1** | $5 - 3 = $ **2** | $6 - 3 = $ **3** |

Subtraction

**74**

---

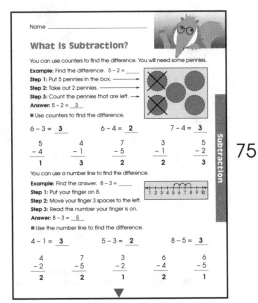

Name _____

## What Is Subtraction?

You can use counters to find the difference. You will need some pennies.

**Example:** Find the difference. $5 - 2 = $

**Step 1:** Put 5 pennies in the box. →

**Step 2:** Take out 2 pennies. →

**Step 3:** Count the pennies that are left. →

**Answer:** $5 - 2 = $ __3__

■ Use counters to find the difference.

| $6 - 3 = $ **3** | $6 - 4 = $ **2** | $7 - 4 = $ **3** |
|---|---|---|

| | | | |
|---|---|---|---|
| 5 | 4 | 7 | 3 | 5 |
| -4 | -1 | -5 | -1 | -2 |
| **1** | **3** | **2** | **2** | **3** |

You can use a number line to find the difference.

**Example:** Find the answer. $8 - 3 = $

**Step 1:** Put your finger on 8.

**Step 2:** Move your finger 3 spaces to the left.

**Step 3:** Read the number your finger is on.

**Answer:** $8 - 3 = $ __5__

■ Use the number line to find the difference.

| $4 - 1 = $ **3** | $5 - 3 = $ **2** | $8 - 5 = $ **3** |
|---|---|---|

| | | | |
|---|---|---|---|
| 4 | 7 | 3 | 6 | 6 |
| -2 | -5 | -2 | -4 | -5 |
| **2** | **2** | **1** | **2** | **1** |

Subtraction

**75**

---

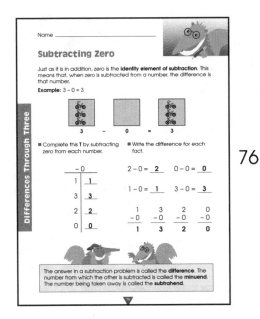

Name _____

## Subtracting Zero

Just as it is in addition, zero is the **identity element of subtraction**. This means that, when zero is subtracted from a number, the difference is that number.

**Example:** $3 - 0 = 3$

$$3 \quad - \quad 0 \quad = \quad 3$$

■ Complete this **T** by subtracting zero from each number.

| -0 | |
|---|---|
| 1 | **1** |
| 3 | **3** |
| 2 | **2** |
| 0 | **0** |

■ Write the difference for each fact.

$2 - 0 = $ **2**     $0 - 0 = $ **0**

$1 - 0 = $ **1**     $3 - 0 = $ **3**

| | | | |
|---|---|---|---|
| 1 | 3 | 2 | 0 |
| -0 | -0 | -0 | -0 |
| **1** | **3** | **2** | **0** |

The answer in a subtraction problem is called the **difference**. The number from which the other is subtracted is called the **minuend**. The number being taken away is called the **subtrahend**.

Differences Through Three

**76**

---

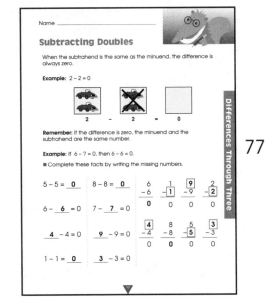

Name _____

## Subtracting Doubles

When the subtrahend is the same as the minuend, the difference is always zero.

**Example:** $2 - 2 = 0$

$$2 \quad - \quad 2 \quad = \quad 0$$

**Remember:** If the difference is zero, the minuend and the subtrahend are the same number.

**Example:** If $6 - ? = 0$, then $6 - 6 = 0$.

■ Complete these facts by writing the missing numbers.

$5 - 5 = $ **0**     $8 - 8 = $ **0**

| | | | |
|---|---|---|---|
| 6 | **1** | **9** | 2 |
| -6 | -**1** | -9 | -**2** |
| **0** | **0** | **0** | **0** |

$6 - $ **6** $= 0$     $7 - $ **7** $= 0$

| | | | |
|---|---|---|---|
| **4** | 8 | 5 | **3** |
| -4 | -8 | -**5** | -3 |
| **0** | **0** | **0** | **0** |

__**4**__ $- 4 = 0$     __**9**__ $- 9 = 0$

$1 - 1 = $ **0**     __**3**__ $- 3 = 0$

Differences Through Three

**77**

---

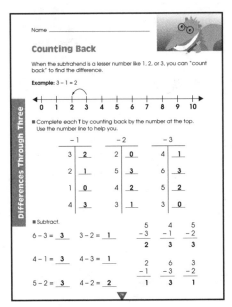

Name _____

## Counting Back

When the subtrahend is a lesser number like 1, 2, or 3, you can "count back" to find the difference.

**Example:** $3 - 1 = 2$

■ Complete each **T** by counting back by the number at the top. Use the number line to help you.

| -1 | | | -2 | | | -3 | |
|---|---|---|---|---|---|---|---|
| 3 | **2** | | 2 | **0** | | 4 | **1** |
| 2 | **1** | | 5 | **3** | | 6 | **3** |
| 1 | **0** | | 4 | **2** | | 5 | **2** |
| 4 | **3** | | 3 | **1** | | 3 | **0** |

■ Subtract.

$6 - 3 = $ **3**     $3 - 2 = $ **1**

| | |
|---|---|
| 5 | 4 | 5 |
| -3 | -1 | -2 |
| **2** | **3** | **3** |

$4 - 1 = $ **3**     $4 - 3 = $ **1**

| | |
|---|---|
| 2 | 6 | 3 |
| -1 | -3 | -2 |
| **1** | **3** | **1** |

$5 - 2 = $ **3**     $4 - 2 = $ **2**

Differences Through Three

**78**

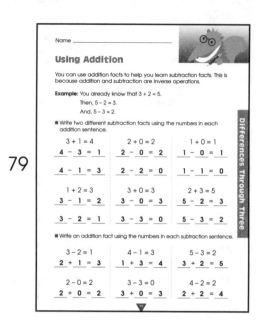

**79**

Name _____

## Using Addition

You can use addition facts to help you learn subtraction facts. This is because addition and subtraction are inverse operations.

**Example:** You already know that $3 + 2 = 5$.
Then, $5 - 2 = 3$.
And, $5 - 3 = 2$.

■ Write two different subtraction facts using the numbers in each addition sentence.

| $3 + 1 = 4$ | $2 + 0 = 2$ | $1 + 0 = 1$ |
|---|---|---|
| $4 - 3 = \underline{1}$ | $2 - 0 = \underline{2}$ | $1 - 0 = \underline{1}$ |
| $4 - 1 = \underline{3}$ | $2 - 2 = \underline{0}$ | $1 - 1 = \underline{0}$ |

| $1 + 2 = 3$ | $3 + 0 = 3$ | $2 + 3 = 5$ |
|---|---|---|
| $3 - 1 = \underline{2}$ | $3 - 0 = \underline{3}$ | $5 - 2 = \underline{3}$ |
| $3 - 2 = \underline{1}$ | $3 - 3 = \underline{0}$ | $5 - 3 = \underline{2}$ |

■ Write an addition fact using the numbers in each subtraction sentence.

| $3 - 2 = 1$ | $4 - 1 = 3$ | $5 - 3 = 2$ |
|---|---|---|
| $2 + 1 = \underline{3}$ | $1 + 3 = \underline{4}$ | $3 + 2 = \underline{5}$ |

| $2 - 0 = 2$ | $3 - 3 = 0$ | $4 - 2 = 2$ |
|---|---|---|
| $2 + 0 = \underline{2}$ | $3 + 0 = \underline{3}$ | $2 + 2 = \underline{4}$ |

*Differences Through Three*

---

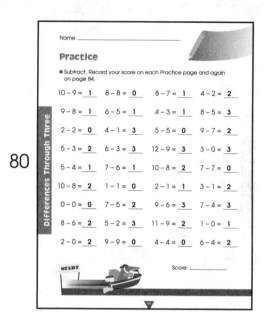

**80**

Name _____

## Practice

■ Subtract. Record your score on each Practice page and again on page 84.

| | | | |
|---|---|---|---|
| $10 - 9 = \underline{1}$ | $8 - 8 = \underline{0}$ | $8 - 7 = \underline{1}$ | $4 - 2 = \underline{2}$ |
| $9 - 8 = \underline{1}$ | $6 - 5 = \underline{1}$ | $4 - 3 = \underline{1}$ | $8 - 5 = \underline{3}$ |
| $2 - 2 = \underline{0}$ | $4 - 1 = \underline{3}$ | $5 - 5 = \underline{0}$ | $9 - 7 = \underline{2}$ |
| $5 - 3 = \underline{2}$ | $6 - 3 = \underline{3}$ | $12 - 9 = \underline{3}$ | $3 - 0 = \underline{3}$ |
| $5 - 4 = \underline{1}$ | $7 - 6 = \underline{1}$ | $10 - 8 = \underline{2}$ | $7 - 7 = \underline{0}$ |
| $10 - 8 = \underline{2}$ | $1 - 1 = \underline{0}$ | $2 - 1 = \underline{1}$ | $3 - 1 = \underline{2}$ |
| $0 - 0 = \underline{0}$ | $7 - 5 = \underline{2}$ | $9 - 6 = \underline{3}$ | $7 - 4 = \underline{3}$ |
| $8 - 6 = \underline{2}$ | $5 - 2 = \underline{3}$ | $11 - 9 = \underline{2}$ | $1 - 0 = \underline{1}$ |
| $2 - 0 = \underline{2}$ | $9 - 9 = \underline{0}$ | $4 - 4 = \underline{0}$ | $6 - 4 = \underline{2}$ |

START

Score: _____

*Differences Through Three*

---

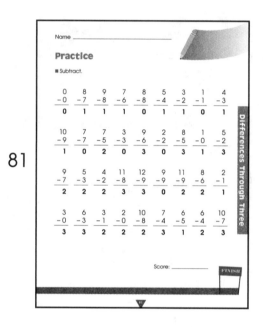

**81**

Name _____

## Practice

■ Subtract.

| 0 | 8 | 9 | 7 | 8 | 5 | 3 | 1 | 4 |
|---|---|---|---|---|---|---|---|---|
| $-0$ | $-7$ | $-8$ | $-6$ | $-8$ | $-4$ | $-2$ | $-1$ | $-3$ |
| **0** | **1** | **1** | **1** | **0** | **1** | **1** | **0** | **1** |

| 10 | 7 | 7 | 3 | 9 | 2 | 8 | 1 | 5 |
|---|---|---|---|---|---|---|---|---|
| $-9$ | $-7$ | $-5$ | $-3$ | $-6$ | $-2$ | $-5$ | $-0$ | $-2$ |
| **1** | **0** | **2** | **0** | **3** | **0** | **3** | **1** | **3** |

| 9 | 5 | 4 | 11 | 12 | 9 | 11 | 8 | 2 |
|---|---|---|---|---|---|---|---|---|
| $-7$ | $-3$ | $-2$ | $-8$ | $-9$ | $-9$ | $-9$ | $-6$ | $-1$ |
| **2** | **2** | **2** | **3** | **3** | **0** | **2** | **2** | **1** |

| 3 | 6 | 3 | 2 | 10 | 7 | 6 | 6 | 10 |
|---|---|---|---|---|---|---|---|---|
| $-0$ | $-3$ | $-1$ | $-0$ | $-8$ | $-4$ | $-5$ | $-4$ | $-7$ |
| **3** | **3** | **2** | **2** | **2** | **3** | **1** | **2** | **3** |

Score: _____

FINISH

*Differences Through Three*

---

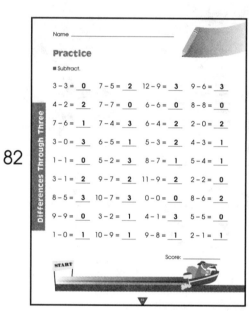

**82**

Name _____

## Practice

■ Subtract.

| | | | |
|---|---|---|---|
| $3 - 3 = \underline{0}$ | $7 - 5 = \underline{2}$ | $12 - 9 = \underline{3}$ | $9 - 6 = \underline{3}$ |
| $4 - 2 = \underline{2}$ | $7 - 7 = \underline{0}$ | $6 - 6 = \underline{0}$ | $8 - 8 = \underline{0}$ |
| $7 - 6 = \underline{1}$ | $7 - 4 = \underline{3}$ | $6 - 4 = \underline{2}$ | $2 - 0 = \underline{2}$ |
| $3 - 0 = \underline{3}$ | $6 - 5 = \underline{1}$ | $5 - 3 = \underline{2}$ | $4 - 3 = \underline{1}$ |
| $1 - 1 = \underline{0}$ | $5 - 2 = \underline{3}$ | $8 - 7 = \underline{1}$ | $5 - 4 = \underline{1}$ |
| $3 - 1 = \underline{2}$ | $9 - 7 = \underline{2}$ | $11 - 9 = \underline{2}$ | $2 - 2 = \underline{0}$ |
| $8 - 5 = \underline{3}$ | $10 - 7 = \underline{3}$ | $0 - 0 = \underline{0}$ | $8 - 6 = \underline{2}$ |
| $9 - 9 = \underline{0}$ | $3 - 2 = \underline{1}$ | $4 - 1 = \underline{3}$ | $5 - 5 = \underline{0}$ |
| $1 - 0 = \underline{1}$ | $10 - 9 = \underline{1}$ | $9 - 8 = \underline{1}$ | $2 - 1 = \underline{1}$ |

Score: _____

START

*Differences Through Three*

---

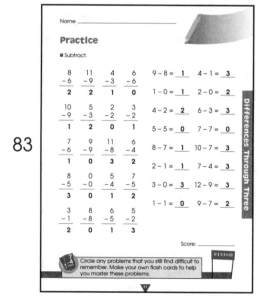

**83**

Name _____

## Practice

■ Subtract.

| 8 | 11 | 4 | 6 |
|---|---|---|---|
| $-6$ | $-9$ | $-3$ | $-6$ |
| **2** | **2** | **1** | **0** |

| 10 | 5 | 2 | 3 |
|---|---|---|---|
| $-9$ | $-3$ | $-2$ | $-2$ |
| **1** | **2** | **0** | **1** |

| 7 | 9 | 11 | 6 |
|---|---|---|---|
| $-6$ | $-9$ | $-8$ | $-4$ |
| **1** | **0** | **3** | **2** |

| 8 | 0 | 5 | 7 |
|---|---|---|---|
| $-5$ | $-0$ | $-4$ | $-5$ |
| **3** | **0** | **1** | **2** |

| 3 | 8 | 6 | 5 |
|---|---|---|---|
| $-1$ | $-8$ | $-5$ | $-2$ |
| **2** | **0** | **1** | **3** |

| | |
|---|---|
| $9 - 8 = \underline{1}$ | $4 - 1 = \underline{3}$ |
| $1 - 0 = \underline{1}$ | $2 - 0 = \underline{2}$ |
| $4 - 2 = \underline{2}$ | $6 - 3 = \underline{3}$ |
| $5 - 5 = \underline{0}$ | $7 - 7 = \underline{0}$ |
| $8 - 7 = \underline{1}$ | $10 - 7 = \underline{3}$ |
| $2 - 1 = \underline{1}$ | $7 - 4 = \underline{3}$ |
| $3 - 0 = \underline{3}$ | $12 - 9 = \underline{3}$ |
| $1 - 1 = \underline{0}$ | $9 - 7 = \underline{2}$ |

Circle any problems that you still find difficult to remember. Make your own flash cards to help you master these problems.

Score: _____

FINISH

*Differences Through Three*

---

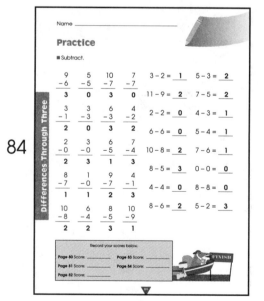

**84**

Name _____

## Practice

■ Subtract.

| 9 | 5 | 10 | 7 |
|---|---|---|---|
| $-6$ | $-5$ | $-7$ | $-7$ |
| **3** | **0** | **3** | **0** |

| 3 | 3 | 6 | 4 |
|---|---|---|---|
| $-1$ | $-3$ | $-3$ | $-2$ |
| **2** | **0** | **3** | **2** |

| 2 | 3 | 6 | 7 |
|---|---|---|---|
| $-0$ | $-0$ | $-5$ | $-4$ |
| **2** | **3** | **1** | **3** |

| 8 | 1 | 9 | 4 |
|---|---|---|---|
| $-7$ | $-0$ | $-7$ | $-1$ |
| **1** | **1** | **2** | **3** |

| 10 | 6 | 8 | 10 |
|---|---|---|---|
| $-8$ | $-4$ | $-5$ | $-9$ |
| **2** | **2** | **3** | **1** |

| | |
|---|---|
| $3 - 2 = \underline{1}$ | $5 - 3 = \underline{2}$ |
| $11 - 9 = \underline{2}$ | $7 - 5 = \underline{2}$ |
| $2 - 2 = \underline{0}$ | $4 - 3 = \underline{1}$ |
| $6 - 6 = \underline{0}$ | $5 - 4 = \underline{1}$ |
| $10 - 8 = \underline{2}$ | $7 - 6 = \underline{1}$ |
| $8 - 5 = \underline{3}$ | $0 - 0 = \underline{0}$ |
| $4 - 4 = \underline{0}$ | $8 - 8 = \underline{0}$ |
| $8 - 6 = \underline{2}$ | $5 - 2 = \underline{3}$ |

Record your scores below.

| | |
|---|---|
| Page 80 Score: _____ | Page 83 Score: _____ |
| Page 81 Score: _____ | Page 84 Score: _____ |
| Page 82 Score: _____ | |

FINISH

*Differences Through Three*

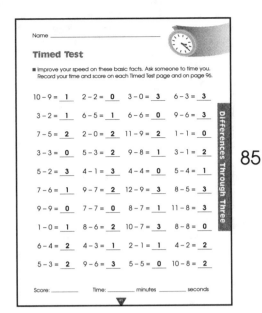

**Page 85 — Timed Test**

■ Improve your speed on these basic facts. Ask someone to time you. Record your time and score on each Timed Test page and on page 96.

10 − 9 = **1**   2 − 2 = **0**   3 − 0 = **3**   6 − 3 = **3**
3 − 2 = **1**   6 − 5 = **1**   6 − 6 = **0**   9 − 6 = **3**
7 − 5 = **2**   2 − 0 = **2**   11 − 9 = **2**   1 − 1 = **0**
3 − 3 = **0**   5 − 3 = **2**   9 − 8 = **1**   3 − 1 = **2**
5 − 2 = **3**   4 − 1 = **3**   4 − 4 = **0**   5 − 4 = **1**
7 − 6 = **1**   9 − 7 = **2**   12 − 9 = **3**   8 − 5 = **3**
9 − 9 = **0**   7 − 7 = **0**   8 − 7 = **1**   11 − 8 = **3**
1 − 0 = **1**   8 − 6 = **2**   10 − 7 = **3**   8 − 8 = **0**
6 − 4 = **2**   4 − 3 = **1**   2 − 1 = **1**   4 − 2 = **2**
5 − 3 = **2**   9 − 6 = **3**   5 − 5 = **0**   10 − 8 = **2**

*Differences Through Three*

Score: _____   Time: _____ minutes _____ seconds

**85**

---

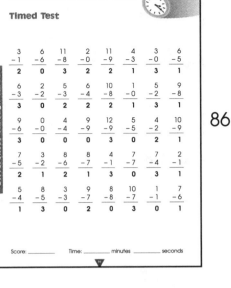

**Page 86 — Timed Test**

| | | | | | | | |
|---|---|---|---|---|---|---|---|
| 3 − 1 = **2** | 6 − 6 = **0** | 11 − 8 = **3** | 2 − 0 = **2** | 11 − 9 = **2** | 4 − 3 = **1** | 3 − 0 = **3** | 6 − 5 = **1** |
| 6 − 3 = **3** | 2 − 2 = **0** | 5 − 3 = **2** | 6 − 4 = **2** | 10 − 8 = **2** | 1 − 0 = **1** | 5 − 2 = **3** | 9 − 8 = **1** |
| 9 − 6 = **3** | 0 − 0 = **0** | 4 − 4 = **0** | 9 − 9 = **0** | 12 − 9 = **3** | 5 − 5 = **0** | 4 − 2 = **2** | 10 − 9 = **1** |
| 7 − 5 = **2** | 3 − 2 = **1** | 8 − 6 = **2** | 8 − 7 = **1** | 4 − 1 = **3** | 7 − 7 = **0** | 7 − 4 = **3** | 2 − 1 = **1** |
| 5 − 4 = **1** | 8 − 5 = **3** | 3 − 3 = **0** | 9 − 7 = **2** | 8 − 8 = **0** | 10 − 7 = **3** | 1 − 1 = **0** | 7 − 6 = **1** |

*Differences Through Three*

Score: _____   Time: _____ minutes _____ seconds

**86**

---

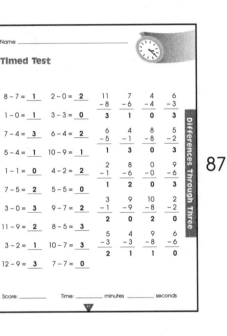

**Page 87 — Timed Test**

8 − 7 = **1**   2 − 0 = **2**
1 − 0 = **1**   3 − 3 = **0**
7 − 4 = **3**   6 − 4 = **2**
5 − 4 = **1**   10 − 9 = **1**
1 − 1 = **0**   4 − 2 = **2**
7 − 5 = **2**   5 − 5 = **0**
3 − 0 = **3**   9 − 7 = **2**
11 − 9 = **2**   8 − 5 = **3**
3 − 2 = **1**   10 − 7 = **3**
12 − 9 = **3**   7 − 7 = **0**

| | | | |
|---|---|---|---|
| 11 − 8 = **3** | 7 − 6 = **1** | 4 − 4 = **0** | 6 − 3 = **3** |
| 6 − 5 = **1** | 4 − 1 = **3** | 8 − 8 = **0** | 5 − 2 = **3** |
| 2 − 1 = **1** | 8 − 6 = **2** | 0 − 0 = **0** | 9 − 6 = **3** |
| 3 − 1 = **2** | 9 − 9 = **0** | 10 − 8 = **2** | 2 − 2 = **0** |
| 5 − 3 = **2** | 4 − 3 = **1** | 9 − 8 = **1** | 6 − 6 = **0** |

*Differences Through Three*

Score: _____   Time: _____ minutes _____ seconds

**87**

---

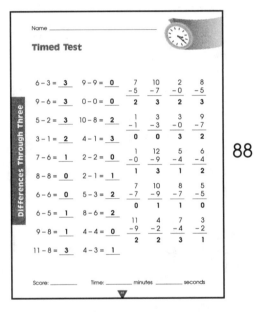

**Page 88 — Timed Test**

6 − 3 = **3**   9 − 9 = **0**
9 − 6 = **3**   0 − 0 = **0**
5 − 2 = **3**   10 − 8 = **2**
3 − 1 = **2**   4 − 1 = **3**
7 − 6 = **1**   2 − 2 = **0**
8 − 8 = **0**   2 − 1 = **1**
6 − 6 = **0**   5 − 3 = **2**
6 − 5 = **1**   8 − 6 = **2**
9 − 8 = **1**   4 − 4 = **0**
11 − 8 = **3**   4 − 3 = **1**

| | | | |
|---|---|---|---|
| 7 − 5 = **2** | 10 − 7 = **3** | 2 − 0 = **2** | 8 − 5 = **3** |
| 1 − 1 = **0** | 3 − 3 = **0** | 3 − 0 = **3** | 9 − 7 = **2** |
| 1 − 0 = **1** | 12 − 9 = **3** | 5 − 4 = **1** | 6 − 4 = **2** |
| 7 − 7 = **0** | 10 − 9 = **1** | 8 − 7 = **1** | 5 − 5 = **0** |
| 11 − 9 = **2** | 4 − 2 = **2** | 7 − 4 = **3** | 3 − 2 = **1** |

*Differences Through Three*

Score: _____   Time: _____ minutes _____ seconds

**88**

---

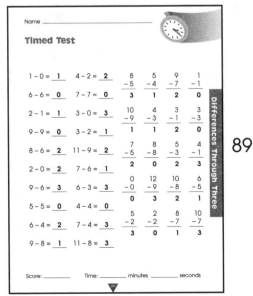

**Page 89 — Timed Test**

1 − 0 = **1**   4 − 2 = **2**
6 − 6 = **0**   7 − 7 = **0**
2 − 1 = **1**   3 − 0 = **3**
9 − 9 = **0**   3 − 2 = **1**
8 − 6 = **2**   11 − 9 = **2**
2 − 0 = **2**   7 − 6 = **1**
9 − 6 = **3**   6 − 3 = **3**
5 − 5 = **0**   4 − 4 = **0**
6 − 4 = **2**   7 − 4 = **3**
9 − 8 = **1**   11 − 8 = **3**

| | | | |
|---|---|---|---|
| 8 − 5 = **3** | 5 − 4 = **1** | 9 − 7 = **2** | 1 − 1 = **0** |
| 10 − 9 = **1** | 4 − 3 = **1** | 3 − 1 = **2** | 3 − 3 = **0** |
| 7 − 5 = **2** | 8 − 8 = **0** | 5 − 3 = **2** | 4 − 1 = **3** |
| 0 − 0 = **0** | 12 − 9 = **3** | 10 − 8 = **2** | 6 − 5 = **1** |
| 5 − 2 = **3** | 2 − 2 = **0** | 8 − 7 = **1** | 10 − 7 = **3** |

*Differences Through Three*

Score: _____   Time: _____ minutes _____ seconds

**89**

---

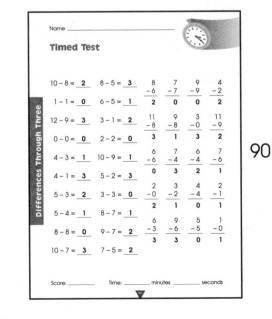

**Page 90 — Timed Test**

10 − 8 = **2**   8 − 5 = **3**
1 − 1 = **0**   6 − 5 = **1**
12 − 9 = **3**   3 − 1 = **2**
0 − 0 = **0**   2 − 2 = **0**
4 − 3 = **1**   10 − 9 = **1**
4 − 1 = **3**   5 − 2 = **3**
5 − 3 = **2**   3 − 3 = **0**
5 − 4 = **1**   8 − 7 = **1**
8 − 8 = **0**   9 − 7 = **2**
10 − 7 = **3**   7 − 5 = **2**

| | | | |
|---|---|---|---|
| 8 − 6 = **2** | 7 − 7 = **0** | 9 − 9 = **0** | 4 − 2 = **2** |
| 11 − 8 = **3** | 9 − 8 = **1** | 3 − 0 = **3** | 11 − 9 = **2** |
| 6 − 6 = **0** | 7 − 4 = **3** | 6 − 4 = **2** | 7 − 6 = **1** |
| 2 − 0 = **2** | 3 − 2 = **1** | 4 − 4 = **0** | 2 − 1 = **1** |
| 6 − 3 = **3** | 9 − 6 = **3** | 5 − 5 = **0** | 1 − 0 = **1** |

*Differences Through Three*

Score: _____   Time: _____ minutes _____ seconds

**90**

**91**

Name _____

**Timed Test**

8 − 8 = **0**   11 − 9 = **2**

| 0 | 4 | 2 | 8 |
|---|---|---|---|
| −0 | −3 | −0 | −5 |
| **0** | **1** | **2** | **3** |

3 − 1 = **2**   3 − 3 = **0**

7 − 4 = **3**   1 − 0 = **1**

| 4 | 2 | 9 | 10 |
|---|---|---|---|
| −4 | −1 | −7 | −9 |
| **0** | **1** | **2** | **1** |

1 − 1 = **0**   6 − 4 = **2**

3 − 2 = **1**   8 − 7 = **1**

| 8 | 9 | 2 | 12 |
|---|---|---|---|
| −6 | −9 | −2 | −9 |
| **2** | **0** | **0** | **3** |

10 − 8 = **2**   5 − 3 = **2**

6 − 3 = **3**   6 − 5 = **1**

| 4 | 9 | 7 | 3 |
|---|---|---|---|
| −2 | −8 | −5 | −0 |
| **2** | **1** | **2** | **3** |

7 − 7 = **0**   5 − 5 = **0**

5 − 2 = **3**   9 − 6 = **3**

| 5 | 6 | 4 | 11 |
|---|---|---|---|
| −4 | −6 | −1 | −8 |
| **1** | **0** | **3** | **3** |

7 − 6 = **1**   10 − 7 = **3**

Score: _____   Time: _____ minutes _____ seconds

*Differences Through Three*

---

**92**

Name _____

**Timed Test**

2 − 0 = **2**   4 − 1 = **3**

| 1 | 3 | 8 | 6 |
|---|---|---|---|
| −1 | −3 | −8 | −3 |
| **0** | **0** | **0** | **3** |

9 − 9 = **0**   12 − 9 = **3**

10 − 9 = **1**   11 − 8 = **3**

| 7 | 10 | 3 | 5 |
|---|---|---|---|
| −7 | −8 | −2 | −5 |
| **0** | **2** | **1** | **0** |

7 − 5 = **2**   5 − 4 = **1**

9 − 7 = **2**   0 − 0 = **0**

| 1 | 6 | 6 | 11 |
|---|---|---|---|
| −0 | −5 | −4 | −9 |
| **1** | **1** | **2** | **2** |

2 − 2 = **0**   4 − 2 = **2**

9 − 8 = **1**   8 − 6 = **2**

| 7 | 7 | 5 | 3 |
|---|---|---|---|
| −4 | −6 | −2 | −1 |
| **3** | **1** | **3** | **2** |

3 − 0 = **3**   4 − 4 = **0**

4 − 3 = **1**   8 − 5 = **3**

| 10 | 9 | 5 | 8 |
|---|---|---|---|
| −7 | −6 | −3 | −7 |
| **3** | **3** | **2** | **1** |

2 − 1 = **1**   6 − 6 = **0**

*Differences Through Three*

Score: _____   Time: _____ minutes _____ seconds

---

**93**

Name _____

**Timed Test**

11 − 9 = **2**   3 − 2 = **1**   7 − 4 = **3**   9 − 6 = **3**

4 − 2 = **2**   7 − 5 = **2**   10 − 8 = **2**   10 − 9 = **1**

1 − 1 = **0**   3 − 3 = **0**   2 − 2 = **0**   6 − 5 = **1**

1 − 0 = **1**   9 − 9 = **0**   2 − 1 = **1**   4 − 1 = **3**

12 − 9 = **3**   9 − 8 = **1**   11 − 8 = **3**   5 − 3 = **2**

3 − 1 = **2**   5 − 4 = **1**   9 − 7 = **2**   4 − 4 = **0**

10 − 7 = **3**   3 − 0 = **3**   2 − 0 = **2**   8 − 8 = **0**

6 − 6 = **0**   5 − 5 = **0**   8 − 6 = **2**   5 − 2 = **3**

7 − 7 = **0**   6 − 4 = **2**   0 − 0 = **0**   8 − 7 = **1**

6 − 3 = **3**   7 − 6 = **1**   4 − 3 = **1**   8 − 5 = **3**

*Differences Through Three*

Score: _____   Time: _____ minutes _____ seconds

---

**94**

Name _____

**Timed Test**

*Differences Through Three*

| 5 | 12 | 4 | 5 | 2 | 11 | 3 | 4 |
|---|---|---|---|---|---|---|---|
| −3 | −9 | −3 | −5 | −1 | −9 | −3 | −1 |
| **2** | **3** | **1** | **0** | **1** | **2** | **0** | **3** |

| 10 | 9 | 6 | 9 | 7 | 8 | 3 | 7 |
|---|---|---|---|---|---|---|---|
| −9 | −7 | −5 | −9 | −5 | −7 | −1 | −7 |
| **1** | **2** | **1** | **0** | **2** | **1** | **2** | **0** |

| 6 | 10 | 1 | 8 | 8 | 5 | 5 | 0 |
|---|---|---|---|---|---|---|---|
| −3 | −7 | −1 | −5 | −8 | −4 | −2 | −0 |
| **3** | **3** | **0** | **3** | **0** | **1** | **3** | **0** |

| 2 | 10 | 6 | 1 | 7 | 9 | 3 | 2 |
|---|---|---|---|---|---|---|---|
| −0 | −8 | −6 | −0 | −4 | −8 | −0 | −2 |
| **2** | **2** | **0** | **1** | **3** | **1** | **3** | **0** |

| 7 | 8 | 4 | 9 | 4 | 3 | 6 | 11 |
|---|---|---|---|---|---|---|---|
| −6 | −6 | −2 | −6 | −4 | −2 | −4 | −8 |
| **1** | **2** | **2** | **3** | **0** | **1** | **2** | **3** |

Score: _____   Time: _____ minutes _____ seconds

---

**95**

Name _____

**Timed Test**

12 − 9 = **3**   7 − 5 = **2**   5 − 2 = **3**   2 − 2 = **0**

1 − 1 = **0**   6 − 5 = **1**   6 − 4 = **2**   7 − 4 = **3**

9 − 7 = **2**   6 − 3 = **3**   4 − 2 = **2**   3 − 0 = **3**

3 − 3 = **0**   3 − 1 = **2**   9 − 6 = **3**   5 − 4 = **1**

7 − 7 = **0**   4 − 3 = **1**   0 − 0 = **0**   3 − 2 = **1**

4 − 1 = **3**   11 − 9 = **2**   8 − 6 = **2**   4 − 4 = **0**

8 − 5 = **3**   10 − 9 = **1**   6 − 6 = **0**   8 − 8 = **0**

8 − 7 = **1**   2 − 1 = **1**   10 − 8 = **2**   11 − 8 = **3**

5 − 3 = **2**   10 − 7 = **3**   2 − 0 = **2**   1 − 0 = **1**

9 − 9 = **0**   5 − 5 = **0**   7 − 6 = **1**   9 − 8 = **1**

*Differences Through Three*

Score: _____   Time: _____ minutes _____ seconds

---

**96**

Name _____

**Timed Test**

*Differences Through Three*

| 8 | 5 | 5 | 1 | 5 | 7 | 9 | 1 |
|---|---|---|---|---|---|---|---|
| −7 | −3 | −5 | −0 | −2 | −6 | −6 | −1 |
| **1** | **2** | **0** | **1** | **3** | **1** | **3** | **0** |

| 2 | 6 | 10 | 3 | 12 | 2 | 8 | 3 |
|---|---|---|---|---|---|---|---|
| −0 | −3 | −9 | −1 | −9 | −2 | −8 | −2 |
| **2** | **3** | **1** | **2** | **3** | **0** | **0** | **1** |

| 7 | 9 | 6 | 0 | 4 | 4 | 10 | 6 |
|---|---|---|---|---|---|---|---|
| −5 | −8 | −4 | −0 | −4 | −1 | −7 | −5 |
| **2** | **1** | **2** | **0** | **0** | **3** | **3** | **1** |

| 8 | 4 | 6 | 9 | 2 | 11 | 5 | 8 |
|---|---|---|---|---|---|---|---|
| −5 | −2 | −6 | −9 | −1 | −9 | −4 | −6 |
| **3** | **2** | **0** | **0** | **1** | **2** | **1** | **2** |

| 4 | 10 | 3 | 7 | 11 | 3 | 9 | 7 |
|---|---|---|---|---|---|---|---|
| −3 | −8 | −0 | −4 | −8 | −3 | −7 | −7 |
| **1** | **2** | **3** | **3** | **3** | **0** | **2** | **0** |

| Record your scores and times below. | |
|---|---|
| **Page 85** Score: _____ Time: ____ min. ____ sec. | **Page 91** Score: _____ Time: ____ min. ____ sec. |
| **Page 86** Score: _____ Time: ____ min. ____ sec. | **Page 92** Score: _____ Time: ____ min. ____ sec. |
| **Page 87** Score: _____ Time: ____ min. ____ sec. | **Page 93** Score: _____ Time: ____ min. ____ sec. |
| **Page 88** Score: _____ Time: ____ min. ____ sec. | **Page 94** Score: _____ Time: ____ min. ____ sec. |
| **Page 89** Score: _____ Time: ____ min. ____ sec. | **Page 95** Score: _____ Time: ____ min. ____ sec. |
| **Page 90** Score: _____ Time: ____ min. ____ sec. | **Page 96** Score: _____ Time: ____ min. ____ sec. |

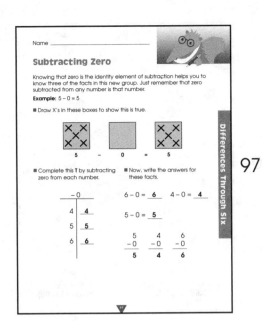

## Subtracting Zero

Knowing that zero is the identity element of subtraction helps you to know three of the facts in this new group. Just remember that zero subtracted from any number is that number.

**Example:** $5 - 0 = 5$

■ Draw X's in these boxes to show this is true.

$$5 - 0 = 5$$

■ Complete this **T** by subtracting zero from each number.

| $-0$ | |
|---|---|
| 4 | **4** |
| 5 | **5** |
| 6 | **6** |

■ Now, write the answers for these facts.

$6 - 0 =$ **6**   $4 - 0 =$ **4**

$5 - 0 =$ **5**

| 5 | 4 | 6 |
|---|---|---|
| $-0$ | $-0$ | $-0$ |
| **5** | **4** | **6** |

**Differences Through Six**

97

---

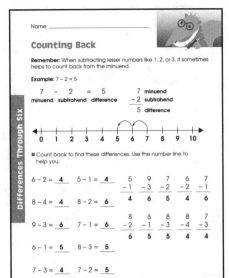

## Counting Back

**Remember:** When subtracting lesser numbers like 1, 2, or 3, it sometimes helps to count back from the minuend.

**Example:** $7 - 2 = 5$

$$7 - 2 = 5$$

minuend   subtrahend   difference

| 7 | minuend |
|---|---|
| $-2$ | subtrahend |
| 5 | difference |

$$0\ 1\ 2\ 3\ 4\ 5\ 6\ 7\ 8\ 9\ 10$$

■ Count back to find these differences. Use the number line to help you.

$6 - 2 =$ **4**   $5 - 1 =$ **4**

$8 - 4 =$ **4**   $8 - 2 =$ **6**

$9 - 3 =$ **6**   $7 - 1 =$ **6**

$6 - 1 =$ **5**   $8 - 3 =$ **5**

$7 - 3 =$ **4**   $7 - 2 =$ **5**

| 5 | 9 | 7 | 6 | 7 |
|---|---|---|---|---|
| $-1$ | $-3$ | $-2$ | $-2$ | $-1$ |
| **4** | **6** | **5** | **4** | **6** |

| 8 | 6 | 8 | 8 | 7 |
|---|---|---|---|---|
| $-2$ | $-1$ | $-3$ | $-4$ | $-3$ |
| **6** | **5** | **5** | **4** | **4** |

**Differences Through Six**

98

---

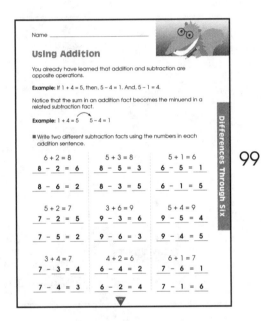

## Using Addition

You already have learned that addition and subtraction are opposite operations.

**Example:** If $1 + 4 = 5$, then, $5 - 4 = 1$. And, $5 - 1 = 4$.

Notice that the sum in an addition fact becomes the minuend in a related subtraction fact.

**Example:** $1 + 4 = 5$   $5 - 4 = 1$

■ Write two different subtraction facts using the numbers in each addition sentence.

$6 + 2 = 8$        $5 + 3 = 8$        $5 + 1 = 6$
**8** $-$ **2** $=$ **6**   **8** $-$ **5** $=$ **3**   **6** $-$ **5** $=$ **1**
**8** $-$ **6** $=$ **2**   **8** $-$ **3** $=$ **5**   **6** $-$ **1** $=$ **5**

$5 + 2 = 7$        $3 + 6 = 9$        $5 + 4 = 9$
**7** $-$ **2** $=$ **5**   **9** $-$ **3** $=$ **6**   **9** $-$ **5** $=$ **4**
**7** $-$ **5** $=$ **2**   **9** $-$ **6** $=$ **3**   **9** $-$ **4** $=$ **5**

$3 + 4 = 7$        $4 + 2 = 6$        $6 + 1 = 7$
**7** $-$ **3** $=$ **4**   **6** $-$ **4** $=$ **2**   **7** $-$ **6** $=$ **1**
**7** $-$ **4** $=$ **3**   **6** $-$ **2** $=$ **4**   **7** $-$ **1** $=$ **6**

**Differences Through Six**

99

---

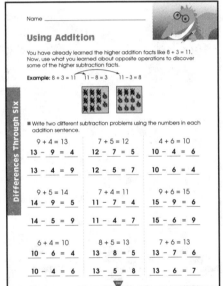

## Using Addition

You have already learned the higher addition facts like $8 + 3 = 11$. Now, use what you learned about opposite operations to discover some of the higher subtraction facts.

**Example:** $8 + 3 = 11$   $11 - 8 = 3$   $11 - 3 = 8$

■ Write two different subtraction problems using the numbers in each addition sentence.

$9 + 4 = 13$        $7 + 5 = 12$        $4 + 6 = 10$
**13** $-$ **9** $=$ **4**   **12** $-$ **7** $=$ **5**   **10** $-$ **4** $=$ **6**
**13** $-$ **4** $=$ **9**   **12** $-$ **5** $=$ **7**   **10** $-$ **6** $=$ **4**

$9 + 5 = 14$        $7 + 4 = 11$        $9 + 6 = 15$
**14** $-$ **9** $=$ **5**   **11** $-$ **7** $=$ **4**   **15** $-$ **9** $=$ **6**
**14** $-$ **5** $=$ **9**   **11** $-$ **4** $=$ **7**   **15** $-$ **6** $=$ **9**

$6 + 4 = 10$        $8 + 5 = 13$        $7 + 6 = 13$
**10** $-$ **6** $=$ **4**   **13** $-$ **8** $=$ **5**   **13** $-$ **7** $=$ **6**
**10** $-$ **4** $=$ **6**   **13** $-$ **5** $=$ **8**   **13** $-$ **6** $=$ **7**

**Differences Through Six**

100

---

## Practice

■ Subtract. Record your score on each Practice page and on page 106.

$13 - 8 =$ **5**   $7 - 1 =$ **6**   $6 - 1 =$ **5**   $11 - 5 =$ **6**

$5 - 1 =$ **4**   $12 - 8 =$ **4**   $12 - 6 =$ **6**   $10 - 6 =$ **4**

$6 - 0 =$ **6**   $8 - 2 =$ **6**   $11 - 7 =$ **4**   $14 - 9 =$ **5**

$13 - 9 =$ **4**   $10 - 5 =$ **5**   $9 - 4 =$ **5**   $8 - 4 =$ **4**

$5 - 0 =$ **5**   $15 - 9 =$ **6**   $7 - 3 =$ **4**   $13 - 8 =$ **5**

$11 - 6 =$ **5**   $6 - 2 =$ **4**   $9 - 5 =$ **4**   $10 - 5 =$ **5**

$4 - 0 =$ **4**   $9 - 3 =$ **6**   $8 - 3 =$ **5**   $7 - 1 =$ **6**

$14 - 8 =$ **6**   $13 - 7 =$ **6**   $10 - 4 =$ **6**   $12 - 7 =$ **5**

$12 - 7 =$ **5**   $8 - 4 =$ **4**   $7 - 2 =$ **5**   $13 - 9 =$ **4**

**START**   Score: _____

**Differences Through Six**

101

---

## Practice

■ Subtract:

| 5 | 13 | 7 | 15 | 12 | 12 | 6 | 11 | 9 |
|---|---|---|---|---|---|---|---|---|
| $-0$ | $-9$ | $-3$ | $-9$ | $-7$ | $-6$ | $-2$ | $-6$ | $-3$ |
| **5** | **4** | **4** | **6** | **5** | **6** | **4** | **5** | **6** |

| 10 | 7 | 6 | 13 | 4 | 9 | 8 | 13 | 5 |
|---|---|---|---|---|---|---|---|---|
| $-6$ | $-2$ | $-0$ | $-7$ | $-0$ | $-4$ | $-2$ | $-8$ | $-1$ |
| **4** | **5** | **6** | **6** | **4** | **5** | **6** | **5** | **4** |

| 12 | 6 | 10 | 14 | 11 | 14 | 10 | 11 | 8 |
|---|---|---|---|---|---|---|---|---|
| $-8$ | $-1$ | $-5$ | $-9$ | $-7$ | $-8$ | $-4$ | $-5$ | $-4$ |
| **4** | **5** | **5** | **5** | **4** | **6** | **6** | **6** | **4** |

| 7 | 9 | 8 | 9 | 7 | 15 | 8 | 13 | 11 |
|---|---|---|---|---|---|---|---|---|
| $-1$ | $-5$ | $-3$ | $-4$ | $-0$ | $-9$ | $-4$ | $-9$ | $-6$ |
| **6** | **4** | **5** | **5** | **7** | **6** | **4** | **4** | **5** |

**START**   Score: _____

**Differences Through Six**

102

## 103

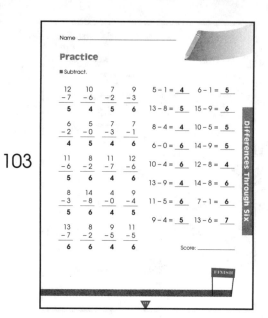

**Practice**

■ Subtract.

| | | | |
|---|---|---|---|
| 12 −7 = 5 | 10 −6 = 4 | 7 −2 = 5 | 9 −3 = 6 |
| 6 −2 = 4 | 5 −0 = 5 | 7 −3 = 4 | 7 −1 = 6 |
| 11 −6 = 5 | 8 −2 = 6 | 11 −7 = 4 | 12 −6 = 6 |
| 8 −3 = 5 | 14 −8 = 6 | 4 −0 = 4 | 9 −4 = 5 |
| 13 −7 = 6 | 8 −2 = 6 | 9 −5 = 4 | 11 −5 = 6 |

5 − 1 = **4**   6 − 1 = **5**
13 − 8 = **5**   15 − 9 = **6**
8 − 4 = **4**   10 − 5 = **5**
6 − 0 = **6**   14 − 9 = **5**
10 − 4 = **6**   12 − 8 = **4**
13 − 9 = **4**   14 − 8 = **6**
11 − 5 = **6**   7 − 1 = **6**
9 − 4 = **5**   13 − 6 = **7**

Differences Through Six

Score: _____

FINISH

## 104

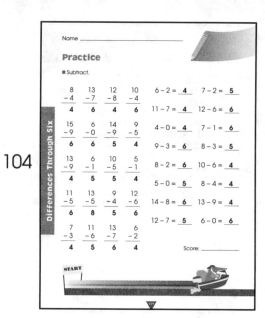

**Practice**

■ Subtract.

| | | | |
|---|---|---|---|
| 8 −4 = 4 | 13 −7 = 6 | 12 −8 = 4 | 10 −4 = 6 |
| 15 −9 = 6 | 6 −0 = 6 | 14 −9 = 5 | 9 −5 = 4 |
| 13 −9 = 4 | 6 −1 = 5 | 10 −5 = 5 | 5 −1 = 4 |
| 11 −5 = 6 | 13 −5 = 8 | 9 −4 = 5 | 12 −6 = 6 |
| 7 −3 = 4 | 11 −6 = 5 | 13 −7 = 6 | 6 −2 = 4 |

6 − 2 = **4**   7 − 2 = **5**
11 − 7 = **4**   12 − 6 = **6**
4 − 0 = **4**   7 − 1 = **6**
9 − 3 = **6**   8 − 3 = **5**
8 − 2 = **6**   10 − 6 = **4**
5 − 0 = **5**   8 − 4 = **4**
14 − 8 = **6**   13 − 9 = **4**
12 − 7 = **5**   6 − 0 = **6**

Differences Through Six

START

Score: _____

## 105

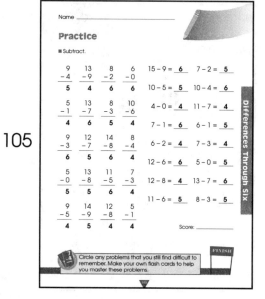

**Practice**

■ Subtract.

| | | | |
|---|---|---|---|
| 9 −4 = 5 | 13 −9 = 4 | 8 −2 = 6 | 6 −0 = 6 |
| 5 −1 = 4 | 13 −7 = 6 | 8 −3 = 5 | 10 −6 = 4 |
| 9 −3 = 6 | 12 −7 = 5 | 14 −8 = 6 | 8 −4 = 4 |
| 5 −0 = 5 | 13 −8 = 5 | 11 −5 = 6 | 7 −3 = 4 |
| 9 −5 = 4 | 14 −9 = 5 | 12 −8 = 4 | 5 −1 = 4 |

15 − 9 = **6**   7 − 2 = **5**
10 − 5 = **5**   10 − 4 = **6**
4 − 0 = **4**   11 − 7 = **4**
7 − 1 = **6**   6 − 1 = **5**
6 − 2 = **4**   7 − 3 = **4**
12 − 6 = **6**   5 − 0 = **5**
12 − 8 = **4**   13 − 7 = **6**
11 − 6 = **5**   8 − 3 = **5**

Differences Through Six

Circle any problems that you still find difficult to remember. Make your own flash cards to help you master these problems.

Score: _____

FINISH

## 106

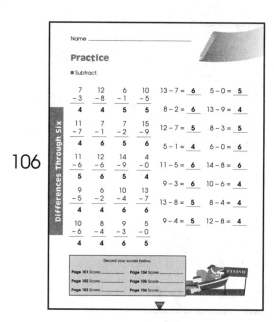

**Practice**

■ Subtract.

| | | | |
|---|---|---|---|
| 7 −3 = 4 | 12 −8 = 4 | 6 −1 = 5 | 10 −5 = 5 |
| 11 −7 = 4 | 7 −1 = 6 | 7 −2 = 5 | 15 −9 = 6 |
| 11 −6 = 5 | 12 −6 = 6 | 14 −9 = 5 | 4 −0 = 4 |
| 9 −5 = 4 | 6 −2 = 4 | 10 −4 = 6 | 13 −7 = 6 |
| 10 −6 = 4 | 8 −4 = 4 | 9 −3 = 6 | 5 −0 = 5 |

13 − 7 = **6**   5 − 0 = **5**
8 − 2 = **6**   13 − 9 = **4**
12 − 7 = **5**   8 − 3 = **5**
5 − 1 = **4**   6 − 0 = **6**
11 − 5 = **6**   14 − 8 = **6**
9 − 3 = **6**   10 − 6 = **4**
13 − 8 = **5**   8 − 4 = **4**
9 − 4 = **5**   12 − 8 = **4**

Differences Through Six

| Record your scores below. | |
|---|---|
| Page 101 Score: _____ | Page 104 Score: _____ |
| Page 102 Score: _____ | Page 105 Score: _____ |
| Page 103 Score: _____ | Page 106 Score: _____ |

FINISH

## 107

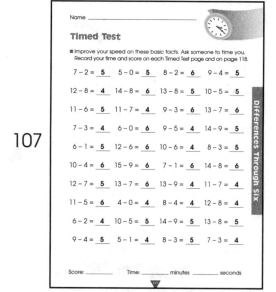

**Timed Test**

■ Improve your speed on these basic facts. Ask someone to time you. Record your time and score on each Timed Test page and on page 118.

7 − 2 = **5**   5 − 0 = **5**   8 − 2 = **6**   9 − 4 = **5**
12 − 8 = **4**   14 − 8 = **6**   13 − 8 = **5**   10 − 5 = **5**
11 − 6 = **5**   11 − 7 = **4**   9 − 3 = **6**   13 − 7 = **6**
7 − 3 = **4**   6 − 0 = **6**   9 − 5 = **4**   14 − 9 = **5**
6 − 1 = **5**   12 − 6 = **6**   10 − 6 = **4**   8 − 3 = **5**
10 − 4 = **6**   15 − 9 = **6**   7 − 1 = **6**   14 − 8 = **6**
12 − 7 = **5**   13 − 7 = **6**   13 − 9 = **4**   11 − 7 = **4**
11 − 5 = **6**   4 − 0 = **4**   8 − 4 = **4**   12 − 8 = **4**
6 − 2 = **4**   10 − 5 = **5**   14 − 9 = **5**   13 − 8 = **5**
9 − 4 = **5**   5 − 1 = **4**   8 − 3 = **5**   7 − 3 = **4**

Differences Through Six

Score: _____   Time: _____ minutes _____ seconds

## 108

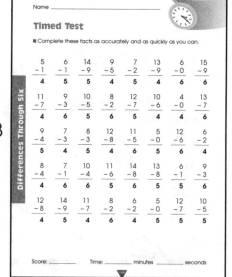

**Timed Test**

■ Complete these facts as accurately and as quickly as you can.

| | | | | | | | |
|---|---|---|---|---|---|---|---|
| 5 −1 = 4 | 6 −1 = 5 | 14 −9 = 5 | 9 −5 = 4 | 7 −2 = 5 | 13 −9 = 4 | 6 −0 = 6 | 15 −9 = 6 |
| 11 −7 = 4 | 9 −3 = 6 | 10 −5 = 5 | 8 −2 = 6 | 12 −7 = 5 | 10 −6 = 4 | 4 −0 = 4 | 13 −7 = 6 |
| 9 −4 = 5 | 7 −3 = 4 | 8 −3 = 5 | 12 −8 = 4 | 11 −5 = 6 | 5 −0 = 5 | 12 −6 = 6 | 6 −2 = 4 |
| 8 −4 = 4 | 7 −1 = 6 | 10 −4 = 6 | 11 −6 = 5 | 14 −8 = 6 | 13 −8 = 5 | 6 −1 = 5 | 9 −3 = 6 |
| 12 −8 = 4 | 14 −9 = 5 | 11 −7 = 4 | 8 −2 = 6 | 6 −2 = 4 | 5 −0 = 5 | 12 −7 = 5 | 10 −5 = 5 |

Differences Through Six

Score: _____   Time: _____ minutes _____ seconds

## 109

**Timed Test** — Differences Through Six

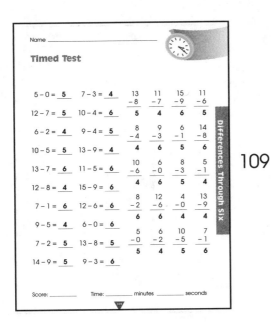

5 − 0 = **5**    7 − 3 = **4**

12 − 7 = **5**    10 − 4 = **6**

6 − 2 = **4**    9 − 4 = **5**

10 − 5 = **5**    13 − 9 = **4**

13 − 7 = **6**    11 − 5 = **6**

12 − 8 = **4**    15 − 9 = **6**

7 − 1 = **6**    12 − 6 = **6**

9 − 5 = **4**    6 − 0 = **6**

7 − 2 = **5**    13 − 8 = **5**

14 − 9 = **5**    9 − 3 = **6**

```
13   11   15   11
-8   -7   -9   -6
 5    4    6    5

 8    9    6   14
-4   -3   -1   -8
 4    6    5    6

10    6    8    5
-6   -0   -3   -1
 4    6    5    4

 8   12    4   13
-2   -6   -0   -9
 6    6    4    4

 5    6   10    7
-0   -2   -5   -1
 5    4    5    6
```

Score: _____    Time: _____ minutes _____ seconds

## 110

**Timed Test** — Differences Through Six

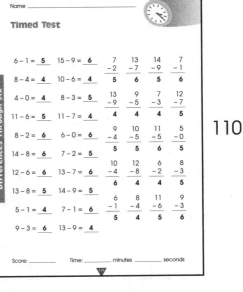

6 − 1 = **5**    15 − 9 = **6**

8 − 4 = **4**    10 − 6 = **4**

4 − 0 = **4**    8 − 3 = **5**

11 − 6 = **5**    11 − 7 = **4**

8 − 2 = **6**    6 − 0 = **6**

14 − 8 = **6**    7 − 2 = **5**

12 − 6 = **6**    13 − 7 = **6**

13 − 8 = **5**    14 − 9 = **5**

5 − 1 = **4**    7 − 1 = **6**

9 − 3 = **6**    13 − 9 = **4**

```
 7   13   14    7
-2   -7   -9   -1
 5    6    5    6

13    9    7   12
-9   -5   -3   -7
 4    4    4    5

 9   10   11    5
-4   -5   -5   -0
 5    5    6    5

10   12    6    8
-4   -8   -2   -3
 6    4    4    5

 6    8   11    9
-1   -4   -6   -3
 5    4    5    6
```

Score: _____    Time: _____ minutes _____ seconds

## 111

**Timed Test** — Differences Through Six

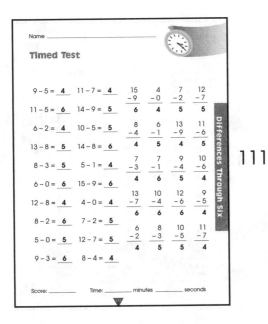

9 − 5 = **4**    11 − 7 = **4**

11 − 5 = **6**    14 − 9 = **5**

6 − 2 = **4**    10 − 5 = **5**

13 − 8 = **5**    14 − 8 = **6**

8 − 3 = **5**    5 − 1 = **4**

6 − 0 = **6**    15 − 9 = **6**

12 − 8 = **4**    4 − 0 = **4**

8 − 2 = **6**    7 − 2 = **5**

5 − 0 = **5**    12 − 7 = **5**

9 − 3 = **6**    8 − 4 = **4**

```
15    4    7   12
-9   -0   -2   -7
 6    4    5    5

 8    6   13   11
-4   -1   -9   -6
 4    5    4    5

 7    7    9   10
-3   -1   -4   -6
 4    6    5    4

13   10   12    9
-7   -4   -6   -5
 6    6    6    4

 6    8   10   11
-2   -3   -5   -7
 4    5    5    4
```

Score: _____    Time: _____ minutes _____ seconds

## 112

**Timed Test** — Differences Through Six

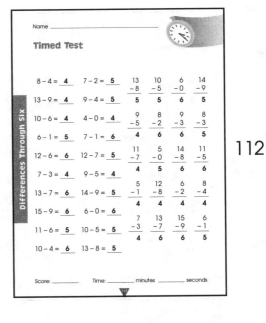

8 − 4 = **4**    7 − 2 = **5**

13 − 9 = **4**    9 − 4 = **5**

10 − 6 = **4**    4 − 0 = **4**

6 − 1 = **5**    7 − 1 = **6**

12 − 6 = **6**    12 − 7 = **5**

7 − 3 = **4**    9 − 5 = **4**

13 − 7 = **6**    14 − 9 = **5**

15 − 9 = **6**    6 − 0 = **6**

11 − 6 = **5**    10 − 5 = **5**

10 − 4 = **6**    13 − 8 = **5**

```
13   10    6   14
-8   -5   -0   -9
 5    5    6    5

 9    8    9    8
-5   -2   -3   -3
 4    6    6    5

11    5   14   11
-7   -0   -8   -5
 4    5    6    6

 5   12    6    8
-1   -8   -2   -4
 4    4    4    4

 7   13   15    6
-3   -7   -9   -1
 4    6    6    5
```

Score: _____    Time: _____ minutes _____ seconds

## 113

**Timed Test** — Differences Through Six

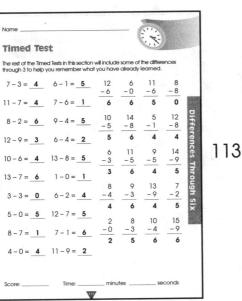

The rest of the Timed Tests in this section will include some of the differences through 3 to help you remember what you have already learned.

7 − 3 = **4**    6 − 1 = **5**

11 − 7 = **4**    7 − 6 = **1**

8 − 2 = **6**    9 − 4 = **5**

12 − 9 = **3**    6 − 4 = **2**

10 − 6 = **4**    13 − 8 = **5**

13 − 7 = **6**    1 − 0 = **1**

3 − 3 = **0**    6 − 2 = **4**

5 − 0 = **5**    12 − 7 = **5**

8 − 7 = **1**    7 − 1 = **6**

4 − 0 = **4**    11 − 9 = **2**

```
12    6   11    8
-6   -0   -6   -8
 6    6    5    0

10   14    5   12
-5   -8   -1   -8
 5    6    4    4

 6   11    9   14
-3   -5   -5   -9
 3    6    4    5

 8    9   13    7
-4   -3   -9   -2
 4    6    4    5

 2    8   10   15
-0   -3   -4   -9
 2    5    6    6
```

Score: _____    Time: _____ minutes _____ seconds

## 114

**Timed Test** — Differences Through Six

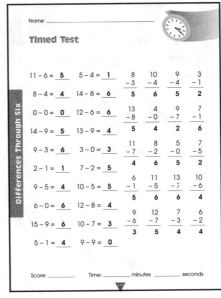

11 − 6 = **5**    5 − 4 = **1**

8 − 4 = **4**    14 − 8 = **6**

0 − 0 = **0**    12 − 6 = **6**

14 − 9 = **5**    13 − 9 = **4**

9 − 3 = **6**    3 − 0 = **3**

2 − 1 = **1**    7 − 2 = **5**

9 − 5 = **4**    10 − 5 = **5**

6 − 0 = **6**    12 − 8 = **4**

15 − 9 = **6**    10 − 7 = **3**

5 − 1 = **4**    9 − 9 = **0**

```
 8   10    9    3
-3   -4   -4   -1
 5    6    5    2

13    4    9    7
-8   -0   -7   -1
 5    4    2    6

11    8    5    7
-7   -2   -0   -5
 4    6    5    2

 6   11   13   10
-1   -5   -7   -6
 5    6    6    4

 9   12    7    6
-6   -7   -3   -2
 3    5    4    4
```

Score: _____    Time: _____ minutes _____ seconds

## 115 — Timed Test — Differences Through Six

Name _____

11 − 5 = **6**    4 − 0 = **4**    4 − 2 = **2**    5 − 1 = **4**
9 − 4 = **5**    12 − 7 = **5**    10 − 4 = **6**    13 − 8 = **5**
8 − 4 = **4**    6 − 1 = **5**    7 − 3 = **4**    5 − 2 = **3**
3 − 2 = **1**    5 − 5 = **0**    15 − 9 = **6**    11 − 6 = **5**
9 − 3 = **6**    5 − 0 = **5**    10 − 5 = **5**    10 − 6 = **4**
13 − 7 = **6**    9 − 5 = **4**    7 − 7 = **0**    14 − 9 = **5**
8 − 3 = **5**    6 − 0 = **6**    12 − 8 = **4**    7 − 2 = **5**
6 − 2 = **4**    11 − 8 = **3**    13 − 9 = **4**    8 − 5 = **3**
11 − 7 = **4**    12 − 6 = **6**    8 − 2 = **6**    7 − 1 = **6**
10 − 8 = **2**    1 − 1 = **0**    6 − 5 = **1**    14 − 8 = **6**

Score: _____    Time: _____ minutes _____ seconds

## 116 — Timed Test — Differences Through Six

Name _____

| 5<br>−0<br>**5** | 8<br>−4<br>**4** | 8<br>−2<br>**6** | 12<br>−5<br>**7** | 6<br>−0<br>**6** | 12<br>−9<br>**3** | 11<br>−6<br>**5** | 9<br>−4<br>**5** |
|---|---|---|---|---|---|---|---|
| 10<br>−4<br>**6** | 6<br>−2<br>**4** | 9<br>−9<br>**0** | 13<br>−8<br>**5** | 7<br>−6<br>**1** | 7<br>−2<br>**5** | 11<br>−9<br>**2** | 4<br>−0<br>**4** |
| 14<br>−8<br>**6** | 10<br>−6<br>**4** | 12<br>−6<br>**6** | 10<br>−7<br>**3** | 10<br>−8<br>**2** | 13<br>−9<br>**4** | 15<br>−9<br>**6** | 8<br>−6<br>**2** |
| 10<br>−5<br>**5** | 14<br>−9<br>**5** | 9<br>−5<br>**4** | 7<br>−1<br>**6** | 5<br>−5<br>**0** | 7<br>−3<br>**4** | 13<br>−7<br>**6** | 6<br>−1<br>**5** |
| 11<br>−5<br>**6** | 11<br>−8<br>**3** | 5<br>−1<br>**4** | 9<br>−3<br>**6** | 11<br>−7<br>**4** | 5<br>−4<br>**1** | 8<br>−3<br>**5** | 12<br>−7<br>**5** |

Score: _____    Time: _____ minutes _____ seconds

## 117 — Timed Test — Differences Through Six

Name _____

15 − 9 = **6**    8 − 5 = **3**    7 − 5 = **2**    10 − 4 = **6**
10 − 5 = **5**    12 − 7 = **5**    9 − 4 = **5**    14 − 8 = **6**
14 − 9 = **5**    5 − 1 = **4**    8 − 4 = **4**    9 − 8 = **1**
8 − 7 = **1**    13 − 7 = **6**    9 − 7 = **2**    4 − 0 = **4**
9 − 5 = **4**    7 − 3 = **4**    10 − 6 = **4**    7 − 2 = **5**
9 − 3 = **6**    8 − 3 = **5**    5 − 0 = **5**    12 − 6 = **6**
11 − 7 = **4**    10 − 9 = **1**    13 − 8 = **5**    8 − 2 = **6**
9 − 6 = **3**    13 − 9 = **4**    7 − 4 = **3**    6 − 2 = **4**
6 − 1 = **5**    7 − 1 = **6**    6 − 0 = **6**    6 − 5 = **1**
11 − 5 = **6**    8 − 8 = **0**    11 − 6 = **5**    12 − 8 = **4**

Score: _____    Time: _____ minutes _____ seconds

## 118 — Timed Test — Differences Through Six

Name _____

| 4<br>−0<br>**4** | 12<br>−6<br>**6** | 5<br>−3<br>**2** | 9<br>−5<br>**4** | 11<br>−7<br>**4** | 10<br>−5<br>**5** | 4<br>−3<br>**1** | 9<br>−4<br>**5** |
|---|---|---|---|---|---|---|---|
| 7<br>−4<br>**3** | 5<br>−0<br>**5** | 2<br>−2<br>**0** | 5<br>−1<br>**4** | 12<br>−8<br>**4** | 12<br>−7<br>**5** | 9<br>−3<br>**6** | 13<br>−9<br>**4** |
| 9<br>−8<br>**1** | 13<br>−8<br>**5** | 7<br>−1<br>**6** | 10<br>−4<br>**6** | 14<br>−8<br>**6** | 11<br>−5<br>**6** | 6<br>−6<br>**0** | 10<br>−6<br>**4** |
| 6<br>−0<br>**6** | 14<br>−9<br>**5** | 11<br>−6<br>**5** | 8<br>−6<br>**2** | 4<br>−4<br>**0** | 6<br>−2<br>**4** | 8<br>−4<br>**4** | 13<br>−7<br>**6** |
| 7<br>−2<br>**5** | 6<br>−1<br>**5** | 10<br>−9<br>**1** | 8<br>−3<br>**5** | 7<br>−3<br>**4** | 5<br>−1<br>**4** | 8<br>−2<br>**6** | 15<br>−9<br>**6** |

Record your scores and times below.

Page 107 Score: _____ Time: _____ min. _____ sec.    Page 113 Score: _____ Time: _____ min. _____ sec.
Page 108 Score: _____ Time: _____ min. _____ sec.    Page 114 Score: _____ Time: _____ min. _____ sec.
Page 109 Score: _____ Time: _____ min. _____ sec.    Page 115 Score: _____ Time: _____ min. _____ sec.
Page 110 Score: _____ Time: _____ min. _____ sec.    Page 116 Score: _____ Time: _____ min. _____ sec.
Page 111 Score: _____ Time: _____ min. _____ sec.    Page 117 Score: _____ Time: _____ min. _____ sec.
Page 112 Score: _____ Time: _____ min. _____ sec.    Page 118 Score: _____ Time: _____ min. _____ sec.

## 119 — Subtracting Zero — Differences Through Nine

Name _____

If you remember that zero is the identity element of subtraction, you already know three of the facts in this new group.

**Example:** 8 − 0 = 8

■ Draw small circles in these boxes to show this is true.

8 − 0 = 8

■ Complete this T by subtracting zero from each number.

| − 0 | |
|---|---|
| 7 | **7** |
| 8 | **8** |
| 9 | **9** |

■ Write the difference for each fact.

9 − 0 = **9**    7 − 0 = **7**
8 − 0 = **8**

7<br>−0<br>**7**    9<br>−0<br>**9**    8<br>−0<br>**8**

## 120 — Counting Back — Differences Through Nine

Name _____

**Remember:** You can count back to find the difference when the subtrahend is a lesser number like 1, 2, or 3.

**Example:** 10 − 1 = 9

0  1  2  3  4  5  6  7  8  9  10  11  12

■ Complete these T's by subtracting the numbers at the top from those along the side. You may use the number line to help you count.

| − 1 | | − 2 | | − 3 | |
|---|---|---|---|---|---|
| 10 | **9** | 11 | **9** | 10 | **7** |
| 9 | **8** | 9 | **7** | 12 | **9** |
| 8 | **7** | 10 | **8** | 11 | **8** |

■ Subtract.

9 − 2 = **7**    11 − 3 = **8**
10 − 3 = **7**    8 − 1 = **7**
11 − 2 = **9**    12 − 3 = **9**

8<br>−1<br>**7**    10<br>−2<br>**8**    11<br>−3<br>**8**
10<br>−1<br>**9**    12<br>−3<br>**9**    9<br>−1<br>**8**

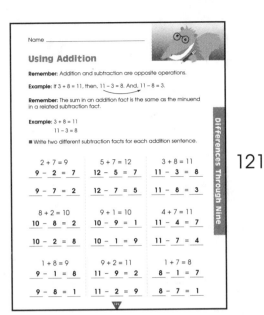

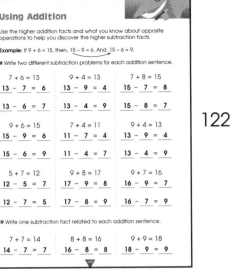

## Using Addition (121)

**Remember:** Addition and subtraction are opposite operations.

**Example:** If 3 + 8 = 11, then, 11 − 3 = 8. And, 11 − 8 = 3.

**Remember:** The sum in an addition fact is the same as the minuend in a related subtraction fact.

**Example:** 3 + 8 = 11
11 − 3 = 8

■ Write two different subtraction facts for each addition sentence.

| 2 + 7 = 9 | 5 + 7 = 12 | 3 + 8 = 11 |
|---|---|---|
| 9 − 2 = **7** | 12 − 5 = **7** | 11 − 3 = **8** |
| 9 − 7 = **2** | 12 − 7 = **5** | 11 − 8 = **3** |

| 8 + 2 = 10 | 9 + 1 = 10 | 4 + 7 = 11 |
|---|---|---|
| 10 − 8 = **2** | 10 − 9 = **1** | 11 − 4 = **7** |
| 10 − 2 = **8** | 10 − 1 = **9** | 11 − 7 = **4** |

| 1 + 8 = 9 | 9 + 2 = 11 | 1 + 7 = 8 |
|---|---|---|
| 9 − 1 = **8** | 11 − 9 = **2** | 8 − 1 = **7** |
| 9 − 8 = **1** | 11 − 2 = **9** | 8 − 7 = **1** |

*Differences Through Nine*

---

## Using Addition (122)

Use the higher addition facts and what you know about opposite operations to help you discover the higher subtraction facts.

**Example:** If 9 + 6 = 15, then, 15 − 9 = 6. And, 15 − 6 = 9.

■ Write two different subtraction problems for each addition sentence.

| 7 + 6 = 13 | 9 + 4 = 13 | 7 + 8 = 15 |
|---|---|---|
| 13 − 7 = **6** | 13 − 9 = **4** | 15 − 7 = **8** |
| 13 − 6 = **7** | 13 − 4 = **9** | 15 − 8 = **7** |

| 9 + 6 = 15 | 7 + 4 = 11 | 9 + 4 = 13 |
|---|---|---|
| 15 − 9 = **6** | 11 − 7 = **4** | 13 − 9 = **4** |
| 15 − 6 = **9** | 11 − 4 = **7** | 13 − 4 = **9** |

| 5 + 7 = 12 | 9 + 8 = 17 | 9 + 7 = 16 |
|---|---|---|
| 12 − 5 = **7** | 17 − 9 = **8** | 16 − 9 = **7** |
| 12 − 7 = **5** | 17 − 8 = **9** | 16 − 7 = **9** |

■ Write one subtraction fact related to each addition sentence.

| 7 + 7 = 14 | 8 + 8 = 16 | 9 + 9 = 18 |
|---|---|---|
| 14 − 7 = **7** | 16 − 8 = **8** | 18 − 9 = **9** |

*Differences Through Nine*

---

## Practice (123)

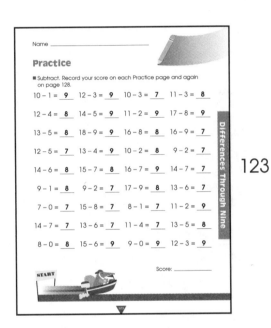

■ Subtract. Record your score on each Practice page and again on page 128.

| 10 − 1 = **9** | 12 − 3 = **9** | 10 − 3 = **7** | 11 − 3 = **8** |
|---|---|---|---|
| 12 − 4 = **8** | 14 − 5 = **9** | 11 − 2 = **9** | 17 − 8 = **9** |
| 13 − 5 = **8** | 18 − 9 = **9** | 16 − 8 = **8** | 16 − 9 = **7** |
| 12 − 5 = **7** | 13 − 4 = **9** | 10 − 2 = **8** | 9 − 2 = **7** |
| 14 − 6 = **8** | 15 − 7 = **8** | 16 − 7 = **9** | 14 − 7 = **7** |
| 9 − 1 = **8** | 9 − 2 = **7** | 17 − 9 = **8** | 13 − 6 = **7** |
| 7 − 0 = **7** | 15 − 8 = **7** | 8 − 1 = **7** | 11 − 2 = **9** |
| 14 − 7 = **7** | 13 − 6 = **7** | 11 − 4 = **7** | 13 − 5 = **8** |
| 8 − 0 = **8** | 15 − 6 = **9** | 9 − 0 = **9** | 12 − 3 = **9** |

Score: _____

*Differences Through Nine*

---

## Practice (124)

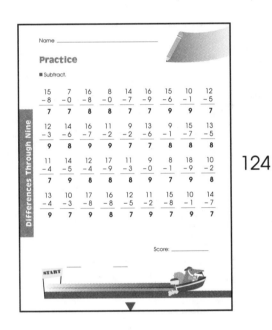

■ Subtract.

| 15 | 7 | 16 | 8 | 14 | 16 | 15 | 10 | 12 |
|---|---|---|---|---|---|---|---|---|
| −8 | −0 | −8 | −0 | −7 | −9 | −6 | −1 | −5 |
| **7** | **7** | **8** | **8** | **7** | **7** | **9** | **9** | **7** |

| 12 | 14 | 16 | 11 | 9 | 13 | 9 | 15 | 13 |
|---|---|---|---|---|---|---|---|---|
| −3 | −6 | −7 | −2 | −2 | −6 | −1 | −7 | −5 |
| **9** | **8** | **9** | **9** | **7** | **7** | **8** | **8** | **8** |

| 11 | 14 | 12 | 17 | 11 | 9 | 8 | 18 | 10 |
|---|---|---|---|---|---|---|---|---|
| −4 | −5 | −4 | −9 | −3 | −0 | −1 | −9 | −2 |
| **7** | **9** | **8** | **8** | **8** | **9** | **7** | **9** | **8** |

| 13 | 10 | 17 | 16 | 12 | 11 | 15 | 10 | 14 |
|---|---|---|---|---|---|---|---|---|
| −4 | −3 | −8 | −8 | −5 | −2 | −8 | −1 | −7 |
| **9** | **7** | **9** | **8** | **7** | **9** | **7** | **9** | **7** |

Score: _____

*Differences Through Nine*

---

## Practice (125)

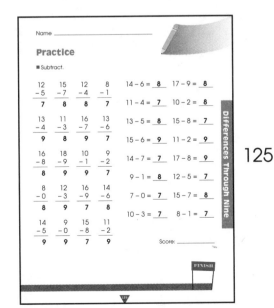

■ Subtract.

| 12 | 15 | 12 | 8 |
|---|---|---|---|
| −5 | −7 | −4 | −1 |
| **7** | **8** | **8** | **7** |

| 13 | 11 | 16 | 13 |
|---|---|---|---|
| −4 | −3 | −7 | −6 |
| **9** | **8** | **9** | **7** |

| 16 | 18 | 10 | 9 |
|---|---|---|---|
| −8 | −9 | −1 | −2 |
| **8** | **9** | **9** | **7** |

| 8 | 12 | 16 | 14 |
|---|---|---|---|
| −0 | −3 | −9 | −6 |
| **8** | **9** | **7** | **8** |

| 14 | 9 | 15 | 11 |
|---|---|---|---|
| −5 | −0 | −8 | −2 |
| **9** | **9** | **7** | **9** |

| 14 − 6 = **8** | 17 − 9 = **8** |
|---|---|
| 11 − 4 = **7** | 10 − 2 = **8** |
| 13 − 5 = **8** | 15 − 8 = **7** |
| 15 − 6 = **9** | 11 − 2 = **9** |
| 14 − 7 = **7** | 17 − 8 = **9** |
| 9 − 1 = **8** | 12 − 5 = **7** |
| 7 − 0 = **7** | 15 − 7 = **8** |
| 10 − 3 = **7** | 8 − 1 = **7** |

Score: _____

*Differences Through Nine*

---

## Practice (126)

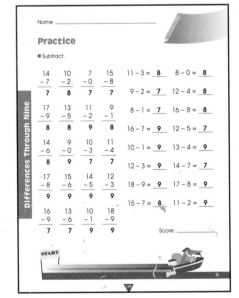

■ Subtract.

| 14 | 10 | 7 | 15 |
|---|---|---|---|
| −7 | −2 | −0 | −8 |
| **7** | **8** | **7** | **7** |

| 17 | 13 | 11 | 9 |
|---|---|---|---|
| −9 | −5 | −2 | −1 |
| **8** | **8** | **9** | **8** |

| 14 | 9 | 10 | 11 |
|---|---|---|---|
| −6 | −0 | −3 | −4 |
| **8** | **9** | **7** | **7** |

| 17 | 15 | 14 | 12 |
|---|---|---|---|
| −8 | −6 | −5 | −3 |
| **9** | **9** | **9** | **9** |

| 16 | 13 | 10 | 18 |
|---|---|---|---|
| −9 | −6 | −1 | −9 |
| **7** | **7** | **9** | **9** |

| 11 − 3 = **8** | 8 − 0 = **8** |
|---|---|
| 9 − 2 = **7** | 12 − 4 = **8** |
| 8 − 1 = **7** | 16 − 8 = **8** |
| 16 − 7 = **9** | 12 − 5 = **7** |
| 10 − 1 = **9** | 13 − 4 = **9** |
| 12 − 3 = **9** | 14 − 7 = **7** |
| 18 − 9 = **9** | 17 − 8 = **9** |
| 15 − 7 = **8** | 11 − 2 = **9** |

Score: _____

*Differences Through Nine*

---

**Timed Test Answer Key**

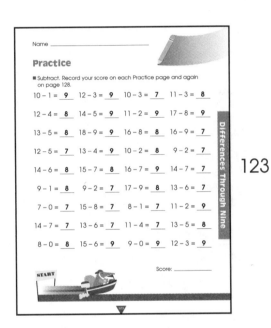

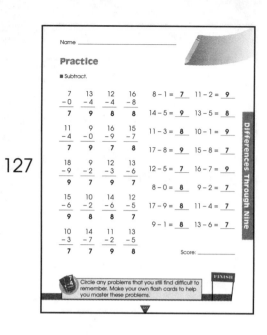

**127**

Name _____

### Practice

■ Subtract.

```
  7     13    12    16        8 - 1 = _7_    11 - 2 = _9_
- 0    - 4   - 4   - 8
  7      9     8     8        14 - 5 = _9_   13 - 5 = _8_

 11      9    16    15        11 - 3 = _8_   10 - 1 = _9_
- 4    - 0   - 9   - 7
  7      9     7     8        17 - 8 = _9_   15 - 8 = _7_

 18      9    12    13        12 - 5 = _7_   16 - 7 = _9_
- 9    - 2   - 3   - 6
  9      7     9     7         8 - 0 = _8_    9 - 2 = _7_

 15     10    14    12        17 - 9 = _8_   11 - 4 = _7_
- 6    - 2   - 6   - 5
  9      8     8     7

 10     14    11    13         9 - 1 = _8_   13 - 6 = _7_
- 3    - 7   - 2   - 5
  7      7     9     8        Score: _____
```

*Differences Through Nine*

Circle any problems that you still find difficult to remember. Make your own flash cards to help you master these problems.

FINISH

---

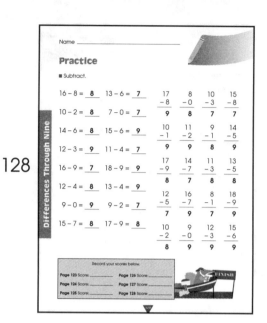

**128**

Name _____

### Practice

■ Subtract.

```
16 - 8 = _8_   13 - 6 = _7_      17     8    10    15
                                - 8   - 0   - 3   - 8
10 - 2 = _8_    7 - 0 = _7_       9     8     7     7

14 - 6 = _8_   15 - 6 = _9_      10    11     9    14
                                - 1   - 2   - 1   - 5
12 - 3 = _9_   11 - 4 = _7_       9     9     8     9

16 - 9 = _7_   18 - 9 = _9_      17    14    11    13
                                - 9   - 7   - 3   - 5
12 - 4 = _8_   13 - 4 = _9_       8     7     8     8

 9 - 0 = _9_    9 - 2 = _7_      12    16     8    18
                                - 5   - 7   - 1   - 9
15 - 7 = _8_   17 - 9 = _8_       7     9     7     9

                                10     9    12    15
                                - 2   - 0   - 3   - 6
                                 8     9     9     9
```

*Differences Through Nine*

Record your scores below.
Page 123 Score: _____   Page 126 Score: _____
Page 124 Score: _____   Page 127 Score: _____
Page 125 Score: _____   Page 128 Score: _____

FINISH

---

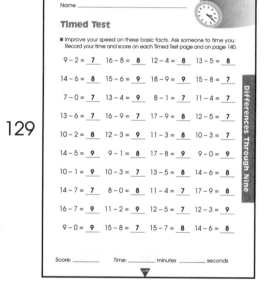

**129**

Name _____

### Timed Test

■ Improve your speed on these basic facts. Ask someone to time you. Record your time and score on each Timed Test page and on page 140.

```
 9 - 2 = _7_   16 - 8 = _8_   12 - 4 = _8_   13 - 5 = _8_
14 - 6 = _8_   15 - 6 = _9_   18 - 9 = _9_   15 - 8 = _7_
 7 - 0 = _7_   13 - 4 = _9_    8 - 1 = _7_   11 - 4 = _7_
13 - 6 = _7_   16 - 9 = _7_   17 - 9 = _8_   12 - 5 = _7_
10 - 2 = _8_   12 - 3 = _9_   11 - 3 = _8_   10 - 3 = _7_
14 - 5 = _9_    9 - 1 = _8_   17 - 8 = _9_    9 - 0 = _9_
10 - 1 = _9_   10 - 3 = _7_   13 - 5 = _8_   14 - 6 = _8_
14 - 7 = _7_    8 - 0 = _8_   11 - 4 = _7_   17 - 9 = _8_
16 - 7 = _9_   11 - 2 = _9_   12 - 5 = _7_   12 - 3 = _9_
 9 - 0 = _9_   15 - 8 = _7_   15 - 7 = _8_   14 - 6 = _8_
```

*Differences Through Nine*

Score: _____   Time: _____ minutes _____ seconds

---

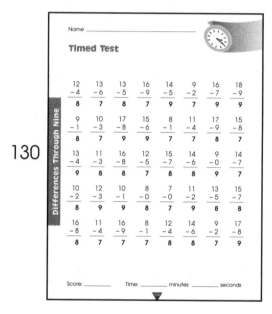

**130**

Name _____

### Timed Test

```
12    13    13    16    14     9    16    18
-4    -6    -5    -9    -5    -2    -7    -9
 8     7     8     7     9     7     9     9

 9    10    17    15     8    11    17    15
-1    -3    -8    -6    -1    -4    -9    -8
 8     7     9     9     7     7     8     7

13    11    16    12    15    14     9    14
-4    -3    -8    -5    -7    -6    -0    -7
 9     8     8     7     8     8     9     7

10    12    10     8     7    11     9    13
-2    -3    -1    -0    -0    -2    -5    -7
 8     9     9     8     7     9     8     8

16    11    16     8    12    14     9    17
-8    -4    -9    -1    -4    -6    -2    -8
 8     7     7     7     8     8     7     9
```

*Differences Through Nine*

Score: _____   Time: _____ minutes _____ seconds

---

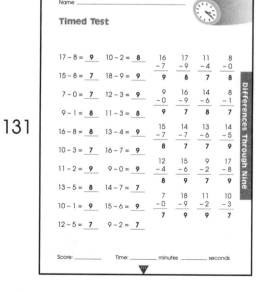

**131**

Name _____

### Timed Test

```
17 - 8 = _9_   10 - 2 = _8_      16    17    11     8
                                - 7   - 9   - 4   - 0
15 - 8 = _7_   18 - 9 = _9_       9     8     7     8

 7 - 0 = _7_   12 - 3 = _9_       9    16    14     8
                                - 0   - 9   - 6   - 1
 9 - 1 = _8_   11 - 3 = _8_       9     7     8     7

16 - 8 = _8_   13 - 4 = _9_      15    14    13    14
                                - 7   - 7   - 6   - 5
10 - 3 = _7_   16 - 7 = _9_       8     7     7     9

11 - 2 = _9_    9 - 0 = _9_      12    15     9    17
                                - 4   - 6   - 2   - 8
13 - 5 = _8_   14 - 7 = _7_       8     9     7     9

10 - 1 = _9_   15 - 6 = _9_       7    18    11    10
                                - 0   - 9   - 2   - 3
12 - 5 = _7_    9 - 2 = _7_       7     9     9     7
```

*Differences Through Nine*

Score: _____   Time: _____ minutes _____ seconds

---

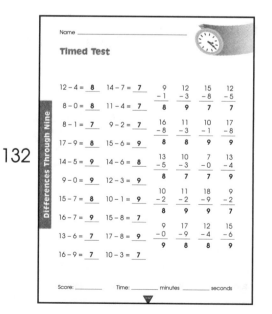

**132**

Name _____

### Timed Test

```
12 - 4 = _8_   14 - 7 = _7_       9    12    15    12
                                - 1   - 3   - 8   - 5
 8 - 0 = _8_   11 - 4 = _7_       8     9     7     7

 8 - 1 = _7_    9 - 2 = _7_      16    11    10    17
                                - 8   - 3   - 1   - 8
17 - 9 = _8_   15 - 6 = _9_       8     8     9     9

14 - 5 = _9_   14 - 6 = _8_      13    10     7    13
                                - 5   - 3   - 0   - 4
 9 - 0 = _9_   12 - 3 = _9_       8     7     7     9

15 - 7 = _8_   10 - 1 = _9_      10    11    18     9
                                - 2   - 2   - 9   - 2
16 - 7 = _9_   15 - 8 = _7_       8     9     9     7

13 - 6 = _7_   17 - 8 = _9_       9    17    12    15
                                - 0   - 9   - 4   - 6
16 - 9 = _7_   10 - 3 = _7_       9     8     8     9
```

*Differences Through Nine*

Score: _____   Time: _____ minutes _____ seconds

## Timed Test — 133
*Differences Through Nine*

Name _____

12 - 5 = **7**   14 - 6 = **8**
16 - 7 = **9**   10 - 1 = **9**
9 - 2 = **7**    8 - 1 = **7**
11 - 2 = **9**   7 - 0 = **7**
13 - 5 = **8**   15 - 8 = **7**
9 - 1 = **8**    12 - 4 = **8**
14 - 5 = **9**   11 - 3 = **8**
13 - 6 = **7**   18 - 9 = **9**
9 - 0 = **9**    15 - 7 = **8**
10 - 2 = **8**   16 - 8 = **8**

17 - 8 = **9**   12 - 4 = **8**   15 - 6 = **9**   14 - 7 = **7**
13 - 4 = **9**   11 - 3 = **8**   18 - 9 = **9**   10 - 3 = **7**
15 - 7 = **8**   8 - 0 = **8**    12 - 3 = **9**   16 - 8 = **8**
16 - 9 = **7**   11 - 4 = **7**   17 - 9 = **8**   12 - 5 = **7**
14 - 5 = **9**   8 - 1 = **7**    10 - 2 = **8**   13 - 6 = **7**

Score: _____   Time: _____ minutes _____ seconds

## Timed Test — 134
*Differences Through Nine*

Name _____

18 - 9 = **9**   12 - 3 = **9**
11 - 3 = **8**   16 - 9 = **7**
17 - 9 = **8**   15 - 6 = **9**
15 - 7 = **8**   16 - 8 = **8**
12 - 4 = **8**   13 - 4 = **9**
10 - 3 = **7**   11 - 2 = **9**
14 - 7 = **7**   9 - 1 = **8**
11 - 4 = **7**   16 - 7 = **9**
8 - 0 = **8**    14 - 5 = **9**
17 - 8 = **9**   9 - 0 = **9**

14 - 5 = **9**   11 - 2 = **9**   14 - 6 = **8**   9 - 0 = **9**
12 - 5 = **7**   9 - 1 = **8**    10 - 2 = **8**   13 - 5 = **8**
7 - 0 = **7**    10 - 1 = **9**   16 - 7 = **9**   8 - 1 = **7**
13 - 6 = **7**   15 - 8 = **7**   9 - 2 = **7**    11 - 3 = **8**
17 - 8 = **9**   15 - 7 = **8**   11 - 4 = **7**   8 - 0 = **8**

Score: _____   Time: _____ minutes _____ seconds

## Timed Test — 135
*Differences Through Nine*

Name _____

The rest of the Timed Tests in this section will include some of the differences through 6 to help you remember what you have already learned.

11 - 3 = **8**   12 - 6 = **6**
14 - 7 = **7**   7 - 0 = **7**
4 - 0 = **4**    9 - 1 = **8**
11 - 4 = **7**   14 - 9 = **5**
9 - 4 = **5**    15 - 7 = **8**
10 - 1 = **9**   11 - 5 = **6**
14 - 6 = **8**   12 - 3 = **9**
6 - 1 = **5**    18 - 9 = **9**
15 - 8 = **7**   15 - 6 = **9**
16 - 7 = **9**   12 - 5 = **7**

11 - 2 = **9**   12 - 4 = **8**   9 - 3 = **6**    13 - 5 = **8**
13 - 6 = **7**   10 - 2 = **8**   12 - 7 = **5**   9 - 0 = **9**
10 - 3 = **7**   17 - 8 = **9**   14 - 5 = **9**   9 - 5 = **4**
8 - 1 = **7**    17 - 9 = **8**   16 - 9 = **7**   8 - 0 = **8**
9 - 2 = **7**    15 - 9 = **6**   16 - 8 = **8**   13 - 4 = **9**

Score: _____   Time: _____ minutes _____ seconds

## Timed Test — 136
*Differences Through Nine*

Name _____

14 - 5 = **9**   6 - 2 = **4**
17 - 8 = **9**   11 - 6 = **5**
12 - 8 = **4**   17 - 9 = **8**
10 - 2 = **8**   10 - 3 = **7**
13 - 4 = **9**   6 - 0 = **6**
8 - 1 = **7**    16 - 9 = **7**
14 - 8 = **6**   12 - 4 = **8**
13 - 5 = **8**   9 - 2 = **7**
16 - 8 = **8**   13 - 6 = **7**
9 - 0 = **9**    8 - 0 = **8**

15 - 6 = **9**   7 - 3 = **4**    16 - 7 = **9**   11 - 3 = **8**
15 - 8 = **7**   18 - 9 = **9**   12 - 5 = **7**   11 - 7 = **4**
14 - 6 = **8**   5 - 0 = **5**    11 - 4 = **7**   13 - 7 = **6**
7 - 0 = **7**    15 - 7 = **8**   11 - 2 = **9**   9 - 1 = **8**
12 - 3 = **9**   10 - 1 = **9**   14 - 7 = **7**   7 - 1 = **6**

Score: _____   Time: _____ minutes _____ seconds

## Timed Test — 137
*Differences Through Nine*

Name _____

7 - 2 = **5**    15 - 6 = **9**
8 - 0 = **8**    8 - 1 = **7**
18 - 9 = **9**   12 - 5 = **7**
9 - 2 = **7**    10 - 2 = **8**
14 - 5 = **9**   8 - 3 = **5**
16 - 8 = **8**   16 - 7 = **9**
5 - 1 = **4**    13 - 8 = **5**
16 - 9 = **7**   11 - 3 = **8**
10 - 5 = **5**   14 - 7 = **7**
9 - 1 = **8**    8 - 4 = **4**

17 - 8 = **9**   10 - 4 = **6**   17 - 9 = **8**   13 - 4 = **9**
12 - 4 = **8**   13 - 6 = **7**   12 - 3 = **9**   13 - 5 = **8**
10 - 6 = **4**   11 - 2 = **9**   9 - 0 = **9**    13 - 9 = **4**
10 - 3 = **7**   15 - 7 = **8**   8 - 2 = **6**    11 - 4 = **7**
14 - 6 = **8**   10 - 1 = **9**   15 - 8 = **7**   7 - 0 = **7**

Score: _____   Time: _____ minutes _____ seconds

## Timed Test — 138
*Differences Through Nine*

Name _____

7 - 0 = **7**    10 - 4 = **6**   17 - 9 = **8**   13 - 5 = **8**   14 - 5 = **9**   12 - 6 = **6**   16 - 9 = **7**   11 - 4 = **7**
12 - 3 = **9**   9 - 1 = **8**    9 - 4 = **5**    15 - 8 = **7**   11 - 3 = **8**   16 - 7 = **9**   9 - 2 = **7**    10 - 6 = **4**
15 - 7 = **8**   13 - 6 = **7**   10 - 1 = **9**   6 - 6 = **0**    18 - 9 = **9**   9 - 5 = **4**    9 - 0 = **9**    7 - 7 = **0**
12 - 5 = **7**   15 - 6 = **9**   13 - 4 = **9**   8 - 4 = **4**    12 - 4 = **8**   8 - 1 = **7**    16 - 8 = **8**   14 - 6 = **8**
11 - 2 = **9**   8 - 0 = **8**    10 - 3 = **7**   14 - 7 = **7**   10 - 2 = **8**   11 - 5 = **6**   17 - 8 = **9**   10 - 5 = **5**

Score: _____   Time: _____ minutes _____ seconds

## 139

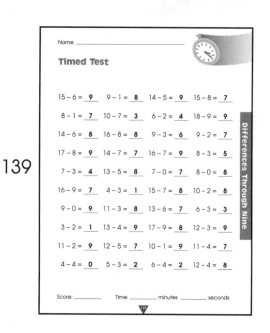

**Timed Test**

*Differences Through Nine*

$15-6=\underline{9}$  $9-1=\underline{8}$  $14-5=\underline{9}$  $15-8=\underline{7}$

$8-1=\underline{7}$  $10-7=\underline{3}$  $6-2=\underline{4}$  $18-9=\underline{9}$

$14-6=\underline{8}$  $16-8=\underline{8}$  $9-3=\underline{6}$  $9-2=\underline{7}$

$17-8=\underline{9}$  $14-7=\underline{7}$  $16-7=\underline{9}$  $8-3=\underline{5}$

$7-3=\underline{4}$  $13-5=\underline{8}$  $7-0=\underline{7}$  $8-0=\underline{8}$

$16-9=\underline{7}$  $4-3=\underline{1}$  $15-7=\underline{8}$  $10-2=\underline{8}$

$9-0=\underline{9}$  $11-3=\underline{8}$  $13-6=\underline{7}$  $6-3=\underline{3}$

$3-2=\underline{1}$  $13-4=\underline{9}$  $17-9=\underline{8}$  $12-3=\underline{9}$

$11-2=\underline{9}$  $12-5=\underline{7}$  $10-1=\underline{9}$  $11-4=\underline{7}$

$4-4=\underline{0}$  $5-3=\underline{2}$  $6-4=\underline{2}$  $12-4=\underline{8}$

Score: _____  Time: _____ minutes _____ seconds

## 140

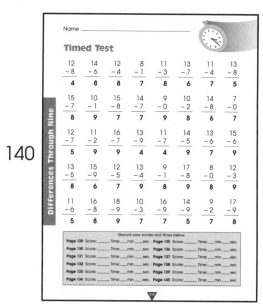

**Timed Test**

*Differences Through Nine*

| | | | | | | | |
|---|---|---|---|---|---|---|---|
| $12-8$ | $14-6$ | $12-4$ | $8-1$ | $11-3$ | $13-7$ | $11-4$ | $13-8$ |
| **4** | **8** | **8** | **7** | **8** | **6** | **7** | **5** |
| $15-7$ | $10-1$ | $15-8$ | $14-7$ | $9-0$ | $10-2$ | $14-8$ | $7-0$ |
| **8** | **9** | **7** | **7** | **9** | **8** | **6** | **7** |
| $12-7$ | $11-2$ | $16-7$ | $13-9$ | $11-7$ | $14-5$ | $13-6$ | $15-6$ |
| **5** | **9** | **9** | **4** | **4** | **9** | **7** | **9** |
| $13-5$ | $15-9$ | $12-5$ | $13-4$ | $9-1$ | $17-8$ | $8-0$ | $12-3$ |
| **8** | **6** | **7** | **9** | **8** | **9** | **8** | **9** |
| $11-6$ | $16-8$ | $18-9$ | $10-3$ | $16-9$ | $14-9$ | $9-2$ | $17-9$ |
| **5** | **8** | **9** | **7** | **7** | **5** | **7** | **8** |

Record your scores and times below.

Page 129 Score: _____ Time: ___ min. ___ sec.  Page 135 Score: _____ Time: ___ min. ___ sec.
Page 130 Score: _____ Time: ___ min. ___ sec.  Page 136 Score: _____ Time: ___ min. ___ sec.
Page 131 Score: _____ Time: ___ min. ___ sec.  Page 137 Score: _____ Time: ___ min. ___ sec.
Page 132 Score: _____ Time: ___ min. ___ sec.  Page 138 Score: _____ Time: ___ min. ___ sec.
Page 133 Score: _____ Time: ___ min. ___ sec.  Page 139 Score: _____ Time: ___ min. ___ sec.
Page 134 Score: _____ Time: ___ min. ___ sec.  Page 140 Score: _____ Time: ___ min. ___ sec.

## 141

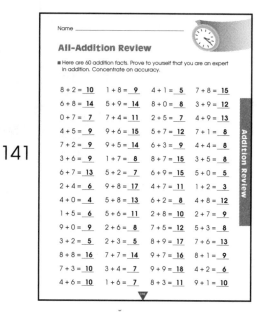

**All-Addition Review**

*Addition Review*

■ Here are 60 addition facts. Prove to yourself that you are an expert in addition. Concentrate on accuracy.

$8+2=\underline{10}$  $1+8=\underline{9}$  $4+1=\underline{5}$  $7+8=\underline{15}$

$6+8=\underline{14}$  $5+9=\underline{14}$  $8+0=\underline{8}$  $3+9=\underline{12}$

$0+7=\underline{7}$  $7+4=\underline{11}$  $2+5=\underline{7}$  $4+9=\underline{13}$

$4+5=\underline{9}$  $9+6=\underline{15}$  $5+7=\underline{12}$  $7+1=\underline{8}$

$7+2=\underline{9}$  $9+5=\underline{14}$  $6+3=\underline{9}$  $4+4=\underline{8}$

$3+6=\underline{9}$  $1+7=\underline{8}$  $8+7=\underline{15}$  $3+5=\underline{8}$

$6+7=\underline{13}$  $5+2=\underline{7}$  $6+9=\underline{15}$  $5+0=\underline{5}$

$2+4=\underline{6}$  $9+8=\underline{17}$  $4+7=\underline{11}$  $1+2=\underline{3}$

$4+0=\underline{4}$  $5+8=\underline{13}$  $6+2=\underline{8}$  $4+8=\underline{12}$

$1+5=\underline{6}$  $5+6=\underline{11}$  $2+8=\underline{10}$  $2+7=\underline{9}$

$9+0=\underline{9}$  $2+6=\underline{8}$  $7+5=\underline{12}$  $5+3=\underline{8}$

$3+2=\underline{5}$  $2+3=\underline{5}$  $8+9=\underline{17}$  $7+6=\underline{13}$

$8+8=\underline{16}$  $7+7=\underline{14}$  $9+7=\underline{16}$  $8+1=\underline{9}$

$7+3=\underline{10}$  $3+4=\underline{7}$  $9+9=\underline{18}$  $4+2=\underline{6}$

$4+6=\underline{10}$  $1+6=\underline{7}$  $8+3=\underline{11}$  $9+1=\underline{10}$

## 142

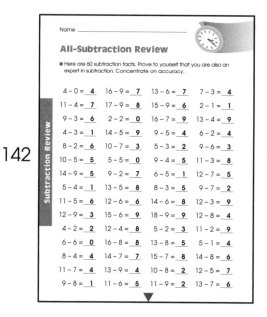

**All-Subtraction Review**

*Subtraction Review*

■ Here are 60 subtraction facts. Prove to yourself that you are also an expert in subtraction. Concentrate on accuracy.

$4-0=\underline{4}$  $16-9=\underline{7}$  $13-6=\underline{7}$  $7-3=\underline{4}$

$11-4=\underline{7}$  $17-9=\underline{8}$  $15-9=\underline{6}$  $2-1=\underline{1}$

$9-3=\underline{6}$  $2-2=\underline{0}$  $16-7=\underline{9}$  $13-4=\underline{9}$

$4-3=\underline{1}$  $14-5=\underline{9}$  $9-5=\underline{4}$  $6-2=\underline{4}$

$8-2=\underline{6}$  $10-7=\underline{3}$  $5-3=\underline{2}$  $9-6=\underline{3}$

$10-5=\underline{5}$  $5-5=\underline{0}$  $9-4=\underline{5}$  $11-3=\underline{8}$

$14-9=\underline{5}$  $9-2=\underline{7}$  $6-5=\underline{1}$  $12-7=\underline{5}$

$5-4=\underline{1}$  $13-5=\underline{8}$  $8-3=\underline{5}$  $9-7=\underline{2}$

$11-5=\underline{6}$  $12-6=\underline{6}$  $14-6=\underline{8}$  $12-3=\underline{9}$

$12-9=\underline{3}$  $15-6=\underline{9}$  $18-9=\underline{9}$  $12-8=\underline{4}$

$4-2=\underline{2}$  $12-4=\underline{8}$  $5-2=\underline{3}$  $11-2=\underline{9}$

$6-6=\underline{0}$  $16-8=\underline{8}$  $13-8=\underline{5}$  $5-1=\underline{4}$

$8-4=\underline{4}$  $14-7=\underline{7}$  $15-7=\underline{8}$  $14-8=\underline{6}$

$11-7=\underline{4}$  $13-9=\underline{4}$  $10-8=\underline{2}$  $12-5=\underline{7}$

$9-8=\underline{1}$  $11-6=\underline{5}$  $11-9=\underline{2}$  $13-7=\underline{6}$

## 144

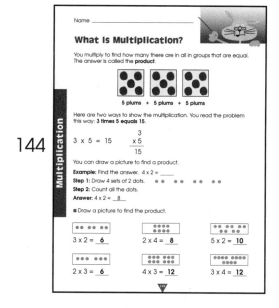

**What Is Multiplication?**

*Multiplication*

You multiply to find how many there are in all in groups that are equal. The answer is called the **product**.

5 plums + 5 plums + 5 plums

Here are two ways to show the multiplication. You read the problem this way: **3 times 5 equals 15**.

$3 \times 5 = 15$

$$\begin{array}{r} 3 \\ \times 5 \\ \hline 15 \end{array}$$

You can draw a picture to find a product.

**Example:** Find the answer. $4 \times 2 =$ ____

**Step 1:** Draw 4 sets of 2 dots.

**Step 2:** Count all the dots.

**Answer:** $4 \times 2 = \underline{8}$

■ Draw a picture to find the product.

$3 \times 2 = \underline{6}$   $2 \times 4 = \underline{8}$   $5 \times 2 = \underline{10}$

$2 \times 3 = \underline{6}$   $4 \times 3 = \underline{12}$   $3 \times 4 = \underline{12}$

## 145

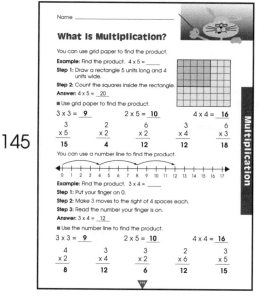

**What Is Multiplication?**

*Multiplication*

You can use grid paper to find the product.

**Example:** Find the product. $4 \times 5 =$ ____

**Step 1:** Draw a rectangle 5 units long and 4 units wide.

**Step 2:** Count the squares inside the rectangle.

**Answer:** $4 \times 5 = \underline{20}$

■ Use grid paper to find the product.

$3 \times 3 = \underline{9}$   $2 \times 5 = \underline{10}$   $4 \times 4 = \underline{16}$

| $\times 5$ | $\times 2$ | $\times 2$ | $\times 4$ | $\times 3$ |
|---|---|---|---|---|
| **15** | **4** | **12** | **12** | **18** |

(3, 2, 6, 3, 6)

You can use a number line to find the product.

0 1 2 3 4 5 6 7 8 9 10 11 12 13 14 15 16 17

**Example:** Find the product. $3 \times 4 =$ ____

**Step 1:** Put your finger on 0.

**Step 2:** Make 3 moves to the right of 4 spaces each.

**Step 3:** Read the number your finger is on.

**Answer:** $3 \times 4 = \underline{12}$

■ Use the number line to find the product.

$3 \times 3 = \underline{9}$   $2 \times 5 = \underline{10}$   $4 \times 4 = \underline{16}$

| $\times 2$ | $\times 4$ | $\times 2$ | $\times 6$ | $\times 5$ |
|---|---|---|---|---|
| **8** | **12** | **6** | **12** | **15** |

(4, 3, 3, 2, 3)

## Page 146

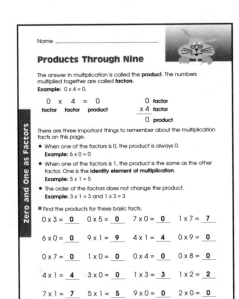

Name _____

### Products Through Nine

The answer in multiplication is called the **product**. The numbers multiplied together are called **factors**.

**Example:** 0 x 4 = 0.

0  x  4  =  0       0 factor
factor factor product    x 4 factor
                          0 product

There are three important things to remember about the multiplication facts on this page.

- When one of the factors is 0, the product is always 0.
  **Example:** 6 x 0 = 0
- When one of the factors is 1, the product is the same as the other factor. One is the **identity element of multiplication**.
  **Example:** 5 x 1 = 5
- The order of the factors does not change the product.
  **Example:** 3 x 1 = 3 and 1 x 3 = 3

■ Find the products for these basic facts.

| | | | |
|---|---|---|---|
| 0 x 3 = **0** | 0 x 5 = **0** | 7 x 0 = **0** | 1 x 7 = **7** |
| 6 x 0 = **0** | 9 x 1 = **9** | 4 x 1 = **4** | 0 x 9 = **0** |
| 0 x 7 = **0** | 1 x 0 = **0** | 0 x 4 = **0** | 0 x 8 = **0** |
| 4 x 1 = **4** | 3 x 0 = **0** | 1 x 3 = **3** | 1 x 2 = **2** |
| 7 x 1 = **7** | 5 x 1 = **5** | 9 x 0 = **0** | 2 x 0 = **0** |

*Zero and One as Factors*

## Page 147

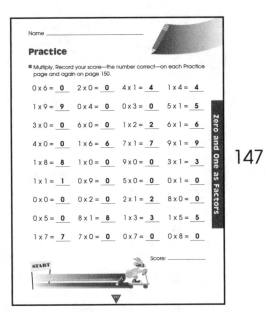

Name _____

### Practice

■ Multiply. Record your score—the number correct—on each Practice page and again on page 150.

| | | | |
|---|---|---|---|
| 0 x 6 = **0** | 2 x 0 = **0** | 4 x 1 = **4** | 1 x 4 = **4** |
| 1 x 9 = **9** | 0 x 4 = **0** | 0 x 3 = **0** | 5 x 1 = **5** |
| 3 x 0 = **0** | 6 x 0 = **0** | 1 x 2 = **2** | 6 x 1 = **6** |
| 4 x 0 = **0** | 1 x 6 = **6** | 7 x 1 = **7** | 9 x 1 = **9** |
| 1 x 8 = **8** | 1 x 0 = **0** | 9 x 0 = **0** | 3 x 1 = **3** |
| 1 x 1 = **1** | 0 x 9 = **0** | 5 x 0 = **0** | 0 x 1 = **0** |
| 0 x 0 = **0** | 0 x 2 = **0** | 2 x 1 = **2** | 8 x 0 = **0** |
| 0 x 5 = **0** | 8 x 1 = **8** | 1 x 3 = **3** | 1 x 5 = **5** |
| 1 x 7 = **7** | 7 x 0 = **0** | 0 x 7 = **0** | 0 x 8 = **0** |

Score: _____

START

*Zero and One as Factors*

## Page 148

Name _____

### Practice

■ Multiply.

| 0 | 1 | 2 | 4 | 9 | 5 | 0 | 1 | 0 |
|---|---|---|---|---|---|---|---|---|
| x0 | x2 | x0 | x1 | x0 | x1 | x3 | x9 | x5 |
| **0** | **2** | **0** | **4** | **0** | **5** | **0** | **9** | **0** |

| 1 | 5 | 1 | 0 | 9 | 7 | 1 | 0 | 0 |
|---|---|---|---|---|---|---|---|---|
| x1 | x0 | x8 | x7 | x1 | x1 | x7 | x9 | x8 |
| **1** | **0** | **8** | **0** | **9** | **7** | **7** | **0** | **0** |

| 4 | 8 | 1 | 1 | 3 | 1 | 3 | 0 | 0 |
|---|---|---|---|---|---|---|---|---|
| x0 | x0 | x4 | x0 | x1 | x3 | x0 | x1 | x4 |
| **0** | **0** | **4** | **0** | **3** | **3** | **0** | **0** | **0** |

| 2 | 6 | 8 | 1 | 0 | 6 | 7 | 0 | 1 |
|---|---|---|---|---|---|---|---|---|
| x1 | x0 | x1 | x5 | x6 | x1 | x0 | x2 | x6 |
| **2** | **0** | **8** | **5** | **0** | **6** | **0** | **0** | **6** |

Score: _____

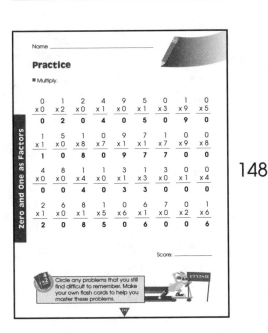

Circle any problems that you still find difficult to remember. Make your own flash cards to help you master these problems.

FINISH

*Zero and One as Factors*

## Page 149

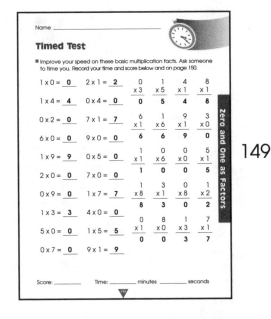

Name _____

### Timed Test

■ Improve your speed on these basic multiplication facts. Ask someone to time you. Record your time and score below and on page 150.

| 1 x 0 = **0** | 2 x 1 = **2** | 0 x3 | 1 x5 | 4 x1 | 8 x1 |
|---|---|---|---|---|---|
| | | **0** | **5** | **4** | **8** |

| 1 x 4 = **4** | 0 x 4 = **0** | | | | |
|---|---|---|---|---|---|

| 0 x 2 = **0** | 7 x 1 = **7** | 6 x1 | 1 x6 | 9 x1 | 3 x0 |
|---|---|---|---|---|---|
| | | **6** | **6** | **9** | **0** |

| 6 x 0 = **0** | 9 x 0 = **0** | | | | |
|---|---|---|---|---|---|

| 1 x 9 = **9** | 0 x 5 = **0** | 1 x1 | 0 x6 | 0 x0 | 5 x1 |
|---|---|---|---|---|---|
| | | **1** | **0** | **0** | **5** |

| 2 x 0 = **0** | 7 x 0 = **0** | | | | |
|---|---|---|---|---|---|

| 0 x 9 = **0** | 1 x 7 = **7** | 1 x8 | 3 x1 | 0 x8 | 1 x2 |
|---|---|---|---|---|---|
| | | **8** | **3** | **0** | **2** |

| 1 x 3 = **3** | 4 x 0 = **0** | | | | |
|---|---|---|---|---|---|

| 5 x 0 = **0** | 1 x 5 = **5** | 0 x1 | 8 x0 | 1 x3 | 7 x1 |
|---|---|---|---|---|---|
| | | **0** | **0** | **3** | **7** |

| 0 x 7 = **0** | 9 x 1 = **9** | | | | |
|---|---|---|---|---|---|

Score: _____    Time: _____ minutes _____ seconds

*Zero and One as Factors*

## Page 150

Name _____

### Timed Test

■ Complete these facts as accurately and as quickly as you can.

| 9 x 1 = **9** | 7 x 1 = **7** | 5 x0 | 1 x5 | 8 x1 | 0 x4 |
|---|---|---|---|---|---|
| | | **0** | **5** | **8** | **0** |

| 2 x 0 = **0** | 8 x 0 = **0** | | | | |
|---|---|---|---|---|---|

| 1 x 7 = **7** | 1 x 4 = **4** | 0 x6 | 1 x0 | 6 x1 | 2 x1 |
|---|---|---|---|---|---|
| | | **0** | **0** | **6** | **2** |

| 0 x 1 = **0** | 3 x 0 = **0** | | | | |
|---|---|---|---|---|---|

| 6 x 0 = **0** | 1 x 3 = **3** | 1 x6 | 1 x2 | 9 x0 | 0 x7 |
|---|---|---|---|---|---|
| | | **6** | **2** | **0** | **0** |

| 0 x 2 = **0** | 5 x 1 = **5** | | | | |
|---|---|---|---|---|---|

| 0 x 9 = **0** | 0 x 0 = **0** | 1 x1 | 1 x4 | 1 x8 | 0 x5 |
|---|---|---|---|---|---|
| | | **1** | **4** | **8** | **0** |

| 4 x 0 = **0** | 0 x 3 = **0** | | | | |
|---|---|---|---|---|---|

| 1 x 9 = **9** | 8 x 1 = **8** | 7 x0 | 3 x1 | 9 x1 | 1 x4 |
|---|---|---|---|---|---|
| | | **0** | **3** | **9** | **4** |

| 0 x 8 = **0** | 1 x 2 = **2** | | | | |
|---|---|---|---|---|---|

Record your scores and times below.

| Page 147 Score: _____ | Page 149 Score: _____ Time: ___ min. ___ sec. |
|---|---|
| Page 148 Score: _____ | Page 150 Score: _____ Time: ___ min. ___ sec. |

*Zero and One as Factors*

## Page 151

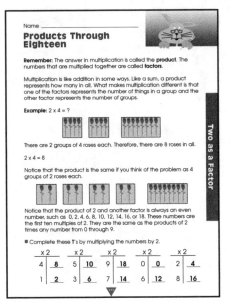

Name _____

### Products Through Eighteen

**Remember:** The answer in multiplication is called the **product**. The numbers that are multiplied together are called **factors**.

Multiplication is like addition in some ways. Like a sum, a product represents how many in all. What makes multiplication different is that one of the factors represents the number of things in a group and the other factor represents the number of groups.

**Example:** 2 x 4 = ?

There are 2 groups of 4 roses each. Therefore, there are 8 roses in all.

2 x 4 = 8

Notice that the product is the same if you think of the problem as 4 groups of 2 roses each.

Notice that the product of 2 and another factor is always an even number, such as 0, 2, 4, 6, 8, 10, 12, 14, 16, or 18. These numbers are the first ten multiples of 2. They are the same as the products of 2 times any number from 0 through 9.

■ Complete these T's by multiplying the numbers by 2.

| x2 | | x2 | | x2 | | x2 | | x2 | |
|---|---|---|---|---|---|---|---|---|---|
| 4 | **8** | 5 | **10** | 9 | **18** | 0 | **0** | 2 | **4** |
| 1 | **2** | 3 | **6** | 7 | **14** | 6 | **12** | 8 | **16** |

*Two as a Factor*

327

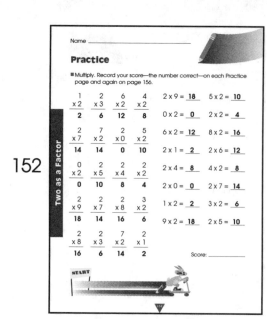

**152**

Name _____

## Practice

■ Multiply. Record your score—the number correct—on each Practice page and again on page 156.

Two as a Factor

| | | | | |
|---|---|---|---|---|
| 1 ×2 = **2** | 2 ×3 = **6** | 6 ×2 = **12** | 4 ×2 = **8** | 2 x 9 = **18**   5 x 2 = **10** |

2 x 9 = **18**   5 x 2 = **10**

2 ×7 = **14**   7 ×2 = **14**   2 ×0 = **0**   5 ×2 = **10**
0 x 2 = **0**   2 x 2 = **4**

6 x 2 = **12**   8 x 2 = **16**

0 ×2 = **0**   2 ×5 = **10**   2 ×4 = **8**   2 ×2 = **4**
2 x 1 = **2**   2 x 6 = **12**

2 x 4 = **8**   4 x 2 = **8**

2 ×9 = **18**   2 ×7 = **14**   2 ×8 = **16**   3 ×2 = **6**
2 x 0 = **0**   2 x 7 = **14**

1 x 2 = **2**   3 x 2 = **6**

2 ×8 = **16**   2 ×3 = **6**   7 ×2 = **14**   2 ×1 = **2**

9 x 2 = **18**   2 x 5 = **10**

START

---

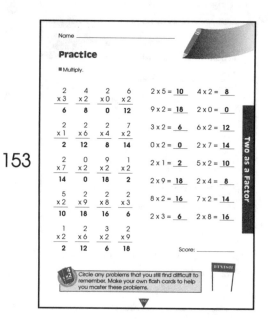

**153**

Name _____

## Practice

■ Multiply.

Two as a Factor

2 ×3 = **6**   4 ×2 = **8**   2 ×0 = **0**   6 ×2 = **12**
2 x 5 = **10**   4 x 2 = **8**
9 x 2 = **18**   2 x 0 = **0**

2 ×1 = **2**   2 ×6 = **12**   2 ×4 = **8**   7 ×2 = **14**
3 x 2 = **6**   6 x 2 = **12**
0 x 2 = **0**   2 x 7 = **14**

2 ×7 = **14**   0 ×2 = **0**   9 ×2 = **18**   1 ×2 = **2**
2 x 1 = **2**   5 x 2 = **10**
2 x 9 = **18**   2 x 4 = **8**

5 ×2 = **10**   9 ×2 = **18**   8 ×2 = **16**   2 ×3 = **6**
8 x 2 = **16**   7 x 2 = **14**
2 x 3 = **6**   2 x 8 = **16**

1 ×2 = **2**   2 ×6 = **12**   3 ×2 = **6**   2 ×9 = **18**

Score: _____

Circle any problems that you still find difficult to remember. Make your own flash cards to help you master these problems.

FINISH

---

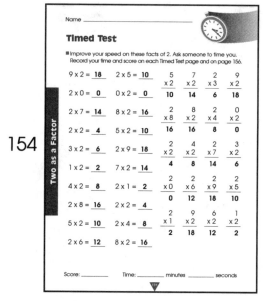

**154**

Name _____

## Timed Test

■ Improve your speed on these facts of 2. Ask someone to time you. Record your time and score on each Timed Test page and on page 156.

Two as a Factor

9 x 2 = **18**   2 x 5 = **10**

5 ×2 = **10**   7 ×2 = **14**   2 ×3 = **6**   9 ×2 = **18**

2 x 0 = **0**   0 x 2 = **0**

2 x 7 = **14**   8 x 2 = **16**

2 ×8 = **16**   8 ×2 = **16**   2 ×4 = **8**   0 ×2 = **0**

2 x 2 = **4**   5 x 2 = **10**

3 x 2 = **6**   2 x 9 = **18**

2 ×2 = **4**   4 ×2 = **8**   2 ×7 = **14**   3 ×2 = **6**

1 x 2 = **2**   7 x 2 = **14**

4 x 2 = **8**   2 x 1 = **2**

2 ×0 = **0**   6 ×2 = **12**   9 ×2 = **18**   5 ×2 = **10**

2 x 8 = **16**   2 x 2 = **4**

5 x 2 = **10**   2 x 4 = **8**

2 ×1 = **2**   9 ×2 = **18**   6 ×2 = **12**   1 ×2 = **2**

2 x 6 = **12**   8 x 2 = **16**

Score: _____   Time: _____ minutes _____ seconds

---

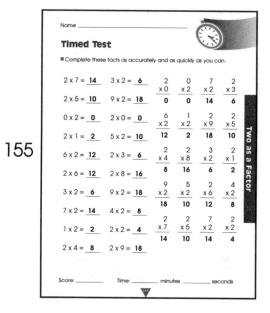

**155**

Name _____

## Timed Test

■ Complete these facts as accurately and as quickly as you can.

Two as a Factor

2 x 7 = **14**   3 x 2 = **6**

2 ×0 = **0**   2 ×2 = **0**   7 ×2 = **14**   2 ×3 = **6**

2 x 5 = **10**   9 x 2 = **18**

0 x 2 = **0**   2 x 0 = **0**

6 ×2 = **12**   1 ×2 = **2**   2 ×9 = **18**   2 ×5 = **10**

2 x 1 = **2**   5 x 2 = **10**

6 x 2 = **12**   2 x 3 = **6**

2 ×4 = **8**   2 ×8 = **16**   3 ×2 = **6**   2 ×1 = **2**

2 x 6 = **12**   2 x 8 = **16**

9 ×2 = **18**   5 ×2 = **10**   2 ×2 = **4**   4 ×2 = **8**

3 x 2 = **6**   9 x 2 = **18**

7 x 2 = **14**   4 x 2 = **8**

2 ×7 = **14**   2 ×5 = **10**   7 ×2 = **14**   2 ×2 = **4**

1 x 2 = **2**   2 x 2 = **4**

2 x 4 = **8**   2 x 9 = **18**

Score: _____   Time: _____ minutes _____ seconds

---

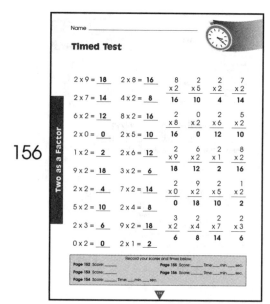

**156**

Name _____

## Timed Test

Two as a Factor

2 x 9 = **18**   2 x 8 = **16**

8 ×2 = **16**   2 ×5 = **10**   2 ×2 = **4**   7 ×2 = **14**

2 x 7 = **14**   4 x 2 = **8**

6 x 2 = **12**   8 x 2 = **16**

2 ×8 = **16**   0 ×2 = **0**   2 ×6 = **12**   5 ×2 = **10**

2 x 0 = **0**   2 x 5 = **10**

1 x 2 = **2**   2 x 6 = **12**

2 ×9 = **18**   6 ×2 = **12**   2 ×1 = **2**   8 ×2 = **16**

9 x 2 = **18**   3 x 2 = **6**

2 ×0 = **0**   9 ×2 = **18**   2 ×5 = **10**   1 ×2 = **2**

2 x 2 = **4**   7 x 2 = **14**

5 x 2 = **10**   2 x 4 = **8**

2 ×3 = **6**   2 ×4 = **8**   2 ×7 = **14**   2 ×3 = **6**

2 x 3 = **6**   9 x 2 = **18**

0 x 2 = **0**   2 x 1 = **2**

**Record your scores and times below.**

| | |
|---|---|
| Page 152 Score: _____ | Page 155 Score: _____ Time: ___ min ___ sec. |
| Page 153 Score: _____ | Page 156 Score: _____ Time: ___ min ___ sec. |
| Page 154 Score: _____ Time: ___ min ___ sec. | |

---

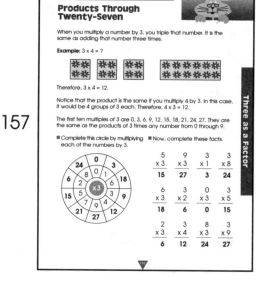

**157**

Name _____

## Products Through Twenty-Seven

When you multiply a number by 3, you triple that number. It is the same as adding that number three times.

**Example:** 3 x 4 = ?

Therefore, 3 x 4 = 12.

Notice that the product is the same if you multiply 4 by 3. In this case, it would be 4 groups of 3 each. Therefore, 4 x 3 = 12.

The first ten multiples of 3 are 0, 3, 6, 9, 12, 15, 18, 21, 24, 27. They are the same as the products of 3 times any number from 0 through 9.

■ Complete this circle by multiplying each of the numbers by 3.

■ Now, complete these facts.

Three as a Factor

5 ×3 = **15**   9 ×3 = **27**   3 ×1 = **3**   3 ×8 = **24**

6 ×3 = **18**   3 ×2 = **6**   0 ×3 = **0**   3 ×5 = **15**

2 ×3 = **6**   3 ×4 = **12**   8 ×3 = **24**   3 ×9 = **27**

---

328

## Page 158

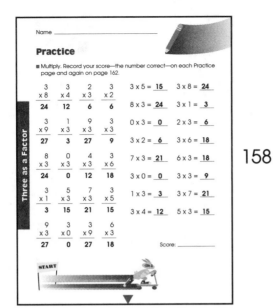

**Name** _____

### Practice

■ Multiply. Record your score—the number correct—on each Practice page and again on page 162.

Three as a Factor

| 3 ×8 = 24 | 3 ×4 = 12 | 2 ×3 = 6 | 3 ×2 = 6 |

3 x 5 = **15**    3 x 8 = **24**
8 x 3 = **24**    3 x 1 = **3**

| 3 ×9 = 27 | 1 ×3 = 3 | 9 ×3 = 27 | 3 ×3 = 9 |

0 x 3 = **0**    2 x 3 = **6**
3 x 2 = **6**    3 x 6 = **18**

| 8 ×3 = 24 | 0 ×3 = 0 | 4 ×3 = 12 | 3 ×6 = 18 |

7 x 3 = **21**    6 x 3 = **18**

| 3 ×1 = 3 | 5 ×3 = 15 | 7 ×3 = 21 | 3 ×5 = 15 |

3 x 0 = **0**    3 x 3 = **9**
1 x 3 = **3**    3 x 7 = **21**
3 x 4 = **12**    5 x 3 = **15**

| 9 ×3 = 27 | 3 ×0 = 0 | 3 ×9 = 27 | 6 ×3 = 18 |

Score: _____

START

**158**

## Page 159

**Name** _____

### Practice

■ Multiply.

Three as a Factor

| 3 ×3 = 9 | 3 ×0 = 0 | 5 ×3 = 15 | 3 ×2 = 6 |

3 x 0 = **0**    6 x 3 = **18**
0 x 3 = **0**    3 x 1 = **3**

| 9 ×3 = 27 | 3 ×6 = 18 | 2 ×3 = 6 | 3 ×7 = 21 |

3 x 8 = **24**    3 x 5 = **15**
3 x 7 = **21**    4 x 3 = **12**

| 3 ×4 = 12 | 8 ×3 = 24 | 1 ×3 = 3 | 3 ×9 = 27 |

8 x 3 = **24**    9 x 3 = **27**
3 x 4 = **12**    3 x 2 = **6**

| 6 ×3 = 18 | 4 ×3 = 12 | 3 ×5 = 15 | 7 ×3 = 21 |

1 x 3 = **3**    5 x 3 = **15**
7 x 3 = **21**    3 x 3 = **9**

| 0 ×3 = 0 | 2 ×3 = 6 | 3 ×1 = 3 | 3 ×8 = 24 |

Circle any problems that you still find difficult to remember. Make your own flash cards to help you master these problems.

FINISH

**159**

## Page 160

**Name** _____

### Timed Test

■ Improve your speed on these facts of 3. Ask someone to time you. Record your time and score on each Timed Test page and on page 162.

Three as a Factor

3 x 5 = **15**    3 x 0 = **0**
3 x 4 = **12**    3 x 9 = **27**

| 9 ×3 = 27 | 3 ×0 = 0 | 2 ×3 = 6 | 3 ×8 = 24 |

0 x 3 = **0**    8 x 3 = **24**
5 x 3 = **15**    3 x 2 = **6**

| 6 ×3 = 18 | 3 ×4 = 12 | 3 ×7 = 21 | 5 ×3 = 15 |

3 x 3 = **9**    3 x 8 = **24**
9 x 3 = **27**    2 x 3 = **6**

| 3 ×1 = 3 | 3 ×6 = 18 | 7 ×3 = 21 | 3 ×2 = 6 |

6 x 3 = **18**    7 x 3 = **21**
3 x 6 = **18**    3 x 1 = **3**

| 3 ×5 = 15 | 0 ×3 = 0 | 3 ×9 = 27 | 5 ×3 = 15 |

1 x 3 = **3**    8 x 3 = **24**

| 3 ×3 = 9 | 8 ×3 = 24 | 1 ×3 = 3 | 4 ×3 = 12 |

4 x 3 = **12**    3 x 7 = **21**

Score: _____    Time: _____ minutes _____ seconds

**160**

## Page 161

**Name** _____

### Timed Test

■ Complete these facts as accurately and as quickly as you can.

Three as a Factor

3 x 6 = **18**    3 x 3 = **9**

| 3 ×8 = 24 | 5 ×3 = 15 | 4 ×3 = 12 | 0 ×3 = 0 |

3 x 5 = **15**    3 x 1 = **3**
0 x 3 = **0**    3 x 4 = **12**

| 3 ×1 = 3 | 1 ×3 = 3 | 3 ×4 = 12 | 6 ×3 = 18 |

3 x 2 = **6**    1 x 3 = **3**
3 x 0 = **0**    3 x 9 = **27**

| 3 ×6 = 18 | 7 ×3 = 21 | 3 ×0 = 0 | 9 ×3 = 27 |

6 x 3 = **18**    2 x 3 = **6**

| 2 ×3 = 6 | 3 ×3 = 9 | 8 ×3 = 24 | 3 ×7 = 21 |

3 x 8 = **24**    3 x 3 = **9**
9 x 3 = **27**    8 x 3 = **24**

| 3 ×5 = 15 | 3 ×2 = 6 | 3 ×9 = 27 | 3 ×6 = 18 |

3 x 7 = **21**    4 x 3 = **12**
5 x 3 = **15**    3 x 1 = **3**

Score: _____    Time: _____ minutes _____ seconds

**161**

## Page 162

**Name** _____

### Timed Test

Three as a Factor

3 x 4 = **12**    3 x 9 = **27**

| 9 ×3 = 27 | 3 ×8 = 24 | 3 ×5 = 15 | 3 ×0 = 0 |

4 x 3 = **12**    5 x 3 = **15**
8 x 3 = **24**    3 x 0 = **0**

| 2 ×3 = 6 | 1 ×3 = 3 | 3 ×6 = 18 | 3 ×4 = 12 |

3 x 5 = **15**    6 x 3 = **18**
9 x 3 = **27**    3 x 7 = **21**

| 8 ×3 = 24 | 0 ×3 = 0 | 2 ×3 = 6 | 6 ×3 = 18 |

2 x 3 = **6**    1 x 3 = **3**

| 3 ×1 = 3 | 3 ×3 = 9 | 4 ×3 = 12 | 7 ×3 = 21 |

3 x 1 = **3**    3 x 8 = **24**
3 x 3 = **9**    7 x 3 = **21**

| 3 ×2 = 6 | 3 ×7 = 21 | 3 ×5 = 15 | 3 ×9 = 27 |

3 x 6 = **18**    3 x 2 = **6**
0 x 3 = **0**    6 x 3 = **18**

| Record your scores and times below. |
| Page 158 Score: _____ | Page 161 Score: _____ Time: _____ min. _____ sec. |
| Page 159 Score: _____ | Page 162 Score: _____ Time: _____ min. _____ sec. |
| Page 160 Score: _____ Time: _____ min. _____ sec. | |

**162**

## Page 163

**Name** _____

### Products Through Thirty-Six

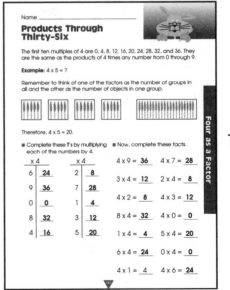

The first ten multiples of 4 are 0, 4, 8, 12, 16, 20, 24, 28, 32, and 36. They are the same as the products of 4 times any number from 0 through 9.

**Example:** 4 x 5 = ?

Remember to think of one of the factors as the number of groups in all and the other as the number of objects in one group.

Therefore, 4 x 5 = 20.

Four as a Factor

■ Complete these T's by multiplying each of the numbers by 4.

| x 4 | | x 4 | |
| 6 | **24** | 2 | **8** |
| 9 | **36** | 7 | **28** |
| 0 | **0** | 1 | **4** |
| 8 | **32** | 3 | **12** |
| 4 | **16** | 5 | **20** |

■ Now, complete these facts.

4 x 9 = **36**    4 x 7 = **28**
3 x 4 = **12**    2 x 4 = **8**
4 x 2 = **8**    4 x 3 = **12**
8 x 4 = **32**    4 x 0 = **0**
1 x 4 = **4**    5 x 4 = **20**
6 x 4 = **24**    0 x 4 = **0**
4 x 1 = **4**    4 x 6 = **24**

**163**

## 164

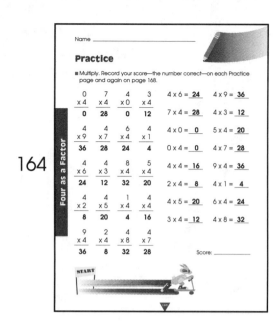

Name _____

### Practice

■ Multiply. Record your score—the number correct—on each Practice page and again on page 168.

**Four as a Factor**

| 0 ×4 | 7 ×4 | 4 ×0 | 3 ×4 | 4 × 6 = **24** | 4 × 9 = **36** |
|---|---|---|---|---|---|
| 0 | 28 | 0 | 12 | 7 × 4 = **28** | 4 × 3 = **12** |

| 4 ×9 | 4 ×7 | 6 ×4 | 4 ×1 | 4 × 0 = **0** | 5 × 4 = **20** |
|---|---|---|---|---|---|
| 36 | 28 | 24 | 4 | 0 × 4 = **0** | 4 × 7 = **28** |

| 4 ×6 | 4 ×3 | 8 ×4 | 5 ×4 | 4 × 4 = **16** | 9 × 4 = **36** |
|---|---|---|---|---|---|
| 24 | 12 | 32 | 20 | 2 × 4 = **8** | 4 × 1 = **4** |

| 4 ×2 | 4 ×5 | 1 ×4 | 4 ×4 | 4 × 5 = **20** | 6 × 4 = **24** |
|---|---|---|---|---|---|
| 8 | 20 | 4 | 16 | 3 × 4 = **12** | 4 × 8 = **32** |

| 9 ×4 | 2 ×4 | 4 ×8 | 4 ×7 |
|---|---|---|---|
| 36 | 8 | 32 | 28 |

START

Score: _____

## 165

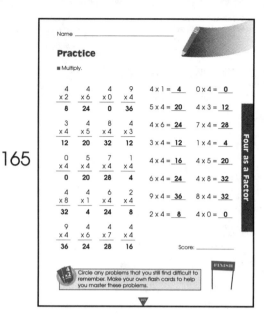

Name _____

### Practice

■ Multiply.

**Four as a Factor**

| 4 ×2 | 4 ×6 | 4 ×0 | 9 ×4 | 4 × 1 = **4** | 0 × 4 = **0** |
|---|---|---|---|---|---|
| 8 | 24 | 0 | 36 | 5 × 4 = **20** | 4 × 3 = **12** |

| 3 ×4 | 4 ×5 | 8 ×4 | 4 ×3 | 4 × 6 = **24** | 7 × 4 = **28** |
|---|---|---|---|---|---|
| 12 | 20 | 32 | 12 | 3 × 4 = **12** | 1 × 4 = **4** |

| 0 ×4 | 5 ×4 | 7 ×4 | 1 ×4 | 4 × 4 = **16** | 4 × 5 = **20** |
|---|---|---|---|---|---|
| 0 | 20 | 28 | 4 | 6 × 4 = **24** | 4 × 8 = **32** |

| 4 ×8 | 4 ×1 | 6 ×4 | 2 ×4 | 9 × 4 = **36** | 8 × 4 = **32** |
|---|---|---|---|---|---|
| 32 | 4 | 24 | 8 | 2 × 4 = **8** | 4 × 0 = **0** |

| 9 ×4 | 4 ×6 | 4 ×7 | 4 ×4 |
|---|---|---|---|
| 36 | 24 | 28 | 16 |

Circle any problems that you still find difficult to remember. Make your own flash cards to help you master these problems.

FINISH

Score: _____

## 166

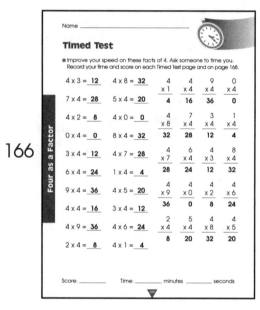

Name _____

### Timed Test

■ Improve your speed on these facts of 4. Ask someone to time you. Record your time and score on each Timed Test page and on page 168.

**Four as a Factor**

4 × 3 = **12**    4 × 8 = **32**

7 × 4 = **28**    5 × 4 = **20**

| 4 ×1 | 4 ×4 | 9 ×4 | 0 |
|---|---|---|---|
| 4 | 16 | 36 | 0 |

4 × 2 = **8**    4 × 0 = **0**

0 × 4 = **0**    8 × 4 = **32**

| 4 ×8 | 7 ×4 | 3 ×4 | 1 ×4 |
|---|---|---|---|
| 32 | 28 | 12 | 4 |

3 × 4 = **12**    4 × 7 = **28**

6 × 4 = **24**    1 × 4 = **4**

| 4 ×7 | 6 ×4 | 4 ×3 | 8 ×4 |
|---|---|---|---|
| 28 | 24 | 12 | 32 |

9 × 4 = **36**    4 × 5 = **20**

4 × 4 = **16**    3 × 4 = **12**

| 4 ×9 | 4 ×0 | 4 ×2 | 4 ×6 |
|---|---|---|---|
| 36 | 0 | 8 | 24 |

4 × 9 = **36**    4 × 6 = **24**

2 × 4 = **8**    4 × 1 = **4**

| 2 ×4 | 4 ×4 | 5 ×4 | 4 ×5 |
|---|---|---|---|
| 8 | 20 | 32 | 20 |

Score: _____    Time: _____ minutes _____ seconds

## 167

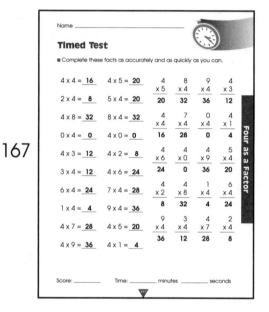

Name _____

### Timed Test

■ Complete these facts as accurately and as quickly as you can.

**Four as a Factor**

4 × 4 = **16**    4 × 5 = **20**

2 × 4 = **8**    5 × 4 = **20**

| 4 ×5 | 8 ×4 | 9 ×4 | 4 ×3 |
|---|---|---|---|
| 20 | 32 | 36 | 12 |

4 × 8 = **32**    8 × 4 = **32**

0 × 4 = **0**    4 × 0 = **0**

| 4 ×4 | 7 ×4 | 0 ×4 | 4 ×1 |
|---|---|---|---|
| 16 | 28 | 0 | 4 |

4 × 3 = **12**    4 × 2 = **8**

3 × 4 = **12**    4 × 6 = **24**

| 4 ×6 | 4 ×0 | 4 ×9 | 5 ×4 |
|---|---|---|---|
| 24 | 0 | 36 | 20 |

6 × 4 = **24**    7 × 4 = **28**

1 × 4 = **4**    9 × 4 = **36**

| 4 ×2 | 4 ×8 | 1 ×4 | 4 ×4 |
|---|---|---|---|
| 8 | 32 | 4 | 12 |

4 × 7 = **28**    4 × 5 = **20**

4 × 9 = **36**    4 × 1 = **4**

| 9 ×4 | 3 ×4 | 4 ×7 | 2 ×4 |
|---|---|---|---|
| 36 | 12 | 28 | 8 |

Score: _____    Time: _____ minutes _____ seconds

## 168

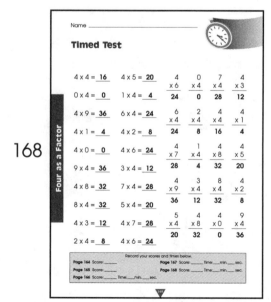

Name _____

### Timed Test

**Four as a Factor**

4 × 4 = **16**    4 × 5 = **20**

0 × 4 = **0**    1 × 4 = **4**

| 4 ×6 | 0 ×4 | 7 ×4 | 4 ×3 |
|---|---|---|---|
| 24 | 0 | 28 | 12 |

4 × 9 = **36**    6 × 4 = **24**

4 × 1 = **4**    4 × 2 = **8**

| 6 ×4 | 2 ×4 | 4 ×4 | 4 ×1 |
|---|---|---|---|
| 24 | 8 | 16 | 4 |

4 × 0 = **0**    4 × 6 = **24**

9 × 4 = **36**    3 × 4 = **12**

| 4 ×7 | 1 ×4 | 4 ×8 | 4 ×5 |
|---|---|---|---|
| 28 | 4 | 32 | 20 |

4 × 8 = **32**    7 × 4 = **28**

8 × 4 = **32**    5 × 4 = **20**

| 4 ×9 | 4 ×4 | 8 ×4 | 4 ×2 |
|---|---|---|---|
| 36 | 12 | 32 | 8 |

4 × 3 = **12**    4 × 7 = **28**

2 × 4 = **8**    4 × 6 = **24**

| 5 ×4 | 4 ×8 | 4 ×0 | 9 ×4 |
|---|---|---|---|
| 20 | 32 | 0 | 36 |

Record your scores and times below.

| | |
|---|---|
| Page 164 Score: _____ | Page 167 Score: _____ Time: ___ min. ___ sec. |
| Page 165 Score: _____ | Page 168 Score: _____ Time: ___ min. ___ sec. |
| Page 166 Score: _____ Time: ___ min. ___ sec. | |

## 169

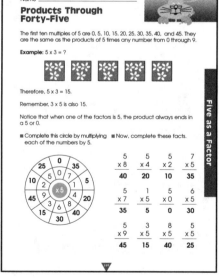

Name _____

### Products Through Forty-Five

The first ten multiples of 5 are 0, 5, 10, 15, 20, 25, 30, 35, 40, and 45. They are the same as the products of 5 times any number from 0 through 9.

**Example:** 5 × 3 = ?

Therefore, 5 × 3 = 15.

Remember, 3 × 5 is also 15.

Notice that when one of the factors is 5, the product always ends in a 5 or 0.

■ Complete this circle by multiplying each of the numbers by 5.

(circle: ×5 — 0, 7, 5, 5, 20, 40, 30, 15, 45, 10, 25, 35)

**Five as a Factor**

■ Now, complete these facts.

| 5 ×8 | 5 ×4 | 5 ×2 | 7 ×5 |
|---|---|---|---|
| 40 | 20 | 10 | 35 |

| 5 ×7 | 1 ×5 | 5 ×0 | 6 ×5 |
|---|---|---|---|
| 35 | 5 | 0 | 30 |

| 5 ×9 | 3 ×5 | 8 ×5 | 5 ×5 |
|---|---|---|---|
| 45 | 15 | 40 | 25 |

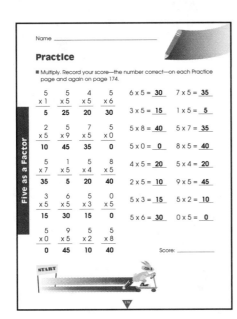

## Practice

■ Multiply. Record your score—the number correct—on each Practice page and again on page 174.

**Five as a Factor**

| | | | |
|---|---|---|---|
| 5 ×1 | 5 ×5 | 4 ×5 | 5 ×6 |
| **5** | **25** | **20** | **30** |

| | | | |
|---|---|---|---|
| 2 ×5 | 5 ×9 | 7 ×5 | 5 ×0 |
| **10** | **45** | **35** | **0** |

| | | | |
|---|---|---|---|
| 5 ×7 | 1 ×5 | 5 ×4 | 8 ×5 |
| **35** | **5** | **20** | **40** |

| | | | |
|---|---|---|---|
| 3 ×5 | 6 ×5 | 5 ×3 | 0 ×5 |
| **15** | **30** | **15** | **0** |

| | | | |
|---|---|---|---|
| 5 ×0 | 9 ×5 | 5 ×2 | 5 ×8 |
| **0** | **45** | **10** | **40** |

6 x 5 = **30**    7 x 5 = **35**
3 x 5 = **15**    1 x 5 = **5**
5 x 8 = **40**    5 x 7 = **35**
5 x 0 = **0**     8 x 5 = **40**
4 x 5 = **20**    5 x 4 = **20**
2 x 5 = **10**    9 x 5 = **45**
5 x 3 = **15**    5 x 2 = **10**
5 x 6 = **30**    0 x 5 = **0**

START    FINISH

Score: _____

**170**

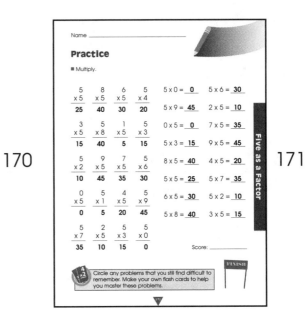

## Practice

■ Multiply.

**Five as a Factor**

| | | | |
|---|---|---|---|
| 5 ×5 | 8 ×5 | 6 ×5 | 5 ×4 |
| **25** | **40** | **30** | **20** |

| | | | |
|---|---|---|---|
| 3 ×5 | 5 ×8 | 1 ×5 | 5 ×3 |
| **15** | **40** | **5** | **15** |

| | | | |
|---|---|---|---|
| 5 ×2 | 9 ×5 | 7 ×5 | 5 ×6 |
| **10** | **45** | **35** | **30** |

| | | | |
|---|---|---|---|
| 0 ×5 | 5 ×1 | 4 ×5 | 5 ×9 |
| **0** | **5** | **20** | **45** |

| | | | |
|---|---|---|---|
| 5 ×7 | 2 ×5 | 5 ×3 | 5 ×0 |
| **35** | **10** | **15** | **0** |

5 x 0 = **0**     5 x 6 = **30**
5 x 9 = **45**    2 x 5 = **10**
0 x 5 = **0**     7 x 5 = **35**
5 x 3 = **15**    9 x 5 = **45**
8 x 5 = **40**    4 x 5 = **20**
5 x 5 = **25**    5 x 7 = **35**
6 x 5 = **30**    5 x 2 = **10**
5 x 8 = **40**    3 x 5 = **15**

Circle any problems that you still find difficult to remember. Make your own flash cards to help you master these problems.

Score: _____

**171**

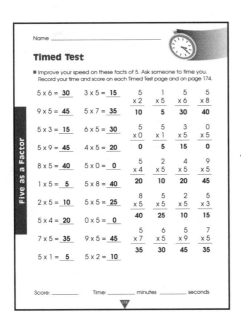

## Timed Test

■ Improve your speed on these facts of 5. Ask someone to time you. Record your time and score on each Timed Test page and on page 174.

**Five as a Factor**

5 x 6 = **30**    3 x 5 = **15**
9 x 5 = **45**    5 x 7 = **35**
5 x 3 = **15**    6 x 5 = **30**
5 x 9 = **45**    4 x 5 = **20**
8 x 5 = **40**    5 x 0 = **0**
1 x 5 = **5**     5 x 8 = **40**
2 x 5 = **10**    5 x 5 = **25**
5 x 4 = **20**    0 x 5 = **0**
7 x 5 = **35**    9 x 5 = **45**
5 x 1 = **5**     5 x 2 = **10**

| | | | |
|---|---|---|---|
| 5 ×2 | 1 ×5 | 5 ×6 | 5 ×8 |
| **10** | **5** | **30** | **40** |

| | | | |
|---|---|---|---|
| 5 ×0 | 5 ×1 | 3 ×5 | 0 ×5 |
| **0** | **5** | **15** | **0** |

| | | | |
|---|---|---|---|
| 5 ×4 | 2 ×5 | 4 ×5 | 9 ×5 |
| **20** | **10** | **20** | **45** |

| | | | |
|---|---|---|---|
| 8 ×5 | 5 ×5 | 2 ×5 | 5 ×3 |
| **40** | **25** | **10** | **15** |

| | | | |
|---|---|---|---|
| 5 ×7 | 6 ×5 | 5 ×9 | 5 ×5 |
| **35** | **30** | **45** | **35** |

Score: _____    Time: _____ minutes _____ seconds

**172**

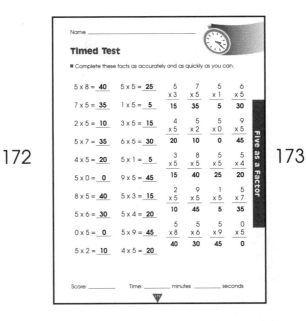

## Timed Test

■ Complete these facts as accurately and as quickly as you can.

**Five as a Factor**

5 x 8 = **40**    5 x 5 = **25**
7 x 5 = **35**    1 x 5 = **5**
2 x 5 = **10**    3 x 5 = **15**
5 x 7 = **35**    6 x 5 = **30**
4 x 5 = **20**    5 x 1 = **5**
5 x 0 = **0**     9 x 5 = **45**
8 x 5 = **40**    5 x 3 = **15**
5 x 6 = **30**    5 x 4 = **20**
0 x 5 = **0**     5 x 9 = **45**
5 x 2 = **10**    4 x 5 = **20**

| | | | |
|---|---|---|---|
| 5 ×3 | 7 ×5 | 5 ×1 | 6 ×5 |
| **15** | **35** | **5** | **30** |

| | | | |
|---|---|---|---|
| 4 ×5 | 5 ×2 | 5 ×0 | 9 ×5 |
| **20** | **10** | **0** | **45** |

| | | | |
|---|---|---|---|
| 3 ×5 | 8 ×5 | 5 ×5 | 5 ×4 |
| **15** | **40** | **25** | **20** |

| | | | |
|---|---|---|---|
| 2 ×5 | 9 ×5 | 1 ×5 | 5 ×7 |
| **10** | **45** | **5** | **35** |

| | | | |
|---|---|---|---|
| 5 ×8 | 5 ×6 | 5 ×9 | 0 ×5 |
| **40** | **30** | **45** | **0** |

Score: _____    Time: _____ minutes _____ seconds

**173**

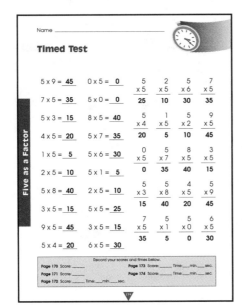

## Timed Test

**Five as a Factor**

5 x 9 = **45**    0 x 5 = **0**
7 x 5 = **35**    5 x 0 = **0**
5 x 3 = **15**    8 x 5 = **40**
4 x 5 = **20**    5 x 7 = **35**
1 x 5 = **5**     5 x 6 = **30**
2 x 5 = **10**    5 x 1 = **5**
5 x 8 = **40**    2 x 5 = **10**
3 x 5 = **15**    5 x 5 = **25**
9 x 5 = **45**    3 x 5 = **15**
5 x 4 = **20**    6 x 5 = **30**

| | | | |
|---|---|---|---|
| 5 ×5 | 2 ×5 | 5 ×6 | 7 ×5 |
| **25** | **10** | **30** | **35** |

| | | | |
|---|---|---|---|
| 5 ×4 | 1 ×5 | 5 ×2 | 9 ×5 |
| **20** | **5** | **10** | **45** |

| | | | |
|---|---|---|---|
| 0 ×5 | 5 ×7 | 8 ×5 | 3 ×5 |
| **0** | **35** | **40** | **15** |

| | | | |
|---|---|---|---|
| 5 ×3 | 5 ×8 | 4 ×5 | 5 ×9 |
| **15** | **40** | **20** | **45** |

| | | | |
|---|---|---|---|
| 7 ×5 | 5 ×5 | 5 ×1 | 6 ×5 |
| **35** | **5** | **0** | **30** |

Record your scores and times below.

Page 170 Score: _____    Page 173 Score: _____ Time: ___min. ___sec.
Page 171 Score: _____    Page 174 Score: _____ Time: ___min. ___sec.
Page 172 Score: _____ Time: ___min. ___sec.

**174**

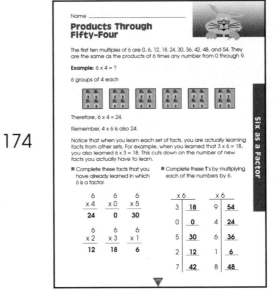

## Products Through Fifty-Four

The first ten multiples of 6 are 0, 6, 12, 18, 24, 30, 36, 42, 48, and 54. They are the same as the products of 6 times any number from 0 through 9.

**Example:** 6 x 4 = ?

6 groups of 4 each

Therefore, 6 x 4 = 24.

Remember, 4 x 6 is also 24.

Notice that when you learn each set of facts, you are actually learning facts from other sets. For example, when you learned that 3 x 6 = 18, you also learned 6 x 3 = 18. This cuts down on the number of new facts you actually have to learn.

**Six as a Factor**

■ Complete these facts that you have already learned in which 6 is a factor.

| | | |
|---|---|---|
| 6 ×4 | 6 ×0 | 6 ×5 |
| **24** | **0** | **30** |

| | | |
|---|---|---|
| 6 ×2 | 6 ×3 | 6 ×1 |
| **12** | **18** | **6** |

■ Complete these T's by multiplying each of the numbers by 6.

| ×6 | | ×6 | |
|---|---|---|---|
| 3 | **18** | 9 | **54** |
| 0 | **0** | 4 | **24** |
| 5 | **30** | 6 | **36** |
| 2 | **12** | 1 | **6** |
| 7 | **42** | 8 | **48** |

**175**

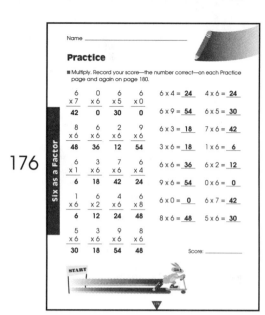

**176** — Six as a Factor

## Practice

■ Multiply. Record your score—the number correct—on each Practice page and again on page 180.

| | | | | | |
|---|---|---|---|---|---|
| 6 ×7 = **42** | 0 ×6 = **0** | 6 ×5 = **30** | 6 ×0 = **0** | 6 × 4 = **24** | 4 × 6 = **24** |

6 × 9 = **54**   6 × 5 = **30**

| 8 ×6 = **48** | 6 ×6 = **36** | 2 ×6 = **12** | 9 ×6 = **54** |
|---|---|---|---|

6 × 3 = **18**   7 × 6 = **42**

3 × 6 = **18**   1 × 6 = **6**

| 6 ×1 = **6** | 3 ×6 = **18** | 7 ×6 = **42** | 6 ×4 = **24** |
|---|---|---|---|

6 × 6 = **36**   6 × 2 = **12**

9 × 6 = **54**   0 × 6 = **0**

| 1 ×6 = **6** | 6 ×2 = **12** | 4 ×6 = **24** | 6 ×8 = **48** |
|---|---|---|---|

6 × 0 = **0**   6 × 7 = **42**

8 × 6 = **48**   5 × 6 = **30**

| 5 ×6 = **30** | 3 ×6 = **18** | 9 ×6 = **54** | 8 ×6 = **48** |
|---|---|---|---|

Score: _____

START / FINISH

---

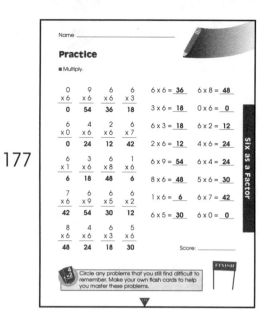

**177** — Six as a Factor

## Practice

■ Multiply.

| 0 ×6 = **0** | 9 ×6 = **54** | 6 ×6 = **36** | 6 ×3 = **18** |
|---|---|---|---|

6 × 6 = **36**   6 × 8 = **48**

3 × 6 = **18**   0 × 6 = **0**

| 6 ×0 = **0** | 4 ×6 = **24** | 2 ×6 = **12** | 6 ×7 = **42** |
|---|---|---|---|

6 × 3 = **18**   6 × 2 = **12**

2 × 6 = **12**   4 × 6 = **24**

| 6 ×1 = **6** | 3 ×6 = **18** | 6 ×8 = **48** | 1 ×6 = **6** |
|---|---|---|---|

6 × 9 = **54**   6 × 4 = **24**

8 × 6 = **48**   5 × 6 = **30**

| 7 ×6 = **42** | 6 ×9 = **54** | 6 ×5 = **30** | 6 ×2 = **12** |
|---|---|---|---|

1 × 6 = **6**   6 × 7 = **42**

6 × 5 = **30**   6 × 0 = **0**

| 8 ×6 = **48** | 4 ×6 = **24** | 6 ×3 = **18** | 5 ×6 = **30** |
|---|---|---|---|

Score: _____

Circle any problems that you still find difficult to remember. Make your own flash cards to help you master these problems.

---

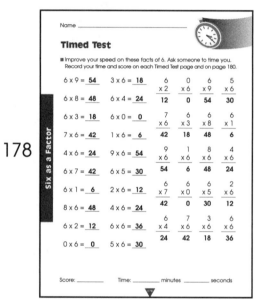

**178** — Six as a Factor

## Timed Test

■ Improve your speed on these facts of 6. Ask someone to time you. Record your time and score on each Timed Test page and on page 180.

6 × 9 = **54**   3 × 6 = **18**

| 6 ×2 = **12** | 0 ×6 = **0** | 6 ×9 = **54** | 5 ×6 = **30** |
|---|---|---|---|

6 × 8 = **48**   6 × 4 = **24**

| 7 ×6 = **42** | 6 ×3 = **18** | 6 ×8 = **48** | 6 ×1 = **6** |
|---|---|---|---|

6 × 3 = **18**   6 × 0 = **0**

| 9 ×6 = **54** | 1 ×6 = **6** | 8 ×6 = **48** | 4 ×6 = **24** |
|---|---|---|---|

7 × 6 = **42**   1 × 6 = **6**

4 × 6 = **24**   9 × 6 = **54**

| 6 ×7 = **42** | 6 ×0 = **0** | 6 ×5 = **30** | 2 ×6 = **12** |
|---|---|---|---|

6 × 7 = **42**   6 × 5 = **30**

6 × 1 = **6**   2 × 6 = **12**

| 6 ×4 = **24** | 7 ×6 = **42** | 3 ×6 = **18** | 6 ×6 = **36** |
|---|---|---|---|

8 × 6 = **48**   4 × 6 = **24**

6 × 2 = **12**   6 × 6 = **36**

0 × 6 = **0**   5 × 6 = **30**

Score: _____   Time: _____ minutes _____ seconds

---

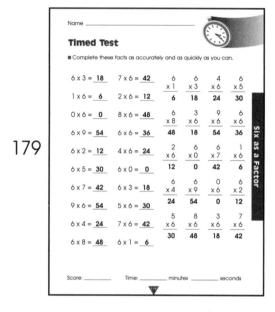

**179** — Six as a Factor

## Timed Test

■ Complete these facts as accurately and as quickly as you can.

6 × 3 = **18**   7 × 6 = **42**

| 6 ×1 = **6** | 6 ×3 = **18** | 4 ×6 = **24** | 6 ×5 = **30** |
|---|---|---|---|

1 × 6 = **6**   2 × 6 = **12**

0 × 6 = **0**   8 × 6 = **48**

| 6 ×8 = **48** | 3 ×6 = **18** | 9 ×6 = **54** | 6 ×6 = **36** |
|---|---|---|---|

6 × 9 = **54**   6 × 6 = **36**

6 × 2 = **12**   4 × 6 = **24**

| 2 ×6 = **12** | 6 ×0 = **0** | 6 ×7 = **42** | 1 ×6 = **6** |
|---|---|---|---|

6 × 5 = **30**   6 × 0 = **0**

6 × 7 = **42**   6 × 3 = **18**

| 6 ×4 = **24** | 6 ×9 = **54** | 6 ×6 = **0** | 6 ×2 = **12** |
|---|---|---|---|

9 × 6 = **54**   5 × 6 = **30**

6 × 4 = **24**   7 × 6 = **42**

| 5 ×6 = **30** | 8 ×6 = **48** | 3 ×6 = **18** | 7 ×6 = **42** |
|---|---|---|---|

6 × 8 = **48**   6 × 1 = **6**

Score: _____   Time: _____ minutes _____ seconds

---

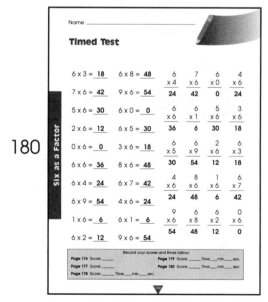

**180** — Six as a Factor

## Timed Test

6 × 3 = **18**   6 × 8 = **48**

| 6 ×4 = **24** | 7 ×6 = **42** | 6 ×0 = **0** | 4 ×6 = **24** |
|---|---|---|---|

7 × 6 = **42**   9 × 6 = **54**

5 × 6 = **30**   6 × 0 = **0**

| 6 ×6 = **36** | 6 ×1 = **6** | 5 ×6 = **30** | 3 ×6 = **18** |
|---|---|---|---|

2 × 6 = **12**   6 × 5 = **30**

0 × 6 = **0**   3 × 6 = **18**

| 6 ×5 = **30** | 6 ×9 = **54** | 2 ×6 = **12** | 6 ×3 = **18** |
|---|---|---|---|

6 × 6 = **36**   8 × 6 = **48**

6 × 4 = **24**   6 × 7 = **42**

| 4 ×6 = **24** | 8 ×6 = **48** | 1 ×6 = **6** | 6 ×7 = **42** |
|---|---|---|---|

6 × 9 = **54**   4 × 6 = **24**

| 9 ×6 = **54** | 6 ×8 = **48** | 6 ×2 = **12** | 6 ×0 = **0** |
|---|---|---|---|

1 × 6 = **6**   6 × 1 = **6**

6 × 2 = **12**   9 × 6 = **54**

**Record your scores and times below.**

Page 176 Score: _____   Page 179 Score: _____ Time: ____ min. ____ sec.
Page 177 Score: _____   Page 180 Score: _____ Time: ____ min. ____ sec.
Page 178 Score: _____ Time: ____ min. ____ sec.

---

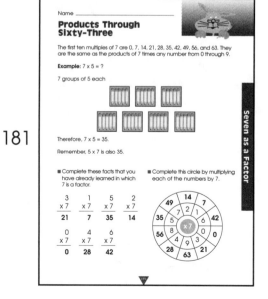

**181** — Seven as a Factor

## Products Through Sixty-Three

The first ten multiples of 7 are 0, 7, 14, 21, 28, 35, 42, 49, 56, and 63. They are the same as the products of 7 times any number from 0 through 9.

**Example:** 7 × 5 = ?

7 groups of 5 each

Therefore, 7 × 5 = 35.

Remember, 5 × 7 is also 35.

■ Complete these facts that you have already learned in which 7 is a factor.

| 3 ×7 = **21** | 1 ×7 = **7** | 5 ×7 = **35** | 2 ×7 = **14** |
|---|---|---|---|

| 0 ×7 = **0** | 4 ×7 = **28** | 6 ×7 = **42** |
|---|---|---|

■ Complete this circle by multiplying each of the numbers by 7.

(×7 circle: 49, 14, 7, 35, 42, 56, 28, 63, 21)

---

## Page 182

**Practice**

Seven as a Factor

■ Multiply. Record your score—the number correct—on each Practice page and again on page 188.

| | | | | |
|---|---|---|---|---|
| 6 ×7 = 42 | 7 ×0 = 0 | 7 ×8 = 56 | 4 ×7 = 28 | 7 x 2 = **14**   1 x 7 = **7** |
| 7 ×7 = 49 | 8 ×3 = 21 | 7 ×8 = 56 | 3 ×7 = 21 | 5 x 7 = **35**   7 x 3 = **21** |

7 ×7 = 49   8 ×3 = 21   7 ×8 = 56   3 ×7 = 21
0 x 7 = **0**   7 x 7 = **49**

7 ×6 = 42   7 ×9 = 63   7 ×4 = 28   5 ×7 = 35
7 x 9 = **63**   8 x 7 = **56**

7 ×5 = 35   7 ×1 = 7

7 ×2 = 14   0 ×7 = 0   7 ×1 = 7   7 ×5 = 35
6 x 7 = **42**   9 x 7 = **63**

4 x 7 = **28**   7 x 8 = **56**

1 ×7 = 7   9 ×7 = 63   8 ×7 = 56   2 ×7 = 14
7 x 0 = **0**   2 x 7 = **14**

Score: _____

**START**

## Page 183

**Practice**

Seven as a Factor

■ Multiply.

7 ×7 = 49   5 ×7 = 35   7 ×4 = 28   9 ×7 = 63
7 x 4 = **28**   7 x 5 = **35**
2 x 7 = **14**   3 x 7 = **21**

7 ×0 = 0   3 ×7 = 21   7 ×8 = 56   4 ×7 = 28
7 x 1 = **7**   9 x 7 = **63**
7 x 7 = **49**   7 x 2 = **14**

7 ×3 = 21   6 ×7 = 42   1 ×7 = 7   7 ×9 = 63
7 x 8 = **56**   5 x 7 = **35**
1 x 7 = **7**   0 x 7 = **0**

7 ×5 = 35   8 ×7 = 56   7 ×2 = 14   0 ×7 = 0
7 x 3 = **21**   7 x 6 = **42**
8 x 7 = **56**   4 x 7 = **28**

2 ×7 = 14   7 ×6 = 42   7 ×8 = 56   7 ×1 = 7

Score: _____

Circle any problems that you still find difficult to remember. Make your own flash cards to help you master these problems.

**FINISH**

## Page 184

**Timed Test**

Seven as a Factor

■ Improve your speed on these facts of 7. Ask someone to time you. Record your time and score on each Timed Test page and on page 188.

7 x 3 = **21**   7 x 6 = **42**
5 x 7 = **35**   2 x 7 = **14**
7 ×3 = 21   9 ×7 = 63   3 ×7 = 21   7 ×8 = 56

7 x 8 = **56**   7 x 1 = **7**
7 x 5 = **35**   7 x 9 = **63**
7 ×1 = 7   7 ×6 = 42   7 ×9 = 63   6 ×7 = 42

0 x 7 = **0**   7 x 7 = **49**
6 x 7 = **42**   7 x 2 = **14**
2 ×7 = 14   7 ×4 = 28   7 ×1 = 7   7 ×0 = 0

7 x 4 = **28**   8 x 7 = **56**
3 x 7 = **21**   7 x 8 = **56**
7 ×7 = 49   7 ×0 = 0   8 ×7 = 56   7 ×2 = 14

7 x 0 = **0**   1 x 7 = **7**
9 x 7 = **63**   4 x 7 = **28**
4 ×7 = 28   7 ×5 = 35   5 ×7 = 35   1 ×7 = 7

Score: _____   Time: _____ minutes _____ seconds

## Page 185

**Timed Test**

Seven as a Factor

■ Complete these facts as accurately and as quickly as you can.

7 x 6 = **42**   1 x 7 = **7**
8 x 7 = **56**   7 x 9 = **63**
0 ×7 = 0   7 ×3 = 21   7 ×8 = 56   7 ×6 = 42

2 x 7 = **14**   3 x 7 = **21**
5 x 7 = **35**   7 x 1 = **7**
7 ×2 = 14   6 ×7 = 42   7 ×5 = 35   7 ×4 = 28

0 x 7 = **0**   6 x 7 = **42**
7 x 2 = **14**   7 x 8 = **56**
7 ×9 = 63   5 ×7 = 35   7 ×7 = 7   1 ×7 = 28

7 x 0 = **0**   9 x 7 = **63**
4 x 7 = **28**   7 x 4 = **28**
7 ×1 = 7   9 ×7 = 63   2 ×7 = 14   7 ×7 = 21

7 x 7 = **49**   2 x 7 = **14**
7 x 5 = **35**   7 x 3 = **21**
8 ×7 = 56   7 ×5 = 35   7 ×7 = 49   7 ×0 = 0

Score: _____   Time: _____ minutes _____ seconds

## Page 186

**Timed Test**

Seven as a Factor

7 x 8 = **56**   7 x 4 = **28**
7 ×6 = 42   0 ×7 = 0   7 ×1 = 7   4 ×7 = 28

7 x 2 = **14**   7 x 1 = **7**
7 ×8 = 56   9 ×7 = 63   7 ×3 = 21   2 ×7 = 14

5 x 7 = **35**   7 x 9 = **63**

1 x 7 = **7**   7 x 2 = **14**
6 ×7 = 42   7 ×7 = 49   3 ×7 = 21   5 ×7 = 35

3 x 7 = **21**   7 x 3 = **21**
7 ×2 = 14   4 ×7 = 28   1 ×7 = 7   7 ×5 = 35

7 x 0 = **0**   7 x 5 = **35**

6 x 7 = **42**   0 x 7 = **0**
7 ×9 = 63   7 ×7 = 56   7 ×4 = 28   7 ×0 = 0

7 x 7 = **49**   4 x 7 = **28**

2 x 7 = **14**   9 x 7 = **63**

8 x 7 = **56**   7 x 6 = **42**

Score: _____   Time: _____ minutes _____ seconds

## Page 187

**Timed Test**

Seven as a Factor

7 x 2 = **14**   7 x 4 = **28**
7 ×0 = 0   2 ×7 = 14   7 ×7 = 49   5 ×7 = 35

4 x 7 = **28**   7 x 0 = **0**

7 x 9 = **63**   2 x 7 = **14**
0 ×7 = 0   7 ×3 = 21   7 ×9 = 63   7 ×5 = 35

7 x 6 = **42**   7 x 7 = **49**

7 x 5 = **35**   7 x 1 = **7**
7 ×1 = 7   7 ×6 = 42   1 ×7 = 7   7 ×7 = 63

3 x 7 = **21**   8 x 7 = **56**

5 x 7 = **35**   1 x 7 = **7**
4 ×7 = 28   7 ×8 = 56   3 ×7 = 21   8 ×7 = 56

7 x 8 = **56**   7 x 3 = **21**

0 x 7 = **0**   9 x 7 = **63**
7 ×2 = 14   7 ×7 = 42   7 ×4 = 28   2 ×7 = 14

6 x 7 = **42**   7 x 6 = **42**

Score: _____   Time: _____ minutes _____ seconds

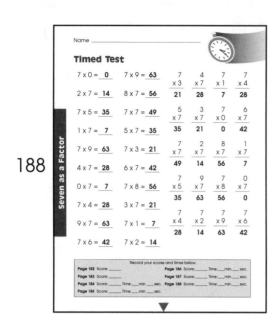

**188**

Name _____

## Timed Test

Seven as a Factor

$7 \times 0 = \underline{0}$   $7 \times 9 = \underline{63}$

| | | | |
|---|---|---|---|
| 7 | 4 | 7 | 7 |
| ×3 | ×7 | ×1 | ×4 |
| 21 | 28 | 7 | 28 |

$2 \times 7 = \underline{14}$   $8 \times 7 = \underline{56}$

$7 \times 5 = \underline{35}$   $7 \times 7 = \underline{49}$

| | | | |
|---|---|---|---|
| 5 | 3 | 7 | 6 |
| ×7 | ×7 | ×0 | ×7 |
| 35 | 21 | 0 | 42 |

$1 \times 7 = \underline{7}$   $5 \times 7 = \underline{35}$

$7 \times 9 = \underline{63}$   $7 \times 3 = \underline{21}$

| | | | |
|---|---|---|---|
| 7 | 2 | 8 | 1 |
| ×7 | ×7 | ×7 | ×7 |
| 49 | 14 | 56 | 7 |

$4 \times 7 = \underline{28}$   $6 \times 7 = \underline{42}$

$0 \times 7 = \underline{7}$   $7 \times 8 = \underline{56}$

| | | | |
|---|---|---|---|
| 7 | 9 | 7 | 0 |
| ×5 | ×7 | ×8 | ×7 |
| 35 | 63 | 56 | 0 |

$7 \times 4 = \underline{28}$   $3 \times 7 = \underline{21}$

$9 \times 7 = \underline{63}$   $7 \times 1 = \underline{7}$

| | | | |
|---|---|---|---|
| 7 | 7 | 7 | 7 |
| ×4 | ×2 | ×9 | ×6 |
| 28 | 14 | 63 | 42 |

$7 \times 6 = \underline{42}$   $7 \times 2 = \underline{14}$

Record your scores and times below.

| Page 182 Score: _____ | Page 186 Score: _____ Time:___min.___sec. |
| Page 183 Score: _____ | Page 187 Score: _____ Time:___min.___sec. |
| Page 184 Score: _____ Time:___min.___sec. | Page 188 Score: _____ Time:___min.___sec. |
| Page 185 Score: _____ | |

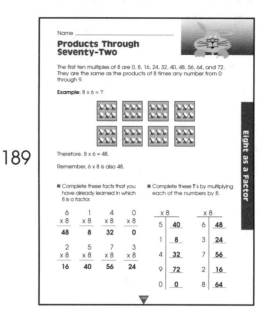

**189**

Name _____

## Products Through Seventy-Two

Eight as a Factor

The first ten multiples of 8 are 0, 8, 16, 24, 32, 40, 48, 56, 64, and 72. They are the same as the products of 8 times any number from 0 through 9.

**Example:** $8 \times 6 = ?$

Therefore, $8 \times 6 = 48$.

Remember, $6 \times 8$ is also 48.

■ Complete these facts that you have already learned in which 8 is a factor.

| 6 | 1 | 4 | 0 |
|---|---|---|---|
| ×8 | ×8 | ×8 | ×8 |
| 48 | 8 | 32 | 0 |

| 2 | 5 | 7 | 3 |
|---|---|---|---|
| ×8 | ×8 | ×8 | ×8 |
| 16 | 40 | 56 | 24 |

■ Complete these T's by multiplying each of the numbers by 8.

| ×8 | | ×8 | |
|---|---|---|---|
| 5 | 40 | 6 | 48 |
| 1 | 8 | 3 | 24 |
| 4 | 32 | 7 | 56 |
| 9 | 72 | 2 | 16 |
| 0 | 0 | 8 | 64 |

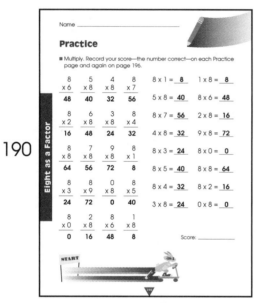

**190**

Name _____

## Practice

Eight as a Factor

■ Multiply. Record your score—the number correct—on each Practice page and again on page 196.

| 8 | 5 | 4 | 8 |
|---|---|---|---|
| ×6 | ×8 | ×8 | ×7 |
| 48 | 40 | 32 | 56 |

| 8 | 6 | 3 | 8 |
|---|---|---|---|
| ×2 | ×8 | ×8 | ×4 |
| 16 | 48 | 24 | 32 |

| 8 | 7 | 9 | 8 |
|---|---|---|---|
| ×8 | ×8 | ×8 | ×1 |
| 64 | 56 | 72 | 8 |

| 8 | 8 | 0 | 8 |
|---|---|---|---|
| ×3 | ×9 | ×8 | ×5 |
| 24 | 72 | 0 | 40 |

| 8 | 2 | 8 | 1 |
|---|---|---|---|
| ×0 | ×8 | ×6 | ×8 |
| 0 | 16 | 48 | 8 |

$8 \times 1 = \underline{8}$   $1 \times 8 = \underline{8}$

$5 \times 8 = \underline{40}$   $8 \times 6 = \underline{48}$

$8 \times 7 = \underline{56}$   $2 \times 8 = \underline{16}$

$4 \times 8 = \underline{32}$   $9 \times 8 = \underline{72}$

$8 \times 3 = \underline{24}$   $8 \times 0 = \underline{0}$

$8 \times 5 = \underline{40}$   $8 \times 8 = \underline{64}$

$8 \times 4 = \underline{32}$   $8 \times 2 = \underline{16}$

$3 \times 8 = \underline{24}$   $0 \times 8 = \underline{0}$

Score: _____

START   FINISH

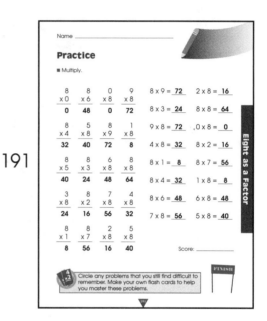

**191**

Name _____

## Practice

Eight as a Factor

■ Multiply.

| 8 | 8 | 0 | 9 |
|---|---|---|---|
| ×0 | ×6 | ×8 | ×8 |
| 0 | 48 | 0 | 72 |

| 8 | 5 | 8 | 1 |
|---|---|---|---|
| ×4 | ×8 | ×9 | ×8 |
| 32 | 40 | 72 | 8 |

| 8 | 8 | 6 | 8 |
|---|---|---|---|
| ×5 | ×3 | ×8 | ×8 |
| 40 | 24 | 48 | 64 |

| 3 | 8 | 7 | 4 |
|---|---|---|---|
| ×8 | ×2 | ×8 | ×8 |
| 24 | 16 | 56 | 32 |

| 8 | 8 | 2 | 5 |
|---|---|---|---|
| ×1 | ×7 | ×8 | ×8 |
| 8 | 56 | 16 | 40 |

$8 \times 9 = \underline{72}$   $2 \times 8 = \underline{16}$

$8 \times 3 = \underline{24}$   $8 \times 8 = \underline{64}$

$9 \times 8 = \underline{72}$   $0 \times 8 = \underline{0}$

$4 \times 8 = \underline{32}$   $8 \times 2 = \underline{16}$

$8 \times 1 = \underline{8}$   $8 \times 7 = \underline{56}$

$8 \times 4 = \underline{32}$   $1 \times 8 = \underline{8}$

$8 \times 6 = \underline{48}$   $6 \times 8 = \underline{48}$

$7 \times 8 = \underline{56}$   $5 \times 8 = \underline{40}$

Score: _____

Circle any problems that you still find difficult to remember. Make your own flash cards to help you master these problems.

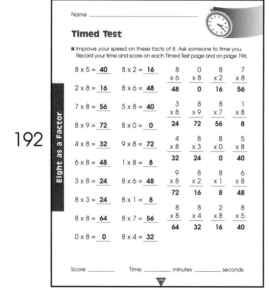

**192**

Name _____

## Timed Test

Eight as a Factor

■ Improve your speed on these facts of 8. Ask someone to time you. Record your time and score on each Timed Test page and on page 196.

$8 \times 5 = \underline{40}$   $8 \times 2 = \underline{16}$

| 8 | 0 | 8 | 7 |
|---|---|---|---|
| ×6 | ×8 | ×2 | ×8 |
| 48 | 0 | 16 | 56 |

$2 \times 8 = \underline{16}$   $8 \times 6 = \underline{48}$

$7 \times 8 = \underline{56}$   $5 \times 8 = \underline{40}$

| 3 | 8 | 8 | 1 |
|---|---|---|---|
| ×8 | ×9 | ×7 | ×8 |
| 24 | 72 | 56 | 8 |

$8 \times 9 = \underline{72}$   $8 \times 0 = \underline{0}$

$4 \times 8 = \underline{32}$   $9 \times 8 = \underline{72}$

| 4 | 8 | 8 | 5 |
|---|---|---|---|
| ×8 | ×3 | ×0 | ×8 |
| 32 | 24 | 0 | 40 |

$6 \times 8 = \underline{48}$   $1 \times 8 = \underline{8}$

| 9 | 8 | 8 | 6 |
|---|---|---|---|
| ×8 | ×2 | ×1 | ×8 |
| 72 | 16 | 8 | 48 |

$3 \times 8 = \underline{24}$   $8 \times 1 = \underline{8}$

| 8 | 8 | 2 | 8 |
|---|---|---|---|
| ×8 | ×4 | ×8 | ×5 |
| 64 | 32 | 16 | 40 |

$8 \times 8 = \underline{64}$   $8 \times 7 = \underline{56}$

$0 \times 8 = \underline{0}$   $8 \times 4 = \underline{32}$

Score: _____   Time: _____ minutes _____ seconds

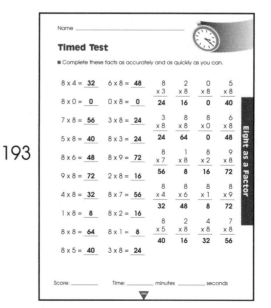

**193**

Name _____

## Timed Test

Eight as a Factor

■ Complete these facts as accurately and as quickly as you can.

$8 \times 4 = \underline{32}$   $6 \times 8 = \underline{48}$

| 8 | 2 | 0 | 5 |
|---|---|---|---|
| ×3 | ×8 | ×8 | ×8 |
| 24 | 16 | 0 | 40 |

$8 \times 0 = \underline{0}$   $0 \times 8 = \underline{0}$

$7 \times 8 = \underline{56}$   $3 \times 8 = \underline{24}$

| 3 | 8 | 8 | 6 |
|---|---|---|---|
| ×8 | ×9 | ×0 | ×8 |
| 24 | 64 | 0 | 48 |

$5 \times 8 = \underline{40}$   $8 \times 3 = \underline{24}$

$8 \times 6 = \underline{48}$   $8 \times 9 = \underline{72}$

| 8 | 1 | 8 | 9 |
|---|---|---|---|
| ×7 | ×8 | ×2 | ×8 |
| 56 | 8 | 16 | 72 |

$9 \times 8 = \underline{72}$   $2 \times 8 = \underline{16}$

$4 \times 8 = \underline{32}$   $8 \times 7 = \underline{56}$

| 8 | 8 | 8 | 8 |
|---|---|---|---|
| ×4 | ×6 | ×1 | ×9 |
| 32 | 48 | 8 | 72 |

$1 \times 8 = \underline{8}$   $8 \times 2 = \underline{16}$

$8 \times 8 = \underline{64}$   $8 \times 1 = \underline{8}$

| 8 | 2 | 4 | 7 |
|---|---|---|---|
| ×5 | ×8 | ×8 | ×8 |
| 40 | 16 | 32 | 56 |

$8 \times 5 = \underline{40}$   $3 \times 8 = \underline{24}$

Score: _____   Time: _____ minutes _____ seconds

## Page 194 — Timed Test (Eight as a Factor)

Name _____

**Timed Test**

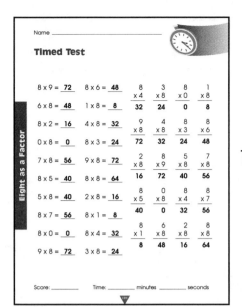

| | |
|---|---|
| 8 x 9 = **72** | 8 x 6 = **48** |
| 6 x 8 = **48** | 1 x 8 = **8** |
| 8 x 2 = **16** | 4 x 8 = **32** |
| 0 x 8 = **0** | 8 x 3 = **24** |
| 7 x 8 = **56** | 9 x 8 = **72** |
| 8 x 5 = **40** | 8 x 8 = **64** |
| 5 x 8 = **40** | 2 x 8 = **16** |
| 8 x 7 = **56** | 8 x 1 = **8** |
| 8 x 0 = **0** | 8 x 4 = **32** |
| 9 x 8 = **72** | 3 x 8 = **24** |

```
 8    3    8    1
x4   x8   x0   x8
32   24    0    8

 9    4    8    8
x8   x8   x3   x6
72   32   24   48

 2    8    5    7
x8   x9   x8   x8
16   72   40   56

 8    0    8    8
x5   x8   x4   x7
40    0   32   56

 8    6    2    8
x1   x8   x8   x8
 8   48   16   64
```

Score: _____  Time: _____ minutes _____ seconds

194

## Page 195 — Timed Test (Eight as a Factor)

Name _____

**Timed Test**

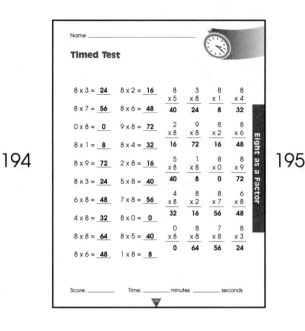

| | |
|---|---|
| 8 x 3 = **24** | 8 x 2 = **16** |
| 8 x 7 = **56** | 8 x 6 = **48** |
| 0 x 8 = **0** | 9 x 8 = **72** |
| 8 x 1 = **8** | 8 x 4 = **32** |
| 8 x 9 = **72** | 2 x 8 = **16** |
| 8 x 3 = **24** | 5 x 8 = **40** |
| 6 x 8 = **48** | 7 x 8 = **56** |
| 4 x 8 = **32** | 8 x 0 = **0** |
| 8 x 8 = **64** | 8 x 5 = **40** |
| 8 x 6 = **48** | 1 x 8 = **8** |

```
 8    3    8    8
x5   x8   x1   x4
40   24    8   32

 2    9    8    8
x8   x8   x2   x6
16   72   16   48

 5    1    8    8
x8   x8   x0   x9
40    8    0   72

 4    8    8    6
x8   x2   x7   x8
32   16   56   48

 0    8    7    8
x8   x8   x8   x3
 0   64   56   24
```

Score: _____  Time: _____ minutes _____ seconds

195

## Page 196 — Timed Test (Eight as a Factor)

Name _____

**Timed Test**

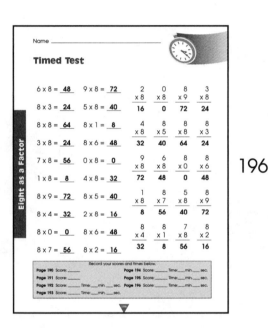

| | |
|---|---|
| 6 x 8 = **48** | 9 x 8 = **72** |
| 8 x 3 = **24** | 5 x 8 = **40** |
| 8 x 8 = **64** | 8 x 1 = **8** |
| 3 x 8 = **24** | 8 x 6 = **48** |
| 7 x 8 = **56** | 0 x 8 = **0** |
| 1 x 8 = **8** | 4 x 8 = **32** |
| 8 x 9 = **72** | 8 x 5 = **40** |
| 8 x 4 = **32** | 2 x 8 = **16** |
| 8 x 0 = **0** | 8 x 6 = **48** |
| 8 x 7 = **56** | 8 x 2 = **16** |

```
 2    0    8    3
x8   x8   x9   x8
16    0   72   24

 4    8    8    8
x8   x5   x8   x3
32   40   64   24

 9    6    8    8
x8   x8   x0   x6
72   48    0   48

 1    8    5    8
x8   x7   x8   x9
 8   56   40   72

 8    8    7    8
x4   x1   x8   x2
32    8   56   16
```

Record your scores and times below.

| | |
|---|---|
| Page 190 Score: _____ | Page 194 Score: _____ Time:___min.___ sec. |
| Page 191 Score: _____ | Page 195 Score: _____ Time:___min.___ sec. |
| Page 192 Score: _____ Time:___min.___ sec. | Page 196 Score: _____ Time:___min.___ sec. |
| Page 193 Score: _____ Time:___min.___ sec. | |

196

## Page 197 — Products Through Eighty-One (Nine as a Factor)

Name _____

### Products Through Eighty-One

The first ten multiples of 9 are 0, 9, 18, 27, 36, 45, 54, 63, 72, and 81. They are the same as the products of 9 times any number from 0 through 9.

**Example:** 9 x 4 = ?

9 groups of 4 each

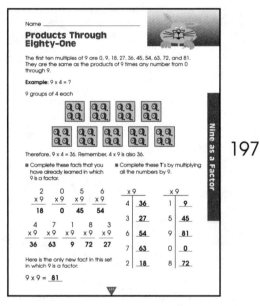

Therefore, 9 x 4 = 36. Remember, 4 x 9 is also 36.

■ Complete these facts that you have already learned in which 9 is a factor.

■ Complete these T's by multiplying all the numbers by 9.

```
 2    0    5    6
x9   x9   x9   x9
18    0   45   54

 4    7    1    8    3
x9   x9   x9   x9   x9
36   63    9   72   27
```

| x9 | | x9 | |
|---|---|---|---|
| 4 | **36** | 1 | **9** |
| 3 | **27** | 5 | **45** |
| 6 | **54** | 9 | **81** |
| 7 | **63** | 0 | **0** |
| 2 | **18** | 8 | **72** |

Here is the only new fact in this set in which 9 is a factor:

9 x 9 = **81**

197

## Page 198 — Practice (Nine as a Factor)

Name _____

**Practice**

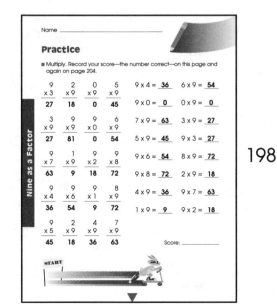

■ Multiply. Record your score—the number correct—on this page and again on page 204.

```
 9    2    0    5
x3   x9   x9   x9
27   18    0   45

 3    9    9    6
x9   x9   x0   x9
27   81    0   54

 9    1    9    9
x7   x9   x2   x8
63    9   18   72

 9    9    9    8
x4   x6   x1   x9
36   54    9   72

 9    2    4    7
x5   x9   x9   x9
45   18   36   63
```

| | |
|---|---|
| 9 x 4 = **36** | 6 x 9 = **54** |
| 9 x 0 = **0** | 0 x 9 = **0** |
| 7 x 9 = **63** | 3 x 9 = **27** |
| 5 x 9 = **45** | 9 x 3 = **27** |
| 9 x 6 = **54** | 8 x 9 = **72** |
| 9 x 8 = **72** | 2 x 9 = **18** |
| 4 x 9 = **36** | 9 x 7 = **63** |
| 1 x 9 = **9** | 9 x 2 = **18** |

Score: _____

START   FINISH

198

## Page 199 — Practice (Nine as a Factor)

Name _____

**Practice**

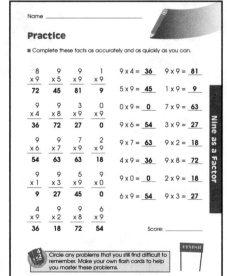

■ Complete these facts as accurately and as quickly as you can.

```
 8    9    9    1
x9   x5   x9   x9
72   45   81    9

 9    9    3    0
x4   x8   x9   x9
36   72   27    0

 9    9    7    2
x6   x7   x9   x9
54   63   63   18

 9    9    5    9
x1   x3   x9   x0
 9   27   45    0

 4    9    9    6
x9   x2   x8   x9
36   18   72   54
```

| | |
|---|---|
| 9 x 4 = **36** | 9 x 9 = **81** |
| 5 x 9 = **45** | 1 x 9 = **9** |
| 0 x 9 = **0** | 7 x 9 = **63** |
| 9 x 6 = **54** | 3 x 9 = **27** |
| 9 x 7 = **63** | 9 x 2 = **18** |
| 4 x 9 = **36** | 9 x 8 = **72** |
| 9 x 0 = **0** | 2 x 9 = **18** |
| 6 x 9 = **54** | 9 x 3 = **27** |

Score: _____

Circle any problems that you still find difficult to remember. Make your own flash cards to help you master these problems.

199

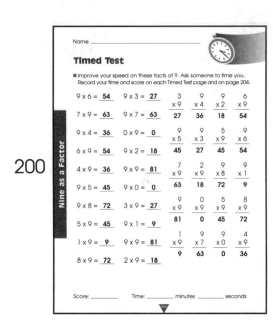

**200** — Nine as a Factor

### Timed Test

■ Improve your speed on these facts of 9. Ask someone to time you. Record your time and score on each Timed Test page and on page 204.

Name _____

$9 \times 6 = \underline{54}$   $9 \times 3 = \underline{27}$

$7 \times 9 = \underline{63}$   $9 \times 7 = \underline{63}$

$9 \times 4 = \underline{36}$   $0 \times 9 = \underline{0}$

$6 \times 9 = \underline{54}$   $9 \times 2 = \underline{18}$

$4 \times 9 = \underline{36}$   $9 \times 9 = \underline{81}$

$9 \times 5 = \underline{45}$   $9 \times 0 = \underline{0}$

$9 \times 8 = \underline{72}$   $3 \times 9 = \underline{27}$

$5 \times 9 = \underline{45}$   $9 \times 1 = \underline{9}$

$1 \times 9 = \underline{9}$   $9 \times 9 = \underline{81}$

$8 \times 9 = \underline{72}$   $2 \times 9 = \underline{18}$

| $\begin{array}{r}3\\ \times 9\end{array}$ | $\begin{array}{r}9\\ \times 4\end{array}$ | $\begin{array}{r}9\\ \times 2\end{array}$ | $\begin{array}{r}6\\ \times 9\end{array}$ |
|---|---|---|---|
| **27** | **36** | **18** | **54** |
| $\begin{array}{r}9\\ \times 5\end{array}$ | $\begin{array}{r}9\\ \times 3\end{array}$ | $\begin{array}{r}5\\ \times 9\end{array}$ | $\begin{array}{r}9\\ \times 6\end{array}$ |
| **45** | **27** | **45** | **54** |
| $\begin{array}{r}7\\ \times 9\end{array}$ | $\begin{array}{r}2\\ \times 9\end{array}$ | $\begin{array}{r}9\\ \times 8\end{array}$ | $\begin{array}{r}9\\ \times 1\end{array}$ |
| **63** | **18** | **72** | **9** |
| $\begin{array}{r}9\\ \times 9\end{array}$ | $\begin{array}{r}0\\ \times 9\end{array}$ | $\begin{array}{r}5\\ \times 9\end{array}$ | $\begin{array}{r}8\\ \times 9\end{array}$ |
| **81** | **0** | **45** | **72** |
| $\begin{array}{r}1\\ \times 9\end{array}$ | $\begin{array}{r}9\\ \times 7\end{array}$ | $\begin{array}{r}9\\ \times 0\end{array}$ | $\begin{array}{r}4\\ \times 9\end{array}$ |
| **9** | **63** | **0** | **36** |

Score: _____   Time: _____ minutes _____ seconds

---

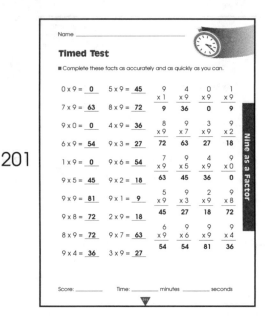

**201** — Nine as a Factor

### Timed Test

■ Complete these facts as accurately and as quickly as you can.

Name _____

$0 \times 9 = \underline{0}$   $5 \times 9 = \underline{45}$

$7 \times 9 = \underline{63}$   $8 \times 9 = \underline{72}$

$9 \times 0 = \underline{0}$   $4 \times 9 = \underline{36}$

$6 \times 9 = \underline{54}$   $9 \times 3 = \underline{27}$

$1 \times 9 = \underline{0}$   $9 \times 6 = \underline{54}$

$9 \times 5 = \underline{45}$   $9 \times 2 = \underline{18}$

$9 \times 9 = \underline{81}$   $9 \times 1 = \underline{9}$

$9 \times 8 = \underline{72}$   $2 \times 9 = \underline{18}$

$8 \times 9 = \underline{72}$   $9 \times 7 = \underline{63}$

$9 \times 4 = \underline{36}$   $3 \times 9 = \underline{27}$

| $\begin{array}{r}9\\ \times 1\end{array}$ | $\begin{array}{r}4\\ \times 9\end{array}$ | $\begin{array}{r}0\\ \times 9\end{array}$ | $\begin{array}{r}1\\ \times 9\end{array}$ |
|---|---|---|---|
| **9** | **36** | **0** | **9** |
| $\begin{array}{r}8\\ \times 9\end{array}$ | $\begin{array}{r}9\\ \times 7\end{array}$ | $\begin{array}{r}3\\ \times 9\end{array}$ | $\begin{array}{r}9\\ \times 2\end{array}$ |
| **72** | **63** | **27** | **18** |
| $\begin{array}{r}7\\ \times 9\end{array}$ | $\begin{array}{r}9\\ \times 5\end{array}$ | $\begin{array}{r}4\\ \times 9\end{array}$ | $\begin{array}{r}9\\ \times 0\end{array}$ |
| **63** | **45** | **36** | **0** |
| $\begin{array}{r}5\\ \times 9\end{array}$ | $\begin{array}{r}9\\ \times 3\end{array}$ | $\begin{array}{r}2\\ \times 9\end{array}$ | $\begin{array}{r}9\\ \times 8\end{array}$ |
| **45** | **27** | **18** | **72** |
| $\begin{array}{r}6\\ \times 9\end{array}$ | $\begin{array}{r}9\\ \times 6\end{array}$ | $\begin{array}{r}9\\ \times 9\end{array}$ | $\begin{array}{r}9\\ \times 4\end{array}$ |
| **54** | **54** | **81** | **36** |

Score: _____   Time: _____ minutes _____ seconds

---

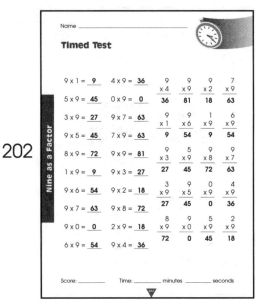

**202** — Nine as a Factor

### Timed Test

Name _____

$9 \times 1 = \underline{9}$   $4 \times 9 = \underline{36}$

$5 \times 9 = \underline{45}$   $0 \times 9 = \underline{0}$

$3 \times 9 = \underline{27}$   $9 \times 7 = \underline{63}$

$9 \times 5 = \underline{45}$   $7 \times 9 = \underline{63}$

$8 \times 9 = \underline{72}$   $9 \times 9 = \underline{81}$

$1 \times 9 = \underline{9}$   $9 \times 3 = \underline{27}$

$9 \times 6 = \underline{54}$   $9 \times 2 = \underline{18}$

$9 \times 7 = \underline{63}$   $9 \times 8 = \underline{72}$

$9 \times 0 = \underline{0}$   $2 \times 9 = \underline{18}$

$6 \times 9 = \underline{54}$   $9 \times 4 = \underline{36}$

| $\begin{array}{r}9\\ \times 4\end{array}$ | $\begin{array}{r}9\\ \times 9\end{array}$ | $\begin{array}{r}9\\ \times 2\end{array}$ | $\begin{array}{r}7\\ \times 9\end{array}$ |
|---|---|---|---|
| **36** | **81** | **18** | **63** |
| $\begin{array}{r}9\\ \times 1\end{array}$ | $\begin{array}{r}9\\ \times 6\end{array}$ | $\begin{array}{r}1\\ \times 9\end{array}$ | $\begin{array}{r}6\\ \times 9\end{array}$ |
| **9** | **54** | **9** | **54** |
| $\begin{array}{r}9\\ \times 3\end{array}$ | $\begin{array}{r}9\\ \times 9\end{array}$ | $\begin{array}{r}9\\ \times 8\end{array}$ | $\begin{array}{r}9\\ \times 7\end{array}$ |
| **27** | **45** | **72** | **63** |
| $\begin{array}{r}3\\ \times 9\end{array}$ | $\begin{array}{r}9\\ \times 5\end{array}$ | $\begin{array}{r}9\\ \times 9\end{array}$ | $\begin{array}{r}4\\ \times 9\end{array}$ |
| **27** | **45** | **0** | **36** |
| $\begin{array}{r}8\\ \times 9\end{array}$ | $\begin{array}{r}9\\ \times 0\end{array}$ | $\begin{array}{r}5\\ \times 9\end{array}$ | $\begin{array}{r}2\\ \times 9\end{array}$ |
| **72** | **0** | **45** | **18** |

Score: _____   Time: _____ minutes _____ seconds

---

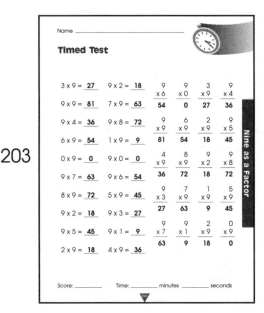

**203** — Nine as a Factor

### Timed Test

Name _____

$3 \times 9 = \underline{27}$   $9 \times 2 = \underline{18}$

$9 \times 9 = \underline{81}$   $7 \times 9 = \underline{63}$

$9 \times 4 = \underline{36}$   $9 \times 8 = \underline{72}$

$6 \times 9 = \underline{54}$   $1 \times 9 = \underline{9}$

$0 \times 9 = \underline{0}$   $9 \times 0 = \underline{0}$

$9 \times 7 = \underline{63}$   $9 \times 6 = \underline{54}$

$8 \times 9 = \underline{72}$   $5 \times 9 = \underline{45}$

$9 \times 2 = \underline{18}$   $9 \times 3 = \underline{27}$

$9 \times 5 = \underline{45}$   $9 \times 1 = \underline{9}$

$2 \times 9 = \underline{18}$   $4 \times 9 = \underline{36}$

| $\begin{array}{r}9\\ \times 6\end{array}$ | $\begin{array}{r}9\\ \times 0\end{array}$ | $\begin{array}{r}3\\ \times 9\end{array}$ | $\begin{array}{r}9\\ \times 4\end{array}$ |
|---|---|---|---|
| **54** | **0** | **27** | **36** |
| $\begin{array}{r}9\\ \times 9\end{array}$ | $\begin{array}{r}6\\ \times 9\end{array}$ | $\begin{array}{r}2\\ \times 9\end{array}$ | $\begin{array}{r}9\\ \times 5\end{array}$ |
| **81** | **54** | **18** | **45** |
| $\begin{array}{r}4\\ \times 9\end{array}$ | $\begin{array}{r}8\\ \times 9\end{array}$ | $\begin{array}{r}9\\ \times 2\end{array}$ | $\begin{array}{r}9\\ \times 8\end{array}$ |
| **36** | **72** | **18** | **72** |
| $\begin{array}{r}9\\ \times 3\end{array}$ | $\begin{array}{r}9\\ \times 9\end{array}$ | $\begin{array}{r}1\\ \times 9\end{array}$ | $\begin{array}{r}5\\ \times 9\end{array}$ |
| **27** | **63** | **9** | **45** |
| $\begin{array}{r}9\\ \times 7\end{array}$ | $\begin{array}{r}9\\ \times 1\end{array}$ | $\begin{array}{r}9\\ \times 9\end{array}$ | $\begin{array}{r}0\\ \times 9\end{array}$ |
| **63** | **9** | **18** | **0** |

Score: _____   Time: _____ minutes _____ seconds

---

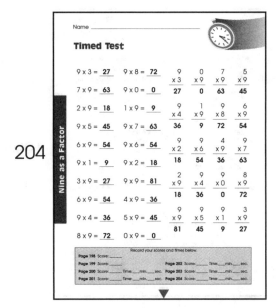

**204** — Nine as a Factor

### Timed Test

Name _____

$9 \times 3 = \underline{27}$   $9 \times 8 = \underline{72}$

$7 \times 9 = \underline{63}$   $9 \times 0 = \underline{0}$

$2 \times 9 = \underline{18}$   $1 \times 9 = \underline{9}$

$9 \times 5 = \underline{45}$   $9 \times 7 = \underline{63}$

$6 \times 9 = \underline{54}$   $9 \times 6 = \underline{54}$

$9 \times 1 = \underline{9}$   $9 \times 2 = \underline{18}$

$3 \times 9 = \underline{27}$   $9 \times 9 = \underline{81}$

$6 \times 9 = \underline{54}$   $4 \times 9 = \underline{36}$

$9 \times 4 = \underline{36}$   $5 \times 9 = \underline{45}$

$8 \times 9 = \underline{72}$   $0 \times 9 = \underline{0}$

| $\begin{array}{r}9\\ \times 3\end{array}$ | $\begin{array}{r}0\\ \times 9\end{array}$ | $\begin{array}{r}7\\ \times 9\end{array}$ | $\begin{array}{r}5\\ \times 9\end{array}$ |
|---|---|---|---|
| **27** | **0** | **63** | **45** |
| $\begin{array}{r}9\\ \times 4\end{array}$ | $\begin{array}{r}9\\ \times 9\end{array}$ | $\begin{array}{r}9\\ \times 8\end{array}$ | $\begin{array}{r}6\\ \times 9\end{array}$ |
| **36** | **9** | **72** | **54** |
| $\begin{array}{r}9\\ \times 2\end{array}$ | $\begin{array}{r}9\\ \times 6\end{array}$ | $\begin{array}{r}4\\ \times 9\end{array}$ | $\begin{array}{r}9\\ \times 7\end{array}$ |
| **18** | **54** | **36** | **63** |
| $\begin{array}{r}2\\ \times 9\end{array}$ | $\begin{array}{r}9\\ \times 4\end{array}$ | $\begin{array}{r}9\\ \times 0\end{array}$ | $\begin{array}{r}8\\ \times 9\end{array}$ |
| **18** | **36** | **0** | **72** |
| $\begin{array}{r}9\\ \times 9\end{array}$ | $\begin{array}{r}9\\ \times 5\end{array}$ | $\begin{array}{r}9\\ \times 1\end{array}$ | $\begin{array}{r}9\\ \times 9\end{array}$ |
| **81** | **45** | **9** | **27** |

Record your scores and times below.

Page 198 Score: _____
Page 199 Score: _____
Page 200 Score: _____ Time: _____ min. _____ sec.   Page 202 Score: _____ Time: _____ min. _____ sec.
Page 201 Score: _____ Time: _____ min. _____ sec.   Page 204 Score: _____ Time: _____ min. _____ sec.

---

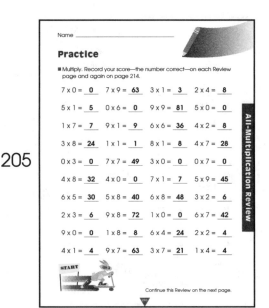

**205** — All-Multiplication Review

### Practice

■ Multiply. Record your score—the number correct—on each Review page and again on page 214.

Name _____

$7 \times 0 = \underline{0}$   $7 \times 9 = \underline{63}$   $3 \times 1 = \underline{3}$   $2 \times 4 = \underline{8}$

$5 \times 1 = \underline{5}$   $0 \times 6 = \underline{0}$   $9 \times 9 = \underline{81}$   $5 \times 0 = \underline{0}$

$1 \times 7 = \underline{7}$   $9 \times 1 = \underline{9}$   $6 \times 6 = \underline{36}$   $4 \times 2 = \underline{8}$

$3 \times 8 = \underline{24}$   $1 \times 1 = \underline{1}$   $8 \times 1 = \underline{8}$   $4 \times 7 = \underline{28}$

$0 \times 3 = \underline{0}$   $7 \times 7 = \underline{49}$   $3 \times 0 = \underline{0}$   $0 \times 7 = \underline{0}$

$4 \times 8 = \underline{32}$   $4 \times 0 = \underline{0}$   $7 \times 1 = \underline{7}$   $5 \times 9 = \underline{45}$

$6 \times 5 = \underline{30}$   $5 \times 8 = \underline{40}$   $6 \times 8 = \underline{48}$   $3 \times 2 = \underline{6}$

$2 \times 3 = \underline{6}$   $9 \times 8 = \underline{72}$   $1 \times 0 = \underline{0}$   $6 \times 7 = \underline{42}$

$9 \times 0 = \underline{0}$   $1 \times 8 = \underline{8}$   $6 \times 4 = \underline{24}$   $2 \times 2 = \underline{4}$

$4 \times 1 = \underline{4}$   $9 \times 7 = \underline{63}$   $3 \times 7 = \underline{21}$   $1 \times 4 = \underline{4}$

START

Continue this Review on the next page.

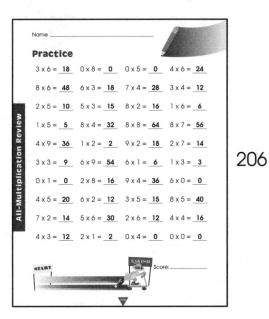

## Practice

$3 \times 6 = \underline{18}$   $0 \times 8 = \underline{0}$   $0 \times 5 = \underline{0}$   $4 \times 6 = \underline{24}$

$8 \times 6 = \underline{48}$   $6 \times 3 = \underline{18}$   $7 \times 4 = \underline{28}$   $3 \times 4 = \underline{12}$

$2 \times 5 = \underline{10}$   $5 \times 3 = \underline{15}$   $8 \times 2 = \underline{16}$   $1 \times 6 = \underline{6}$

$1 \times 5 = \underline{5}$   $8 \times 4 = \underline{32}$   $8 \times 8 = \underline{64}$   $8 \times 7 = \underline{56}$

$4 \times 9 = \underline{36}$   $1 \times 2 = \underline{2}$   $9 \times 2 = \underline{18}$   $2 \times 7 = \underline{14}$

$3 \times 3 = \underline{9}$   $6 \times 9 = \underline{54}$   $6 \times 1 = \underline{6}$   $1 \times 3 = \underline{3}$

$0 \times 1 = \underline{0}$   $2 \times 8 = \underline{16}$   $9 \times 4 = \underline{36}$   $6 \times 0 = \underline{0}$

$4 \times 5 = \underline{20}$   $6 \times 2 = \underline{12}$   $3 \times 5 = \underline{15}$   $8 \times 5 = \underline{40}$

$7 \times 2 = \underline{14}$   $5 \times 6 = \underline{30}$   $2 \times 6 = \underline{12}$   $4 \times 4 = \underline{16}$

$4 \times 3 = \underline{12}$   $2 \times 1 = \underline{2}$   $0 \times 4 = \underline{0}$   $0 \times 0 = \underline{0}$

Score:

**All-Multiplication Review**

**206**

---

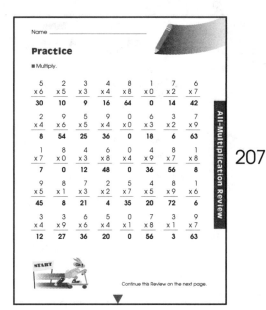

## Practice

■ Multiply.

| 5 ×6 | 2 ×5 | 3 ×3 | 4 ×4 | 8 ×8 | 1 ×0 | 7 ×2 | 6 ×7 |
|---|---|---|---|---|---|---|---|
| **30** | **10** | **9** | **16** | **64** | **0** | **14** | **42** |

| 2 ×4 | 9 ×6 | 5 ×5 | 9 ×4 | 0 ×0 | 6 ×3 | 3 ×2 | 7 ×9 |
|---|---|---|---|---|---|---|---|
| **8** | **54** | **25** | **36** | **0** | **18** | **6** | **63** |

| 1 ×7 | 8 ×0 | 4 ×3 | 6 ×8 | 0 ×4 | 4 ×9 | 8 ×7 | 1 ×8 |
|---|---|---|---|---|---|---|---|
| **7** | **0** | **12** | **48** | **0** | **36** | **56** | **8** |

| 9 ×5 | 8 ×1 | 7 ×3 | 2 ×2 | 5 ×7 | 4 ×5 | 8 ×9 | 1 ×6 |
|---|---|---|---|---|---|---|---|
| **45** | **8** | **21** | **4** | **35** | **20** | **72** | **6** |

| 3 ×4 | 9 ×9 | 6 ×6 | 5 ×4 | 0 ×1 | 7 ×8 | 1 ×1 | 9 ×7 |
|---|---|---|---|---|---|---|---|
| **12** | **27** | **36** | **20** | **0** | **56** | **3** | **63** |

Continue this Review on the next page.

**All-Multiplication Review**

**207**

---

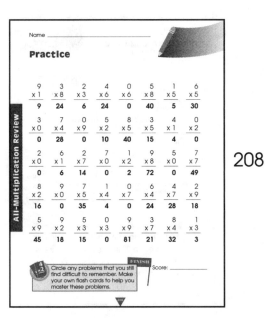

## Practice

| 9 ×1 | 3 ×8 | 2 ×3 | 4 ×6 | 0 ×6 | 5 ×8 | 1 ×5 | 6 ×5 |
|---|---|---|---|---|---|---|---|
| **9** | **24** | **6** | **24** | **0** | **40** | **5** | **30** |

| 3 ×0 | 7 ×4 | 0 ×9 | 5 ×2 | 8 ×5 | 3 ×5 | 4 ×1 | 0 ×2 |
|---|---|---|---|---|---|---|---|
| **0** | **28** | **0** | **10** | **40** | **15** | **4** | **0** |

| 2 ×0 | 6 ×1 | 2 ×7 | 7 ×0 | 1 ×2 | 9 ×8 | 5 ×0 | 7 ×7 |
|---|---|---|---|---|---|---|---|
| **0** | **6** | **14** | **0** | **2** | **72** | **0** | **49** |

| 8 ×2 | 9 ×0 | 7 ×5 | 1 ×4 | 0 ×7 | 6 ×4 | 4 ×7 | 2 ×9 |
|---|---|---|---|---|---|---|---|
| **16** | **0** | **35** | **4** | **0** | **24** | **28** | **18** |

| 5 ×9 | 9 ×2 | 5 ×3 | 0 ×3 | 9 ×9 | 3 ×7 | 8 ×4 | 1 ×3 |
|---|---|---|---|---|---|---|---|
| **45** | **18** | **15** | **0** | **81** | **21** | **32** | **3** |

Circle any problems that you still find difficult to remember. Make your own flash cards to help you master these problems.   Score:

**All-Multiplication Review**

**208**

---

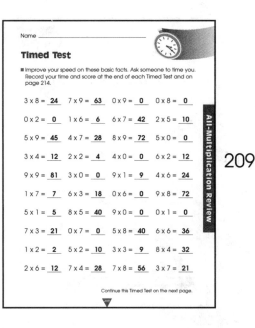

## Timed Test

■ Improve your speed on these basic facts. Ask someone to time you. Record your time and score at the end of each Timed Test and on page 214.

$3 \times 8 = \underline{24}$   $7 \times 9 = \underline{63}$   $0 \times 9 = \underline{0}$   $0 \times 8 = \underline{0}$

$0 \times 2 = \underline{0}$   $1 \times 6 = \underline{6}$   $6 \times 7 = \underline{42}$   $2 \times 5 = \underline{10}$

$5 \times 9 = \underline{45}$   $4 \times 7 = \underline{28}$   $8 \times 9 = \underline{72}$   $5 \times 0 = \underline{0}$

$3 \times 4 = \underline{12}$   $2 \times 2 = \underline{4}$   $4 \times 0 = \underline{0}$   $6 \times 2 = \underline{12}$

$9 \times 9 = \underline{81}$   $3 \times 0 = \underline{0}$   $9 \times 1 = \underline{9}$   $4 \times 6 = \underline{24}$

$1 \times 7 = \underline{7}$   $6 \times 3 = \underline{18}$   $0 \times 6 = \underline{0}$   $9 \times 8 = \underline{72}$

$5 \times 1 = \underline{5}$   $8 \times 5 = \underline{40}$   $9 \times 0 = \underline{0}$   $0 \times 1 = \underline{0}$

$7 \times 3 = \underline{21}$   $0 \times 7 = \underline{0}$   $5 \times 8 = \underline{40}$   $6 \times 6 = \underline{36}$

$1 \times 2 = \underline{2}$   $5 \times 2 = \underline{10}$   $3 \times 3 = \underline{9}$   $8 \times 4 = \underline{32}$

$2 \times 6 = \underline{12}$   $7 \times 4 = \underline{28}$   $7 \times 8 = \underline{56}$   $3 \times 7 = \underline{21}$

Continue this Timed Test on the next page.

**All-Multiplication Review**

**209**

---

## Timed Test

$7 \times 6 = \underline{42}$   $1 \times 0 = \underline{0}$   $0 \times 5 = \underline{0}$   $9 \times 6 = \underline{54}$

$6 \times 5 = \underline{30}$   $8 \times 3 = \underline{24}$   $7 \times 1 = \underline{7}$   $7 \times 5 = \underline{35}$

$5 \times 7 = \underline{35}$   $6 \times 9 = \underline{54}$   $2 \times 8 = \underline{16}$   $6 \times 0 = \underline{0}$

$4 \times 4 = \underline{16}$   $0 \times 0 = \underline{0}$   $1 \times 4 = \underline{4}$   $4 \times 5 = \underline{20}$

$3 \times 2 = \underline{6}$   $5 \times 4 = \underline{20}$   $4 \times 9 = \underline{36}$   $1 \times 1 = \underline{1}$

$8 \times 7 = \underline{56}$   $3 \times 6 = \underline{18}$   $1 \times 8 = \underline{8}$   $2 \times 7 = \underline{14}$

$9 \times 7 = \underline{63}$   $8 \times 2 = \underline{16}$   $2 \times 3 = \underline{6}$   $4 \times 8 = \underline{32}$

$7 \times 7 = \underline{49}$   $1 \times 9 = \underline{9}$   $6 \times 4 = \underline{24}$   $5 \times 6 = \underline{30}$

$6 \times 1 = \underline{6}$   $9 \times 3 = \underline{27}$   $0 \times 4 = \underline{0}$   $8 \times 0 = \underline{0}$

$2 \times 4 = \underline{8}$   $4 \times 2 = \underline{8}$   $3 \times 9 = \underline{27}$   $3 \times 5 = \underline{15}$

Score: _____   Time: _____ minutes _____ seconds

**All-Multiplication Review**

**210**

---

## Timed Test

■ Complete these facts as accurately and as quickly as you can.

$5 \times 4 = \underline{20}$   $2 \times 1 = \underline{2}$   $0 \times 1 = \underline{0}$   $5 \times 5 = \underline{25}$

$1 \times 0 = \underline{0}$   $0 \times 4 = \underline{0}$   $7 \times 3 = \underline{21}$   $4 \times 1 = \underline{4}$

$9 \times 6 = \underline{54}$   $6 \times 3 = \underline{18}$   $8 \times 0 = \underline{0}$   $9 \times 2 = \underline{18}$

$4 \times 4 = \underline{16}$   $9 \times 8 = \underline{72}$   $9 \times 1 = \underline{9}$   $5 \times 3 = \underline{15}$

$9 \times 3 = \underline{27}$   $4 \times 2 = \underline{8}$   $9 \times 7 = \underline{63}$   $4 \times 5 = \underline{20}$

$3 \times 4 = \underline{12}$   $8 \times 3 = \underline{24}$   $2 \times 8 = \underline{16}$   $6 \times 4 = \underline{24}$

$0 \times 9 = \underline{0}$   $2 \times 7 = \underline{14}$   $8 \times 1 = \underline{8}$   $2 \times 0 = \underline{0}$

$3 \times 3 = \underline{9}$   $7 \times 4 = \underline{28}$   $3 \times 5 = \underline{15}$   $3 \times 2 = \underline{6}$

$9 \times 9 = \underline{81}$   $8 \times 4 = \underline{32}$   $1 \times 1 = \underline{1}$   $6 \times 0 = \underline{0}$

$1 \times 3 = \underline{3}$   $6 \times 2 = \underline{12}$   $7 \times 9 = \underline{63}$   $0 \times 2 = \underline{0}$

Continue this Timed Test on the next page.

**All-Multiplication Review**

**211**

**Timed Test Answer Key**

## 212

### Timed Test

All-Multiplication Review

6 x 9 = **54**    6 x 6 = **36**    2 x 4 = **8**    8 x 6 = **48**

4 x 0 = **0**    4 x 6 = **24**    7 x 1 = **7**    5 x 7 = **35**

5 x 6 = **30**    0 x 3 = **0**    1 x 9 = **9**    2 x 9 = **18**

4 x 9 = **36**    5 x 9 = **45**    8 x 9 = **72**    7 x 7 = **49**

1 x 4 = **4**    2 x 6 = **12**    9 x 5 = **45**    4 x 8 = **32**

3 x 1 = **3**    8 x 5 = **40**    8 x 7 = **56**    1 x 7 = **7**

2 x 2 = **4**    5 x 2 = **10**    1 x 5 = **5**    6 x 8 = **48**

7 x 6 = **42**    1 x 8 = **8**    7 x 8 = **56**    3 x 9 = **27**

0 x 7 = **0**    3 x 7 = **21**    3 x 0 = **0**    2 x 3 = **6**

3 x 6 = **18**    5 x 0 = **0**    0 x 8 = **0**    9 x 0 = **0**

Score: _____    Time: _____ minutes _____ seconds

## 213

### Timed Test

All-Multiplication Review

0 x 0 = **0**    5 x 7 = **35**    8 x 8 = **64**    0 x 5 = **0**

1 x 7 = **7**    0 x 9 = **0**    0 x 4 = **0**    5 x 8 = **40**

4 x 5 = **20**    6 x 1 = **6**    3 x 3 = **9**    2 x 6 = **12**

2 x 9 = **18**    8 x 0 = **0**    4 x 9 = **36**    8 x 5 = **40**

3 x 7 = **21**    2 x 5 = **10**    0 x 7 = **0**    1 x 8 = **8**

8 x 4 = **32**    7 x 6 = **42**    2 x 2 = **4**    7 x 9 = **63**

2 x 1 = **2**    9 x 2 = **18**    1 x 0 = **0**    9 x 8 = **72**

7 x 0 = **0**    1 x 3 = **0**    4 x 6 = **24**    5 x 4 = **20**

5 x 3 = **15**    6 x 5 = **30**    8 x 1 = **8**    6 x 9 = **54**

9 x 9 = **81**    4 x 1 = **1**    6 x 2 = **12**    0 x 1 = **0**

Continue this Timed Test on the next page.

## 214

### Timed Test

All-Multiplication Review

4 x 7 = **28**    1 x 1 = **1**    5 x 1 = **5**    5 x 2 = **10**

5 x 9 = **45**    9 x 7 = **63**    1 x 9 = **9**    2 x 0 = **0**

2 x 3 = **6**    7 x 1 = **7**    8 x 6 = **48**    3 x 6 = **18**

0 x 2 = **0**    6 x 7 = **42**    2 x 7 = **14**    0 x 8 = **0**

6 x 3 = **18**    5 x 5 = **25**    9 x 0 = **0**    7 x 7 = **49**

3 x 5 = **15**    1 x 5 = **5**    6 x 0 = **0**    6 x 4 = **24**

7 x 8 = **56**    8 x 2 = **16**    2 x 8 = **16**    9 x 6 = **54**

3 x 1 = **3**    4 x 3 = **12**    4 x 0 = **0**    3 x 2 = **6**

7 x 4 = **28**    9 x 4 = **36**    8 x 7 = **56**    9 x 5 = **45**

3 x 9 = **27**    0 x 6 = **0**    1 x 2 = **2**    4 x 4 = **16**

Record your scores and times below.

| Page 205–206 | Score:____ | Page 211–212 | Score:____ Time:___min.___sec. |
| Page 207–208 | Score:____ | Page 213–214 | Score:____ Time:___min.___sec. |
| Page 209–210 | Score:____ Time:___min.___sec. | | |

## 215

### Products Through One Hundred Twenty

Ten as a Factor

Now you will learn about some higher facts.

The first thirteen multiples of 10 are 0, 10, 20, 30, 40, 50, 60, 70, 80, 90, 100, 110, and 120. They are the same as the products of 10 times any number from 0 through 12.

Here are some things to remember about the basic facts in which 10 is one of the factors:

● The product of 10 and another counting number always ends in 0. Here's a shortcut to find a product of 10 and another number: Simply annex (attach) a zero at the end of the other factor.

**Examples:** 10 x 6 = 60, 10 x 3 = 30, and 10 x 10 = 100

● Changing the order of the factors does not change the product. So, 10 x 7 is the same as 7 x 10.

● As you have learned with other facts, 10 x 0 is 0 and 10 x 1 is 10.

■ Complete these T's by multiplying each of the numbers by 10.

| x 10 | |
|---|---|
| 6 | **60** |
| 2 | **20** |
| 12 | **120** |
| 4 | **40** |
| 7 | **70** |
| 9 | **90** |
| 1 | **10** |

| x 10 | |
|---|---|
| 5 | **50** |
| 3 | **30** |
| 11 | **110** |
| 0 | **0** |
| 8 | **80** |
| 10 | **100** |

■ Now, complete these facts.

10 x 5 = **50**    10 x 9 = **90**

4 x 10 = **40**    10 x 3 = **30**

10 x 12 = **120**    10 x 7 = **70**

10 x 11 = **110**    2 x 10 = **20**

10 x 10 = **100**    10 x 8 = **80**

6 x 10 = **60**    7 x 10 = **70**

10 x 0 = **0**    10 x 2 = **20**

11 x 10 = **110**    1 x 10 = **10**

## 216

### Practice

Ten as a Factor

■ Multiply. Record your score—the number correct—on each Practice page and again on page 220.

| 10<br>x 2 | 11<br>x 10 | 10<br>x 10 | 10<br>x 8 |
|---|---|---|---|
| **20** | **110** | **100** | **80** |

10 x 5 = **50**    10 x 9 = **90**

10 x 6 = **60**    4 x 10 = **40**

| 10<br>x 0 | 10<br>x 1 | 10<br>x 11 | 10<br>x 7 |
|---|---|---|---|
| **0** | **10** | **110** | **70** |

10 x 1 = **10**    10 x 3 = **30**

0 x 10 = **0**    10 x 7 = **70**

| 10<br>x 4 | 10<br>x 6 | 10<br>x 0 | 10<br>x 8 |
|---|---|---|---|
| **40** | **60** | **0** | **80** |

5 x 10 = **50**    10 x 10 = **100**

6 x 10 = **60**    11 x 10 = **110**

| 10<br>x 3 | 10<br>x 12 | 10<br>x 4 | 12<br>x 10 |
|---|---|---|---|
| **30** | **120** | **40** | **120** |

10 x 5 = **50**    10 x 2 = **20**

10 x 12 = **120**    3 x 10 = **30**

| 10<br>x 6 | 10<br>x 5 | 10<br>x 2 | 10<br>x 1 |
|---|---|---|---|
| **60** | **50** | **20** | **10** |

Score: _____

START    FINISH

## 217

### Practice

Ten as a Factor

■ Complete these facts as accurately and as quickly as you can.

| 10<br>x 8 | 10<br>x 5 | 10<br>x 3 | 10<br>x 12 |
|---|---|---|---|
| **80** | **50** | **30** | **120** |

10 x 6 = **60**    7 x 10 = **70**

0 x 10 = **0**    10 x 12 = **120**

| 11<br>x 10 | 10<br>x 8 | 12<br>x 10 | 10<br>x 4 |
|---|---|---|---|
| **110** | **80** | **120** | **40** |

10 x 2 = **20**    10 x 4 = **40**

6 x 10 = **60**    1 x 10 = **10**

| 10<br>x 9 | 10<br>x 2 | 10<br>x 4 | 10<br>x 0 |
|---|---|---|---|
| **90** | **20** | **40** | **100** |

3 x 10 = **30**    12 x 10 = **120**

10 x 7 = **70**    10 x 10 = **100**

| 10<br>x 7 | 10<br>x 6 | 10<br>x 2 | 10<br>x 9 |
|---|---|---|---|
| **70** | **60** | **20** | **90** |

10 x 11 = **110**    11 x 10 = **110**

10 x 0 = **0**    10 x 1 = **10**

| 10<br>x 5 | 10<br>x 1 | 10<br>x 12 | 10<br>x 7 |
|---|---|---|---|
| **50** | **10** | **120** | **70** |

Score: _____

Circle any problems that you still find difficult to remember. Make your own flash cards to help you master these problems.

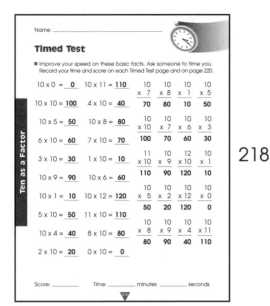

**Ten as a Factor**

Name _____

### Timed Test

■ Improve your speed on these basic facts. Ask someone to time you. Record your time and score on each Timed Test page and on page 220.

10 x 0 = **0**   10 x 11 = **110**

| 10 | 10 | 10 | 10 |
|---|---|---|---|
| x 7 | x 8 | x 1 | x 5 |
| 70 | 80 | 10 | 50 |

10 x 10 = **100**   4 x 10 = **40**

| 10 | 10 | 10 | 10 |
|---|---|---|---|
| x 10 | x 7 | x 6 | x 3 |
| 100 | 70 | 60 | 30 |

10 x 5 = **50**   10 x 8 = **80**

6 x 10 = **60**   7 x 10 = **70**

3 x 10 = **30**   1 x 10 = **10**

| 11 | 10 | 12 | 10 |
|---|---|---|---|
| x 10 | x 9 | x 10 | x 1 |
| 110 | 90 | 120 | 10 |

10 x 9 = **90**   10 x 6 = **60**

10 x 1 = **10**   10 x 12 = **120**

| 10 | 10 | 10 | 10 |
|---|---|---|---|
| x 5 | x 2 | x 12 | x 0 |
| 50 | 20 | 120 | 0 |

5 x 10 = **50**   11 x 10 = **110**

| 10 | 10 | 10 | 10 |
|---|---|---|---|
| x 8 | x 9 | x 4 | x 11 |
| 80 | 90 | 40 | 110 |

10 x 4 = **40**   8 x 10 = **80**

2 x 10 = **20**   0 x 10 = **0**

Score: _____   Time: _____ minutes _____ seconds

**218**

---

**Ten as a Factor**

Name _____

### Timed Test

■ Complete these facts as accurately and as quickly as you can.

10 x 4 = **40**   2 x 10 = **20**

| 10 | 11 | 10 | 10 |
|---|---|---|---|
| x 1 | x 10 | x 5 | x 9 |
| 10 | 110 | 50 | 90 |

12 x 10 = **120**   10 x 8 = **80**

| 10 | 12 | 10 | 10 |
|---|---|---|---|
| x 7 | x 10 | x 9 | x 8 |
| 70 | 120 | 90 | 80 |

10 x 1 = **10**   10 x 11 = **110**

10 x 3 = **30**   8 x 10 = **80**

5 x 10 = **50**   10 x 5 = **50**

| 10 | 10 | 10 | 10 |
|---|---|---|---|
| x 0 | x 4 | x 11 | x 5 |
| 0 | 40 | 110 | 50 |

10 x 9 = **90**   6 x 10 = **60**

3 x 10 = **30**   10 x 10 = **100**

| 10 | 10 | 10 | 10 |
|---|---|---|---|
| x 6 | x 3 | x 10 | x 7 |
| 60 | 30 | 100 | 70 |

10 x 2 = **20**   1 x 10 = **10**

10 x 12 = **120**   10 x 7 = **70**

| 10 | 10 | 10 | 10 |
|---|---|---|---|
| x 2 | x 4 | x 12 | x 1 |
| 20 | 40 | 120 | 10 |

4 x 10 = **40**   10 x 6 = **60**

Score: _____   Time: _____ minutes _____ seconds

**219**

---

**Ten as a Factor**

Name _____

### Timed Test

10 x 8 = **80**   10 x 2 = **20**

| 10 | 12 | 10 | 10 |
|---|---|---|---|
| x 4 | x 10 | x 0 | x 9 |
| 40 | 120 | 0 | 90 |

0 x 10 = **0**   10 x 12 = **120**

10 x 4 = **40**   10 x 6 = **60**

| 10 | 5 | 10 | 10 |
|---|---|---|---|
| x 5 | x 10 | x 8 | x 3 |
| 50 | 110 | 80 | 30 |

8 x 10 = **80**   5 x 10 = **50**

10 x 11 = **110**   10 x 3 = **30**

| 10 | 10 | 10 | 10 |
|---|---|---|---|
| x 0 | x 8 | x 5 | x 2 |
| 0 | 80 | 50 | 20 |

4 x 10 = **40**   9 x 10 = **90**

10 x 5 = **50**   1 x 10 = **10**

| 10 | 10 | 10 | 10 |
|---|---|---|---|
| x 10 | x 12 | x 1 | x 4 |
| 100 | 120 | 10 | 40 |

7 x 10 = **70**   11 x 10 = **110**

10 x 9 = **90**   10 x 0 = **0**

| 10 | 10 | 10 | 10 |
|---|---|---|---|
| x 7 | x 6 | x 2 | x 3 |
| 70 | 60 | 20 | 30 |

3 x 10 = **30**   2 x 10 = **20**

Record your scores and times below.

Page 216 Score: _____
Page 217 Score: _____
Page 218 Score: _____ Time: ___min. ___sec.
Page 219 Score: _____ Time: ___min. ___sec.
Page 220 Score: _____ Time: ___min. ___sec.

**220**

---

**Eleven as a Factor**

Name _____

### Products Through One Hundred Thirty-Two

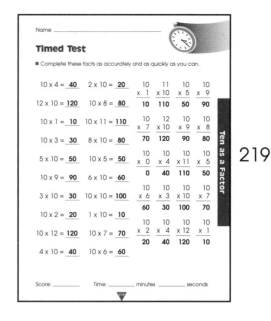

The first thirteen multiples of 11 are 0, 11, 22, 33, 44, 55, 66, 77, 88, 99, 110, 121, and 132. They are the same as the products of 11 times any number from 0 through 12.

Here are some things to remember about the basic facts in which 11 is one of the factors:

● All of the products from 11 x 2 through 11 x 9 are easy to remember because both digits in each product are the same as the second factor. Thus, 11 x 2 is 22, 11 x 5 is 55, and 11 x 9 is 99.

● That leaves only three other facts to learn. The first of these you already know: 11 x 10 is 110. The other two are new: 11 x 11 is 121 and 11 x 12 is 132.

● Changing the order of the factors does not change the product. So, 11 x 7 is the same as 7 x 11.

● As you have learned with other facts, 11 x 0 is 0 and 11 x 1 is 11.

■ Complete this circle by multiplying each of the numbers by 11.
■ Now, complete these facts.

11 x 3 = **33**   2 x 11 = **22**
8 x 11 = **88**   11 x 7 = **77**
11 x 6 = **66**   4 x 11 = **44**
0 x 11 = **0**   10 x 11 = **110**
11 x 2 = **22**   6 x 11 = **66**
7 x 11 = **77**   11 x 12 = **132**
11 x 5 = **55**   9 x 11 = **99**

**221**

---

**Eleven as a Factor**

Name _____

### Practice

■ Multiply. Record your score—the number correct—on each Practice page and again on page 226.

| 11 | 11 | 11 | 11 |
|---|---|---|---|
| x 7 | x 0 | x 1 | x 8 |
| 77 | 0 | 11 | 88 |

11 x 2 = **22**   7 x 11 = **77**
9 x 11 = **99**   5 x 11 = **55**

| 11 | 11 | 11 | 10 |
|---|---|---|---|
| x 4 | x 12 | x 9 | x 11 |
| 44 | 132 | 99 | 110 |

11 x 10 = **110**   12 x 11 = **132**
3 x 11 = **33**   0 x 11 = **0**

| 11 | 11 | 11 | 11 |
|---|---|---|---|
| x 5 | x 4 | x 3 | x 10 |
| 55 | 44 | 33 | 110 |

11 x 5 = **55**   11 x 6 = **66**
2 x 11 = **22**   11 x 9 = **99**

| 11 | 11 | 11 | 12 |
|---|---|---|---|
| x 2 | x 5 | x 0 | x 11 |
| 22 | 55 | 0 | 132 |

11 x 8 = **88**   11 x 12 = **132**
1 x 11 = **11**   4 x 11 = **44**

| 11 | 11 | 11 | 11 |
|---|---|---|---|
| x 3 | x 11 | x 6 | x 2 |
| 33 | 121 | 66 | 22 |

Score: _____

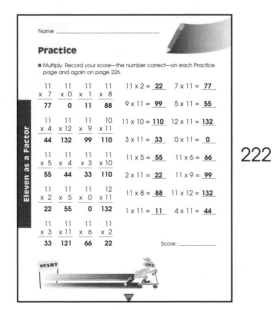

START   FINISH

**222**

---

**Eleven as a Factor**

Name _____

### Practice

■ Multiply.

| 12 | 11 | 11 | 11 |
|---|---|---|---|
| x 11 | x 10 | x 0 | x 4 |
| 132 | 110 | 0 | 44 |

11 x 1 = **11**   11 x 5 = **55**
12 x 11 = **132**   1 x 11 = **11**

| 11 | 10 | 11 | 11 |
|---|---|---|---|
| x 6 | x 11 | x 9 | x 5 |
| 66 | 110 | 99 | 55 |

3 x 11 = **33**   4 x 11 = **44**
11 x 8 = **88**   11 x 10 = **110**

| 11 | 11 | 11 | 11 |
|---|---|---|---|
| x 5 | x 8 | x 3 | x 7 |
| 55 | 88 | 33 | 77 |

2 x 11 = **22**   11 x 2 = **22**
9 x 11 = **99**   11 x 11 = **121**

| 11 | 11 | 11 | 11 |
|---|---|---|---|
| x 1 | x 8 | x 3 | x 12 |
| 11 | 88 | 33 | 132 |

11 x 0 = **0**   11 x 7 = **77**

| 11 | 11 | 11 | 11 |
|---|---|---|---|
| x 4 | x 2 | x 11 | x 5 |
| 44 | 22 | 121 | 55 |

Score: _____

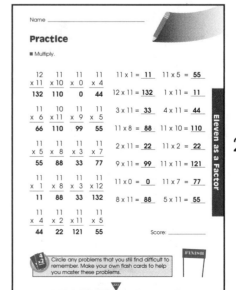

Circle any problems that you still find difficult to remember. Make your own flash cards to help you master these problems.

**223**

# Timed Test Answer Key

---

## 224 — Eleven as a Factor

**Timed Test**

Improve your speed on these facts of 11. Ask someone to time you. Record your time and score on each Timed Test page and on page 226.

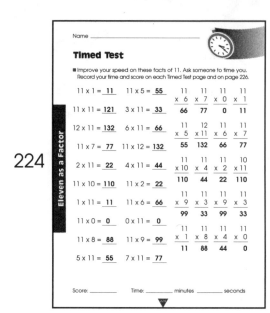

| | | | | | |
|---|---|---|---|---|---|
| 11 x 1 = **11** | 11 x 5 = **55** | 11 x6 = 66 | 11 x7 = 77 | 11 x0 = 0 | 11 x1 = 11 |
| 11 x 11 = **121** | 3 x 11 = **33** | 11 x5 = 55 | 12 x11 = 132 | 11 x6 = 66 | 11 x7 = 77 |
| 12 x 11 = **132** | 6 x 11 = **66** | | | | |
| 11 x 7 = **77** | 11 x 12 = **132** | | | | |
| 2 x 11 = **22** | 4 x 11 = **44** | 11 x10 = 110 | 11 x4 = 44 | 11 x2 = 22 | 10 x11 = 110 |
| 11 x 10 = **110** | 11 x 2 = **22** | | | | |
| 1 x 11 = **11** | 11 x 6 = **66** | 11 x9 = 99 | 11 x3 = 33 | 11 x9 = 99 | 11 x3 = 33 |
| 11 x 0 = **0** | 0 x 11 = **0** | | | | |
| 11 x 8 = **88** | 11 x 9 = **99** | 11 x1 = 11 | 11 x8 = 88 | 11 x4 = 44 | 11 x0 = 0 |
| 5 x 11 = **55** | 7 x 11 = **77** | | | | |

Score: _____   Time: _____ minutes _____ seconds

---

## 225 — Eleven as a Factor

**Timed Test**

Complete these facts as accurately and as quickly as you can.

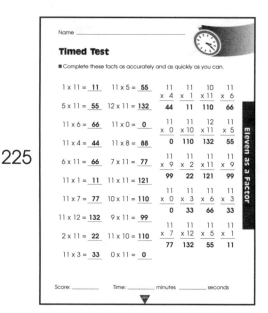

| | | | | | |
|---|---|---|---|---|---|
| 1 x 11 = **11** | 11 x 5 = **55** | 11 x4 = 44 | 11 x1 = 11 | 10 x11 = 110 | 11 x6 = 66 |
| 5 x 11 = **55** | 12 x 11 = **132** | | | | |
| 11 x 6 = **66** | 11 x 0 = **0** | 11 x0 = 0 | 11 x10 = 110 | 12 x11 = 132 | 11 x5 = 55 |
| 11 x 4 = **44** | 11 x 8 = **88** | | | | |
| 6 x 11 = **66** | 7 x 11 = **77** | 11 x9 = 99 | 11 x2 = 22 | 11 x11 = 121 | 11 x9 = 99 |
| 11 x 1 = **11** | 11 x 11 = **121** | | | | |
| 11 x 7 = **77** | 10 x 11 = **110** | 11 x0 = 0 | 11 x3 = 33 | 11 x6 = 66 | 11 x3 = 33 |
| 11 x 12 = **132** | 9 x 11 = **99** | | | | |
| 2 x 11 = **22** | 11 x 10 = **110** | 11 x7 = 77 | 11 x12 = 132 | 11 x5 = 55 | 11 x1 = 11 |
| 11 x 3 = **33** | 0 x 11 = **0** | | | | |

Score: _____   Time: _____ minutes _____ seconds

---

## 226 — Eleven as a Factor

**Timed Test**

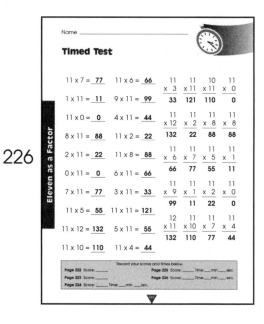

| | | | | | |
|---|---|---|---|---|---|
| 11 x 7 = **77** | 11 x 6 = **66** | 11 x3 = 33 | 11 x11 = 121 | 10 x11 = 110 | 11 x0 = 0 |
| 1 x 11 = **11** | 9 x 11 = **99** | | | | |
| 11 x 0 = **0** | 4 x 11 = **44** | 11 x12 = 132 | 11 x2 = 22 | 11 x8 = 88 | 11 x8 = 88 |
| 8 x 11 = **88** | 11 x 2 = **22** | | | | |
| 2 x 11 = **22** | 11 x 8 = **88** | 11 x6 = 66 | 11 x7 = 77 | 11 x5 = 55 | 11 x1 = 11 |
| 0 x 11 = **0** | 6 x 11 = **66** | | | | |
| 7 x 11 = **77** | 3 x 11 = **33** | 11 x9 = 99 | 11 x1 = 11 | 11 x2 = 22 | 11 x0 = 0 |
| 11 x 5 = **55** | 11 x 11 = **121** | | | | |
| 11 x 12 = **132** | 5 x 11 = **55** | 12 x11 = 132 | 11 x10 = 110 | 11 x7 = 77 | 11 x4 = 44 |
| 11 x 10 = **110** | 11 x 4 = **44** | | | | |

Record your scores and times below.

| | |
|---|---|
| **Page 222** Score: _____ | **Page 225** Score: _____ Time: ____min. ____sec. |
| **Page 223** Score: _____ | **Page 226** Score: _____ Time: ____min. ____sec. |
| **Page 224** Score: _____ Time: ____min. ____sec. | |

---

## 227 — Twelve as a Factor

**Products Through One Hundred Forty-Four**

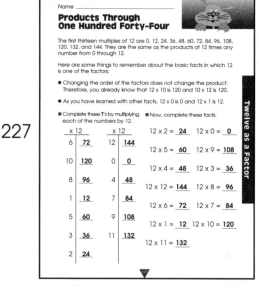

The first thirteen multiples of 12 are 0, 12, 24, 36, 48, 60, 72, 84, 96, 108, 120, 132, and 144. They are the same as the products of 12 times any number from 0 through 12.

Here are some things to remember about the basic facts in which 12 is one of the factors:

- Changing the order of the factors does not change the product. Therefore, you already know that 12 x 10 is 120 and 10 x 12 is 120.
- As you have learned with other facts, 12 x 0 is 0 and 12 x 1 is 12.

Complete these T's by multiplying each of the numbers by 12.   Now, complete these facts.

| x 12 | | x 12 | |
|---|---|---|---|
| 6 | **72** | 12 | **144** |
| 10 | **120** | 0 | **0** |
| 8 | **96** | 4 | **48** |
| 1 | **12** | 7 | **84** |
| 5 | **60** | 9 | **108** |
| 3 | **36** | 11 | **132** |
| 2 | **24** | | |

| | |
|---|---|
| 12 x 2 = **24** | 12 x 0 = **0** |
| 12 x 5 = **60** | 12 x 9 = **108** |
| 12 x 4 = **48** | 12 x 3 = **36** |
| 12 x 12 = **144** | 12 x 8 = **96** |
| 12 x 6 = **72** | 12 x 7 = **84** |
| 12 x 1 = **12** | 12 x 10 = **120** |
| 12 x 11 = **132** | |

---

## 228 — Twelve as a Factor

**Practice**

Multiply. Record your score—the number correct—on each Practice page and again on page 232.

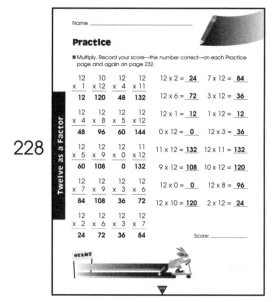

| | | | | | |
|---|---|---|---|---|---|
| 12 x1 = 12 | 10 x12 = 120 | 12 x4 = 48 | 12 x11 = 132 | 12 x 2 = **24** | 7 x 12 = **84** |
| 12 x4 = 48 | 12 x8 = 96 | 12 x5 = 60 | 12 x12 = 144 | 12 x 6 = **72** | 3 x 12 = **36** |
| 12 x5 = 60 | 12 x9 = 108 | 12 x0 = 0 | 11 x12 = 132 | 12 x 1 = **12** | 1 x 12 = **12** |
| 12 x7 = 84 | 12 x9 = 108 | 12 x3 = 36 | 12 x6 = 72 | 0 x 12 = **0** | 12 x 3 = **36** |
| 12 x2 = 24 | 12 x6 = 72 | 12 x3 = 36 | 12 x7 = 84 | 11 x 12 = **132** | 12 x 11 = **132** |
| | | | | 9 x 12 = **108** | 10 x 12 = **120** |
| | | | | 12 x 0 = **0** | 12 x 8 = **96** |
| | | | | 12 x 10 = **120** | 2 x 12 = **24** |

Score: _____

---

## 229 — Twelve as a Factor

**Practice**

Multiply.

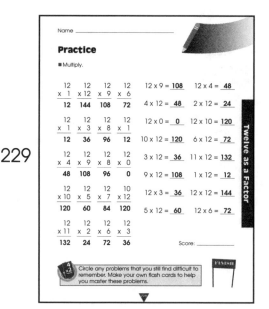

| | | | | | |
|---|---|---|---|---|---|
| 12 x1 = 12 | 12 x12 = 144 | 12 x9 = 108 | 12 x6 = 72 | 12 x 9 = **108** | 12 x 4 = **48** |
| 12 x1 = 12 | 12 x3 = 36 | 12 x8 = 96 | 12 x1 = 12 | 4 x 12 = **48** | 2 x 12 = **24** |
| 12 x4 = 48 | 12 x9 = 108 | 12 x8 = 96 | 12 x0 = 0 | 12 x 0 = **0** | 12 x 10 = **120** |
| 12 x10 = 120 | 12 x5 = 60 | 12 x7 = 84 | 10 x12 = 120 | 10 x 12 = **120** | 6 x 12 = **72** |
| 12 x11 = 132 | 12 x2 = 24 | 12 x6 = 72 | 12 x3 = 36 | 3 x 12 = **36** | 11 x 12 = **132** |
| | | | | 9 x 12 = **108** | 1 x 12 = **12** |
| | | | | 12 x 3 = **36** | 12 x 12 = **144** |
| | | | | 5 x 12 = **60** | 12 x 6 = **72** |

Score: _____

Circle any problems that you still find difficult to remember. Make your own flash cards to help you master these problems.

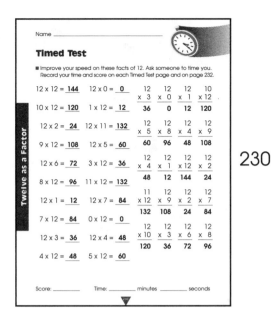

**Timed Test**

■ Improve your speed on these facts of 12. Ask someone to time you. Record your time and score on each Timed Test page and on page 232.

12 x 12 = **144**   12 x 0 = **0**

10 x 12 = **120**   1 x 12 = **12**

12 x 2 = **24**   12 x 11 = **132**

9 x 12 = **108**   12 x 5 = **60**

12 x 6 = **72**   3 x 12 = **36**

8 x 12 = **96**   11 x 12 = **132**

12 x 1 = **12**   12 x 7 = **84**

7 x 12 = **84**   0 x 12 = **0**

12 x 3 = **36**   12 x 4 = **48**

4 x 12 = **48**   5 x 12 = **60**

| 12<br>x 3 | 12<br>x 0 | 12<br>x 1 | 10<br>x 12 |
|---|---|---|---|
| 36 | 0 | 12 | 120 |
| 12<br>x 5 | 12<br>x 8 | 12<br>x 4 | 12<br>x 9 |
| 60 | 96 | 48 | 108 |
| 12<br>x 4 | 12<br>x 1 | 12<br>x 12 | 12<br>x 2 |
| 48 | 12 | 144 | 24 |
| 11<br>x 12 | 12<br>x 9 | 12<br>x 2 | 12<br>x 7 |
| 132 | 108 | 24 | 84 |
| 12<br>x 10 | 12<br>x 3 | 12<br>x 6 | 12<br>x 8 |
| 120 | 36 | 72 | 96 |

*Twelve as a Factor*

Score: _____   Time: _____ minutes _____ seconds

**230**

---

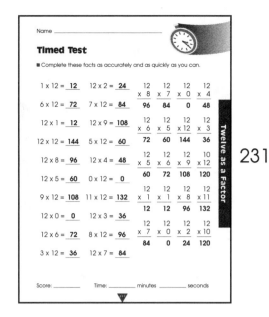

**Timed Test**

■ Complete these facts as accurately and as quickly as you can.

1 x 12 = **12**   12 x 2 = **24**

6 x 12 = **72**   7 x 12 = **84**

12 x 1 = **12**   12 x 9 = **108**

12 x 12 = **144**   5 x 12 = **60**

12 x 8 = **96**   12 x 4 = **48**

12 x 5 = **60**   0 x 12 = **0**

9 x 12 = **108**   11 x 12 = **132**

12 x 0 = **0**   12 x 3 = **36**

12 x 6 = **72**   8 x 12 = **96**

3 x 12 = **36**   12 x 7 = **84**

| 12<br>x 8 | 12<br>x 7 | 12<br>x 0 | 12<br>x 4 |
|---|---|---|---|
| 96 | 84 | 0 | 48 |
| 12<br>x 6 | 12<br>x 5 | 12<br>x 12 | 12<br>x 3 |
| 72 | 60 | 144 | 36 |
| 12<br>x 5 | 12<br>x 6 | 12<br>x 9 | 10<br>x 12 |
| 60 | 72 | 108 | 120 |
| 12<br>x 1 | 12<br>x 1 | 12<br>x 8 | 12<br>x 11 |
| 12 | 12 | 96 | 132 |
| 12<br>x 7 | 12<br>x 0 | 12<br>x 2 | 12<br>x 10 |
| 84 | 0 | 24 | 120 |

*Twelve as a Factor*

Score: _____   Time: _____ minutes _____ seconds

**231**

---

**Timed Test**

12 x 7 = **84**   12 x 6 = **72**

3 x 12 = **36**   12 x 11 = **132**

12 x 1 = **12**   11 x 12 = **132**

2 x 12 = **24**   12 x 0 = **0**

12 x 12 = **144**   12 x 3 = **36**

7 x 12 = **84**   4 x 12 = **48**

12 x 5 = **60**   12 x 10 = **120**

1 x 12 = **12**   12 x 3 = **36**

12 x 8 = **96**   4 x 12 = **48**

6 x 12 = **72**   12 x 10 = **120**

| 12<br>x 9 | 12<br>x 10 | 12<br>x 0 | 12<br>x 11 |
|---|---|---|---|
| 108 | 120 | 0 | 132 |
| 12<br>x 8 | 12<br>x 9 | 12<br>x 1 | 12<br>x 8 |
| 96 | 108 | 12 | 96 |
| 10<br>x 12 | 12<br>x 0 | 12<br>x 7 | 12<br>x 2 |
| 120 | 0 | 84 | 24 |
| 12<br>x 1 | 12<br>x 12 | 12<br>x 7 | 11<br>x 12 |
| 12 | 144 | 84 | 132 |
| 12<br>x 6 | 12<br>x 5 | 12<br>x 3 | 12<br>x 2 |
| 72 | 60 | 36 | 24 |

*Twelve as a Factor*

| Record your scores and times below. | | | | |
|---|---|---|---|---|
| **Page 228** Score: _____ | | **Page 231** Score: _____ | Time: _____ min. _____ sec. | |
| **Page 229** Score: _____ | | **Page 232** Score: _____ | Time: _____ min. _____ sec. | |
| **Page 230** Score: _____ | Time: _____ min. _____ sec. | | | |

**232**

---

**Timed Test**

■ Improve your speed on these facts of 12. Ask someone to time you. Record your time and score on each Timed Test page and on page 234.

12 x 10 = **120**   1 x 12 = **12**   12 x 2 = **24**   4 x 10 = **40**

10 x 9 = **90**   11 x 6 = **66**   6 x 11 = **66**   11 x 7 = **77**

2 x 10 = **20**   10 x 12 = **120**   11 x 8 = **88**   8 x 11 = **88**

11 x 9 = **99**   5 x 11 = **55**   0 x 11 = **0**   11 x 0 = **0**

10 x 5 = **50**   11 x 1 = **11**   10 x 4 = **40**   10 x 2 = **20**

4 x 11 = **44**   8 x 12 = **96**   12 x 11 = **132**   12 x 4 = **48**

12 x 1 = **12**   10 x 8 = **80**   7 x 11 = **77**   11 x 5 = **55**

6 x 10 = **60**   3 x 10 = **30**   12 x 5 = **60**   10 x 7 = **70**

12 x 6 = **72**   12 x 3 = **36**   7 x 12 = **84**   10 x 3 = **30**

10 x 1 = **10**   3 x 12 = **36**   10 x 0 = **0**   11 x 9 = **99**

*All-Multiplication Review*

Continue this Timed Test on the next page.

**233**

---

**Timed Test**

11 x 11 = **121**   12 x 8 = **96**   1 x 11 = **11**   9 x 10 = **90**

3 x 11 = **33**   2 x 11 = **22**   2 x 10 = **20**   11 x 5 = **55**

10 x 3 = **30**   10 x 7 = **70**   7 x 10 = **70**   9 x 11 = **99**

8 x 10 = **80**   0 x 12 = **0**   11 x 10 = **110**   12 x 0 = **0**

12 x 12 = **144**   11 x 12 = **132**   6 x 12 = **72**   10 x 10 = **100**

5 x 12 = **60**   12 x 4 = **48**   10 x 6 = **60**   11 x 8 = **88**

11 x 3 = **33**   1 x 10 = **10**   0 x 10 = **0**   12 x 3 = **36**

11 x 4 = **44**   12 x 9 = **108**   12 x 7 = **84**   11 x 5 = **55**

5 x 10 = **50**   4 x 12 = **48**   9 x 12 = **108**   10 x 4 = **40**

10 x 11 = **110**   11 x 2 = **22**   10 x 2 = **20**   11 x 6 = **66**

*All-Multiplication Review*

Score: _____   Time: _____ minutes _____ seconds

**234**

---

**What Is Division?**

You divide to answer questions such as how many groups of 3's are there in 12. The answer is called the **quotient**.

12 grapes divided into groups of 3 equals 4 equal groups.

Here are two ways to show the division.

$12 \div 3 = 4$   $3\overline{)12}$ ... $\frac{4}{}$

You read the problem this way: **12 divided by 3 equals 4.**

You can draw a picture to find a quotient.

**Example:** Find the quotient. 8 ÷ 2 = _____

**Step 1:** Draw 8 dots. Group them into 2's.

**Step 2:** Count all the groups.

**Answer:** 8 ÷ 2 = **4**

■ Draw a picture to find the quotient.

6 ÷ 2 = **3**   8 ÷ 4 = **2**   10 ÷ 2 = **5**

6 ÷ 3 = **2**   12 ÷ 3 = **4**   12 ÷ 4 = **3**

*Division*

**236**

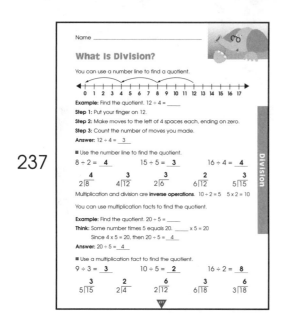

**237**

### What Is Division?

You can use a number line to find a quotient.

0 1 2 3 4 5 6 7 8 9 10 11 12 13 14 15 16 17

**Example:** Find the quotient. 12 ÷ 4 = ___
**Step 1:** Put your finger on 12.
**Step 2:** Make moves to the left of 4 spaces each, ending on zero.
**Step 3:** Count the number of moves you made.
**Answer:** 12 ÷ 4 = **3**

■ Use the number line to find the quotient.

8 ÷ 2 = **4**    15 ÷ 5 = **3**    16 ÷ 4 = **4**

$\frac{4}{2\overline{)8}}$   $\frac{3}{4\overline{)12}}$   $\frac{3}{2\overline{)6}}$   $\frac{2}{6\overline{)12}}$   $\frac{3}{5\overline{)15}}$

Multiplication and division are **inverse operations.** 10 ÷ 2 = 5   5 x 2 = 10

You can use multiplication facts to find the quotient.

**Example:** Find the quotient. 20 ÷ 5 = ___
**Think:** Some number times 5 equals 20.   ___ x 5 = 20
Since 4 x 5 = 20, then 20 ÷ 5 = **4**
**Answer:** 20 ÷ 5 = **4**

■ Use a multiplication fact to find the quotient.

9 ÷ 3 = **3**    10 ÷ 5 = **2**    16 ÷ 2 = **8**

$\frac{3}{5\overline{)15}}$   $\frac{2}{2\overline{)4}}$   $\frac{6}{2\overline{)12}}$   $\frac{6}{3\overline{)18}}$   $\frac{6}{3\overline{)18}}$

**Division**

---

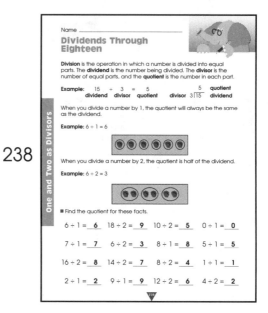

**238**

### Dividends Through Eighteen

**Division** is the operation in which a number is divided into equal parts. The **dividend** is the number being divided. The **divisor** is the number of equal parts, and the **quotient** is the number in each part.

**Example:**  15 ÷ 3 = 5
dividend divisor quotient    $3\overline{)15}$ with quotient 5 and dividend

When you divide a number by 1, the quotient will always be the same as the dividend.

**Example:** 6 ÷ 1 = 6

When you divide a number by 2, the quotient is half of the dividend.

**Example:** 6 ÷ 2 = 3

■ Find the quotient for these facts.

6 ÷ 1 = **6**    18 ÷ 2 = **9**    10 ÷ 2 = **5**    0 ÷ 1 = **0**

7 ÷ 1 = **7**    6 ÷ 2 = **3**    8 ÷ 1 = **8**    5 ÷ 1 = **5**

16 ÷ 2 = **8**    14 ÷ 2 = **7**    8 ÷ 2 = **4**    1 ÷ 1 = **1**

2 ÷ 1 = **2**    9 ÷ 1 = **9**    12 ÷ 2 = **6**    4 ÷ 2 = **2**

**One and Two as Divisors**

---

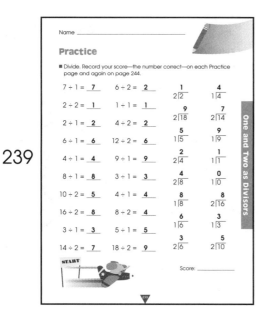

**239**

### Practice

■ Divide. Record your score—the number correct—on each Practice page and again on page 244.

7 ÷ 1 = **7**    6 ÷ 2 = **2**    $\frac{1}{2\overline{)2}}$   $\frac{4}{1\overline{)4}}$

2 ÷ 2 = **1**    1 ÷ 1 = **1**    $\frac{9}{2\overline{)18}}$   $\frac{7}{2\overline{)14}}$

2 ÷ 1 = **2**    4 ÷ 2 = **2**    $\frac{5}{1\overline{)5}}$   $\frac{9}{1\overline{)9}}$

6 ÷ 1 = **6**    12 ÷ 2 = **6**    $\frac{2}{2\overline{)4}}$   $\frac{1}{1\overline{)1}}$

4 ÷ 1 = **4**    9 ÷ 1 = **9**    $\frac{4}{2\overline{)8}}$   $\frac{0}{1\overline{)0}}$

8 ÷ 1 = **8**    3 ÷ 1 = **3**    $\frac{8}{1\overline{)8}}$   $\frac{8}{2\overline{)16}}$

10 ÷ 2 = **5**    4 ÷ 1 = **4**    $\frac{6}{1\overline{)6}}$   $\frac{3}{1\overline{)3}}$

16 ÷ 2 = **8**    8 ÷ 2 = **4**

3 ÷ 1 = **3**    5 ÷ 1 = **5**    $\frac{5}{2\overline{)6}}$   $\frac{5}{2\overline{)10}}$

14 ÷ 2 = **7**    18 ÷ 2 = **9**

**START**    Score: _____

**One and Two as Divisors**

---

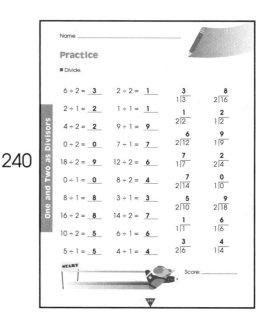

**240**

### Practice

■ Divide.

6 ÷ 2 = **3**    2 ÷ 2 = **1**    $\frac{3}{1\overline{)3}}$   $\frac{8}{2\overline{)16}}$

2 ÷ 1 = **2**    1 ÷ 1 = **1**    $\frac{1}{2\overline{)2}}$   $\frac{2}{1\overline{)2}}$

4 ÷ 2 = **2**    9 ÷ 1 = **9**    $\frac{6}{2\overline{)12}}$   $\frac{9}{1\overline{)9}}$

0 ÷ 2 = **0**    7 ÷ 1 = **7**    $\frac{7}{1\overline{)7}}$   $\frac{2}{2\overline{)4}}$

18 ÷ 2 = **9**    12 ÷ 2 = **6**    $\frac{7}{2\overline{)14}}$   $\frac{0}{1\overline{)0}}$

0 ÷ 1 = **0**    8 ÷ 2 = **4**

8 ÷ 1 = **8**    3 ÷ 1 = **3**    $\frac{5}{2\overline{)10}}$   $\frac{9}{2\overline{)18}}$

16 ÷ 2 = **8**    14 ÷ 2 = **7**

10 ÷ 2 = **5**    6 ÷ 1 = **6**    $\frac{1}{1\overline{)1}}$   $\frac{6}{1\overline{)6}}$

5 ÷ 1 = **5**    4 ÷ 1 = **4**    $\frac{3}{2\overline{)6}}$   $\frac{4}{1\overline{)4}}$

**START**    Score: _____

**One and Two as Divisors**

---

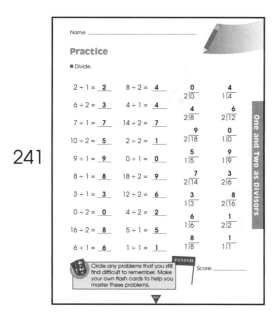

**241**

### Practice

■ Divide.

2 ÷ 1 = **2**    8 ÷ 2 = **4**    $\frac{0}{2\overline{)0}}$   $\frac{4}{1\overline{)4}}$

6 ÷ 2 = **3**    4 ÷ 1 = **4**    $\frac{4}{2\overline{)8}}$   $\frac{6}{2\overline{)12}}$

7 ÷ 1 = **7**    14 ÷ 2 = **7**    $\frac{9}{2\overline{)18}}$   $\frac{0}{1\overline{)0}}$

10 ÷ 2 = **5**    2 ÷ 2 = **1**    $\frac{5}{1\overline{)5}}$   $\frac{9}{1\overline{)9}}$

9 ÷ 1 = **9**    0 ÷ 1 = **0**    $\frac{7}{2\overline{)14}}$   $\frac{3}{2\overline{)6}}$

8 ÷ 1 = **8**    18 ÷ 2 = **9**    $\frac{3}{1\overline{)3}}$   $\frac{8}{2\overline{)16}}$

3 ÷ 1 = **3**    12 ÷ 2 = **6**    $\frac{6}{1\overline{)6}}$   $\frac{1}{2\overline{)2}}$

0 ÷ 2 = **0**    4 ÷ 2 = **2**

16 ÷ 2 = **8**    5 ÷ 1 = **5**    $\frac{8}{1\overline{)8}}$   $\frac{1}{1\overline{)1}}$

6 ÷ 1 = **6**    1 ÷ 1 = **1**

**FINISH**    Circle any problems that you still find difficult to remember. Make your own flash cards to help you master these problems.    Score: _____

**One and Two as Divisors**

---

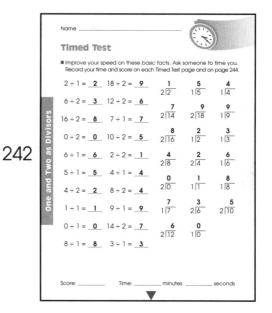

**242**

### Timed Test

■ Improve your speed on these basic facts. Ask someone to time you. Record your time and score on each Timed Test page and on page 244.

2 ÷ 1 = **2**    18 ÷ 2 = **9**    $\frac{1}{2\overline{)2}}$   $\frac{5}{1\overline{)5}}$   $\frac{4}{1\overline{)4}}$

6 ÷ 2 = **3**    12 ÷ 2 = **6**    $\frac{7}{2\overline{)14}}$   $\frac{9}{2\overline{)18}}$   $\frac{9}{1\overline{)9}}$

16 ÷ 2 = **8**    7 ÷ 1 = **7**    $\frac{8}{2\overline{)16}}$   $\frac{1}{2\overline{)2}}$   $\frac{3}{1\overline{)3}}$

0 ÷ 2 = **0**    10 ÷ 2 = **5**    $\frac{4}{2\overline{)8}}$   $\frac{2}{2\overline{)4}}$   $\frac{6}{1\overline{)6}}$

6 ÷ 1 = **6**    2 ÷ 2 = **1**    $\frac{0}{2\overline{)0}}$   $\frac{1}{1\overline{)1}}$   $\frac{8}{1\overline{)8}}$

5 ÷ 1 = **5**    4 ÷ 1 = **4**

4 ÷ 2 = **2**    8 ÷ 2 = **4**    $\frac{7}{1\overline{)7}}$   $\frac{3}{2\overline{)6}}$   $\frac{5}{2\overline{)10}}$

1 ÷ 1 = **1**    9 ÷ 1 = **9**    $\frac{6}{2\overline{)12}}$   $\frac{0}{1\overline{)0}}$

0 ÷ 1 = **0**    14 ÷ 2 = **7**

8 ÷ 1 = **8**    3 ÷ 1 = **3**

Score: _____    Time: _____ minutes _____ seconds

**One and Two as Divisors**

## Page 243

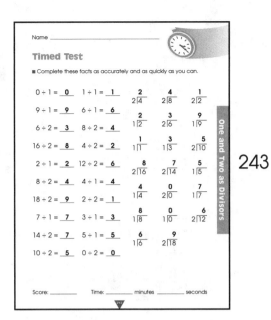

Name _____

**Timed Test**

■ Complete these facts as accurately and as quickly as you can.

| | | | | |
|---|---|---|---|---|
| 0 ÷ 1 = **0** | 1 ÷ 1 = **1** | **2** / 2⟌4 | **4** / 2⟌8 | **1** / 2⟌2 |
| 9 ÷ 1 = **9** | 6 ÷ 1 = **6** | **2** / 1⟌2 | **3** / 2⟌6 | **9** / 1⟌9 |
| 6 ÷ 2 = **3** | 8 ÷ 2 = **4** | **1** / 1⟌1 | **3** / 1⟌3 | **5** / 2⟌10 |
| 16 ÷ 2 = **8** | 4 ÷ 2 = **2** | | | |
| 2 ÷ 1 = **2** | 12 ÷ 2 = **6** | **8** / 2⟌16 | **7** / 2⟌14 | **1** / 1⟌5 |
| 8 ÷ 2 = **4** | 4 ÷ 1 = **4** | | | |
| 18 ÷ 2 = **9** | 2 ÷ 2 = **1** | **4** / 1⟌4 | **0** / 2⟌0 | **7** / 1⟌7 |
| 7 ÷ 1 = **7** | 3 ÷ 1 = **3** | **8** / 1⟌8 | **0** / 1⟌0 | **6** / 2⟌12 |
| 14 ÷ 2 = **7** | 5 ÷ 1 = **5** | **6** / 1⟌6 | **9** / 2⟌18 | |
| 10 ÷ 2 = **5** | 0 ÷ 2 = **0** | | | |

One and Two as Divisors

Score: _____  Time: _____ minutes _____ seconds

## Page 244

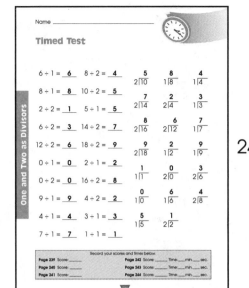

Name _____

**Timed Test**

| | | | | |
|---|---|---|---|---|
| 6 ÷ 1 = **6** | 8 ÷ 2 = **4** | **5** / 2⟌10 | **8** / 1⟌8 | **4** / 1⟌4 |
| 8 ÷ 1 = **8** | 10 ÷ 2 = **5** | **7** / 2⟌14 | **2** / 2⟌4 | **3** / 1⟌3 |
| 2 ÷ 2 = **1** | 5 ÷ 1 = **5** | | | |
| 6 ÷ 2 = **3** | 14 ÷ 2 = **7** | **8** / 2⟌16 | **6** / 2⟌12 | **7** / 1⟌7 |
| 12 ÷ 2 = **6** | 18 ÷ 2 = **9** | **9** / 2⟌18 | **2** / 1⟌2 | **9** / 1⟌9 |
| 0 ÷ 1 = **0** | 2 ÷ 1 = **2** | **1** / 1⟌1 | **0** / 2⟌0 | **3** / 2⟌6 |
| 0 ÷ 2 = **0** | 16 ÷ 2 = **8** | | | |
| 9 ÷ 1 = **9** | 4 ÷ 2 = **2** | **0** / 1⟌0 | **6** / 1⟌6 | **4** / 2⟌8 |
| 4 ÷ 1 = **4** | 3 ÷ 1 = **3** | **5** / 1⟌5 | **1** / 2⟌2 | |
| 7 ÷ 1 = **7** | 1 ÷ 1 = **1** | | | |

One and Two as Divisors

Record your scores and times below.

| | | |
|---|---|---|
| Page 239 Score: ___ | Page 242 Score: ___ Time: ___ min. ___ sec. |
| Page 240 Score: ___ | Page 243 Score: ___ Time: ___ min. ___ sec. |
| Page 241 Score: ___ | Page 244 Score: ___ Time: ___ min. ___ sec. |

## Page 245

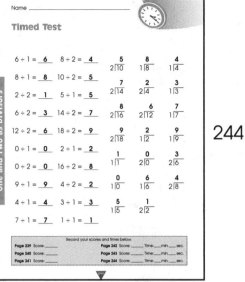

Name _____

**Dividends Through Twenty-Seven**

Now, think about what happens when a number is divided by 3.

**Example:** 18 ÷ 3 = 6

The dividend is 18. If you put 3 objects in each group, you have 6 equal groups.

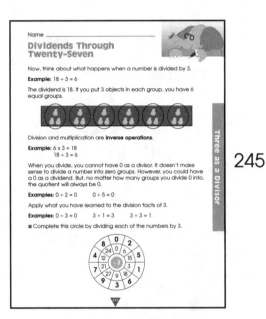

Division and multiplication are **inverse operations**.

**Example:** 6 x 3 = 18
18 ÷ 3 = 6

When you divide, you cannot have 0 as a divisor. It doesn't make sense to divide a number into zero groups. However, you could have a 0 as a dividend. But, no matter how many groups you divide 0 into, the quotient will always be 0.

**Examples:** 0 ÷ 2 = 0    0 ÷ 5 = 0

Apply what you have learned to the division facts of 3.

**Examples:** 0 ÷ 3 = 0    3 ÷ 1 = 3    3 ÷ 3 = 1

■ Complete this circle by dividing each of the numbers by 3.

Three as a Divisor

## Page 246

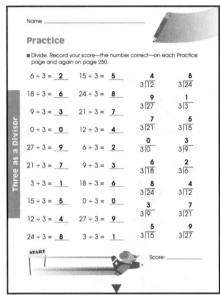

Name _____

**Practice**

■ Divide. Record your score—the number correct—on each Practice page and again on page 250.

| | | | |
|---|---|---|---|
| 6 ÷ 3 = **2** | 15 ÷ 3 = **5** | **4** / 3⟌12 | **8** / 3⟌24 |
| 18 ÷ 3 = **6** | 24 ÷ 3 = **8** | **9** / 3⟌27 | **1** / 3⟌3 |
| 9 ÷ 3 = **3** | 21 ÷ 3 = **7** | **7** / 3⟌21 | **5** / 3⟌15 |
| 0 ÷ 3 = **0** | 12 ÷ 3 = **4** | | |
| 27 ÷ 3 = **9** | 6 ÷ 3 = **2** | **0** / 3⟌0 | **3** / 3⟌9 |
| 21 ÷ 3 = **7** | 9 ÷ 3 = **3** | **6** / 3⟌18 | **2** / 3⟌6 |
| 3 ÷ 3 = **1** | 18 ÷ 3 = **6** | **8** / 3⟌24 | **4** / 3⟌12 |
| 15 ÷ 3 = **5** | 0 ÷ 3 = **0** | **3** / 3⟌9 | **7** / 3⟌21 |
| 12 ÷ 3 = **4** | 27 ÷ 3 = **9** | | |
| 24 ÷ 3 = **8** | 3 ÷ 3 = **1** | **5** / 3⟌15 | **9** / 3⟌27 |

START

Three as a Divisor

Score: _____

## Page 247

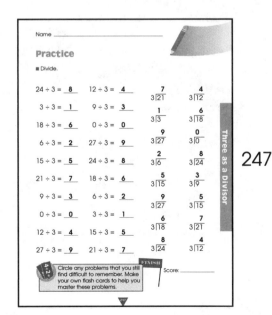

Name _____

**Practice**

■ Divide.

| | | | |
|---|---|---|---|
| 24 ÷ 3 = **8** | 12 ÷ 3 = **4** | **7** / 3⟌21 | **4** / 3⟌12 |
| 3 ÷ 3 = **1** | 9 ÷ 3 = **3** | **1** / 3⟌3 | **6** / 3⟌18 |
| 18 ÷ 3 = **6** | 0 ÷ 3 = **0** | | |
| 6 ÷ 3 = **2** | 27 ÷ 3 = **9** | **9** / 3⟌27 | **0** / 3⟌0 |
| 15 ÷ 3 = **5** | 24 ÷ 3 = **8** | **2** / 3⟌6 | **8** / 3⟌24 |
| 21 ÷ 3 = **7** | 18 ÷ 3 = **6** | **5** / 3⟌15 | **3** / 3⟌9 |
| 9 ÷ 3 = **3** | 6 ÷ 3 = **2** | **9** / 3⟌27 | **5** / 3⟌15 |
| 0 ÷ 3 = **0** | 3 ÷ 3 = **1** | **6** / 3⟌18 | **7** / 3⟌21 |
| 12 ÷ 3 = **4** | 15 ÷ 3 = **5** | | |
| 27 ÷ 3 = **9** | 21 ÷ 3 = **7** | **8** / 3⟌24 | **4** / 3⟌12 |

Three as a Divisor

Circle any problems that you still find difficult to remember. Make your own flash cards to help you master these problems.

FINISH

Score: _____

## Page 248

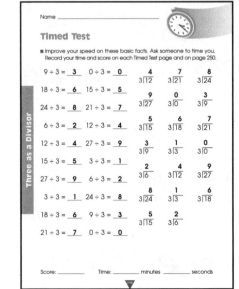

Name _____

**Timed Test**

■ Improve your speed on these basic facts. Ask someone to time you. Record your time and score on each Timed Test page and on page 250.

| | | | | |
|---|---|---|---|---|
| 9 ÷ 3 = **3** | 0 ÷ 3 = **0** | **4** / 3⟌12 | **7** / 3⟌21 | **8** / 3⟌24 |
| 18 ÷ 3 = **6** | 15 ÷ 3 = **5** | **9** / 3⟌27 | **0** / 3⟌0 | **3** / 3⟌9 |
| 24 ÷ 3 = **8** | 21 ÷ 3 = **7** | | | |
| 6 ÷ 3 = **2** | 12 ÷ 3 = **4** | **5** / 3⟌15 | **6** / 3⟌18 | **7** / 3⟌21 |
| 12 ÷ 3 = **4** | 27 ÷ 3 = **9** | **3** / 3⟌9 | **1** / 3⟌3 | **0** / 3⟌0 |
| 15 ÷ 3 = **5** | 3 ÷ 3 = **1** | **2** / 3⟌6 | **4** / 3⟌12 | **9** / 3⟌27 |
| 27 ÷ 3 = **9** | 6 ÷ 3 = **2** | | | |
| 3 ÷ 3 = **1** | 24 ÷ 3 = **8** | **8** / 3⟌24 | **1** / 3⟌3 | **6** / 3⟌18 |
| 18 ÷ 3 = **6** | 9 ÷ 3 = **3** | **5** / 3⟌15 | **2** / 3⟌6 | |
| 21 ÷ 3 = **7** | 0 ÷ 3 = **0** | | | |

Three as a Divisor

Score: _____  Time: _____ minutes _____ seconds

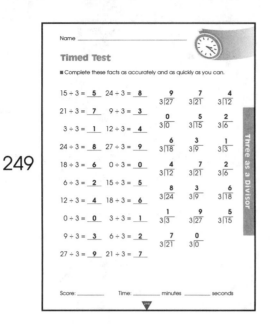

**249**

### Timed Test
*Three as a Divisor*

■ Complete these facts as accurately and as quickly as you can.

15 ÷ 3 = **5**    24 ÷ 3 = **8**    **9** 3)27    **7** 3)21    **4** 3)12
21 ÷ 3 = **7**    9 ÷ 3 = **3**     **0** 3)0     **5** 3)15    **2** 3)6
3 ÷ 3 = **1**     12 ÷ 3 = **4**    **6** 3)18    **3** 3)9     **1** 3)3
24 ÷ 3 = **8**    27 ÷ 3 = **9**    **4** 3)12    **7** 3)21    **2** 3)6
18 ÷ 3 = **6**    0 ÷ 3 = **0**     **8** 3)24    **3** 3)9     **6** 3)18
6 ÷ 3 = **2**     15 ÷ 3 = **5**    **1** 3)3     **9** 3)27    **5** 3)15
12 ÷ 3 = **4**    18 ÷ 3 = **6**    **7** 3)21    **0** 3)0
0 ÷ 3 = **0**     3 ÷ 3 = **1**
9 ÷ 3 = **3**     6 ÷ 3 = **2**
27 ÷ 3 = **9**    21 ÷ 3 = **7**

Score: _____    Time: _____ minutes _____ seconds

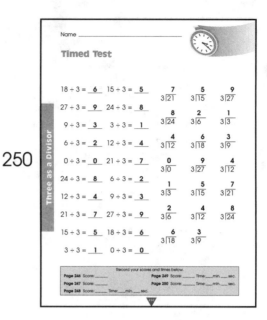

**250**

### Timed Test
*Three as a Divisor*

18 ÷ 3 = **6**    15 ÷ 3 = **5**    **7** 3)21    **5** 3)15    **9** 3)27
27 ÷ 3 = **9**    24 ÷ 3 = **8**    **8** 3)24    **2** 3)6     **1** 3)3
9 ÷ 3 = **3**     3 ÷ 3 = **1**     **4** 3)12    **6** 3)18    **3** 3)9
6 ÷ 3 = **2**     12 ÷ 3 = **4**    **0** 3)0     **9** 3)27    **4** 3)12
0 ÷ 3 = **0**     21 ÷ 3 = **7**    **1** 3)3     **5** 3)15    **7** 3)21
24 ÷ 3 = **8**    6 ÷ 3 = **2**     **2** 3)6     **4** 3)12    **8** 3)24
12 ÷ 3 = **4**    9 ÷ 3 = **3**     **6** 3)18    **3** 3)9
21 ÷ 3 = **7**    27 ÷ 3 = **9**
15 ÷ 3 = **5**    18 ÷ 3 = **6**
3 ÷ 3 = **1**     0 ÷ 3 = **0**

Record your scores and times below.
Page 246 Score:_____     Page 249 Score:_____ Time:___min.___sec.
Page 247 Score:_____     Page 250 Score:_____ Time:___min.___sec.
Page 248 Score:_____ Time:___min.___sec.

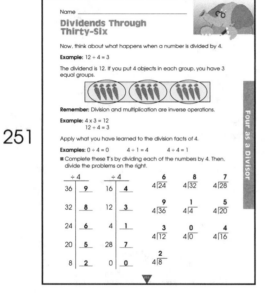

**251**

### Dividends Through Thirty-Six
*Four as a Divisor*

Now, think about what happens when a number is divided by 4.

**Example:** 12 ÷ 4 = 3

The dividend is 12. If you put 4 objects in each group, you have 3 equal groups.

**Remember:** Division and multiplication are inverse operations.

**Example:** 4 x 3 = 12
          12 ÷ 4 = 3

Apply what you have learned to the division facts of 4.

**Examples:** 0 ÷ 4 = 0    4 ÷ 1 = 4    4 ÷ 4 = 1

■ Complete these T's by dividing each of the numbers by 4. Then, divide the problems on the right.

| ÷ 4 | | ÷ 4 | |
|---|---|---|---|
| 36 | **9** | 16 | **4** |
| 32 | **8** | 12 | **3** |
| 24 | **6** | 4 | **1** |
| 20 | **5** | 28 | **7** |
| 8 | **2** | 0 | **0** |

**6** 4)24    **8** 4)32    **7** 4)28
**9** 4)36    **1** 4)4     **5** 4)20
**3** 4)12    **0** 4)0     **4** 4)16
**2** 4)8

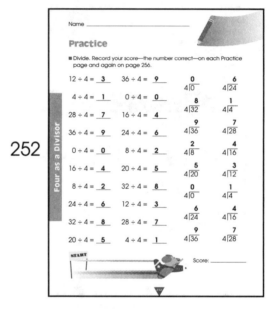

**252**

### Practice
*Four as a Divisor*

■ Divide. Record your score—the number correct—on each Practice page and again on page 256.

12 ÷ 4 = **3**    36 ÷ 4 = **9**    **0** 4)0     **6** 4)24
4 ÷ 4 = **1**     0 ÷ 4 = **0**     **8** 4)32    **1** 4)4
28 ÷ 4 = **7**    16 ÷ 4 = **4**    **9** 4)36    **7** 4)28
36 ÷ 4 = **9**    24 ÷ 4 = **6**    **2** 4)8     **4** 4)16
0 ÷ 4 = **0**     8 ÷ 4 = **2**     **5** 4)20    **3** 4)12
16 ÷ 4 = **4**    20 ÷ 4 = **5**    **0** 4)0     **1** 4)4
8 ÷ 4 = **2**     32 ÷ 4 = **8**    **6** 4)24    **4** 4)16
24 ÷ 4 = **6**    12 ÷ 4 = **3**    **9** 4)36    **7** 4)28
32 ÷ 4 = **8**    28 ÷ 4 = **7**
20 ÷ 4 = **5**    4 ÷ 4 = **1**

START    Score: _____

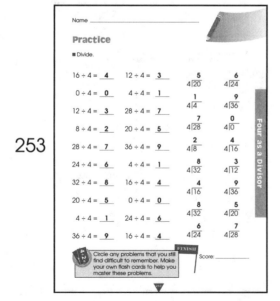

**253**

### Practice
*Four as a Divisor*

■ Divide.

16 ÷ 4 = **4**    12 ÷ 4 = **3**    **5** 4)20    **6** 4)24
0 ÷ 4 = **0**     4 ÷ 4 = **1**     **1** 4)4     **9** 4)36
12 ÷ 4 = **3**    28 ÷ 4 = **7**    **7** 4)28    **0** 4)0
8 ÷ 4 = **2**     20 ÷ 4 = **5**    **2** 4)8     **4** 4)16
28 ÷ 4 = **7**    36 ÷ 4 = **9**    **8** 4)32    **3** 4)12
24 ÷ 4 = **6**    4 ÷ 4 = **1**     **4** 4)16    **9** 4)36
32 ÷ 4 = **8**    16 ÷ 4 = **4**    **4** 4)16    **9** 4)36
20 ÷ 4 = **5**    0 ÷ 4 = **0**     **8** 4)32    **5** 4)20
4 ÷ 4 = **1**     24 ÷ 4 = **6**    **6** 4)24    **7** 4)28
36 ÷ 4 = **9**    16 ÷ 4 = **4**

Circle any problems that you still find difficult to remember. Make your own flash cards to help you master these problems.    Score: _____

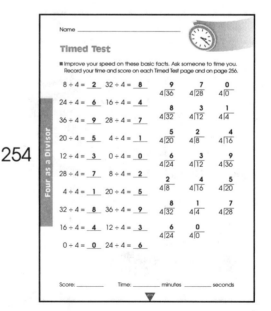

**254**

### Timed Test
*Four as a Divisor*

■ Improve your speed on these basic facts. Ask someone to time you. Record your time and score on each Timed Test page and on page 256.

8 ÷ 4 = **2**     32 ÷ 4 = **8**    **9** 4)36    **7** 4)28    **0** 4)0
24 ÷ 4 = **6**    16 ÷ 4 = **4**    **8** 4)32    **3** 4)12    **1** 4)4
36 ÷ 4 = **9**    28 ÷ 4 = **7**    **5** 4)20    **2** 4)8     **4** 4)16
20 ÷ 4 = **5**    4 ÷ 4 = **1**     **6** 4)24    **3** 4)12    **9** 4)36
12 ÷ 4 = **3**    0 ÷ 4 = **0**     **2** 4)8     **4** 4)16    **5** 4)20
28 ÷ 4 = **7**    8 ÷ 4 = **2**     **8** 4)32    **1** 4)4     **7** 4)28
4 ÷ 4 = **1**     20 ÷ 4 = **5**    **6** 4)24    **0** 4)0
32 ÷ 4 = **8**    36 ÷ 4 = **9**
16 ÷ 4 = **4**    12 ÷ 4 = **3**
0 ÷ 4 = **0**     24 ÷ 4 = **6**

Score: _____    Time: _____ minutes _____ seconds

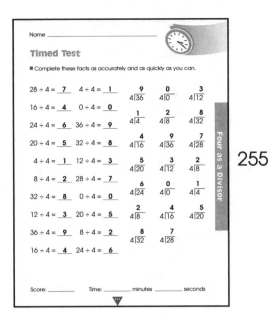

## Timed Test

■ Complete these facts as accurately and as quickly as you can.

| | | 9/4√36 | 0/4√0 | 3/4√12 |
28 ÷ 4 = **7**    4 ÷ 4 = **1**

16 ÷ 4 = **4**    0 ÷ 4 = **0**    1/4√4    2/4√8    8/4√32

24 ÷ 4 = **6**    36 ÷ 4 = **9**

20 ÷ 4 = **5**    32 ÷ 4 = **8**    4/4√16    9/4√36    7/4√28

4 ÷ 4 = **1**    12 ÷ 4 = **3**    5/4√20    3/4√12    2/4√8

8 ÷ 4 = **2**    28 ÷ 4 = **7**

32 ÷ 4 = **8**    0 ÷ 4 = **0**    6/4√24    0/4√0    1/4√4

12 ÷ 4 = **3**    20 ÷ 4 = **5**    2/4√8    4/4√16    5/4√20

36 ÷ 4 = **9**    8 ÷ 4 = **2**    8/4√32    7/4√28

16 ÷ 4 = **4**    24 ÷ 4 = **6**

Score: _____    Time: _____ minutes _____ seconds

**Four as a Divisor**

255

---

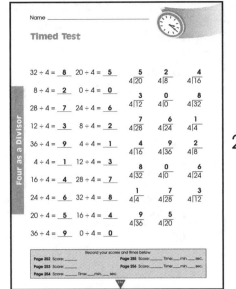

## Timed Test

32 ÷ 4 = **8**    20 ÷ 4 = **5**    5/4√20    2/4√8    4/4√16

8 ÷ 4 = **2**    0 ÷ 4 = **0**    3/4√12    0/4√0    8/4√32

28 ÷ 4 = **7**    24 ÷ 4 = **6**    7/4√28    6/4√24    1/4√4

12 ÷ 4 = **3**    8 ÷ 4 = **2**

36 ÷ 4 = **9**    4 ÷ 4 = **1**    4/4√16    9/4√36    2/4√8

4 ÷ 4 = **1**    12 ÷ 4 = **3**    8/4√32    0/4√0    6/4√24

16 ÷ 4 = **4**    28 ÷ 4 = **7**

24 ÷ 4 = **6**    32 ÷ 4 = **8**    1/4√4    7/4√28    3/4√12

20 ÷ 4 = **5**    16 ÷ 4 = **4**    9/4√36    5/4√20

36 ÷ 4 = **9**    0 ÷ 4 = **0**

**Four as a Divisor**

Record your scores and times below.

Page 252 Score: _____    Page 255 Score: _____ Time: ___ min. ___ sec.
Page 253 Score: _____    Page 256 Score: _____ Time: ___ min. ___ sec.
Page 254 Score: _____ Time: ___ min. ___ sec.

256

---

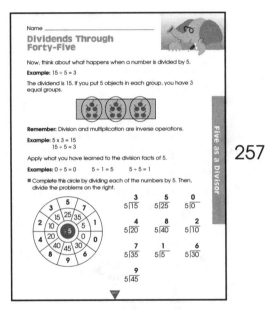

## Dividends Through Forty-Five

Now, think about what happens when a number is divided by 5.

**Example:** 15 ÷ 5 = 3

The dividend is 15. If you put 5 objects in each group, you have 3 equal groups.

**Remember:** Division and multiplication are inverse operations.

**Example:** 5 x 3 = 15
15 ÷ 5 = 3

Apply what you have learned to the division facts of 5.

**Examples:** 0 ÷ 5 = 0    5 ÷ 1 = 5    5 ÷ 5 = 1

■ Complete this circle by dividing each of the numbers by 5. Then, divide the problems on the right.

(circle center: ÷5; outer ring: 3, 5, 25, 35, 1, 0, 0, 30, 45, 40, 20, 10, 2; with answers 15, 25, 0, 20, 40, 10, 35, 5, 30, 45 ...)

3/5√15    5/5√25    0/5√0

4/5√20    8/5√40    2/5√10

7/5√35    1/5√5    6/5√30

9/5√45

**Five as a Divisor**

257

---

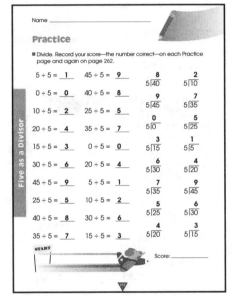

## Practice

■ Divide. Record your score—the number correct—on each Practice page and again on page 262.

5 ÷ 5 = **1**    45 ÷ 5 = **9**    8/5√40    2/5√10

0 ÷ 5 = **0**    40 ÷ 5 = **8**    9/5√45    7/5√35

10 ÷ 5 = **2**    25 ÷ 5 = **5**    0/5√0    5/5√25

20 ÷ 5 = **4**    35 ÷ 5 = **7**

15 ÷ 5 = **3**    0 ÷ 5 = **0**    3/5√15    1/5√5

30 ÷ 5 = **6**    20 ÷ 5 = **4**    6/5√30    4/5√20

45 ÷ 5 = **9**    5 ÷ 5 = **1**    7/5√35    9/5√45

25 ÷ 5 = **5**    10 ÷ 5 = **2**    5/5√25    6/5√30

40 ÷ 5 = **8**    30 ÷ 5 = **6**

35 ÷ 5 = **7**    15 ÷ 5 = **3**    4/5√20    3/5√15

START    Score: _____

**Five as a Divisor**

258

---

## Practice

■ Divide.

10 ÷ 5 = **2**    5 ÷ 5 = **1**    3/5√15    6/5√30

35 ÷ 5 = **7**    45 ÷ 5 = **9**    1/5√5    2/5√10

15 ÷ 5 = **3**    20 ÷ 5 = **4**    9/5√45    5/5√25

30 ÷ 5 = **6**    40 ÷ 5 = **8**    7/5√35    0/5√0

5 ÷ 5 = **1**    0 ÷ 5 = **0**

25 ÷ 5 = **5**    15 ÷ 5 = **3**    8/5√40    4/5√20

45 ÷ 5 = **9**    35 ÷ 5 = **7**    3/5√15    2/5√10

20 ÷ 5 = **4**    10 ÷ 5 = **2**    4/5√20    6/5√30

40 ÷ 5 = **8**    30 ÷ 5 = **6**

0 ÷ 5 = **0**    25 ÷ 5 = **5**    9/5√45    8/5√40

FINISH    Circle any problems that you still find difficult to remember. Make your own flash cards to help you master these problems.    Score: _____

**Five as a Divisor**

259

---

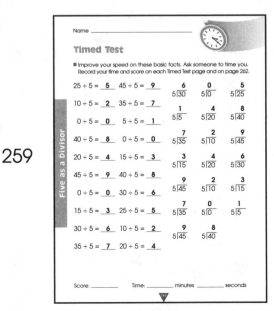

## Timed Test

■ Improve your speed on these basic facts. Ask someone to time you. Record your time and score on each Timed Test page and on page 262.

25 ÷ 5 = **5**    45 ÷ 5 = **9**    6/5√30    0/5√0    5/5√25

10 ÷ 5 = **2**    35 ÷ 5 = **7**    1/5√5    4/5√20    8/5√40

0 ÷ 5 = **0**    5 ÷ 5 = **1**

40 ÷ 5 = **8**    0 ÷ 5 = **0**    7/5√35    2/5√10    9/5√45

20 ÷ 5 = **4**    15 ÷ 5 = **3**    3/5√15    4/5√20    6/5√30

45 ÷ 5 = **9**    40 ÷ 5 = **8**

0 ÷ 5 = **0**    30 ÷ 5 = **6**    9/5√45    2/5√10    3/5√15

15 ÷ 5 = **3**    25 ÷ 5 = **5**    7/5√35    0/5√0    1/5√5

30 ÷ 5 = **6**    10 ÷ 5 = **2**    9/5√45    8/5√40

35 ÷ 5 = **7**    20 ÷ 5 = **4**

Score: _____    Time: _____ minutes _____ seconds

**Five as a Divisor**

260

---

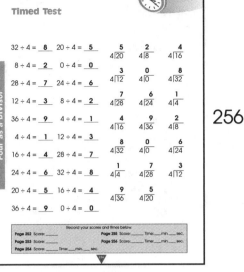

**Timed Test Answer Key**

## 261

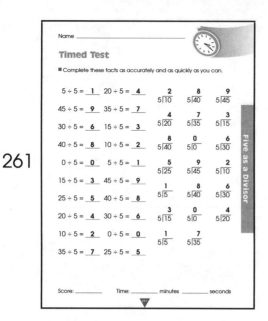

Name _____

### Timed Test

■ Complete these facts as accurately and as quickly as you can.

| | | |
|---|---|---|
| 5 ÷ 5 = **1** | 20 ÷ 5 = **4** | |
| | | 2 / 5)10   8 / 5)40   9 / 5)45 |
| 45 ÷ 5 = **9** | 35 ÷ 5 = **7** | |
| | | 4 / 5)20   7 / 5)35   3 / 5)15 |
| 30 ÷ 5 = **6** | 15 ÷ 5 = **3** | |
| | | 8 / 5)40   0 / 5)0   6 / 5)30 |
| 40 ÷ 5 = **8** | 10 ÷ 5 = **2** | |
| | | 5 / 5)25   9 / 5)45   2 / 5)10 |
| 0 ÷ 5 = **0** | 5 ÷ 5 = **1** | |
| | | 1 / 5)5   8 / 5)40   6 / 5)30 |
| 15 ÷ 5 = **3** | 45 ÷ 5 = **9** | |
| | | 3 / 5)15   0 / 5)0   4 / 5)20 |
| 25 ÷ 5 = **5** | 40 ÷ 5 = **8** | |
| | | 1 / 5)5   7 / 5)35 |
| 20 ÷ 5 = **4** | 30 ÷ 5 = **6** | |
| 10 ÷ 5 = **2** | 0 ÷ 5 = **0** | |
| 35 ÷ 5 = **7** | 25 ÷ 5 = **5** | |

*Five as a Divisor*

Score: _____    Time: _____ minutes _____ seconds

---

## 262

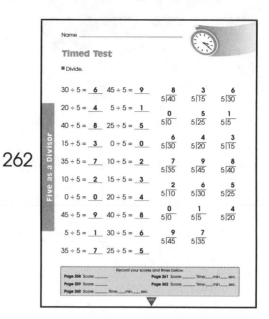

Name _____

### Timed Test

■ Divide.

| | | |
|---|---|---|
| 30 ÷ 5 = **6** | 45 ÷ 5 = **9** | 8 / 5)40   3 / 5)15   6 / 5)30 |
| 20 ÷ 5 = **4** | 5 ÷ 5 = **1** | 0 / 5)0   5 / 5)25   1 / 5)5 |
| 40 ÷ 5 = **8** | 25 ÷ 5 = **5** | 6 / 5)30   4 / 5)20   3 / 5)15 |
| 15 ÷ 5 = **3** | 0 ÷ 5 = **0** | 7 / 5)35   9 / 5)45   8 / 5)40 |
| 35 ÷ 5 = **7** | 10 ÷ 5 = **2** | 6 / 5)30   2 / 5)10   5 / 5)25 |
| 10 ÷ 5 = **2** | 15 ÷ 5 = **3** | 0 / 5)0   1 / 5)5   4 / 5)20 |
| 0 ÷ 5 = **0** | 20 ÷ 5 = **4** | 9 / 5)45   7 / 5)35 |
| 45 ÷ 5 = **9** | 40 ÷ 5 = **8** | |
| 5 ÷ 5 = **1** | 30 ÷ 5 = **6** | |
| 35 ÷ 5 = **7** | 25 ÷ 5 = **5** | |

*Five as a Divisor*

Record your scores and times below.

| | | |
|---|---|---|
| **Page 258** Score: _____ | | **Page 261** Score: _____ Time: ____ min. ____ sec. |
| **Page 259** Score: _____ | | **Page 262** Score: _____ Time: ____ min. ____ sec. |
| **Page 260** Score: _____ Time: ____ min. ____ sec. | | |

---

## 263

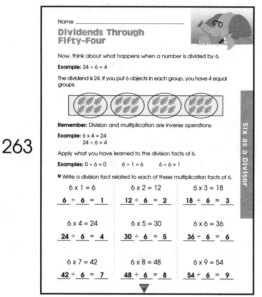

Name _____

### Dividends Through Fifty-Four

Now, think about what happens when a number is divided by 6.

**Example:** 24 ÷ 6 = 4

The dividend is 24. If you put 6 objects in each group, you have 4 equal groups.

**Remember:** Division and multiplication are inverse operations.

**Example:** 6 x 4 = 24
          24 ÷ 6 = 4

Apply what you have learned to the division facts of 6.

**Examples:** 0 ÷ 6 = 0    6 ÷ 1 = 6    6 ÷ 6 = 1

■ Write a division fact related to each of these multiplication facts of 6.

| 6 x 1 = 6 | 6 x 2 = 12 | 6 x 3 = 18 |
|---|---|---|
| **6 ÷ 6 = 1** | **12 ÷ 6 = 2** | **18 ÷ 6 = 3** |
| 6 x 4 = 24 | 6 x 5 = 30 | 6 x 6 = 36 |
| **24 ÷ 6 = 4** | **30 ÷ 6 = 5** | **36 ÷ 6 = 6** |
| 6 x 7 = 42 | 6 x 8 = 48 | 6 x 9 = 54 |
| **42 ÷ 6 = 7** | **48 ÷ 6 = 8** | **54 ÷ 6 = 9** |

*Six as a Divisor*

---

## 264

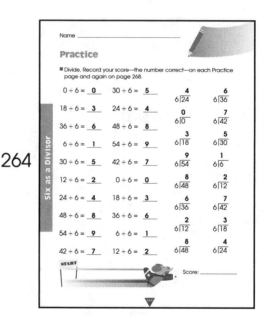

Name _____

### Practice

■ Divide. Record your score—the number correct—on each Practice page and again on page 268.

| | | |
|---|---|---|
| 0 ÷ 6 = **0** | 30 ÷ 6 = **5** | 4 / 6)24   6 / 6)36 |
| 18 ÷ 6 = **3** | 24 ÷ 6 = **4** | 0 / 6)0   7 / 6)42 |
| 36 ÷ 6 = **6** | 48 ÷ 6 = **8** | 3 / 6)18   5 / 6)30 |
| 6 ÷ 6 = **1** | 54 ÷ 6 = **9** | 9 / 6)54   1 / 6)6 |
| 30 ÷ 6 = **5** | 42 ÷ 6 = **7** | 8 / 6)48   2 / 6)12 |
| 12 ÷ 6 = **2** | 0 ÷ 6 = **0** | 6 / 6)36   7 / 6)42 |
| 24 ÷ 6 = **4** | 18 ÷ 6 = **3** | 2 / 6)12   3 / 6)18 |
| 48 ÷ 6 = **8** | 36 ÷ 6 = **6** | 8 / 6)48   4 / 6)24 |
| 54 ÷ 6 = **9** | 6 ÷ 6 = **1** | |
| 42 ÷ 6 = **7** | 12 ÷ 6 = **2** | |

*Six as a Divisor*

START    Score: _____

---

## 265

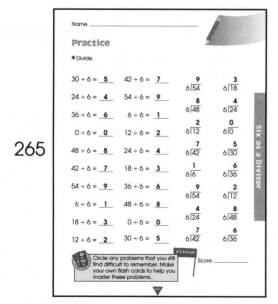

Name _____

### Practice

■ Divide.

| | | |
|---|---|---|
| 30 ÷ 6 = **5** | 42 ÷ 6 = **7** | 9 / 6)54   3 / 6)18 |
| 24 ÷ 6 = **4** | 54 ÷ 6 = **9** | 8 / 6)48   4 / 6)24 |
| 36 ÷ 6 = **6** | 6 ÷ 6 = **1** | 2 / 6)12   0 / 6)0 |
| 0 ÷ 6 = **0** | 12 ÷ 6 = **2** | 7 / 6)42   5 / 6)30 |
| 48 ÷ 6 = **8** | 24 ÷ 6 = **4** | 1 / 6)6   6 / 6)36 |
| 42 ÷ 6 = **7** | 18 ÷ 6 = **3** | 9 / 6)54   2 / 6)12 |
| 54 ÷ 6 = **9** | 36 ÷ 6 = **6** | 4 / 6)24   8 / 6)48 |
| 6 ÷ 6 = **1** | 48 ÷ 6 = **8** | 7 / 6)42   6 / 6)36 |
| 18 ÷ 6 = **3** | 0 ÷ 6 = **0** | |
| 12 ÷ 6 = **2** | 30 ÷ 6 = **5** | |

*Six as a Divisor*

FINISH

Circle any problems that you still find difficult to remember. Make your own flash cards to help you master these problems.

Score: _____

---

## 266

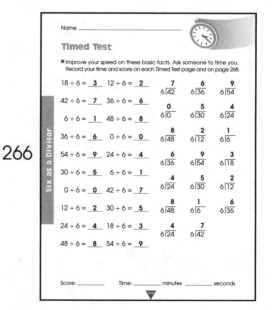

Name _____

### Timed Test

■ Improve your speed on these basic facts. Ask someone to time you. Record your time and score on each Timed Test page and on page 268.

| | | |
|---|---|---|
| 18 ÷ 6 = **3** | 12 ÷ 6 = **2** | 7 / 6)42   6 / 6)36   9 / 6)54 |
| 42 ÷ 6 = **7** | 36 ÷ 6 = **6** | 0 / 6)0   5 / 6)30   4 / 6)24 |
| 6 ÷ 6 = **1** | 48 ÷ 6 = **8** | 8 / 6)48   2 / 6)12   1 / 6)6 |
| 36 ÷ 6 = **6** | 0 ÷ 6 = **0** | 6 / 6)36   9 / 6)54   3 / 6)18 |
| 54 ÷ 6 = **9** | 24 ÷ 6 = **4** | 4 / 6)24   5 / 6)30   2 / 6)12 |
| 30 ÷ 6 = **5** | 6 ÷ 6 = **1** | 8 / 6)48   1 / 6)6   6 / 6)36 |
| 0 ÷ 6 = **0** | 42 ÷ 6 = **7** | 4 / 6)24   7 / 6)42 |
| 12 ÷ 6 = **2** | 30 ÷ 6 = **5** | |
| 24 ÷ 6 = **4** | 18 ÷ 6 = **3** | |
| 48 ÷ 6 = **8** | 54 ÷ 6 = **9** | |

*Six as a Divisor*

Score: _____    Time: _____ minutes _____ seconds

---

**Page 267** — Six as a Divisor

Name _____

## Timed Test

■ Complete these facts as accurately and as quickly as you can.

$6 \div 6 = \underline{1}$   $24 \div 6 = \underline{4}$   $6)\overline{48} = 8$   $6)\overline{42} = 7$   $6)\overline{54} = 9$

$30 \div 6 = \underline{5}$   $48 \div 6 = \underline{8}$   $6)\overline{30} = 5$   $6)\overline{0} = 0$   $6)\overline{18} = 3$

$54 \div 6 = \underline{9}$   $0 \div 6 = \underline{0}$   $6)\overline{6} = 1$   $6)\overline{48} = 8$   $6)\overline{24} = 4$

$42 \div 6 = \underline{7}$   $36 \div 6 = \underline{6}$   $6)\overline{12} = 2$   $6)\overline{54} = 9$   $6)\overline{30} = 5$

$12 \div 6 = \underline{2}$   $18 \div 6 = \underline{3}$   $6)\overline{36} = 6$   $6)\overline{6} = 1$   $6)\overline{18} = 3$

$0 \div 6 = \underline{0}$   $30 \div 6 = \underline{5}$

$36 \div 6 = \underline{6}$   $42 \div 6 = \underline{7}$   $6)\overline{12} = 2$   $6)\overline{24} = 4$   $6)\overline{36} = 6$

$18 \div 6 = \underline{3}$   $54 \div 6 = \underline{9}$   $6)\overline{42} = 7$   $6)\overline{0} = 0$

$24 \div 6 = \underline{4}$   $6 \div 6 = \underline{1}$

$48 \div 6 = \underline{8}$   $12 \div 6 = \underline{2}$

Score: _____   Time: _____ minutes _____ seconds

---

**Page 268** — Six as a Divisor

Name _____

## Timed Test

$24 \div 6 = \underline{4}$   $12 \div 6 = \underline{2}$   $6)\overline{36} = 6$   $6)\overline{54} = 9$   $6)\overline{18} = 3$

$48 \div 6 = \underline{8}$   $6 \div 6 = \underline{1}$   $6)\overline{0} = 0$   $6)\overline{42} = 7$   $6)\overline{6} = 1$

$18 \div 6 = \underline{3}$   $36 \div 6 = \underline{6}$   $6)\overline{24} = 4$   $6)\overline{36} = 6$   $6)\overline{12} = 2$

$54 \div 6 = \underline{9}$   $30 \div 6 = \underline{5}$   $6)\overline{30} = 5$   $6)\overline{48} = 8$   $6)\overline{54} = 9$

$30 \div 6 = \underline{5}$   $48 \div 6 = \underline{8}$

$42 \div 6 = \underline{7}$   $0 \div 6 = \underline{0}$   $6)\overline{42} = 7$   $6)\overline{6} = 1$   $6)\overline{24} = 4$

$6 \div 6 = \underline{1}$   $18 \div 6 = \underline{3}$   $6)\overline{12} = 2$   $6)\overline{18} = 3$   $6)\overline{48} = 8$

$0 \div 6 = \underline{0}$   $24 \div 6 = \underline{4}$

$12 \div 6 = \underline{2}$   $42 \div 6 = \underline{7}$   $6)\overline{30} = 5$   $6)\overline{0} = 0$

$54 \div 6 = \underline{9}$   $36 \div 6 = \underline{6}$

| Record your scores and times below. | |
|---|---|
| **Page 264** Score: _____ | **Page 267** Score: _____ Time: ___min. ___sec. |
| **Page 265** Score: _____ | **Page 268** Score: _____ Time: ___min. ___sec. |
| **Page 266** Score: _____ Time: ___min. ___sec. | |

---

**Page 269** — Seven as a Divisor

Name _____

## Dividends Through Sixty-Three

Now, think about what happens when a number is divided by 7.

**Example:** $63 \div 7 = 9$

The dividend is 63. If you put 7 objects in each group, you have 9 equal groups.

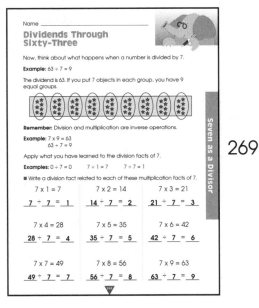

**Remember:** Division and multiplication are inverse operations.

**Example:** $7 \times 9 = 63$
$63 \div 7 = 9$

Apply what you have learned to the division facts of 7.

**Examples:** $0 \div 7 = 0$   $7 \div 1 = 7$   $7 \div 7 = 1$

■ Write a division fact related to each of these multiplication facts of 7.

$7 \times 1 = 7$   $7 \times 2 = 14$   $7 \times 3 = 21$
$\underline{7} \div \underline{7} = \underline{1}$   $\underline{14} \div \underline{7} = \underline{2}$   $\underline{21} \div \underline{7} = \underline{3}$

$7 \times 4 = 28$   $7 \times 5 = 35$   $7 \times 6 = 42$
$\underline{28} \div \underline{7} = \underline{4}$   $\underline{35} \div \underline{7} = \underline{5}$   $\underline{42} \div \underline{7} = \underline{6}$

$7 \times 7 = 49$   $7 \times 8 = 56$   $7 \times 9 = 63$
$\underline{49} \div \underline{7} = \underline{7}$   $\underline{56} \div \underline{7} = \underline{8}$   $\underline{63} \div \underline{7} = \underline{9}$

---

**Page 270** — Seven as a Divisor

Name _____

## Practice

■ Divide. Record your score—the number correct—on each Practice page and again on page 276.

$7 \div 7 = \underline{1}$   $56 \div 7 = \underline{8}$   $7)\overline{14} = 2$   $7)\overline{63} = 9$

$35 \div 7 = \underline{5}$   $49 \div 7 = \underline{7}$   $7)\overline{7} = 1$   $7)\overline{42} = 6$

$0 \div 7 = \underline{0}$   $63 \div 7 = \underline{9}$   $7)\overline{0} = 0$   $7)\overline{35} = 5$

$28 \div 7 = \underline{4}$   $42 \div 7 = \underline{6}$   $7)\overline{56} = 8$   $7)\overline{28} = 4$

$56 \div 7 = \underline{8}$   $49 \div 7 = \underline{7}$   $7)\overline{49} = 7$   $7)\overline{21} = 3$

$14 \div 7 = \underline{2}$   $0 \div 7 = \underline{0}$   $7)\overline{63} = 9$   $7)\overline{7} = 1$

$49 \div 7 = \underline{7}$   $35 \div 7 = \underline{5}$   $7)\overline{35} = 5$   $7)\overline{14} = 2$

$21 \div 7 = \underline{3}$   $7 \div 7 = \underline{1}$

$63 \div 7 = \underline{9}$   $14 \div 7 = \underline{2}$   $7)\overline{21} = 3$   $7)\overline{42} = 6$

$42 \div 7 = \underline{6}$   $28 \div 7 = \underline{4}$

**START**

Score: _____

---

**Page 271** — Seven as a Divisor

Name _____

## Practice

■ Divide.

$14 \div 7 = \underline{2}$   $28 \div 7 = \underline{4}$   $7)\overline{21} = 3$   $7)\overline{49} = 7$

$56 \div 7 = \underline{8}$   $63 \div 7 = \underline{9}$   $7)\overline{14} = 2$   $7)\overline{0} = 0$

$35 \div 7 = \underline{5}$   $7 \div 7 = \underline{1}$   $7)\overline{56} = 8$   $7)\overline{28} = 4$

$0 \div 7 = \underline{0}$   $49 \div 7 = \underline{7}$   $7)\overline{63} = 9$   $7)\overline{35} = 5$

$42 \div 7 = \underline{6}$   $21 \div 7 = \underline{3}$   $7)\overline{42} = 6$   $7)\overline{7} = 1$

$28 \div 7 = \underline{4}$   $35 \div 7 = \underline{5}$   $7)\overline{49} = 7$   $7)\overline{63} = 9$

$63 \div 7 = \underline{9}$   $56 \div 7 = \underline{8}$   $7)\overline{56} = 8$   $7)\overline{21} = 3$

$7 \div 7 = \underline{1}$   $14 \div 7 = \underline{2}$   $7)\overline{14} = 2$   $7)\overline{28} = 4$

$49 \div 7 = \underline{7}$   $0 \div 7 = \underline{0}$

$21 \div 7 = \underline{3}$   $42 \div 7 = \underline{6}$

**FINISH**

Circle any problems that you still find difficult to remember. Make your own flash cards to help you master these problems.

Score: _____

---

**Page 272** — Seven as a Divisor

Name _____

## Timed Test

■ Improve your speed on these basic facts. Ask someone to time you. Record your time and score on each Timed Test page and on page 276.

$63 \div 7 = \underline{9}$   $14 \div 7 = \underline{2}$   $7)\overline{28} = 4$   $7)\overline{7} = 1$   $7)\overline{42} = 6$

$7 \div 7 = \underline{1}$   $35 \div 7 = \underline{5}$   $7)\overline{21} = 3$   $7)\overline{0} = 0$   $7)\overline{35} = 5$

$21 \div 7 = \underline{3}$   $42 \div 7 = \underline{6}$   $7)\overline{49} = 7$   $7)\overline{42} = 6$   $7)\overline{14} = 2$

$56 \div 7 = \underline{8}$   $49 \div 7 = \underline{7}$   $7)\overline{56} = 8$   $7)\overline{28} = 4$   $7)\overline{21} = 3$

$14 \div 7 = \underline{2}$   $63 \div 7 = \underline{9}$

$0 \div 7 = \underline{0}$   $21 \div 7 = \underline{3}$   $7)\overline{63} = 9$   $7)\overline{14} = 2$   $7)\overline{7} = 1$

$28 \div 7 = \underline{4}$   $7 \div 7 = \underline{1}$   $7)\overline{42} = 6$   $7)\overline{7} = 1$   $7)\overline{0} = 0$

$49 \div 7 = \underline{7}$   $56 \div 7 = \underline{8}$

$42 \div 7 = \underline{6}$   $0 \div 7 = \underline{0}$   $7)\overline{49} = 7$   $7)\overline{35} = 5$

$35 \div 7 = \underline{5}$   $28 \div 7 = \underline{4}$

Score: _____   Time: _____ minutes _____ seconds

## 273

Name _____

**Timed Test**

■ Complete these facts as accurately and as quickly as you can.

| | |
|---|---|
| 35 ÷ 7 = **5** | 28 ÷ 7 = **4** |
| 7 ÷ 7 = **1** | 49 ÷ 7 = **7** |
| 56 ÷ 7 = **8** | 21 ÷ 7 = **3** |
| 42 ÷ 7 = **6** | 14 ÷ 7 = **2** |
| 0 ÷ 7 = **0** | 7 ÷ 7 = **1** |
| 63 ÷ 7 = **9** | 35 ÷ 7 = **5** |
| 21 ÷ 7 = **3** | 42 ÷ 7 = **6** |
| 28 ÷ 7 = **4** | 63 ÷ 7 = **9** |
| 49 ÷ 7 = **7** | 0 ÷ 7 = **0** |
| 14 ÷ 7 = **2** | 56 ÷ 7 = **8** |

7)7 = **1**   7)42 = **6**   7)0 = **0**
7)49 = **7**   7)63 = **9**   7)35 = **5**
7)0 = **0**   7)14 = **2**   7)56 = **8**
7)21 = **3**   7)7 = **1**   7)63 = **9**
7)28 = **4**   7)56 = **8**   7)42 = **6**
7)14 = **2**   7)49 = **7**   7)21 = **3**
7)28 = **4**   7)35 = **5**

*Seven as a Divisor*

Score: _____   Time: _____ minutes _____ seconds

## 274

Name _____

**Timed Test**

| | |
|---|---|
| 28 ÷ 7 = **4** | 49 ÷ 7 = **7** |
| 7 ÷ 7 = **1** | 35 ÷ 7 = **5** |
| 42 ÷ 7 = **6** | 56 ÷ 7 = **8** |
| 21 ÷ 7 = **3** | 0 ÷ 7 = **0** |
| 14 ÷ 7 = **2** | 63 ÷ 7 = **9** |
| 35 ÷ 7 = **5** | 28 ÷ 7 = 4 |
| 0 ÷ 7 = **0** | 42 ÷ 7 = **6** |
| 49 ÷ 7 = **7** | 7 ÷ 7 = **1** |
| 63 ÷ 7 = **9** | 14 ÷ 7 = **2** |
| 21 ÷ 7 = **3** | 56 ÷ 7 = **8** |

7)7 = **1**   7)35 = **5**   7)28 = **4**
7)21 = **3**   7)56 = **8**   7)49 = **7**
7)42 = **6**   7)63 = **9**   7)14 = **2**
7)28 = **4**   7)49 = **7**   7)21 = **3**
7)0 = **0**   7)7 = **1**   7)35 = **5**
7)56 = **8**   7)49 = **7**   7)14 = **2**
7)63 = **9**   7)0 = **0**

*Seven as a Divisor*

Score: _____   Time: _____ minutes _____ seconds

## 275

Name _____

**Timed Test**

| | |
|---|---|
| 14 ÷ 7 = **2** | 42 ÷ 7 = **6** |
| 49 ÷ 7 = **7** | 63 ÷ 7 = **9** |
| 21 ÷ 7 = **3** | 35 ÷ 7 = **5** |
| 7 ÷ 7 = **1** | 0 ÷ 7 = **0** |
| 56 ÷ 7 = **8** | 14 ÷ 7 = **2** |
| 28 ÷ 7 = **4** | 35 ÷ 7 = **5** |
| 42 ÷ 7 = **6** | 49 ÷ 7 = **7** |
| 0 ÷ 7 = **0** | 56 ÷ 7 = **8** |
| 63 ÷ 7 = **9** | 28 ÷ 7 = **4** |
| 21 ÷ 7 = **3** | 7 ÷ 7 = **1** |

7)35 = **5**   7)63 = **9**   7)21 = **3**
7)14 = **2**   7)42 = **6**   7)56 = **8**
7)0 = **0**   7)35 = **5**   7)7 = **1**
7)49 = **7**   7)28 = **4**   7)35 = **5**
7)21 = **3**   7)63 = **9**   7)14 = **2**
7)42 = **6**   7)56 = **8**   7)0 = **0**
7)49 = **7**   7)7 = **1**

*Seven as a Divisor*

Score: _____   Time: _____ minutes _____ seconds

## 276

Name _____

**Timed Test**

| | |
|---|---|
| 49 ÷ 7 = **7** | 42 ÷ 7 = **6** |
| 7 ÷ 7 = **1** | 28 ÷ 7 = **4** |
| 63 ÷ 7 = **9** | 0 ÷ 7 = **0** |
| 14 ÷ 7 = **2** | 56 ÷ 7 = **8** |
| 35 ÷ 7 = **5** | 21 ÷ 7 = **3** |
| 28 ÷ 7 = **4** | 7 ÷ 7 = **1** |
| 21 ÷ 7 = **3** | 35 ÷ 7 = **5** |
| 49 ÷ 7 = **7** | 14 ÷ 7 = **2** |
| 42 ÷ 7 = **6** | 63 ÷ 7 = **9** |
| 56 ÷ 7 = **8** | 0 ÷ 7 = **0** |

7)14 = **2**   7)0 = **0**   7)28 = **4**
7)7 = **1**   7)56 = **8**   7)42 = **6**
7)63 = **9**   7)21 = **3**   7)49 = **7**
7)0 = **0**   7)28 = **4**   7)63 = **9**
7)35 = **5**   7)42 = **6**   7)14 = **2**
7)56 = **8**   7)63 = **9**   7)7 = **1**
7)21 = **3**   7)35 = **5**

*Seven as a Divisor*

Record your scores and times below.

| | |
|---|---|
| Page 270 Score: _____ | Page 274 Score: _____ Time: ____ min. ____ sec. |
| Page 271 Score: _____ | Page 275 Score: _____ Time: ____ min. ____ sec. |
| Page 272 Score: _____ Time: ____ min. ____ sec. | Page 276 Score: _____ Time: ____ min. ____ sec. |
| Page 273 Score: _____ Time: ____ min. ____ sec. | |

## 277

Name _____

**Dividends Through Seventy-Two**

Now, think about what happens when a number is divided by 8.

**Example:** 48 ÷ 8 = 6

The dividend is 48. If you put 8 objects in each group, you will have 6 equal groups.

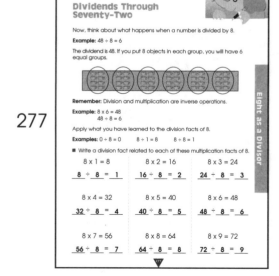

**Remember:** Division and multiplication are inverse operations.

**Example:** 8 x 6 = 48
48 ÷ 8 = 6

Apply what you have learned to the division facts of 8.

**Examples:** 0 ÷ 8 = 0   8 ÷ 1 = 8   8 ÷ 8 = 1

■ Write a division fact related to each of these multiplication facts of 8.

| 8 x 1 = 8 | 8 x 2 = 16 | 8 x 3 = 24 |
|---|---|---|
| **8 ÷ 8 = 1** | **16 ÷ 8 = 2** | **24 ÷ 8 = 3** |
| 8 x 4 = 32 | 8 x 5 = 40 | 8 x 6 = 48 |
| **32 ÷ 8 = 4** | **40 ÷ 8 = 5** | **48 ÷ 8 = 6** |
| 8 x 7 = 56 | 8 x 8 = 64 | 8 x 9 = 72 |
| **56 ÷ 8 = 7** | **64 ÷ 8 = 8** | **72 ÷ 8 = 9** |

*Eight as a Divisor*

## 278

Name _____

**Practice**

■ Divide. Record your score—the number correct—on each Practice page and again on page 284.

| | |
|---|---|
| 32 ÷ 8 = **4** | 56 ÷ 8 = **7** |
| 0 ÷ 8 = **0** | 8 ÷ 8 = **1** |
| 64 ÷ 8 = **8** | 40 ÷ 8 = **5** |
| 24 ÷ 8 = **3** | 16 ÷ 8 = **2** |
| 72 ÷ 8 = **9** | 48 ÷ 8 = **6** |
| 56 ÷ 8 = **7** | 24 ÷ 8 = **3** |
| 8 ÷ 8 = **1** | 64 ÷ 8 = **8** |
| 40 ÷ 8 = **5** | 0 ÷ 8 = **0** |
| 16 ÷ 8 = **2** | 32 ÷ 8 = **4** |
| 48 ÷ 8 = **6** | 72 ÷ 8 = **9** |

8)24 = **3**   8)72 = **9**
8)32 = **4**   8)64 = **8**
8)8 = **1**   8)56 = **7**
8)48 = **6**   8)16 = **2**
8)0 = **0**   8)40 = **5**
8)72 = **9**   8)32 = **4**
8)64 = **8**   8)24 = **3**
8)56 = **7**   8)48 = **6**

*Eight as a Divisor*

START

Score: _____

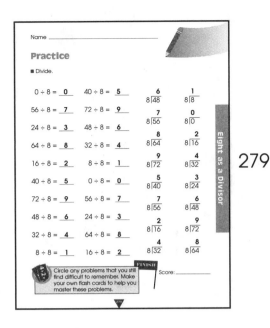

**Practice**

■ Divide.

| | | |
|---|---|---|
| 0 ÷ 8 = **0** | 40 ÷ 8 = **5** | 8)48 **6** |
| 56 ÷ 8 = **7** | 72 ÷ 8 = **9** | 8)56 **7** |
| 24 ÷ 8 = **3** | 48 ÷ 8 = **6** | 8)0 **0** |
| 64 ÷ 8 = **8** | 32 ÷ 8 = **4** | 8)64 **8** |
| 16 ÷ 8 = **2** | 8 ÷ 8 = **1** | 8)72 **9** |
| 40 ÷ 8 = **5** | 0 ÷ 8 = **0** | 8)40 **5** |
| 72 ÷ 8 = **9** | 56 ÷ 8 = **7** | 8)56 **7** |
| 48 ÷ 8 = **6** | 24 ÷ 8 = **3** | 8)16 **2** |
| 32 ÷ 8 = **4** | 64 ÷ 8 = **8** | 8)32 **4** |
| 8 ÷ 8 = **1** | 16 ÷ 8 = **2** | 8)64 **8** |

Second column of answer boxes: 8)8 **1**, 8)0 **0**, 8)16 **2**, 8)32 **4**, 8)24 **3**, 8)48 **6**, 8)72 **9**

Circle any problems that you still find difficult to remember. Make your own flash cards to help you master these problems.

Score: _____

*Eight as a Divisor*

**279**

---

**Timed Test**

■ Improve your speed on these basic facts. Ask someone to time you. Record your time and score on each Timed Test page and on page 284.

| | | | | |
|---|---|---|---|---|
| 16 ÷ 8 = **2** | 56 ÷ 8 = **7** | 8)24 **3** | 8)48 **6** | 8)40 **5** |
| 72 ÷ 8 = **9** | 40 ÷ 8 = **5** | 8)72 **9** | 8)16 **2** | 8)64 **8** |
| 24 ÷ 8 = **3** | 8 ÷ 8 = **1** | 8)8 **1** | 8)0 **0** | 8)56 **7** |
| 64 ÷ 8 = **8** | 32 ÷ 8 = **4** | 8)8 **1** | 8)0 **0** | 8)56 **7** |
| 0 ÷ 8 = **0** | 48 ÷ 8 = **6** | 8)40 **5** | 8)24 **3** | 8)32 **4** |
| 40 ÷ 8 = **5** | 16 ÷ 8 = **2** | 8)64 **8** | 8)72 **9** | 8)8 **1** |
| 48 ÷ 8 = **6** | 64 ÷ 8 = **8** | 8)16 **2** | 8)48 **6** | 8)32 **4** |
| 32 ÷ 8 = **4** | 24 ÷ 8 = **3** | 8)56 **7** | 8)64 **8** | |
| 8 ÷ 8 = **1** | 72 ÷ 8 = **9** | | | |
| 56 ÷ 8 = **7** | 0 ÷ 8 = **0** | | | |

Score: _____    Time: _____ minutes _____ seconds

*Eight as a Divisor*

**280**

---

**Timed Test**

■ Complete these facts as accurately and as quickly as you can.

| | | | | |
|---|---|---|---|---|
| 56 ÷ 8 = **7** | 72 ÷ 8 = **9** | 8)40 **5** | 8)8 **1** | 8)56 **7** |
| 32 ÷ 8 = **4** | 24 ÷ 8 = **3** | 8)32 **4** | 8)72 **9** | 8)0 **0** |
| 16 ÷ 8 = **2** | 0 ÷ 8 = **0** | 8)32 **4** | 8)72 **9** | 8)0 **0** |
| 40 ÷ 8 = **5** | 48 ÷ 8 = **6** | 8)48 **6** | 8)64 **8** | 8)24 **3** |
| 64 ÷ 8 = **8** | 32 ÷ 8 = **4** | 8)16 **2** | 8)32 **4** | 8)40 **5** |
| 72 ÷ 8 = **9** | 8 ÷ 8 = **1** | 8)24 **3** | 8)72 **9** | 8)48 **6** |
| 8 ÷ 8 = **1** | 40 ÷ 8 = **5** | 8)8 **1** | 8)32 **4** | 8)0 **0** |
| 24 ÷ 8 = **3** | 16 ÷ 8 = **2** | 8)64 **8** | 8)56 **7** | |
| 0 ÷ 8 = **0** | 56 ÷ 8 = **7** | | | |
| 48 ÷ 8 = **6** | 64 ÷ 8 = **8** | | | |

Score: _____    Time: _____ minutes _____ seconds

*Eight as a Divisor*

**281**

---

**Timed Test**

| | | | | |
|---|---|---|---|---|
| 32 ÷ 8 = **4** | 56 ÷ 8 = **7** | 8)8 **1** | 8)32 **4** | 8)64 **8** |
| 72 ÷ 8 = **9** | 16 ÷ 8 = **2** | 8)16 **2** | 8)0 **0** | 8)56 **7** |
| 8 ÷ 8 = **1** | 48 ÷ 8 = **6** | 8)16 **2** | 8)0 **0** | 8)56 **7** |
| 0 ÷ 8 = **0** | 40 ÷ 8 = **5** | 8)40 **5** | 8)24 **3** | 8)72 **9** |
| 64 ÷ 8 = **8** | 24 ÷ 8 = **3** | 8)48 **6** | 8)16 **2** | 8)8 **1** |
| 40 ÷ 8 = **5** | 8 ÷ 8 = **1** | 8)24 **3** | 8)32 **4** | 8)0 **0** |
| 56 ÷ 8 = **7** | 0 ÷ 8 = **0** | 8)24 **3** | 8)32 **4** | 8)0 **0** |
| 24 ÷ 8 = **3** | 64 ÷ 8 = **8** | 8)64 **8** | 8)56 **7** | 8)72 **9** |
| 16 ÷ 8 = **2** | 32 ÷ 8 = **4** | 8)40 **5** | 8)48 **6** | |
| 8 ÷ 8 = **1** | 48 ÷ 8 = **6** | | | |

Score: _____    Time: _____ minutes _____ seconds

*Eight as a Divisor*

**282**

---

**Timed Test**

| | | | | |
|---|---|---|---|---|
| 16 ÷ 8 = **2** | 24 ÷ 8 = **3** | 8)40 **5** | 8)56 **7** | 8)8 **1** |
| 40 ÷ 8 = **5** | 32 ÷ 8 = **4** | 8)72 **9** | 8)48 **6** | 8)16 **2** |
| 72 ÷ 8 = **9** | 0 ÷ 8 = **0** | 8)72 **9** | 8)48 **6** | 8)16 **2** |
| 56 ÷ 8 = **7** | 64 ÷ 8 = **8** | 8)32 **4** | 8)0 **0** | 8)24 **3** |
| 48 ÷ 8 = **6** | 24 ÷ 8 = **3** | 8)56 **7** | 8)16 **2** | 8)64 **8** |
| 8 ÷ 8 = **1** | 40 ÷ 8 = **5** | 8)8 **1** | 8)72 **9** | 8)40 **5** |
| 64 ÷ 8 = **8** | 72 ÷ 8 = **9** | 8)8 **1** | 8)72 **9** | 8)40 **5** |
| 32 ÷ 8 = **4** | 0 ÷ 8 = **0** | 8)32 **4** | 8)56 **7** | 8)24 **3** |
| 16 ÷ 8 = **2** | 8 ÷ 8 = **1** | 8)64 **8** | 8)8 **1** | |
| 56 ÷ 8 = **7** | 48 ÷ 8 = **6** | | | |

Score: _____    Time: _____ minutes _____ seconds

*Eight as a Divisor*

**283**

---

**Timed Test**

| | | | | |
|---|---|---|---|---|
| 8 ÷ 8 = **1** | 32 ÷ 8 = **4** | 8)48 **6** | 8)8 **1** | 8)64 **8** |
| 64 ÷ 8 = **8** | 0 ÷ 8 = **0** | 8)16 **2** | 8)0 **0** | 8)56 **7** |
| 48 ÷ 8 = **6** | 24 ÷ 8 = **3** | 8)16 **2** | 8)0 **0** | 8)56 **7** |
| 72 ÷ 8 = **9** | 56 ÷ 8 = **7** | 8)24 **3** | 8)40 **5** | 8)48 **6** |
| 16 ÷ 8 = **2** | 72 ÷ 8 = **9** | 8)56 **7** | 8)32 **4** | 8)72 **9** |
| 40 ÷ 8 = **5** | 48 ÷ 8 = **6** | 8)64 **8** | 8)0 **0** | 8)16 **2** |
| 56 ÷ 8 = **7** | 64 ÷ 8 = **8** | 8)64 **8** | 8)0 **0** | 8)16 **2** |
| 0 ÷ 8 = **0** | 8 ÷ 8 = **1** | 8)8 **1** | 8)24 **3** | 8)32 **4** |
| 32 ÷ 8 = **4** | 40 ÷ 8 = **5** | 8)40 **5** | 8)72 **9** | |
| 72 ÷ 8 = **9** | 16 ÷ 8 = **2** | | | |

Record your scores and times below.

| | |
|---|---|
| Page 278 Score: _____ | Page 282 Score: _____ Time: ____ min. ____ sec. |
| Page 279 Score: _____ | Page 283 Score: _____ Time: ____ min. ____ sec. |
| Page 280 Score: _____ Time: ____ min. ____ sec. | Page 284 Score: _____ Time: ____ min. ____ sec. |
| Page 281 Score: _____ Time: ____ min. ____ sec. | |

*Eight as a Divisor*

**284**

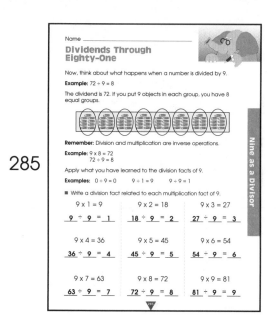

**285**

Name

### Dividends Through Eighty-One

Now, think about what happens when a number is divided by 9.

**Example:** $72 \div 9 = 8$

The dividend is 72. If you put 9 objects in each group, you have 8 equal groups.

**Remember:** Division and multiplication are inverse operations.

**Example:** $9 \times 8 = 72$
$72 \div 9 = 8$

Apply what you have learned to the division facts of 9.

**Examples:** $0 \div 9 = 0$    $9 \div 1 = 9$    $9 \div 9 = 1$

■ Write a division fact related to each multiplication fact of 9.

$9 \times 1 = 9$        $9 \times 2 = 18$        $9 \times 3 = 27$

$\underline{9} \div \underline{9} = \underline{1}$    $\underline{18} \div \underline{9} = \underline{2}$    $\underline{27} \div \underline{9} = \underline{3}$

$9 \times 4 = 36$        $9 \times 5 = 45$        $9 \times 6 = 54$

$\underline{36} \div \underline{9} = \underline{4}$    $\underline{45} \div \underline{9} = \underline{5}$    $\underline{54} \div \underline{9} = \underline{6}$

$9 \times 7 = 63$        $9 \times 8 = 72$        $9 \times 9 = 81$

$\underline{63} \div \underline{9} = \underline{7}$    $\underline{72} \div \underline{9} = \underline{8}$    $\underline{81} \div \underline{9} = \underline{9}$

*Nine as a Divisor*

---

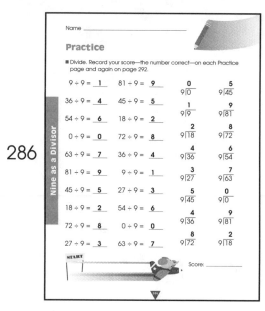

**286**

Name

### Practice

■ Divide. Record your score—the number correct—on each Practice page and again on page 292.

$9 \div 9 = \underline{1}$     $81 \div 9 = \underline{9}$

$36 \div 9 = \underline{4}$     $45 \div 9 = \underline{5}$

$54 \div 9 = \underline{6}$     $18 \div 9 = \underline{2}$

$0 \div 9 = \underline{0}$     $72 \div 9 = \underline{8}$

$63 \div 9 = \underline{7}$     $36 \div 9 = \underline{4}$

$81 \div 9 = \underline{9}$     $9 \div 9 = \underline{1}$

$45 \div 9 = \underline{5}$     $27 \div 9 = \underline{3}$

$18 \div 9 = \underline{2}$     $54 \div 9 = \underline{6}$

$72 \div 9 = \underline{8}$     $0 \div 9 = \underline{0}$

$27 \div 9 = \underline{3}$     $63 \div 9 = \underline{7}$

$9\overline{)0}^{\,0}$   $9\overline{)45}^{\,5}$

$9\overline{)9}^{\,1}$   $9\overline{)81}^{\,9}$

$9\overline{)18}^{\,2}$   $9\overline{)72}^{\,8}$

$9\overline{)36}^{\,4}$   $9\overline{)54}^{\,6}$

$9\overline{)27}^{\,3}$   $9\overline{)63}^{\,7}$

$9\overline{)45}^{\,5}$   $9\overline{)0}^{\,0}$

$9\overline{)36}^{\,4}$   $9\overline{)81}^{\,9}$

$9\overline{)72}^{\,8}$   $9\overline{)18}^{\,2}$

START

Score: _____

*Nine as a Divisor*

---

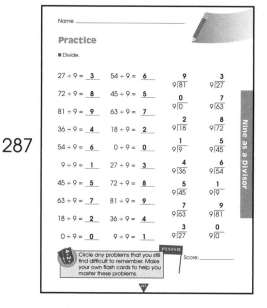

**287**

Name

### Practice

■ Divide.

$27 \div 9 = \underline{3}$     $54 \div 9 = \underline{6}$

$72 \div 9 = \underline{8}$     $45 \div 9 = \underline{5}$

$81 \div 9 = \underline{9}$     $63 \div 9 = \underline{7}$

$36 \div 9 = \underline{4}$     $18 \div 9 = \underline{2}$

$54 \div 9 = \underline{6}$     $0 \div 9 = \underline{0}$

$9 \div 9 = \underline{1}$     $27 \div 9 = \underline{3}$

$45 \div 9 = \underline{5}$     $72 \div 9 = \underline{8}$

$63 \div 9 = \underline{7}$     $81 \div 9 = \underline{9}$

$18 \div 9 = \underline{2}$     $36 \div 9 = \underline{4}$

$0 \div 9 = \underline{0}$     $9 \div 9 = \underline{1}$

$9\overline{)81}^{\,9}$   $9\overline{)27}^{\,3}$

$9\overline{)0}^{\,0}$   $9\overline{)63}^{\,7}$

$9\overline{)18}^{\,2}$   $9\overline{)72}^{\,8}$

$9\overline{)9}^{\,1}$   $9\overline{)45}^{\,5}$

$9\overline{)36}^{\,4}$   $9\overline{)54}^{\,6}$

$9\overline{)45}^{\,5}$   $9\overline{)9}^{\,1}$

$9\overline{)63}^{\,7}$   $9\overline{)81}^{\,9}$

$9\overline{)27}^{\,3}$   $9\overline{)0}^{\,0}$

Circle any problems that you still find difficult to remember. Make your own flash cards to help you master these problems.

FINISH

Score: _____

*Nine as a Divisor*

---

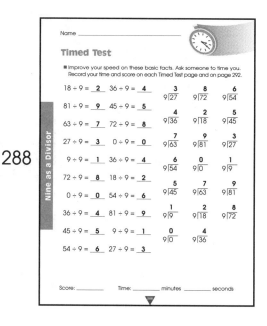

**288**

Name

### Timed Test

■ Improve your speed on these basic facts. Ask someone to time you. Record your time and score on each Timed Test page and on page 292.

$18 \div 9 = \underline{2}$     $36 \div 9 = \underline{4}$

$81 \div 9 = \underline{9}$     $45 \div 9 = \underline{5}$

$63 \div 9 = \underline{7}$     $72 \div 9 = \underline{8}$

$27 \div 9 = \underline{3}$     $0 \div 9 = \underline{0}$

$9 \div 9 = \underline{1}$     $36 \div 9 = \underline{4}$

$72 \div 9 = \underline{8}$     $18 \div 9 = \underline{2}$

$0 \div 9 = \underline{0}$     $54 \div 9 = \underline{6}$

$36 \div 9 = \underline{4}$     $81 \div 9 = \underline{9}$

$45 \div 9 = \underline{5}$     $9 \div 9 = \underline{1}$

$54 \div 9 = \underline{6}$     $27 \div 9 = \underline{3}$

$9\overline{)27}^{\,3}$   $9\overline{)72}^{\,8}$   $9\overline{)54}^{\,6}$

$9\overline{)36}^{\,4}$   $9\overline{)18}^{\,2}$   $9\overline{)45}^{\,5}$

$9\overline{)63}^{\,7}$   $9\overline{)81}^{\,9}$   $9\overline{)27}^{\,3}$

$9\overline{)54}^{\,6}$   $9\overline{)0}^{\,0}$   $9\overline{)9}^{\,1}$

$9\overline{)45}^{\,5}$   $9\overline{)63}^{\,7}$   $9\overline{)81}^{\,9}$

$9\overline{)9}^{\,1}$   $9\overline{)18}^{\,2}$   $9\overline{)72}^{\,8}$

$9\overline{)0}^{\,0}$   $9\overline{)36}^{\,4}$

Score: _____     Time: _____ minutes _____ seconds

*Nine as a Divisor*

---

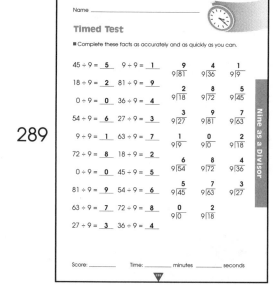

**289**

Name

### Timed Test

■ Complete these facts as accurately and as quickly as you can.

$45 \div 9 = \underline{5}$     $9 \div 9 = \underline{1}$

$18 \div 9 = \underline{2}$     $81 \div 9 = \underline{9}$

$0 \div 9 = \underline{0}$     $36 \div 9 = \underline{4}$

$54 \div 9 = \underline{6}$     $27 \div 9 = \underline{3}$

$9 \div 9 = \underline{1}$     $63 \div 9 = \underline{7}$

$72 \div 9 = \underline{8}$     $18 \div 9 = \underline{2}$

$0 \div 9 = \underline{0}$     $45 \div 9 = \underline{5}$

$81 \div 9 = \underline{9}$     $54 \div 9 = \underline{6}$

$63 \div 9 = \underline{7}$     $72 \div 9 = \underline{8}$

$27 \div 9 = \underline{3}$     $36 \div 9 = \underline{4}$

$9\overline{)81}^{\,9}$   $9\overline{)36}^{\,4}$   $9\overline{)9}^{\,1}$

$9\overline{)18}^{\,2}$   $9\overline{)72}^{\,8}$   $9\overline{)45}^{\,5}$

$9\overline{)27}^{\,3}$   $9\overline{)81}^{\,9}$   $9\overline{)63}^{\,7}$

$9\overline{)9}^{\,1}$   $9\overline{)0}^{\,0}$   $9\overline{)18}^{\,2}$

$9\overline{)54}^{\,6}$   $9\overline{)72}^{\,8}$   $9\overline{)36}^{\,4}$

$9\overline{)45}^{\,5}$   $9\overline{)63}^{\,7}$   $9\overline{)27}^{\,3}$

$9\overline{)0}^{\,0}$   $9\overline{)18}^{\,2}$

Score: _____     Time: _____ minutes _____ seconds

*Nine as a Divisor*

---

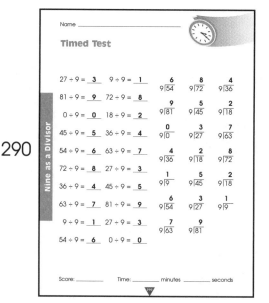

**290**

Name

### Timed Test

$27 \div 9 = \underline{3}$     $9 \div 9 = \underline{1}$

$81 \div 9 = \underline{9}$     $72 \div 9 = \underline{8}$

$0 \div 9 = \underline{0}$     $18 \div 9 = \underline{2}$

$45 \div 9 = \underline{5}$     $36 \div 9 = \underline{4}$

$54 \div 9 = \underline{6}$     $63 \div 9 = \underline{7}$

$72 \div 9 = \underline{8}$     $27 \div 9 = \underline{3}$

$36 \div 9 = \underline{4}$     $45 \div 9 = \underline{5}$

$63 \div 9 = \underline{7}$     $81 \div 9 = \underline{9}$

$9 \div 9 = \underline{1}$     $27 \div 9 = \underline{3}$

$54 \div 9 = \underline{6}$     $0 \div 9 = \underline{0}$

$9\overline{)54}^{\,6}$   $9\overline{)72}^{\,8}$   $9\overline{)36}^{\,4}$

$9\overline{)81}^{\,9}$   $9\overline{)45}^{\,5}$   $9\overline{)18}^{\,2}$

$9\overline{)0}^{\,0}$   $9\overline{)27}^{\,3}$   $9\overline{)63}^{\,7}$

$9\overline{)36}^{\,4}$   $9\overline{)18}^{\,2}$   $9\overline{)72}^{\,8}$

$9\overline{)9}^{\,1}$   $9\overline{)45}^{\,5}$   $9\overline{)18}^{\,2}$

$9\overline{)54}^{\,6}$   $9\overline{)27}^{\,3}$   $9\overline{)9}^{\,1}$

$9\overline{)63}^{\,7}$   $9\overline{)81}^{\,9}$

Score: _____     Time: _____ minutes _____ seconds

*Nine as a Divisor*

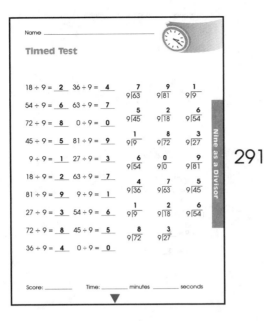

**Timed Test** — Nine as a Divisor — 291

Name _____

18 ÷ 9 = **2**   36 ÷ 9 = **4**
54 ÷ 9 = **6**   63 ÷ 9 = **7**
72 ÷ 9 = **8**   0 ÷ 9 = **0**
45 ÷ 9 = **5**   81 ÷ 9 = **9**
9 ÷ 9 = **1**   27 ÷ 9 = **3**
18 ÷ 9 = **2**   63 ÷ 9 = **7**
81 ÷ 9 = **9**   9 ÷ 9 = **1**
27 ÷ 9 = **3**   54 ÷ 9 = **6**
72 ÷ 9 = **8**   45 ÷ 9 = **5**
36 ÷ 9 = **4**   0 ÷ 9 = **0**

9)63 = **7**   9)81 = **9**   9)9 = **1**
9)45 = **5**   9)18 = **2**   9)54 = **6**
9)9 = **1**   9)72 = **8**   9)27 = **3**
9)54 = **6**   9)0 = **0**   9)81 = **9**
9)36 = **4**   9)63 = **7**   9)45 = **5**
9)9 = **1**   9)18 = **2**   9)54 = **6**
9)72 = **8**   9)27 = **3**

Score: _____   Time: _____ minutes _____ seconds

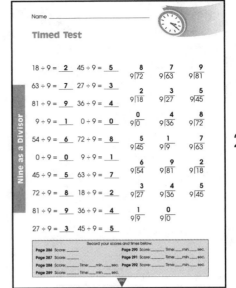

**Timed Test** — Nine as a Divisor — 292

Name _____

18 ÷ 9 = **2**   45 ÷ 9 = **5**
63 ÷ 9 = **7**   27 ÷ 9 = **3**
81 ÷ 9 = **9**   36 ÷ 9 = **4**
9 ÷ 9 = **1**   0 ÷ 9 = **0**
54 ÷ 9 = **6**   72 ÷ 9 = **8**
0 ÷ 9 = **0**   9 ÷ 9 = **1**
45 ÷ 9 = **5**   63 ÷ 9 = **7**
72 ÷ 9 = **8**   18 ÷ 9 = **2**
81 ÷ 9 = **9**   36 ÷ 9 = **4**
27 ÷ 9 = **3**   45 ÷ 9 = **5**

9)72 = **8**   9)63 = **7**   9)81 = **9**
9)18 = **2**   9)27 = **3**   9)45 = **5**
9)0 = **0**   9)36 = **4**   9)72 = **8**
9)45 = **5**   9)9 = **1**   9)63 = **7**
9)54 = **6**   9)81 = **9**   9)18 = **2**
9)27 = **3**   9)36 = **4**   9)45 = **5**
9)9 = **1**   9)0 = **0**

| |  |  | |  |  |
|---|---|---|---|---|---|
| Page 286 | Score: _____ | | Page 290 | Score: _____ | Time:___ min.___ sec. |
| Page 287 | Score: _____ | | Page 291 | Score: _____ | Time:___ min.___ sec. |
| Page 288 | Score: _____ | Time:___min.___sec. | Page 292 | Score: _____ | Time:___ min.___ sec. |
| Page 289 | Score: _____ | Time:___min.___sec. | | | |

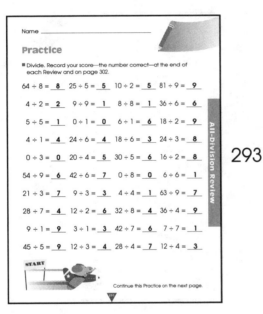

**Practice** — All-Division Review — 293

Name _____

■ Divide. Record your score—the number correct—at the end of each Review and on page 302.

64 ÷ 8 = **8**   25 ÷ 5 = **5**   10 ÷ 2 = **5**   81 ÷ 9 = **9**
4 ÷ 2 = **2**   9 ÷ 9 = **1**   8 ÷ 8 = **1**   36 ÷ 6 = **6**
5 ÷ 5 = **1**   0 ÷ 1 = **0**   6 ÷ 1 = **6**   18 ÷ 2 = **9**
4 ÷ 1 = **4**   24 ÷ 6 = **4**   18 ÷ 6 = **3**   24 ÷ 3 = **8**
0 ÷ 3 = **0**   20 ÷ 4 = **5**   30 ÷ 5 = **6**   16 ÷ 2 = **8**
54 ÷ 9 = **6**   42 ÷ 6 = **7**   0 ÷ 8 = **0**   6 ÷ 6 = **1**
21 ÷ 3 = **7**   9 ÷ 3 = **3**   4 ÷ 4 = **1**   63 ÷ 9 = **7**
28 ÷ 7 = **4**   12 ÷ 2 = **6**   32 ÷ 8 = **4**   36 ÷ 4 = **9**
9 ÷ 1 = **9**   3 ÷ 1 = **3**   42 ÷ 7 = **6**   7 ÷ 7 = **1**
45 ÷ 5 = **9**   12 ÷ 3 = **4**   28 ÷ 4 = **7**   12 ÷ 4 = **3**

Continue this Practice on the next page.

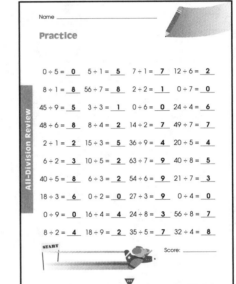

**Practice** — All-Division Review — 294

Name _____

0 ÷ 5 = **0**   5 ÷ 1 = **5**   7 ÷ 1 = **7**   12 ÷ 6 = **2**
8 ÷ 1 = **8**   56 ÷ 7 = **8**   2 ÷ 2 = **1**   0 ÷ 7 = **0**
45 ÷ 9 = **5**   3 ÷ 3 = **1**   0 ÷ 6 = **0**   24 ÷ 4 = **6**
48 ÷ 6 = **8**   8 ÷ 4 = **2**   14 ÷ 2 = **7**   49 ÷ 7 = **7**
2 ÷ 1 = **2**   15 ÷ 3 = **5**   36 ÷ 9 = **4**   20 ÷ 5 = **4**
6 ÷ 2 = **3**   10 ÷ 5 = **2**   63 ÷ 7 = **9**   40 ÷ 8 = **5**
40 ÷ 5 = **8**   6 ÷ 3 = **2**   54 ÷ 6 = **9**   21 ÷ 7 = **3**
18 ÷ 3 = **6**   0 ÷ 2 = **0**   27 ÷ 3 = **9**   0 ÷ 4 = **0**
0 ÷ 9 = **0**   16 ÷ 4 = **4**   24 ÷ 8 = **3**   56 ÷ 8 = **7**
8 ÷ 2 = **4**   18 ÷ 9 = **2**   35 ÷ 5 = **7**   32 ÷ 4 = **8**

Score: _____

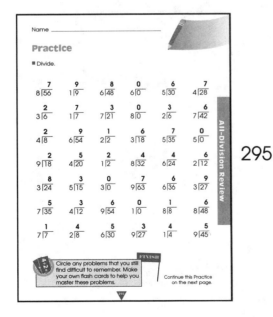

**Practice** — All-Division Review — 295

Name _____

■ Divide.

8)56 = **7**   1)9 = **9**   6)48 = **8**   6)0 = **0**   5)30 = **6**   4)28 = **7**
3)6 = **2**   1)7 = **7**   7)21 = **3**   8)0 = **0**   2)6 = **3**   7)42 = **6**
4)8 = **2**   6)54 = **9**   2)2 = **1**   3)18 = **6**   5)35 = **7**   5)0 = **0**
9)18 = **2**   4)20 = **5**   1)2 = **2**   8)32 = **4**   6)24 = **4**   2)12 = **6**
3)24 = **8**   5)15 = **3**   3)0 = **0**   9)63 = **7**   6)36 = **6**   3)27 = **9**
7)35 = **5**   4)12 = **3**   9)54 = **6**   1)0 = **0**   8)8 = **1**   8)48 = **6**
7)7 = **1**   2)8 = **4**   6)30 = **5**   9)27 = **3**   1)4 = **4**   9)45 = **5**

Circle any problems that you still find difficult to remember. Make your own flash cards to help you master these problems.

Continue this Practice on the next page.

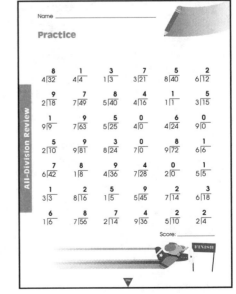

**Practice** — All-Division Review — 296

Name _____

4)32 = **8**   4)4 = **1**   1)3 = **3**   3)21 = **7**   8)40 = **5**   6)12 = **2**
2)18 = **9**   7)49 = **7**   5)40 = **8**   4)16 = **4**   1)1 = **1**   3)15 = **5**
9)9 = **1**   7)63 = **9**   5)25 = **5**   4)0 = **0**   4)24 = **6**   6)0 = **0**
2)10 = **5**   9)81 = **9**   8)24 = **3**   7)0 = **0**   9)72 = **8**   6)6 = **1**
6)42 = **7**   1)8 = **8**   4)36 = **9**   7)28 = **4**   2)0 = **0**   5)5 = **1**
3)3 = **1**   8)16 = **2**   1)5 = **5**   5)45 = **9**   7)14 = **2**   6)18 = **3**
1)6 = **6**   7)56 = **8**   2)14 = **7**   9)36 = **4**   5)10 = **2**   2)4 = **2**

Score: _____

## 297

Name _____

### Timed Test

■ Increase your speed on the basic facts of division. Record your time and score on each Timed Test page and on page 302.

| | | | |
|---|---|---|---|
| 0 ÷ 8 = **0** | 4 ÷ 4 = **1** | 0 ÷ 3 = **0** | 7 ÷ 7 = **1** |
| 21 ÷ 7 = **3** | 3 ÷ 1 = **3** | 32 ÷ 4 = **8** | 27 ÷ 9 = **3** |
| 18 ÷ 2 = **9** | 30 ÷ 5 = **6** | 63 ÷ 9 = **7** | 2 ÷ 2 = **1** |
| 35 ÷ 5 = **7** | 63 ÷ 7 = **9** | 72 ÷ 9 = **8** | 36 ÷ 9 = **4** |
| 5 ÷ 1 = **5** | 24 ÷ 3 = **8** | 0 ÷ 5 = **0** | 64 ÷ 8 = **8** |
| 24 ÷ 4 = **6** | 8 ÷ 8 = **1** | 3 ÷ 3 = **1** | 28 ÷ 7 = **4** |
| 9 ÷ 3 = **3** | 6 ÷ 6 = **1** | 45 ÷ 9 = **5** | 48 ÷ 6 = **8** |
| 54 ÷ 6 = **9** | 56 ÷ 8 = **7** | 12 ÷ 6 = **2** | 8 ÷ 4 = **2** |
| 10 ÷ 2 = **5** | 36 ÷ 6 = **6** | 0 ÷ 1 = **0** | 2 ÷ 1 = **2** |
| 14 ÷ 7 = **2** | 28 ÷ 4 = **7** | 27 ÷ 3 = **9** | 12 ÷ 3 = **4** |

*All-Division Review*

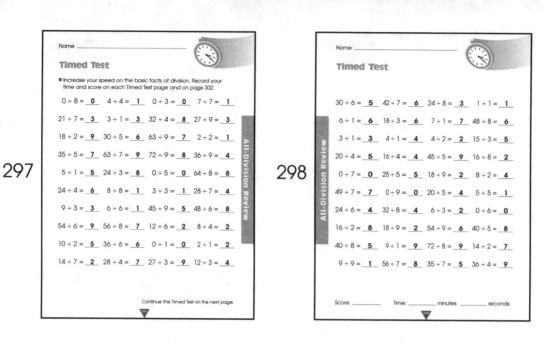

Continue this Timed Test on the next page.

## 298

Name _____

### Timed Test

| | | | |
|---|---|---|---|
| 30 ÷ 6 = **5** | 42 ÷ 7 = **6** | 24 ÷ 8 = **3** | 1 ÷ 1 = **1** |
| 6 ÷ 1 = **6** | 18 ÷ 3 = **6** | 7 ÷ 1 = **7** | 48 ÷ 8 = **6** |
| 3 ÷ 1 = **3** | 4 ÷ 1 = **4** | 4 ÷ 2 = **2** | 15 ÷ 3 = **5** |
| 20 ÷ 4 = **5** | 16 ÷ 4 = **4** | 45 ÷ 5 = **9** | 16 ÷ 8 = **2** |
| 0 ÷ 7 = **0** | 25 ÷ 5 = **5** | 18 ÷ 9 = **2** | 8 ÷ 2 = **4** |
| 49 ÷ 7 = **7** | 0 ÷ 9 = **0** | 20 ÷ 5 = **4** | 5 ÷ 5 = **1** |
| 24 ÷ 6 = **4** | 32 ÷ 8 = **4** | 6 ÷ 3 = **2** | 0 ÷ 6 = **0** |
| 16 ÷ 2 = **8** | 18 ÷ 9 = **2** | 54 ÷ 9 = **6** | 40 ÷ 5 = **8** |
| 40 ÷ 8 = **5** | 9 ÷ 1 = **9** | 72 ÷ 8 = **9** | 14 ÷ 2 = **7** |
| 9 ÷ 9 = **1** | 56 ÷ 7 = **8** | 35 ÷ 7 = **5** | 36 ÷ 4 = **9** |

*All-Division Review*

Score: _____  Time: _____ minutes _____ seconds

## 299

Name _____

### Timed Test

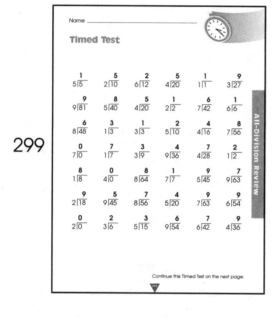

| | | | | | |
|---|---|---|---|---|---|
| 5)5 = **1** | 2)10 = **5** | 6)12 = **2** | 4)20 = **5** | 1)1 = **1** | 3)27 = **9** |
| 9)81 = **9** | 5)40 = **8** | 4)20 = **5** | 2)2 = **1** | 7)42 = **6** | 6)6 = **1** |
| 8)48 = **6** | 1)3 = **3** | 3)3 = **1** | 5)10 = **2** | 4)16 = **4** | 7)56 = **8** |
| 7)0 = **0** | 1)7 = **7** | 3)9 = **3** | 9)36 = **4** | 4)28 = **7** | 1)2 = **2** |
| 1)8 = **8** | 4)0 = **0** | 8)64 = **8** | 7)7 = **1** | 5)45 = **9** | 9)63 = **7** |
| 2)18 = **9** | 9)45 = **5** | 8)56 = **7** | 5)20 = **4** | 7)63 = **9** | 6)54 = **9** |
| 2)0 = **0** | 3)6 = **2** | 5)15 = **3** | 9)54 = **6** | 6)42 = **7** | 4)36 = **9** |

*All-Division Review*

Continue this Timed Test on the next page.

## 300

Name _____

### Timed Test

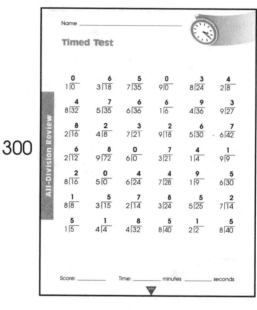

| | | | | | |
|---|---|---|---|---|---|
| 1)0 = **0** | 3)18 = **6** | 7)35 = **5** | 9)0 = **0** | 8)24 = **3** | 2)8 = **4** |
| 8)32 = **4** | 5)35 = **7** | 6)36 = **6** | 1)6 = **6** | 4)36 = **9** | 9)27 = **3** |
| 2)16 = **8** | 4)8 = **2** | 7)21 = **3** | 9)18 = **2** | 5)30 = **6** | 6)42 = **7** |
| 2)12 = **6** | 9)72 = **8** | 6)0 = **0** | 3)21 = **7** | 1)4 = **4** | 9)9 = **1** |
| 8)16 = **2** | 5)0 = **0** | 6)24 = **4** | 7)28 = **4** | 1)9 = **9** | 6)30 = **5** |
| 8)8 = **1** | 3)15 = **5** | 2)14 = **7** | 3)24 = **8** | 5)25 = **5** | 7)14 = **2** |
| 1)5 = **5** | 4)4 = **1** | 4)32 = **8** | 8)40 = **5** | 2)2 = **1** | 8)40 = **5** |

*All-Division Review*

Score: _____  Time: _____ minutes _____ seconds

## 301

Name _____

### Timed Test

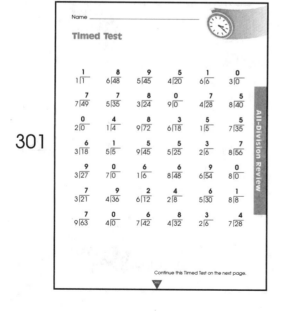

| | | | | | |
|---|---|---|---|---|---|
| 1)1 = **1** | 6)48 = **8** | 5)45 = **9** | 4)20 = **5** | 6)6 = **1** | 3)0 = **0** |
| 7)49 = **7** | 5)35 = **7** | 3)24 = **8** | 9)0 = **0** | 4)28 = **7** | 8)40 = **5** |
| 2)0 = **0** | 1)4 = **4** | 9)72 = **8** | 6)18 = **3** | 1)5 = **5** | 7)35 = **5** |
| 3)18 = **6** | 5)5 = **1** | 9)45 = **5** | 5)25 = **5** | 2)6 = **3** | 8)56 = **7** |
| 3)27 = **9** | 7)0 = **0** | 1)6 = **6** | 6)48 = **8** | 6)54 = **9** | 8)0 = **0** |
| 3)21 = **7** | 4)36 = **9** | 6)12 = **2** | 2)8 = **4** | 5)30 = **6** | 8)8 = **1** |
| 9)63 = **7** | 4)0 = **0** | 7)42 = **6** | 4)32 = **8** | 2)6 = **3** | 7)28 = **4** |

*All-Division Review*

Continue this Timed Test on the next page.

## 302

Name _____

### Timed Test

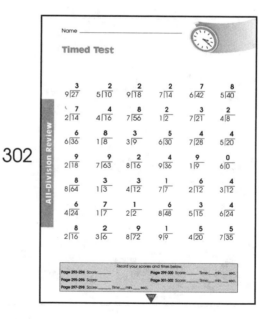

| | | | | | |
|---|---|---|---|---|---|
| 9)27 = **3** | 5)10 = **2** | 9)18 = **2** | 7)14 = **2** | 6)42 = **7** | 5)40 = **8** |
| 2)14 = **7** | 4)16 = **4** | 7)56 = **8** | 1)2 = **2** | 7)21 = **3** | 4)8 = **2** |
| 6)36 = **6** | 1)8 = **8** | 3)9 = **3** | 6)30 = **5** | 7)28 = **4** | 5)20 = **4** |
| 2)18 = **9** | 7)63 = **9** | 8)16 = **2** | 9)36 = **4** | 1)9 = **9** | 6)0 = **0** |
| 8)64 = **8** | 1)3 = **3** | 4)12 = **3** | 7)7 = **1** | 2)12 = **6** | 3)12 = **4** |
| 4)24 = **6** | 1)7 = **7** | 6)48 = **8** | 5)15 = **3** | 6)24 = **4** | 6)24 = **4** |
| 2)16 = **8** | 3)6 = **2** | 8)72 = **9** | 9)9 = **1** | 4)20 = **5** | 7)35 = **5** |

*All-Division Review*

| Record your scores and times below. | | |
|---|---|---|
| **Page 293-294** Score: _____ | | **Page 299-300** Score: _____ Time: ____ min. ____ sec. |
| **Page 295-296** Score: _____ | | **Page 301-302** Score: _____ Time: ____ min. ____ sec. |
| **Page 297-298** Score: _____ Time: ____ min. ____ sec. | | |

## ones

| | | | |
|---|---|---|---|
| 1 | x 1 = | 1 |
| 2 | x 1 = | 2 |
| 3 | x 1 = | 3 |
| 4 | x 1 = | 4 |
| 5 | x 1 = | 5 |
| 6 | x 1 = | 6 |
| 7 | x 1 = | 7 |
| 8 | x 1 = | 8 |
| 9 | x 1 = | 9 |
| 10 | x 1 = | 10 |
| 11 | x 1 = | 11 |
| 12 | x 1 = | 12 |

## twos

| | | |
|---|---|---|
| 1 | x 2 = | 2 |
| 2 | x 2 = | 4 |
| 3 | x 2 = | 6 |
| 4 | x 2 = | 8 |
| 5 | x 2 = | 10 |
| 6 | x 2 = | 12 |
| 7 | x 2 = | 14 |
| 8 | x 2 = | 16 |
| 9 | x 2 = | 18 |
| 10 | x 2 = | 20 |
| 11 | x 2 = | 22 |
| 12 | x 2 = | 24 |

## threes

| | |
|---|---|
| 1 | x 3 = |
| 2 | x 3 = |
| 3 | x 3 = |
| 4 | x 3 = |
| 5 | x 3 = |
| 6 | x 3 = |
| 7 | x 3 = |
| 8 | x 3 = |
| 9 | x 3 = |
| 10 | x 3 = |
| 11 | x 3 = |
| 12 | x 3 = |

## sixes

| | | |
|---|---|---|
| 1 | x 6 = | 6 |
| 2 | x 6 = | 12 |
| 3 | x 6 = | 18 |
| 4 | x 6 = | 24 |
| 5 | x 6 = | 30 |
| 6 | x 6 = | 36 |
| 7 | x 6 = | 42 |
| 8 | x 6 = | 48 |
| 9 | x 6 = | 54 |
| 10 | x 6 = | 60 |
| 11 | x 6 = | 66 |
| 12 | x 6 = | 72 |

## sevens

| | | |
|---|---|---|
| 1 | x 7 = | 7 |
| 2 | x 7 = | 14 |
| 3 | x 7 = | 21 |
| 4 | x 7 = | 28 |
| 5 | x 7 = | 35 |
| 6 | x 7 = | 42 |
| 7 | x 7 = | 49 |
| 8 | x 7 = | 56 |
| 9 | x 7 = | 63 |
| 10 | x 7 = | 70 |
| 11 | x 7 = | 77 |
| 12 | x 7 = | 84 |

## eights

| | |
|---|---|
| 1 | x 8 = |
| 2 | x 8 = |
| 3 | x 8 = |
| 4 | x 8 = |
| 5 | x 8 = |
| 6 | x 8 = |
| 7 | x 8 = |
| 8 | x 8 = |
| 9 | x 8 = |
| 10 | x 8 = |
| 11 | x 8 = |
| 12 | x 8 = |

| | fours | fives |
|---|---|---|
| 3 | 1 x 4 = 4 | 1 x 5 = 5 |
| 6 | 2 x 4 = 8 | 2 x 5 = 10 |
| 9 | 3 x 4 = 12 | 3 x 5 = 15 |
| 12 | 4 x 4 = 16 | 4 x 5 = 20 |
| 15 | 5 x 4 = 20 | 5 x 5 = 25 |
| 18 | 6 x 4 = 24 | 6 x 5 = 30 |
| 21 | 7 x 4 = 28 | 7 x 5 = 35 |
| 24 | 8 x 4 = 32 | 8 x 5 = 40 |
| 27 | 9 x 4 = 36 | 9 x 5 = 45 |
| 30 | 10 x 4 = 40 | 10 x 5 = 50 |
| 33 | 11 x 4 = 44 | 11 x 5 = 55 |
| 36 | 12 x 4 = 48 | 12 x 5 = 60 |

| | nines | tens |
|---|---|---|
| 8 | 1 x 9 = 9 | 1 x 10 = 10 |
| 16 | 2 x 9 = 18 | 2 x 10 = 20 |
| 24 | 3 x 9 = 27 | 3 x 10 = 30 |
| 32 | 4 x 9 = 36 | 4 x 10 = 40 |
| 40 | 5 x 9 = 45 | 5 x 10 = 50 |
| 48 | 6 x 9 = 54 | 6 x 10 = 60 |
| 56 | 7 x 9 = 63 | 7 x 10 = 70 |
| 64 | 8 x 9 = 72 | 8 x 10 = 80 |
| 72 | 9 x 9 = 81 | 9 x 10 = 90 |
| 80 | 10 x 9 = 90 | 10 x 10 = 100 |
| 88 | 11 x 9 = 99 | 11 x 10 = 110 |
| 96 | 12 x 9 = 108 | 12 x 10 = 120 |

MULTIPLICATION TABLE